WHEN

A **COLLECTION** of **SHORT STORIES** to
Help **NAVIGATE** Your **LIFE** and **CAREER**

Things I Wish I Knew
When I Was **STARTING OUT**,
STARTING OVER, and
Trying to **GET AHEAD**

WHEN

A **COLLECTION** of **SHORT STORIES** to
Help **NAVIGATE** Your **LIFE** and **CAREER**

JEFF WELLEN

DALLAS, TEXAS

WHEN—Things I Wish I Knew When I Was STARTING OUT, STARTING OVER, and Trying To GET AHEAD

Published by Jeff Wellen
Dallas, Texas
Printed in the U.S.A.

ISBN (print): 978-1-7379458-0-2
ISBN (kindle): 978-1-7379458-1-9
Library of Congress Control Number: 2021918975

Prepared for publication by: palmtreeproductions.com

To contact the author: **JEFFWELLEN.COM**

DEDICATION

I dedicate this book to my mom and dad—without your love and support, I would not be the man I am today. I wish you were still here and able to read my book, but I know you are looking down on me, feeling proud of your son's accomplishment.

To my sister and brother-in-law—you have always been there for me through my highest of highs and lowest of lows.

To my son, Zachary—I hope and pray you have all the success in the world as you embark on your life's journey. Without your support, love, guidance, editing skills, and willingness to help me during the writing of this book, I would not have been able to accomplish this goal.

And finally, to my wonderful and beautiful wife, Lisa—your steadfast love and unwavering support have been the rock that has enabled me to succeed in my career and push through any challenges I have faced, including the time and investments necessary to write and publish this book.

WHAT PEOPLE ARE SAYING ABOUT JEFF WELLEN AND *WHEN*

In all my associations with Jeff, he always showed himself to be an excellent worker with drive and the ability to think strategically. His strategic skills were always coupled with solid common sense. He was never complacent; instead, he ambitiously dug into every project.

WHEN has all the ingredients for those who have ambition but do not know where to start.

MICHAEL ROULEAU
Former CEO of Michaels Stores & Tuesday Morning Stores

Jeff always had a confident, eager approach to taking on challenges and doing things the right way. He never allowed himself to become complacent and did not confuse activity with accomplishment. He has a unique way of looking at life and uses unusual clarity in how he approaches decisions and opportunities. I've known Jeff throughout his career, and he's demonstrated this focus and commitment that are built on being positive and not being afraid to take the leap when it's the right thing to do.

I remember several of the stories as they occurred, and he always saw the experiences as an opportunity to improve himself with a "can-do," high moral attitude. *WHEN* is a valuable read to anyone beginning their careers or those stuck in jobs and need the confidence to step forward. I highly recommend the book.

CHIP HUMPHREY
Former Vice President of Haggar Clothing Company

In life, as in business, many of the most important lessons are sometimes the simplest. The key is to see through the everyday noise and absorb the experiences. *WHEN* does just that for the reader—it cuts through the noise and teaches a valuable lesson in each short story. Jeff uses his own experiences, concisely telling a story, to make valuable points useful for the reader to navigate their life and career.

LES GARDNER
Former Vice President of Supply Chain for Michaels & Tractor Supply

What I find most compelling about Jeff's book is not the stories per se, but all the life lessons learned—the missteps, successes, and accolades. While structured and formal education is important, life lessons are just as important, perhaps even more so. Jeff's trials and tribulations are a testament to the value of experience and authentic lifelong learning. Reading WHEN, you will gain decades of experience you can only learn by living life.

HARVEY S. KANTER
President and CEO, DXLG at DXL Group

There are a billion business books, millions on leadership, not very many from the heart. *WHEN* speaks from the heart.

AMIR HODA
Co-Founder, TheOne08, Inc.

Jeff is a dedicated family man. He worked hard to build a trusted environment at Michaels Stores that allowed him to collaborate with the CEO and Senior Executives while gaining agreement on a company strategy that saved the retailer. His mission was to leave behind a legacy that enabled the organization to continue to be successful even after he left. During my three-year tenure working with Jeff, I listened to many stories from his past experiences that brought to light his salient points.

He was especially proficient in using diagrams (the whiteboard) and presentations to help others quickly understand his ideas. Jeff's experiences are varied and extensive due to his career in consulting, supply chain, and retailing. He shares these stories not to make himself look more authoritative, but rather to build a variety of formidable visuals that help the reader understand the reason behind an area they too wish to change. *WHEN* is the book of the year to read. If you are looking for solutions, don't let this one pass you by.

MARY KUNISKI
Executive Coach & Former Vice President of Michaels

Everybody needs a mentor! Finding a good one you can rely on and communicate with fully is not easy. **WHEN** is a great resource for those times, or any time you need a different perspective on a challenging situation. Essentially, he is mentoring remotely. Jeff has distilled decades of experience from dozens of mentors into an accessible and entertaining format. The stories he recounts are brief and readily understood, and his occasional injection of humor is also helpful.

The book is focused toward sharing Jeff's experiences and what he has learned not only to individuals who need a mentor but is a great resource for those who do or would love to mentor as well. Either way, this is a book you will read through quickly the first time and find yourself leafing through the stories again and again as time passes.

DAVID LAZOVIK
Former Senior Vice President and General
Merchandise Manager of Gimbels

I was one of the first to help Jeff in the clothing business and watched him grow from a young, naïve man to an accomplished person in the corporate world. Shortly after I met Jeff, I met his parents, and after that meeting, I knew he would be successful. The examples his parents set were a recipe for success, so I knew his future would be bright. Jeff is an intelligent person who doesn't put superfluous spin on life, and thus I knew his book would be honest and heartfelt. It's been my pleasure to be associated with Jeff for so many years!

JIM HERMAN
Former Sales Representative for Haggar Clothing Company

Jeff has written a book that will help you be a better leader and person just by focusing on yourself. There are no new vocabulary or acronyms to learn, no charts or quadrants to think about when looking at how to improve yourself. He just shares practical, easily implemented lessons to help you navigate your life more efficiently and effectively, at work, at home, and in your community.

TOM BAZZONE
President, Frontgate

I first met Jeff 37 years ago when he was a 24-year-old young man who had just moved to Dallas, Texas, for a job with the same company I worked for at the time. I needed a baseball coach that identified with a group of talented but undeveloped 14 and 15-year-old boys on my son's team. Jeff was likable, independent, different, and perfect for the job.

You could see even at that age the joy he had in mentoring and coaching. His thinking was totally outside the box, and he was comfortable with constantly striving for excellence. He had a no-compromise, not-settle-for-average attitude that he used not only to coach those boys, but he uses to this day in his life and career. He is now using his always-striving-for excellence attitude and his desire to mentor individuals in his book to help you.

I can guarantee you; you will not find this type of practical experience and knowledge by searching the internet. Jeff's stories are an honest, interesting, and compelling journey that shows how to handle life's situations and challenges. His collection of stories is an easy, must-read for all of those in search of success.

JIMMY PALASOTA
President, Palasota Property Company, LLC

In the earlier years of our careers, Jeff and I worked together when he was consulting for Michaels and starting his long-lasting relationship with then CEO Michael Rouleau. We worked for the same partner at our firm, Steve Biciocchi, who became a valuable mentor to both of us.

I have always been impressed with Jeff, how he managed his career, took risks, fought battles, came out on top, and lived his life for himself and his family. I don't know how to make a better endorsement of Jeff or this book, WHEN, than to say that I can't wait to get copies into the hands of my children—two of which are young professionals, growing their careers, their families, and living their lives.

Jeff's stories and lessons are what every young (and not so young) person should hear. Our lives are made of our personal and professional decisions. They are intermingled. This book will guide you to through these decisions.

WILL O'BRIEN
CEO, True North Growth Partners

I was impressed with Jeff the moment I first met him in 1985. He always exemplified a sense of confidence, fairness, and a willingness for hard work. I am not surprised that Jeff has been successful in his career, and I believe his book of career experiences will help you in your career.

JAMES THOMPSON
Former Vice President, National Sales
Manager for Haggar Clothing Company

I had the privilege of a front-row seat to Jeff's process as he wrote *WHEN*. He showed up every day with passion, drive, enthusiasm, and a relentless desire to make a positive difference. You are reading the premium cut— the stories that made it through the scrutiny of relevance, concision, and clarity with a powerful and memorable deliverable. This book is a resource not only for those starting out, starting over, and trying to get ahead, but also for mentors, coaches, and executives who need real-world anecdotes to illustrate a powerful principle or life lesson. Prepare to be both inspired and entertained as you journey through *WHEN—A Collection of Short Stories to Help Navigate Your Life and Career.*

WENDY K. WALTERS
Motivational Speaker, Author, Editor,
Master Coach, and Owner of Palm Tree Productions

CONTENTS

CHAPTER 2
STARTING MY FIRST REAL-WORLD JOB

CHAPTER 3   93

MAKING A SIGNIFICANT LIFE AND CAREER CHANGE

CHAPTER 4   157
TRYING IT ON MY OWN

CHAPTER 5   167
MAKING A DRAMATIC CAREER CHANGE IN MID-STREAM

CHAPTER 6 197
YOU HAVE A FRONT ROW SEAT TO THE C-SUITE

CHAPTER 8
NAVIGATING A NEW JOB THAT SEEMED TOO GOOD TO BE TRUE

CHAPTER 9
RUNNING A SIGNIFICANT PART OF A COMPANY

DREAMING OF TOMORROW

REMEMBERING THOSE WHO HELPED YOU ALONG THE WAY

MEET JEFF WELLEN

INTRODUCTION

WHEN

I TOLD MY SON A STORY

"Let me tell you a story," I said to my 22-year-old son Zachary. He had just graduated from college and was sharing with me a challenging situation he was dealing with at his first job. As with many young adults and people in general, he felt like he was the first one ever to experience an event like this.

Feeling his pain, I told him a story about my first job and a situation I experienced at almost the same age. He could not believe how eerily similar our issues were. We talked about how I handled it, and it gave him insight into what he could and should do.

When I was done talking to Zach, I started thinking about our conversation more deeply. I thought about all the knowledge, experiences, and stories I had accumulated over my entire life and career. For the past 38 years, I have worked for some great companies, advancing through the ranks from a rookie trainee to hold several Senior Executive-level positions and even a short entrepreneurial venture out on my own. Along the way, I was fortunate to be mentored by several industry titans, successful colleagues, and friends.

I asked myself, "How could I possibly share all this knowledge I have about life and the business world with my son? Do I wait until he has another issue? Do I wait for him to come to me and ask me how I handled a particular situation?" I concluded that I didn't know if I would live long enough to wait for one situation to arise at a time.

My response was to write a book of short stories as love letters to Zachary about success, failure, friends, foes, the high highs, and the low lows of family, life, and career. Every story could start **"Dear Zachary,"** and end with **"Love Dad."**

I wanted each story not only to tell a tale but also to have a memorable takeaway quote on how to deal with a current situation, prepare for the future, avoid pitfalls, navigate rough seas, take advantage of opportunities, and help understand that the only way to know what you are truly capable of is to try. I shared them with Zach along the way, and his responses lit a fire in me to make them available to others like him.

My hope is that these short stories will inspire, motivate, challenge, and teach you valuable lessons that **you will not find in textbooks or an internet search.** To the very best of my recollection, these are true stories based on living life—a dash of humor, some brutal honesty, a bit of soul-searching, and a commitment to be authentic to my journey— good, bad, ugly, and incredible alike.

Why *WHEN*? The title relates to the time in my life or career that each of these stories took place; from before I began my first job after college to the present day and everything in between.

So, here it is. A collection of motivational short stories based on my real-life and career experiences.

Enjoy!

CHAPTER   1

PREPARING TO ENTER
THE WORKFORCE

When I was just 22, what did I truly know about the real world? Like most young adults, I thought I knew a lot. Though I had graduated from college, the reality was I knew extraordinarily little about how life and the business world worked. I was textbook smart, but not street smart. I did not know then but realize now that only time on this earth allows you to gain experience and apply your knowledge. Some people call this "Adulting."

As you embark on your post-school life, this section is an accelerator to guide you safely through many of those miscellaneous but important lessons it would otherwise take you years to learn on your own. It explains things to know, avoid, experience, share, and never forget. I had to learn the hard way, and you can benefit from my lessons learned. Each story gives you insight, so your path forward might be a little less difficult.

A PEN CAP AND MY DAD

When I was about 23, I worked as an assistant buyer for Gimbels Department Stores in Milwaukee, Wisconsin. Like most people my age, I was challenging the norms concerning my life and career, so when a sales representative handed me a pen as a marketing handout, the saying on the pen cap caught my attention: ***"Success and failure are judged only by those who are willing to try."***

There are many sayings like it, such as "You never miss the shots you don't take," and "Dreams can come true if you have the courage to pursue them," or "Only those who dare to fail greatly can ever achieve greatly." They all basically say the same thing, but I really liked this particular quote, and it has remained my favorite saying to this very day. It provoked the question in me, "What should I try?"

As I searched for that answer, my world was rocked. My dad suffered a heart attack and stroke. For the first time, I realized how fragile life was and how quickly it can hit you over the head like a ten-ton sledgehammer. After he recovered, I began to think more deeply about the word **try**.

I kept wondering if there was more to life than my current situation. I began thinking the only way to see what I was really capable of achieving was to take a chance and explore the world on my own terms. With my dad's trauma etched in my mind and my favorite saying guiding my way, I did not want to have any regrets or be concerned with some unexpected event happening to me. I did not know exactly what the path would or should be, but I felt the only way to move forward was to take a giant, bold step.

The challenge for me was I had a wonderful life. I had a college degree and a great job working for a great company where I was highly thought of. I was part of a supportive family, and I had tremendous friends—some new, but many long-term, some of them friends since the first grade. Still, something was missing, and I had to find out what that was. I needed to see what else was out there, even if that meant embracing the incredible risk and uncertainty involved in leaving this all behind.

So, without having any personal connections or even a job to go to, I left my position at Gimbels and planned a move to Dallas, Texas. Little town Jeff traded a picture-perfect life for a new adventure in the Big D.

Everybody thought I was crazy. No one could understand what I was doing because they did not understand my passion to "try" a different path with a "no regrets" mentality. It is easy to sit back and be a Monday morning quarterback and point out, "You are making a mistake." It is much harder to take the risk, but I chose the harder, less-traveled path.

The worst thing that could happen was it would not work out, and I would have to pick myself up and try something else. The best thing that could happen (which it did) was that it would propel me to meet my wife, have a wonderfully successful career, and see more of the world than I ever thought possible. The quote from that pen cap and my dad's heart attack are the two defining moments that have inspired my entire life. **Almost every decision I have made has been through the lens of these two simple truths; the only way to really have no regrets in life is to try, and life can change in a heartbeat.**

It is okay to challenge the status quo and take risks in your life. That is the only true way to know how far you can really go. If a small-town truck drivers' kid can challenge the world and succeed, so can you. You just have to be willing to try.

POWER OF POSITIVE THINKING

What kind of attitude do you have? Do you look at the glass as half empty or half full? Do you wake up and say, "It is going to be a great day!" or do you find something negative before you make it to the kitchen for a cup of coffee? What about the people around you? Do you know people who always see the world through a negative lens? They can never find a positive thing to say about anything or anyone.

I was struggling a little to make it on my own. With a flick of a switch, I had gone from living with my parents to living 1,000 miles away—a cold turkey reality of being responsible for everything. I wanted this move, but it was quickly becoming crystal clear that this would not be easy.

In 1952 Norman Vincent Peale wrote the best-selling book *The Power of Positive Thinking*. I received this book as a gift during my initial stay in Dallas with the Haggar Company when I began to read as many books as I could get my hands on to help me reach my goals.

This book was a Godsend. It taught me that your attitude in life can make or break you. Lou Holtz, the former Notre Dame coach, once said, **"Virtually nothing is impossible in this world if you just put your mind to it and maintain a positive attitude."**

He was right. I began to focus not on the things that were going wrong or the challenges but on the things that were going right. I tried to avoid negative people and surrounded myself with those who had a positive outlook. I developed a high level of confidence and an ever-growing positive attitude about life and its possibilities—an incredibly dynamic duo.

Confidence and a positive attitude were feeding me more and more energy every day to work towards being the best. They were also a tremendously strong force field to fend off negative thoughts, both the general negativity of the world around me or negative thoughts from myself.

This habit has remained with me throughout my career. Years later, I walked into the Tuesday Morning office to pick up a package, engaging in polite talk with the receptionist. She asked, "Where do you get your positive energy?" "From my beliefs in God and in myself," I replied.

"Well, your attitude and energy are infectious!" she countered, "Do you know how many people want to be near you so they can feed off that energy?"

Talk about a power-up boost! It was one of the greatest compliments I ever received. Knowing that I affected her in that way was pretty awesome. I am high on life. That is my drug. Focusing on all that is negative will weigh you down like an anchor. Seek out positive people, positive energy, and positive thoughts. These will help you rise about all the chaos and soar to unthinkable heights.

> **FOCUSING ON ALL THAT IS NEGATIVE WILL WEIGH YOU DOWN LIKE AN ANCHOR. SEEK OUT POSITIVE PEOPLE, POSITIVE ENERGY, AND POSITIVE THOUGHTS. THESE WILL HELP YOU RISE ABOVE ALL THE CHAOS AND SOAR TO UNTHINKABLE HEIGHTS.**

DREAM THE IMPOSSIBLE

My 23-year-old son Zachary and I were discussing his aspirational goals. He was contemplating his potential next move of either continuing to work as an electrical engineer or taking some time off to get a master's degree. I wanted to discuss how either decision would impact where he thought his career could take him.

I wanted to know his dreams and aspirations. The challenge was the conversation was more a practical analysis of his current skills and not about what was possible. He has a degree in electrical engineering and mathematics, so as a father, I can say he is one smart young man. I know many engineers, and I always kid them that they can only dream if the math worked out in their heads. I could see the mathematical wheels turning in Zach's head as we talked.

I tried a new approach and asked him what he dreams about. He kind of shrugged his shoulders, so I gave him an example. When I was young, I dreamed about playing major league baseball with my favorite player, Roberto Clemente, and hitting the game-winning home run. Sometimes, I dreamed of hitting the game-winning basket for the NBA championship playing for my favorite team, the Milwaukee Bucks.

I told him I played out my dreams in the backyard, acting like I was the play-by-play announcer in the final seconds of the NBA game. I would describe my moves and then countdown, 3,2,1 and take the final shot. Of course, if I missed, I would do it all over again.

When I got older, my dreams shifted to being a leader of a company. We discussed how all my decisions concerning my career path focused on that dream. Now that I have written a book, my dream is to be a best-selling author. Aspirational, crazy, but it is a dream.

Many people cannot drop the anchor of doubt about what they are really capable of doing. This little voice on their shoulder telling them the reason they can't do something restricts them. I encouraged Zach to cut that anchor and start saying, "What can I achieve if I put my mind to it?"

Dream not about the possible but the impossible and see if you can reach it. Elon Musk is not only a visionary and a dreamer; he is a doer. I asked Zach, "Why can't you be the next Elon Musk?" He wanted to tell me all the reasons why he could not instead of the one reason why he could.

Don't restrict your dreams. Cut that anchor of doubts and begin to dream the impossible. Think big. Challenge yourself to achieve something you never thought you were capable of doing—it just might come true.

—•—•—•—

WHAT DO YOU WANT TO BE WHEN YOU GROW UP?

What are your goals? Have you defined them? Zig Ziglar, a world-famous motivational speaker, once said, "You need a plan to build a house. To build a life, it is even more important to have a plan." I put my first goals together when I was about 24. Before that, I was just doing things randomly. There was never a true North Star guiding my life.

Venturing out into the real world after college, I began to understand the need to define more clearly what it was I was working toward. If I were going to spend all this time and energy building my career and personal life, how could I determine if I was a success or not? The answer: Goals!

There is a multitude of self-help books and publications to help you, but here are my reasons for setting goals:

1. **Take control of your life:** These should be your goals, not anyone else's.

2. **Give your life a purpose and meaning:** They give you a reason to get up in the morning.

3. **Provide a laser focus:** They give you target(s) for you to achieve.

4. **Give you energy as you progress:** They motivate you to work harder to achieve those goals.

5. **Self-satisfaction:** Reaching goals builds confidence and motivates you to set new ones.

Here are the goals I wrote down at 24 years old:

- Find that special person to live and share my life
- Have a child (or children)

- Travel the world
- Be a senior leader of a company and have a certain net worth by 40 years old
- Be able to retire at 50
- Teach and motivate as many people as I possibly could

Many people are like zombies throughout their life. Living in some sleepwalking-like trance. All the successful people I personally knew or were reading books about set goals for their lives. So I made sure that I had crystal clear goals and purpose. My path was never a straight line to success. But I always had my North Star as my focus.

Successful people set goals. What are your goals? If you don't have any, start writing.

------•------

WHY ARE THEY SO SUCCESSFUL?

How do you become successful? With my goals in hand, I did not want to fail. What was the best way to learn? How about learning from other successful people?

When I was working at Haggar, I had the chance to get to know Mr. Ed Haggar pretty well. He was the son of the founder of Haggar Apparel Company, President of the company for more than 20 years; he was Chairman of the Board when I initially trained in Dallas in 1985. One of my many duties as a trainee was driving Mr. Ed to the airport, which provided the opportunity to develop a relationship with him as a mentor. Those 20 to 45-minute rides were incredible. On one of those trips, he asked me if I had any goals. Without hesitation, I said yes and listed them off for him. He gave me an incredible compliment, "Son, most people at your age don't have a clue what they want to do."

Here I was sitting in a car with the Chairman of the Board of one of the most successful apparel companies in history. I figured I might as well ask him if he had any insights on reaching my goals. His answer was simple: "Learn how others became successful." Then he asked me if I ever read his dad's book, *That Haggar Man*. I was honest with him. I had been given a copy during my orientation, but I had not read it.

"Read it," he replied, "and any other book you can find on successful people." He started listing off successful people he was friends with as examples: Ross Perot, the founder of Electronic Data Systems, for many years one of the world's largest information technology companies. Trammell Crow, who ran one of the most successful real estate companies. Tom Landry, the legendary coach of the Dallas Cowboys ... the names just kept coming. He said, "Read about them. What they did. How they did it. What they did right. What they did wrong. Read as much as you can and learn from other successful people."

READ EVERY BOOK YOU CAN GET YOUR HANDS ON ABOUT SUCCESSFUL PEOPLE AND MOTIVATIONAL BOOKS ON HOW TO BE A SUCCESS.

So, I did. From that day forward, I read every book I could get my hands on about successful people and motivational books on how to be a success. I read about business leaders, presidents, world leaders, historical figures, college and professional coaches, athletes, doctors, inventors, etc. And of course, I read *That Haggar Man* too. I was a sponge.

Here are some of the common themes from all these successful people:

- They were **driven** to be a success.
- They all **faced obstacles**. Nothing was easy.
- They were **willing to fail**.
- They **set goals**.
- There were **extremely inquisitive** about learning.
- They could **adjust to changes** that were happening around them.
- **Hard work** was a starter. They wanted to outwork anyone else.
- They were **visionary**.
- They knew that they **needed others** to help in their success.

I have not yet become as successful as the people I was reading about or even someone like Mr. Ed Haggar. That did not stop me from using these common themes to strive to reach my goals ... and I am still not done.

AN OPTIMIST, A PESSIMIST, AND A REALIST

It was written on an 8 x 11 laminated piece of paper hung up by the cook in our small cafeteria at Michaels. It read, **"An Optimist Hopes the Wind Will Come; a Pessimist Believes the Wind Will Never Come and a Realist Will Change the Sail."** When I asked him why he liked this quote, he answered, "I thought it might help our employees understand that they could hope for Filet Mignon or be a pessimist that the food would never get any better or maybe be realistic about the cafeteria's budget and just enjoy what we do have."

I found this insightful. It is extremely easy to be a pessimist with so much negative news. It is a challenge just to live your life every day. It can drag you down. On the other hand, I know many optimists who just hope things will get better or change.

I myself like being a realist. I try to understand the challenges, gaps, or issues pertaining to a subject. Then I look to see the best alternative avenues you could take to change the outcome of the issue. Then, I work as hard as I can with my teammates, family, or friends to implement the change necessary to eliminate the issue.

Arizona was my first sales territory for Haggar Apparel Company and was comprised of a mixture of small mom-and-pop stores, military base exchanges, and a nine-store department chain called Goldwater's. They faced two main issues. The small mom-and-pop stores struggled because Wal-Mart was moving into smaller towns and putting tremendous pressure on them. The Peso's devaluation caused prices to rise for my products, hindering the business I had selling to towns like Nogales, Douglass, Bisbee, and San Luis on the US and Mexican border.

I could try to be optimistic and hope that Wal-Mart would stop encroaching on my business or that the Mexican government would rethink its policy. I could be a pessimist and just throw up my hands and call management to give me a new territory. Or I could be realistic and put together a plan to tackle these issues.

With the mom-and-pop stores, I tried adjusting their assortments to not compete on price alone. We worked extremely hard to watch inventory so they would not have to take huge markdowns or have their money tied up with units that were not selling. I highlighted the difference in quality with what they were selling compared to Wal-Mart.

As for the Peso, the reality was the situation was not going to improve. I sold as much as I could to my accounts on the border and then got to work finding other places to replace that business. An example was the casino business in Laughlin, Nevada. I found a contact that introduced me to the purchasing agent for one of the casinos to see if they would buy my basic black pants for their dealers. I also realized that I needed to emphasize getting more business out of my biggest account, Goldwater Department Stores.

Over the next three years, this resulted in my sales nearly doubling. **Hope is not a strategy, and pessimism is a worthless loss of energy. A realist will pick a destination, set their sails to take advantage of the current environment, and get moving.**

────────── • ● • ──────────

THE WISDOM TO KNOW
THE DIFFERENCE

I had only been with Haggar for five months when I was targeted to move to a new territory. I had just returned to Dallas from a trip with a few sales representatives when James Thompson, the National Sales Manager, told me that I had the ability to sell a broader variety of accounts than they first thought. This meant they would need some more time to find me the right territory, and though it was a compliment, I really wanted to get going on my career.

This decision meant I would be spending about seven more months in Dallas. I had exhausted the basic training, so management decided to expose me to more areas, processes, and people within the company. I spent time visiting manufacturing plants, our pieced goods cutting facility, the Information Technology department (called data processing back then), the product development team, marketing, forecasting, and more. It was outstanding because I got to see behind the curtain.

Because I was now being exposed to so many things that the sales force would not have seen, it began to open a pandora's box. I saw a lot of good but also a lot of things that needed to be addressed. During this rotation, people began to show me not only how things worked but also complained about things that needed to change.

I started to lose focus on what I was there for, which was to round out my knowledge to be a better sales representative. I was a young sales trainee now expending a tremendous amount of energy thinking about how to solve a manufacturing defect issue or a forecasting error. I was not focusing my energy and skills like a laser beam on what I could control—being the best-prepared sales representative.

One day I called back home to talk with mom and dad about what was happening. Mom asked if I still had the Serenity Prayer that my teacher Mrs. Rose gave me when I was in third grade.

"God, grant me the serenity to accept the things I cannot change, the courage to change the things I can, and the wisdom to know the difference."

She reminded me of the struggles I had in grade school, constantly trying to solve the problems of the world as a third grader. I would get terribly upset about things I had zero control over. I realized it was happening again.

I remembered that at the tender age of eight years old that I would say this prayer every night. It provided me the guidance to focus my energies and thoughts. I have always had this prayer hanging somewhere in my home. Now I have it permanently hung in my memory.

In this crazy world we live in where you can be so easily distracted, it is a struggle to know what you can and can't control. This simple prayer can help keep you grounded and focused.

———— • ● • ————

THIS IS ME

The Greatest Showman is a fabulous feel-good movie about the life of P.T. Barnum. A highlight is when the rag-tag group of misfits who were bullied and maligned sing "This Is Me" as their anthem of self-acceptance, bravery, and confidence. It is an inspiring scene, and if you have never heard the song, I encourage you to pause right now, search YouTube for a clip from the movie, and watch it.

The bullying started for me in grade school and continued through high school. I was exceedingly small in physique and the youngest person in my class, so I was a prime target to get picked on. I never was physically abused, but cruel words were like bullets that hit deeply and painfully. I could not fight back physically, so I fought with my words. That is why I talk a lot. It has been a tough habit to break after 12 years of pain.

In high school and into college, I also had a terrible case of acne. Nothing would work to make it better. I had very little self-esteem because every time I looked in the mirror, I saw a new breakout or scars from a previous breakout. It was a punch to the gut. Between the bullying and the acne, I was a mess.

Then two things changed my life. The first was the medicine Accutane. (Disclaimer: I am not telling anyone to use a drug). I started taking the medicine late in my final semester of college and into the first few months of my new job. In a matter of 6 months, my skin was completely clear. I could now look in the mirror and not be ashamed of the way I looked.

The second change was I started my new job at Gimbels. The people there did not know me as the frail, small kid picked on for years; they saw me as a new friend and associate. They treated me like a normal individual. I was having some early success at work, and my confidence and self-esteem levels were beginning to rise. It has never stopped growing.

It was a new lease on life. I liked the way I looked; people liked me for who I was, and I was good at what I did. I basically said, "Screw all those people who picked on me—screw all the people who said I could not do something!" Actually, I did not say screw, but I wanted this to be PG-13. I was ready to conquer the world. It was like a switch went from off to on.

If you are having similar challenges, maybe it is time for you to say, "Screw them!" too. I did what was in my control—finding medicine to address an issue, and moved to a new location with fresh faces. I said good-bye to limiting beliefs, anchors of self-doubt, and painful memories from my past, no longer allowing them to hold me back.

What is holding you back? Find out what will turn that light switch on for you, and then flip the switch! **Your success is linked to your confidence and self-esteem. Address the things that sabotage these, and you are on your way to conquering the world or your small piece of it.**

IF YOU STOP LEARNING, YOU DIE

My dad never graduated from high school. He was a really good athlete, and when he was a junior in high school, he got hurt playing football. His father, who owned a small delicatessen, told him that if he could not play sports, there was no need for a high school diploma. He said that he should come work in the family business instead. It was 1947.

Years later, my dad did receive his G.E.D. while in the Army. Throughout his life, I believe he always wondered what would have been different if he would have graduated from high school. He always stressed to me, "Learn as much as you can." He never really talked about learning in terms of getting degrees; he meant never stop trying to gain knowledge. One time when we were talking, he said, "If you stop learning, you die."

I have never forgotten that. Even though I have a college degree, I have never stopped trying to learn and broaden my knowledge of the world around me. I knew many people that thought their college degree was enough. They were done studying. Not me.

When I was selling clothing for Haggar in Arizona, I took a real estate class and got a real estate license. Real estate was on fire at the time, and I wanted to learn more about it for future investment possibilities or maybe even a new career.

When I began to encounter new things that I did not know about, I would take a class or find some books to read on the subject. For example, I encountered issues related to receivables, payables, chargebacks, marketing co-op money, and invoice deductions, to name a few. My one accounting class was not enough, so I took a night class offered by a local community college.

I was also being hit with many transportation chargebacks. My dad was a truck driver, but I was not deeply knowledgeable about all the inner workings of the logistics business. I went to the library and checked out a few books. Whether it was accounting, budgeting, politics, finance, human resources, investing, sourcing, etc., I always wanted to learn more.

An extremely smart young man, my son graduated from SMU in Dallas with a double major, Electrical Engineering and Mathematics. He encountered many finance-related issues surrounding a couple of products he was working on in his first position. I suggested to him that he find a class on YouTube and learn more about this subject. He found an MIT finance class and watched all sixteen sessions.

If you stop learning, you die! Never stop expanding your knowledge. Read, watch, ask questions, listen, be inquisitive and learn. **Learning gives you an advantage—a leg up in life. It increases your value in the marketplace and helps you stand out head and shoulders above those who relax into practicing only what they already know.**

YOU ONLY KNOW WHAT YOU KNOW

Until my mid-teens, I thought my dad was the smartest person I knew. He knew so much about so many things, and I learned something from him every single day. Then starting in my teen years, my attitude shifted a little. I began to think maybe I could hang with or surpass my dad in knowledge because I was learning all this cool stuff in school. As I finished college, I just knew that I was so much smarter than my dad (and most adults) about every subject. I had a college diploma and all this knowledge—who could possibly be smarter than me?

Plus, I had this inquisitive nature. I knew if I kept asking questions, I would fill in some missing blanks in my knowledge database. I was ready to conquer the world in about two years. Then something happened on the way to the top of the world. I slowly began to realize that I did not know everything.

At first, I did not want to admit to myself, but every day there were 5, 10, 15, and more things that I never knew about or experienced before. My first major wave of reality had hit me. I was secure that I knew what I knew, but I quickly realized that I did **not** know what I did **not** know. I needed to step back and take an inventory.

I had to change my attitude about others, especially toward individuals who were more senior to me. They knew a lot more than I did. Having this piece of paper saying that I was a college graduate meant nothing because I was competing with people who had a lot more experience than me, whether or not they were more textbook smart or street smart. If I was going to be successful, I had to learn from all of them.

This concept also applies to companies. All the companies I have worked for or consulted with have had this problem to some degree. A company gets stagnant but doesn't know how to get out of the situation. They become like a young adult. They think they already know it all and are unwilling to realize that someone may have more insight, may have already solved this situation, or have a better way of doing business.

Those in charge can become more and more stubborn, believing they can find the answer. What they fail to realize is that they don't know what they don't know. They may not have the knowledge or experiences they need to solve the problem, and pride keeps them from accepting that others do.

So, whether you are a young adult, older adult, or a company leader, when you think you know it all, you probably don't. **Confidence accepts knowing what you know. Humility accepts knowing what you don't know and being willing to receive that wisdom from another source.**

—————— • ● • ——————

STAND BY ME

In 1986 *Stand by Me* came out. It was such a perfect movie about friendship—true friendship. Not just friendly relationships; I am talking about true friendship.

A true friend is someone who:

- has your back,
- is authentic and honest with you,
- accepts you for who you are,
- genuinely wants the best for you,
- will not abandon you,
- will not ask you to do something wrong,
- will be there for you when you call.

These statements make a pretty tough filter to determine a true friend. I thought many people were my true friends, only to realize all we had was a friendly relationship. I have been burned by many I thought fit the definition but came to find out our relationship was merely one of convenience.

Maybe they wanted to leverage my knowledge, steal an idea, or use me to get their idea funded. The reasons are not important; it sucks being used. I have had more than a few fair-weather friends in my day. Learning the difference between a network connection, an energy vampire, and a true friend was a tough lesson to learn.

In the early years on my own, I was naive to the intentions of many people. As I began to learn from my experiences and my mentors, I began to use the above filters to determine my true friends.

I am fortunate to have many true friends. I will talk about one—the best man at my wedding, Mr. Charles (Chip) Humphrey. Chip and I were Haggar trainees together, and ever since then, we have been best friends. Though we have rarely lived in the same city during most of our 35-year friendship, we have always depended on each other through thick and thin. He is the perfect definition of a true friend, and I know if I needed him to get on a plane tomorrow, he would. I would do the same for him.

My guidance is not to eliminate people in your life who do not make it through the true friend filter. I am also not saying eliminate everybody with whom you associate. Not every superficial connection is bad, and not everyone you work with is destined to become a meaningful friend. I advise caution as you enter the real world. **Not everybody has your best intentions in mind. Being aware of this makes you wise. The simple question I ask concerning a true friend is will this person stand by me?**

———•●•———

EXPERIENCES OR POSSESSIONS, YOU CAN'T HAVE BOTH

My father was a truck driver, and though she worked part-time at a friend's hardware store, my mother was a stay-at-home mom. We were considered lower middle class, which meant we always had what we needed, but not always what we wanted. Unable to have everything, we had to make choices, and one of those was to choose between having experiences or possessions.

My dad was a big believer in the value of experiences and creating memories. When he traveled to the South Pacific for his tour in the Army, it had opened his eyes to a whole different world beyond Wisconsin. He wanted us to take vacations or go to different events to experience as many new ideas and places as we could afford.

The challenge for me was there were things I really wanted to have as a young boy. There were three things I wanted badly. One was a Wilson A2000 baseball glove. It was the glove to have when I was young, and I wanted one. But, this glove was two or three times the cost of the glove I currently had. I did not care. I thought it would make me a better player. I also wanted a Schwinn bike—the bike to have in the late 1960s and early 1970s. The last was an above-ground swimming pool. This would have been the cherry on top of the cake!

My dad had other ideas for us. He wanted us to take some great vacations to places like Mount Rushmore, Pikes Peak, Disney World, Gettysburg, etc. He said, "Not only will you have fun, but you will have memories that will last a lifetime." Then he told us we had to make a choice. As a young kid, I could not understand this memory and experience thing. I wanted my new glove!

Luckily, we all chose memories and experiences. We were like the Griswold's from the movie Vacation. We loaded up our Buick LaSabre family truckster and traveled the country. Dad was 100% right. The memories my sister and I have from those trips live with us to this day.

Memories like the time the muffler on the car fell off driving in Florida right as we were going over a bridge with at least 50 people fishing. Their expressions were priceless. Or the time a Buffalo chased my dad in the Black Hills. Or in 1973, when we stayed at the Contemporary Hotel in Disney World. Or driving up the curvy dirt road to the top of Pikes Peak with my mom screaming at my dad to keep his eyes on the road. I could go on, but they are ingrained into our memories forever.

I never did get that glove, bike, or swimming pool I wanted. As I look back, none of those would have changed my life or added anything to my knowledge of the world compared to the wonderful trips and memories I have.

I know we live in a material world and have for a long time. I know that the latest great toy is fun to have. I also know that our younger generation can't put their phones down long enough to engage meaningfully with the fascinating world around them. I encourage you to live a little. **Possessions cannot enrich your life in the same way that experiences can. There is a great big world out there. Experience It!**

———•●•———

GARDEN OF THE GODS

When I was eight and my sister was eleven, my mom and dad took us on a road trip. We drove through Minnesota, South Dakota, Wyoming, Colorado, Kansas, Missouri, and Illinois. While in Colorado, we visited the wonderful city of Colorado Springs, and on the itinerary was visiting Pikes Peak, the Air Force Academy, and a place called the Garden of the Gods.

The Garden of the Gods is an incredible array of red rock formations. Many of them have been named over the years, including Kissing Camels, White Rock, Siamese Twins, and Cathedral Spires. When my parents were describing this part of the trip, I remember asking myself if this was really going to be as much fun as they were trying to make it out to be.

My instincts at a young age were spot on. The red rocks were definitely something we had never seen before. They were beautiful, but after the second formation, we had seen enough. After the crazy and thrilling drive up Pikes Peak the day before, the Garden of the Gods was falling way short of expectations.

My dad knew we were getting antsy and called a tremendous audible that saved this portion of our trip. He knew there were sections in the park that you could climb up the formations, so he drove us to that area of the park, parked the car, and told us to have fun climbing the formations. We had a blast for the next hour or so.

Fast forward about 25 years. My niece and nephew (who were 11 and 14 at the time) were coming down to Dallas to spend a weekend with my wife and me. We decided to take them to San Antonio, the home of Sea World, the Alamo, and the Riverwalk. Like my dad before me, I had everything mapped out so we could have a tremendous time together.

Our first stop was the Riverwalk. We strolled around the area for a while and then had lunch at a great Mexican restaurant right on the river. Then it was off to the Alamo. The legendary place of Davy Crockett, James Bowie, and General Antonio Lopez de Santa Anna. We began the tour with a short video about the famous battle and then a walkthrough of the buildings with a tour guide. About ten minutes into the tour, my nephew pulls me off to the side and said, "The Garden of the Gods."

I instantly knew what he meant. I asked if my niece agreed, and she said yes. We skipped the rest of the tour, went to the gift shop, and bought a souvenir, then went across the street to Ripley's Believe it or Not. They were thrilled. On the way to Ripley's, my nephew told me that my sister had told him our story and said if we were not having fun, just say, "Garden of the Gods" to Uncle Jeff, and he will know a change of plans is in order!

Whether you are planning vacation locations, giving a presentation, taking part in a discussion group, or teaching a class, know your audience. If not, their brain will be thinking, *Garden of the Gods!*

—————————•◦•—————————

PASSION VS. EMOTIONS

Reed St. James was a small division of the Haggar Apparel Company. Originally, the division was formed to sell lower-priced merchandise such as men's apparel, outwear, etc., under the Reed St. James label. These goods were offered on the downstairs sales floors while the higher-end Haggar labeled merchandise was sold on the department store's main floors.

As mass merchant retailers like Wal-Mart, K-mart, and Target began to grow, the department stores relinquished this strategy. Due to this shift, the Reed St. James division changed its focus and began selling to all the mass merchants in the United States. After selling the Haggar label products for three years, I took a chance and joined this team in 1993. I knew that the mass merchant business was on a roll, and I wanted to be part of that growth.

The entire six-member Reed St. James team assembled to prepare for the upcoming selling season.

We discussed the prices for our upcoming clothing line, and as the meeting went on, I became more and more agitated because I just did not think that we were being competitive enough with our pricing. Before making the big decision to change from selling the established Haggar label product for essentially a startup division, I had been told we could and would be competitive with our pricing. Well, in my opinion, we were not competitive.

Finally, I had enough. "Listen," I shouted, "if we can't get better pricing or shave a little off our margin, I'm not sure I can sell **any** of this product to my accounts!" My voice rose to a fever pitch as my emotions took over. Usually more measured, my mannerisms were completely uncharacteristic. When I finished my rant, the room fell silent until the head of the division, Milton Hickman, answered calmly, "Jeff, I understand your challenges. The team will work diligently to address them the best we can."

Clay Huston was a 30-year Haggar veteran and was one of the founders of the Reed division. After the meeting, he pulled me aside and said, "Let's take a walk." Once away from the others, he continued, "You know everything you said in your rant was 100% correct. The problem was nobody heard you. You were so emotional that all people heard was you complaining. Add in your hand waving and negative body language, and all your points were lost."

I nodded, knowing he was right. "It's good to be passionate," Clay continued, "but not emotional. When emotions come into play, you lose perspective. Your anger causes people to tune you out. Whether your thoughts are correct or not, they never hear you. We need your passion, intelligence, and drive to help this division. We don't need rants like what just happened."

He was right, of course. Navigating the line between passion and emotion has been a challenge for me my entire life, and I have watched countless people do the same thing I did in that meeting.

It's great to be passionate, but when emotions run too hot, they can cloud your perspective and can turn people off to your message. Take a step back from the situation and use your head more than your heart.

I SHOULD HAVE GONE TO THE GAME

After 11 months of training with Haggar, I finally received my sales territory—Phoenix, Arizona. I had one problem; however, I was still coaching a team of 14 and 15-year-old boys with my friend, mentor, and fellow salesperson, Jimmy Palasota. We had a great chance to win the championship, and I was crushed.

Jimmy was awesome about the circumstances. "Don't worry," he said, "go to Phoenix and get set up. I believe we can get through the playoffs without you, but if we make the championship game, I want you here!"

"But I can't afford to fly back from Phoenix."

"Don't worry about it. I'll pay for your ticket!" Everything was set if they made the championship.

My first two weeks in Phoenix were crazy. I had to move into my new apartment and get everything ready for my first selling season. I was calling all my accounts to introduce myself and set up appointments. I had to press all my samples which included about 50 sport coats, suit jackets, and pairs of pants. I had to look at the logistics of my trips, like making hotel reservations. There were no cell phones in those days. Parts of Arizona were hundreds of miles of nothing but desert, and I had no travel apps to rely on for directions or help with finding gas stations.

It was a little overwhelming, but Jim Herman, a fellow sales representative and a new great friend, was mentoring me on how to get these tasks accomplished. Then I received a phone call from Jimmy. The team had made the championship game! He and the boys missed me and wanted me to come back and coach the team.

Before I arrived in Phoenix, it was a no-brainer to go to the game. Now I was unsure. Even though I was only going to be gone a couple of days, I did not feel right about leaving. Jim Herman told me to go. My new regional manager said if I had everything in order, I should go. But something just did not seem right.

I called Jimmy and told him I just could not come. What a huge mistake! The boys lost the game, and to this day, Jimmy has never forgiven me. You only have one chance to live through those super special moments in your life—the birth of a child, a graduation, a wedding, a special dance recital, a Boy Scout camp out, a championship baseball game ... Even in the world we live in with the ability to stream live events, it is not the same.

YOU HAVE ONLY ONCE CHANCE TO LIVE THROUGH LIFE'S SPECIAL MOMENTS; MAKE SURE YOU HAVE YOUR PRIORITIES STRAIGHT. THERE ARE NO DO-OVERS IN LIFE.

I don't have many regrets in my life but missing that game with Jimmy and those great kids is one of them. Even though my professional goals were set really high, I promised myself that I would do my best never to miss something like that again. My attendance record to date on that front is pretty outstanding.

You have only one chance to live through life's special moments; make sure you have your priorities straight. There are no do-overs in life.

———— • ● • ————

DON'T HIT THE SEND BUTTON

It was 1996, and I was a consultant at Electronic Data Systems (EDS) in the Textile and Apparel division. As the only person in the division that had worked in the industry, I was hired into the division as a subject matter expert (SME). Everybody in the division had incredible talents, but no one had my experience. It was a wonderful match of skills.

We had just received a request for proposal (RFP) from a major apparel company. It was a combination of technology and business process assessment. I was focused on the business process part of the response, and I was paired with a gentleman who had great experience responding to RFPs. The challenge was he did not know as much about the apparel industry as I did.

Monday morning, we started strong but soon began to hit a wall. By Friday, we were both a little frustrated with each other and decided to pick it up the following Monday. I determined that we needed some assistance from the other team members since we had tried for a week.

Voicemail was still the dominant form of communication in 1996, and I wanted to leave a message for the boss and the salesman on the account. The process for leaving a message for multiple people was to record the message and then send it to their extensions when prompted. I recorded this very passionate message, and without any hesitation, I sent it to two different extensions.

When I arrived home, I immediately went to listen if I received any responses. The first was from the boss. He completely understood and said that we would deal with it on Monday. Then I listened to the second message. It was the person with whom I was working on the process all week. I had sent the message to his extension by mistake. I felt about a half-inch tall. How embarrassing!

We worked it all out the following week, but it was a massive lesson learned. No matter what kind of message, an email, voicemail, text, Tweet, Facebook post, etc., if you are too passionate or emotional about a subject, DO NOT HIT THE SEND BUTTON. **If there is even a half of a 1% chance you will later regret sending the message, DO NOT HIT THE SEND BUTTON.**

Here are a few tips:

1. I send the message to myself and then sleep on it.
2. I have my wife read the message.
3. I have a colleague or friend read the message.

About half of the time, I rewrite the note before sending it. The other half of the time, I determine it is not worth it even if it is a perfectly written message. I just don't send it. **Think of how much better the world would be if we refrained from hitting the send button.**

NEVER TALK BUSINESS IN
THE BATHROOM

Once a month, on Monday mornings, Michael Rouleau, the CEO of Michaels, ran an Executive Committee meeting. In this particular meeting, we were discussing the upcoming budget process for the 2001 fiscal year. The CFO had just discussed the financial targets that we were challenging ourselves to achieve. As often happens during budget season, the conversation got a little heated because we needed to continue to hold headcount targets flat. Meaning not too many new hires.

After three years of righting the ship, we were no longer taking on water. That did not mean we could spend money indiscriminately. During a break in the meeting, I stayed back to talk with the CFO to discuss what we had just heard and how to handle some of the boss's comments in the meeting. We just wanted to make sure that we were on the same page to support what the boss wanted during the process. We talked for about a minute and then went to take a little bathroom break. As we walked out of the boardroom, we continued to discuss the meeting. We did not want people to hear what we were saying, so we made sure no one was lurking in the hallways and spoke softly.

It looked like no one was in the bathroom when we entered, but I turned around and put my finger to my mouth, signaling him to stop talking. I then pointed to the pair of shoes in one of the bathroom stalls. They belonged to the CEO. No matter how quiet we would have been, he would have heard every word. We were not saying anything negative, but it still would not have gone over too well.

I learned this lesson years earlier. We were on a plane going from Dallas/Fort Worth airport to Las Vegas for a semi-annual men's apparel trade show called M.A.G.I.C. The plane was packed with vendors and retailers from around the country. DFW is a hub for American Airlines, and they have numerous connecting flights. One passenger got up and found a couple of friends near the middle of the plane and started a conversation. They were talking loudly, and you had to be hard of hearing not to be able to hear what they were saying.

The conversation turned to Wal-Mart and how they did not like their business practices and how hard Wal-Mart was making life for suppliers. Not one thing they were saying was false. Wal-Mart was a retail juggernaut, and they were eating the industry alive. There was one major problem that these three gentlemen did not know. About 15 people from Wal-Mart were on the plane, including Wal-Mart's Vice Chairman.

The conversation lasted a few more minutes, and the gentleman returned to his seat. I got up to go to the restroom and walked by his seat. I leaned over and quietly asked, "Do you have a large Wal-Mart business."

He said, "As a matter of fact, I do."

"Well," I told him, "you probably just screwed that up because the plane is full of Wal-Mart people, including the Vice-Chairman, seated just two rows behind where your conversation took place."

He turned as white a ghost. I don't know what happened to his business, but it was a major lesson for me, and I could tell many stories like this. **Be careful when talking in public places. Cell phones make this even more challenging. Not only is it courteous to limit conversations while in public, but it is also wise to use discretion. You never know who is listening or what consequences your words may have.**

———•●•———

BLIND SPOT

I was having dinner with my boss one evening, and we were discussing an upcoming vacation my wife and I were planning. It was a trip around the Baltic Sea. Destinations included Moscow, St. Petersburg, Berlin, Stockholm, and Copenhagen. I told him we were now planning the daily excursions to each city and wanted to make sure that my son had a say in what we did each day.

"How old is your son now?" he interrupted.

"Seventeen. He's a senior in high school," I answered.

"Why are you still taking him on vacations with you? Why don't you just leave him home and enjoy your vacation without him? He doesn't have to go *everywhere* with you."

I was not shocked by his question. My boss had put his career in front of everything, especially his family. He changed companies and moved many times as he rose the corporate ladder. Each position with more power and the financial benefits that come with each role. As CEO of his current company, he had reached the top of the corporate ladder.

In the many years that I worked with him and for him, he expected everyone else to have the same career-first mindset. One time in an Executive Committee meeting, he said, "I want you to be married to the company first, not your spouse." Some people were shocked by his statement, but I was not. It was his blind spot. He was an incredibly successful businessman, but at what cost?

We all have blind spots. These are areas in which we seem to be unable to see or understand a personal constraint or recognize how important that lapse is in our life. One of mine was not understanding the impact my move to Dallas had on my parents. This blind spot was especially glaring when my dad died. I thought I did my best to still take care of my mom from a distance, but I should have done more in retrospect.

What is your blind spot? I can almost guarantee you that you have one. Is it too late, like in my circumstance, to change it? If so, learn from it. I adjusted my blind spot by spending more time with my sister and her family, who still live in Wisconsin. We talk every week and have taken a couple of family vacations together with the whole gang—my wife and son, her two kids, their spouses, and five grandchildren. I fly back once a year to go to a Green Bay Packers' game. I talk and text more with my niece and nephew to be a bigger part of their lives. Spending quality time with my wife and son is even more important to me. My family comes first.

BLIND SPOTS CAUSE YOU TO FOCUS ON THE WRONG PRIORITIES. KEEP LOOKING OVER BOTH SHOULDERS TO SEE WHAT MIGHT BE THERE. ADDRESS IT NOW BEFORE IT IS TOO LATE. YOU'LL BE GLAD YOU DID.

Blind spots cause you to focus on the wrong priorities. Keep looking over both shoulders to see what might be there. Address it now before it is too late. You'll be glad you did.

---•●•---

MAMA'S BOY

We were approaching the first tee, and there were two young guys in their early twenties waiting for us to join them. My mom always got nervous when we had to play golf with someone she did not know. She was concerned that she would play badly and embarrass herself. I always told her if she played her game, no one would say anything other than, "Nice shot, Marilyn."

We got out of the cart, and I introduced myself to the two young men, and then I introduced my 66-year-old mother to them. You could see it in their eyes, but they were polite enough not to say a word about what they were really thinking. They were thinking what bad luck they had to play with this old broad who would probably take all day to play.

What they did not know was that my mom played what I call old lady golf. She may not hit the ball too far, but it is always right down the middle. She rarely, if ever, got in trouble tee to green. For a 66-year-old woman with arthritis in her fingers and wrist, she played a mean game of golf, and these boys were about to be embarrassed for their thoughts.

The first hole was a short par four. The two young men both hit their tee shots way right and into the rough. I hit a solid three medal right down the middle, and mom hit it about 170 yards right down the middle as well. The young men scrambled to get on the green in three shots. Mom hit a low liner that rolled up to about 15 feet of the pin. I hit my second shot within about five feet of the hole. Mom parred the hole; I birdie it, and the two young men each had a double bogey.

The second hole was more of the same. It was a par three, and Mom and I were on the green in one shot, while the two young men hit it way to the left into the woods. Mom and I parred, and the two young men again had double bogeys. It was so awesome!

On the third tee box, both young men came up to our cart and apologized to my mom. "When we saw you coming, we thought you were going to be terrible and ruin our day, but instead, we are the ones embarrassing you!"

"That's so sweet, thank you, boys. Now, we can all just relax and have some fun," she answered. All four of us had a blast the rest of the round. The best part was hearing them say, "Nice shot, Marilyn."

This is one of a million memories I have about my mom. Unfortunately, she passed away about ten years ago, so now all I have are memories. Where my dad was my hero and mentor, my mom was the one who inspired me. She never let me think I could not achieve anything I set my mind to in life. When I struggled with confidence as an adolescent, she was the one who kept telling me things would get better. Her undying confidence in me eventually helped me to build confidence in myself.

She is the one who took care of me when I was sick, helped me with my schoolwork, came to every one of my sports events, gave me a hug when I was down on myself, and she always put my sister and me first before herself. I am proud to say that I am a mama's boy because without her in my life, I know I would not be the person I am today. When people make jokes about turning into your parents, I don't laugh. If I can be half the parents my mom and dad were to me, then I will have been a great parent.

I lost my dad when he was only 63, and my mom was 76 when she passed. It sucks. Even though I tried my best to enjoy every single moment with them, I know I could have done more. **Don't let a moment go by while your parents are alive to tell them that you love them and thank them for their sacrifices. Enjoy every moment you can and take nothing for granted.** If you haven't talked with your parents today, why don't you put the book down and call them right now. Don't text them—actually call them. You will thank me for it after you say goodbye, and I love you to them. Now, start dialing!

———•●•———

GET UP, GET OUT AND GIVE BACK

It was one of the smaller projects I had worked on at Michaels Stores, but it was by far the most fulfilling. The Board and the CEO wanted me to update our donations process for the company. It had become a haphazard mess, and we were starting to hear rumblings from our customers and our associates, wondering why we didn't give back more to the community.

It took me about a month to get my arms around the good, the bad, and the ugly of the current process and another month to come up with a recommendation on how to fix the situation. When I was done, we had come up with specific guidelines for our corporate donations to charities like the North Texas Food Bank, United Way, and programs like Jr. Achievement. I had never felt more satisfaction when a project was over because I knew we were helping charities and people in need.

I picked the North Texas Food Bank to be the non-profit I worked with the most. I volunteer as much as I can, helping sort out food for many needy people in the North Texas region. I started out going to their distribution center in South Dallas and doing a shift or two once every month or so. When my son got older, I took him with me as part of his volunteer hours requirement in school and Boy Scouts.

It was so satisfying after each shift when one of the Food Bank workers would say that we had sorted enough food for 10,521 meals that could help feed over three-quarters of a million hungry people in North Texas. It was a small gesture of appreciation for all the wonderful things that had happened in my life.

My wife's favorite charity is the Children's Hospital of Plano. She started volunteering when she worked at Electronic Data Systems. When our beautiful and healthy son Zachary was born, we started giving financially to the hospital. It is fun to visit and see a plaque with your name on it, showing we played a small part in helping them care for the most vulnerable people in the world. A sick child.

That was not enough for Lisa. She became part of the Women's Auxiliary, which does a variety of wonderful things for the hospital. Lisa chose to concentrate on the Red Cart program. Many times, parents come to the hospital with nothing but the clothes on their backs. The Red Cart Patient Support program provides items such as a toothbrush and toothpaste, a bottle of water, a snack, or a juice drink for both the family members and the children.

It is both heartbreaking and heartwarming to hear Lisa's stories when she comes home from doing one of her volunteer shifts. You want to cry for the pain they are in and also because they are so thankful for something as simple as a toothbrush. You pray for them, and you pray that you are never in that situation.

Our area schools require students to fulfill a certain number of hours volunteering somewhere to graduate. This program is wonderful and reminds young people that there is more to life than social media and video games. Our son, Zachary, has gained an understanding of how fortunate he is, and he is a better person for volunteering.

No matter your age or how busy your life, give back by volunteering your time, talents, or treasure. There is nothing more satisfying than knowing you are helping others in need. I pray that I am never in a situation where I need help, but it comforting to know countless volunteers would be there in my time of need. So, get up, get out, and give back.

NEVER FORGET WHERE
YOU COME FROM

In retail, there is nothing like seeing whether all your hard work to make life a little less hard for stores and managers is actually producing the intended results. It was about a year after the new management team had arrived on the scene to help turn a struggling company around, and I was visiting one of our Tuesday Morning stores on a routine tour.

I walked the backroom with the regional manager and store manager. They explained how some things had improved, but they still needed a lot more help. They listed some things that were on the top of their priority list. I listened intently and took copious notes. If I did not understand the issue, I would interject a question or two to clarify because you cannot get to the root cause without understanding the problem. After about 30 minutes of this, we had a pretty big list.

When we were done, the store manager told me that I was the first Senior Executive to visit her store in almost five years. And when they had come out, they did not listen and absolutely did not do anything differently. She said, "I heard from other people within the organization that you were different, and now that I have spent an hour with you, they were right. You truly do care about us. You are genuine in your compassion for the store associates and management. Where does that come from?"

My answer was simple, "My mom and dad. They always told my sister and me that no matter how much success you have in your life or career, never forget where you came from. No matter how high in the world you get, never look down on anyone."

"Wow," she answered, "your parents taught you well."

"They did," I replied, "and I will never forget that I am a product of a truck-driving dad and a stay-at-home mom.

Not forgetting where I come from has grounded me with a solid foundation. I have never forgotten how hard my dad had to work to give us a home, vacations, food, etc. I will never forget how hard my mom worked taking care of the house, making sure my sister and I were at all our events. She was always in the stands cheering us on, always taking care of all the family finances by pinching pennies the best she could. I will never forget how hard my parents and our blue-collar friends worked to do the same for their families.

I have always been more comfortable talking to the people in the distribution centers, the store associates, the manufacturing workers, the account payable people, the planners, younger workers—the people who actually do all the work and struggle with life's challenges. I have never thought I was better than anyone else due to my current standing in life. This is thanks to my parents' encouragement never to forget where I come from.

VALUE PEOPLE FOR WHO THEY ARE REGARDLESS OF THEIR BACKGROUND, UPBRINGING, SKILLSET, OR PRIORITIES.

Stay grounded. All people are valuable, and you show them dignity when you see and interact with them as your equal. Never allow yourself to look down on people or think you are better than them. Value people for who they are regardless of their background, upbringing, skillset, or priorities. We are all in this together!

AS BEAUTIFUL TODAY AS THE DAY I MET HER

James Thompson was the National Sales Manager at Haggar. He and his wonderful wife, Cissy, invited me to go to church with them one Sunday to hear Zig Ziglar speak. Zig was known for his self-help books and motivational speeches. He told a variety of stories during his talk, but one really hit home.

The story goes something like this: One day, a friend asked how Zig's wife Jean was doing. Zig said, "She is doing wonderfully! She is still as beautiful as the day I met her!" Now Zig and his wife were close to 60 at the time.

Zig's friend said, "I know you are a great motivational speaker and always looking at the world through rose color glasses, but no one is as beautiful in their sixties as they were in their twenties."

Zig said without hesitation, "You are so wrong because you do not see what I see. You are looking at exterior beauty, only looking skin deep. And yes, there are the realities of gravity, but after all these years of marriage, I see an inner beauty that is so much more than just skin deep.

"I see the beauty of a mom that raised four great kids. I see the beauty of a wife who loved, helped, and supported her husband. I see the beauty of a friend who is always there. I see the beauty of a person who does incredible charity work. I see what you do not want to see or do not try to see."

Wow! That was a sledgehammer to the head. How powerful. How true. I was living in Dallas at the height of the TV show *Dallas* which was the glorification of rich and beautiful people in the superficial world. As a 25-year-old young man, I did not look at the inner beauty Zig was talking about. It was all about how a person looked on the outside and not who the entire person was, both inside and out.

Most of us do not take time to look at people for who they are on the inside. We take a shallow look, and if they do not pass a quick "eye test," we move on. After that day, I shifted my thinking. My surface-minded view of people expanded to look at the entire person. I thought about all the great people who had touched my life to date and realized how right Zig was.

A surface look at people is shallow, taking in only their outward appearance or known accomplishments. Look deeper, and you will find the true beauty of who they are and the entirety of their talents and abilities. If you already look at the entire person both inside and out, fantastic. If you don't, start now. Like Zig, I can honestly say that my wife Lisa is more *beautiful* today than when I met her.

THE DAY I FELT 10 FEET TALL

I was always exceedingly small for my age. This meant I was a prime target to be picked on. Being so small, I could not fight back physically, so I either fought back with my words or just took it.

Then one day, everything changed for about a month. During the West Allis summer, you were always doing something at the local elementary school playgrounds. It was *the* place to be. The summer programs were all outstanding. You name it; we did it—baseball, kickball, ping pong, daily crafts, swing sets, basketball, and more.

The playground opened at 9 am and closed at noon for lunch, then reopened at 1 pm and closed at 5 pm for dinner. At 6 pm, it opened once more and closed for the night at 9 pm. You were there when it opened and when it closed.

One day, we were playing baseball on the small ball field at the far south end of the playground. The only people usually in attendance were all the wonderful mothers and a few grandparents of the players. Occasionally, Mr. Kellerman (one of my dad's friends) would get off work and watch a game, but we never saw any other dads.

My dad drove an 18-wheeler semi-trailer truck for a local lumber yard. Most of his routes took him all around Wisconsin and northern Illinois. He left early in the morning (4 or 5 am), and he came home about 4 or 5 in the afternoon. It was a tough job with long hours. He never had a chance to see my sister and me play unless it was on the weekend. That is until arguably, the best day of my young life happened.

It was in the middle innings of the game. My team was on the field. I was playing second base, which meant I was facing south towards Greenfield Avenue, the major street in my neighborhood. It was between pitches when I noticed a flatbed semi-trailer truck turn off Greenfield Avenue and on to 104th street. After the next pitch, I looked up, and I could not believe my eyes—it was my dad!

The game stopped. All eyes were on my dad's truck and trailer. Remember, we were all 10 or 11 years old and loved playing with trucks. Plus, it was so unusual to see anything other than a car on this road. Dad pulled off to the side of the road and parked the truck. The rumbling of the tractor came to a halt when he turned off the engine. Dad opened the door and jumped out. He was only about 5'9" tall, but that day, he looked 6'5" to me. He came over to the fence and watched the rest of the inning.

He told us that he had a city load, which meant he did not leave the Milwaukee area and worked it out so he could come by. All my friends were telling me how cool it must be to have a dad who drives a truck every day. I had a little hop in my step, but the wonderful moment was not over. After the inning was over, dad got back in his truck, did a U-turn, and drove past the ballfield. Every person (including parents) took their arm and made a pull-down motion so he would blow his horn. It was awesome. I was ten feet tall, and the talk of the playground for the next several weeks.

In life, small little gestures of goodwill sometimes have a massive effect. Whether that is doing a wonderful thing for your children, volunteering for a charity, helping someone at work, or just doing something nice for your spouse. It will make them feel ten feet tall.

———————— • ● • ————————

MAJORING IN THE MINOR

We were in a merchandise planning session with a buyer and her team to finalize spring selling season plans. In these meetings, we discussed a buyer's plans by department, classification of products, sub-classification, and sometimes we even went into detail for their bestselling items (called SKUs—stock keeping units).

This particular buyer was incredibly talented and exceptionally passionate about her business. She fought about every single issue that could possibly affect her business. The meeting was run by the Chief Merchant, Greg Sandfort. He was a very detailed boss, but he had his limits.

As the meeting wore on, we began to get worn out from spending too much time on issues not significant enough to warrant that much time. Finally, Greg had enough. He stopped the meeting and asked, "If we give you everything you want, how much sales and profits would you produce?" For this particular category of business, it was insignificant.

Greg responded, "This is a perfect example of majoring in the minor." I had never heard that saying before, but it was perfect for this moment and many moments post this meeting. Greg continued, "We love your passion for the business, but we can't spend an hour discussing something that will generate such a small number of sales when we are a $4 Billion retailer."

As we wrapped up the meeting, I thought about how many times I wished I knew this statement so I could have used it to move a meeting or discussion along. After the meeting, I told Greg how perfect this statement was and how perfect his timing was when he used it. We waste so much time on things that just don't matter in the big picture.

In my non-scientific poll, I believe 99% of the population has a Ph.D. in majoring in the minor. Step back and ask, "Am I majoring

in the minor? Is this discussion worthy of the time and energy I and others are investing?" If not, move on and fight for something bigger another day.

--------- • ● • ---------

IT WAS HARD TO TAKE A BREATH

It was November 2020, and it started like any other common cold or flu I ever had. I had a little scratchy throat with a slight feeling of fatigue but no fever. If this were any normal year, I would have bought some over-the-counter medicine and stayed in bed for a couple of days. 2020 was anything but a normal year. With COVID-19 running rampant, I decided to get tested.

I went to see my doctor on a Wednesday, and she said all my vitals were normal, including that my lungs sounded great. I was hoping if I did test positive that with all my vitals looking good, I would have a mild case and put the virus behind me within ten days or so. On the way home, I received a call from my doctor, "Your test came back positive," she said, "you need to quarantine for ten days. If anything changes, let me know, and I will take the appropriate action."

Well, things did change. By Friday, I began to struggle to take deep breaths. Every time I did, my lungs burned, and I began coughing uncontrollably. My wife called and got a prescription for a steroid, an inhaler, and a cough suppressant. It took them a while to kick in, and when I woke up Saturday, things were even worse.

I could now only take a breath of about 25% capacity before I would start coughing. My oxygen levels were falling, and I really had to think about how to take a breath so I would not cough. Sunday, it remained the status quo. Normal breaths were hard; deep breaths were impossible. Each time I tried, it was painful, and it would make me cough like my lungs were going to burst.

My sister-in-law sent me an article about breathing exercises that helped others with their COVID situation. I thought, *How the heck can I do breathing exercises when I am struggling to breathe, period?!* Then I remembered other rehabilitation situations I had been in during my life with sprained ankles and broken bones and that to get better, you had to endure some pain. I thought about a time when a physical therapist had me in tears because she knew I had to fight through the pain to improve.

For the remainder of Sunday and all day Monday, I fought through the pain in my lungs and forced myself to take long and deep breaths. Yes, it did burn, but by Tuesday morning, the tide had turned. I could now take full deep breaths with less pain than the day before. Each day after that, my breathing improved. By the following Sunday, I was close to 100%. The combination of medicine and those breathing exercises did the trick. What a difference a week makes?

As I was going through this challenging situation, I realized how something that we almost all take for granted was so hard for me to do. To breathe. This simple act fuels us with oxygen—our body's life-sustaining gas. Take the COVID virus out of the conversation for a second and think about your daily activities. You are inundated 24/7 with text messages, emails, Facebook, Twitter, Instagram, 100s of push notifications, and maybe a real live phone call or two. How about the challenges of your job, school, or all the extracurricular activities?

You don't have time to breathe because you cannot or will not turn your life off for five minutes to just take a break from the world. Even if it is just five minutes to put your phone down or find a quiet spot to do nothing other than take a deep, long breath of the body's life-sustaining gas.

You don't realize how important breathing is until you can't do it without a tremendous amount of effort. You must take time to renew and recharge. Don't wait until things spin out of control before you pause, reflect on what is important, and take the time needed to be restored. Start doing your daily deep (I need a break) breathing exercises today. Your mind, body, and spirit will thank you for it.

— • ● • —

BUT I HATE CAMPING

When my son was 11, he joined the Cub Scouts. Since 6 or 7, he had bounced around the usual youth sports circuit; soccer, baseball, and basketball, but never took a liking to any of those activities. The Cub

Scouts were different. He really enjoyed the activities and the group of boys that were in his Den.

One parent asked me if I would like to help with the boys. He said they needed parent sponsors to assist with the weekly meetings, helping boys advance in rank, and monthly campouts. I was okay with the first two, but there was one problem with the last task—I *hate* camping. I mean, I *really hate* camping.

We did some camping back in Wisconsin, and I was not a fan. I loved the outdoors to play golf, baseball, swim, or hike. But I did not want to cook, eat, or sleep in the great outdoors. I had a major problem. The boys really needed parents and my son wanted to be a part of the organization. What was I to do?

For the next five years, until my son earned his Eagle Scout award, I was a parent sponsor. I dove into the manuals like it was my profession. I was never a Boy Scout, so I had a lot to learn. After five years, I even became a surprisingly good outdoorsman. I would never win any outdoor survival contests, but I held my own, and Zachary finished an outstanding achievement. Eagle Scout is a tremendously difficult award to receive. It felt even better because I was able to be part of his journey to Eagle.

Why did I do it? Because I saw my father do the same things for my sister and me. He drove a 40' foot flatbed around Wisconsin about 30,000 miles a year. What do you think he did on his vacation? He drove his wife and two crazy kids in a car around the United States! We would put on close to 4,000 miles over a two-week period. When we went back to the playground to enjoy the rest of the summer, he would go back to driving his truck.

As a young boy, I never thought about what dad did until I had my son. It was then I started to realize I needed to shift my priorities. It was no longer just about me. I needed to think about doing and taking part in what he liked to do and not only what I liked to do.

As a 22-year-old, it was all about me. When I got married and had a family, it was all about us. Priorities shift from ourselves to others as we embrace personal growth, and the sacrifices we make for those we love and care about are definitely worth it. My priorities are faith, family, and friends. What are yours?

TO HELL U RIDE

There is a beautiful little ski resort in the southwest corner of Colorado called Telluride. There are two theories to have the town was named. 1) The name was derived from the mineral tellurium, a non-metallic element often associated with mineral deposits of gold, or 2) it is derived from the phrase, "To Hell You Ride," which described the treacherous journey to get to this remote mountain town back in the day.

I like To Hell U Ride. It describes my adventures to check things off my bucket list now, not when I was 65 and retired. When I was 23, my dad suffered his first heart attack. When I was 33, he died from his second. He was 63 years old and only three months into what was to be a long retirement. So, I started doing things on my bucket list in my mid-30s.

Dad had busted his tail driving a truck for most of his career. In the cold winters of Wisconsin, the crazy rainy spring, and everything in between. He and mom took care of us and saved so they could have a wonderful experience during their golden years. All their plans faded in an instant.

Even though my parents took us on some wonderful vacations, they missed out on so many of their dreams. I realized right then and there that I was not going to wait until my retirement to start checking things off the list. I did not fear the reality that I could have my dad's heart problems, but I also knew that no matter how I changed my diet and exercised, I could fall to the same fate.

Here are a few things I have checked off my bucket list:

- Jumped out of an airplane from 13,500 feet
- Drove a MiG fighter jet going 350 miles per hour
- Bungy jumped from a bridge 143 feet above a river in New Zealand
- Drove a dog sled on a glacier in Alaska
- Snorkeled the Great Barrier Reef
- Played golf at Pebble Beach
- Visited the Kremlin in Moscow
- Saw the Sistine Chapel and the Coliseum of Rome

I have done all of this and more, and I am still not retired! My point is not to brag. My point is to tell you not to wait. Live life along the way. You never know when life will throw you a curveball. Plus, it was such a blast to experience these wonderful events, and those encounters enriched my life in ways that bled over positively into my career. It gave me the motivation to want to do even more now and not wait until later.

LIFE CAN CHANGE IN AN INSTANT. LIVE NOW, DON'T WAIT FOR TOMORROW.

Life can change in an instant. Live now, don't wait for tomorrow. See and experience the world—it is a fun, mysterious, and fascinating place.

———————•●•———————

FATE, CHANCE, OR SOMETHING BIGGER

When people ask me how I met my wife, the easy answer is on a blind date. The real story is one of twists and turns that, for me, was not just fate or chance. There was a Higher Power that played a role. Here is how it happened:

- I was in an elevator going to do an exit interview after resigning from my job at Gimbels. The National Sales Manager for Haggar Apparel company happened to get on that elevator. We talked about my goals, and eight weeks later, I was driving to Dallas to begin work at Haggar.

- I was supposed to get my first territory in Kansas and Missouri, but a late November trip with one of the salesman delayed that move. The salesman told management that I should get a different territory because I had some skills that could be utilized in a different territory.

- I finally got my territory in Arizona. During my stay, I decided to get my real estate license thinking I might be able to that as a side job. On the first day of classes, I met a young lady named Norma. She was late for the meeting, and the only seat available was next to me.

- We dated for a while and then became good friends. When I moved back to Dallas, I called her and asked if she knew anybody in the real estate business that could help me find a place. She had worked in the real estate business there before her move to Phoenix.

- She introduced me to Sandy Woodall and her wonderful

husband, Bill. Sandy showed me around, and I settled on a two-story apartment and condo in North Dallas.

- One day I went to pay my rent to the leasing agent (Jane Rutledge), and she said that she knew a great girl I should meet and that she would get her number and give it to me the next time I came into the office.
- The next time I came, Jane was not there. She had her baby and was out on maternity leave.
- 6 or 8 weeks later, I went to pay my rent, and Jane was back. After we discussed her new baby, she said, "I still must give you my friend's phone number."
- A week later, I called Lisa, and we had our first date!

Some of my friends will say it was luck or fate, or I just happened to be in the right place at that right time. I don't believe that for a second. The sequence of events listed above just doesn't happen by chance.

First, I believe that God had a hand in Lisa and I meeting. Second, I had to put myself in the position to take advantage of His goodness. As I was making some good choices and not-so-good choices, I believe there was a guiding Spirit working hand and hand with me. **I am aware of God's hand of providence at work in my life. His blessings blended with my courage to take risks, willingness to fail, and to try new things has been a partnership that has brought me much success.**

If I had just stayed in my home and waited for the opportunity to knock at my door, it would have been difficult to get the true blessings from God. **I know in the ever-growing secular world we live in that it is hard to believe in a Higher Power. Give it a try. Wonderful things can happen.**

———— • ● • ————

PAY YOURSELF LIKE A BILL

When I was 27, I started to make a very good income as a Haggar sales representative. It was one of the major reasons I wanted to become a sales rep. The challenge was this: what do I do with this newfound prosperity? It was a lot more money than I ever had before. The answer came from a book I received during this time. I can't remember who gave me the book, but it was on wealth management and financial planning.

It was the perfect gift at the perfect time. It discussed in common sense terms how to manage money, invest money, create wealth, manage expenses, and so much more. After reading the book, I wondered why this was not a class taught in college. It sure would have been better than some of the electives they made me take. It was practical, straightforward, and easy-to-understand guide.

One of the best lessons for early wealth creation was to "Pay Yourself as A Bill." Instead of struggling to find a way to save, the premise was to force you to write yourself a check just like the electric bill, rent payment, or your credit card bill. It was such a simple lesson. I added me to my set of bills. I started small at first but as my commission checks rose, so did my bill to myself. I was never delinquent or stopped doing it so I could buy something cool. It was a bill that had to be paid.

The book also contained tips on managing your expenses and lowering your spending. With discipline, expense management, and paying myself as a bill, my wealth began to accumulate. In 1993, I quit my job at Haggar to see if I could make it as an entrepreneur.

There was one simple reason I could take this chance. I loved to save money more than I liked to spend it. I had saved a significant amount of money, and I now had options. Because I had saved and managed my expenses wisely, I now had the ability to leave a job and try something on my own. If I had not had a substantial amount of savings, it would have been exceedingly difficult to take that chance.

When I tell this story, people say, "Well, it is easy to save money when you make a lot of money." My answer Is, "Well, I made only $15,000 per year at my first job." When I moved to Dallas at 25, I had the equivalent of $16,000 in the bank. This was not retirement money, but it was more than enough to help me move to Dallas and then Phoenix the following year.

It takes discipline and desire to find ways to save money, but savings give you options—options that can change your life. Find a good book on money management and start learning how to manage your money significantly better. Start by paying yourself as a bill.

PERSONAL, NOT FINANCIAL

When Lisa and I got married, we wanted children. We discussed whether Lisa would want to continue working if we were blessed with a child. She did not have a definite answer at the time, but she wanted the option to stay at home. Financial factors were a major influence in our decision-making process.

We discussed a variety of options. Both frugal; we were already committed not to live beyond our means, but giving up an entire salary is a whole different topic. We decided that we would try and live on only my salary and save hers to see if we could make it without too much pain. After struggling with various entrepreneurial failures, I now had a good job as a consultant with EDS.

We crunched the numbers and put the plan into action. It was working. We cut back on some things, clipped coupons, looked for deals, did not spend frivolously, and continued to pay ourselves like a bill to add to our savings. Plus, we were saving Lisa's entire salary. Then the big day came. Lisa told me we were expecting a child. We were off the charts excited!

Eight months later, and our beautiful son Zachary was born. Once we got him home, I asked Lisa what she thought about going back to work. She wanted to stay home, but still wasn't sure about the finances.

As each day passed, I saw a joy that was different than anything I had ever seen from Lisa. I knew she was going to choose to stay at home. Because of our propensity to save and be frugal with our money and because we had created a plan, Lisa was able to make a personal decision based on her desires and not forced to make a financial decision based on our needs.

As I started to make more money, we shifted the plan. Whatever raises or bonuses I made were now considered savings or rainy-day money. We went from living off 100% of my income to 95%, then 90%, and then 80%. We were still living comfortably and traveling on our fun vacations, we bought a bigger house, and our net worth was rising exponentially.

I am not telling you whether or not you should be a stay-at-home parent. This story illustrates how managing your money and expenses gives you options. My parents did the same thing on a truck driver's salary and with my mom working part-time at a friend's hardware store. They lived off my dad's base hourly salary. If he received any overtime, they banked it. All my mom's wages were put towards saving, vacations, or emergencies.

We still had everything we needed but not everything we wanted. We still went on great vacations that sometimes took years to save for. Unfortunately, my dad died shortly after retirement, but they had built up a nice amount of money that my mom lived comfortably on for the rest of her life.

Be frugal. Live within (or under) your means. Save before spending. It will give you options allowing your decisions to be personal ones, not financial ones.

> **BE FRUGAL. LIVE WITHIN (OR UNDER) YOUR MEANS. SAVE BEFORE SPENDING. IT WILL GIVE YOU OPTIONS ALLOWING YOUR DECISIONS TO BE PERSONAL ONES, NOT FINANCIAL ONES.**

YOU JUST HAVE TO ASK

Our vacation to Athens, Greece, and a few of the Greek Islands was a combination gift for our 25th wedding anniversary and my son's recent graduation from college. One of the islands, Santorini, was formed after a massive volcanic eruption in 1646, and our hotel was in the center of the beautiful Santorini caldera.

Before we arrived at the area to check-in, I asked my wife Lisa if she would use her magic today. She said, "Of course, you never know what you can get if you don't ask!" We entered a small room with two wonderful young women who were there to check us into our room. We had reserved a suite with two beds. It was basically a slightly oversized hotel room.

One of the women asked for our passports and credit card. Then Lisa tried her magic, "Is there any chance for an upgrade?"

"In fact," she answered, "the Executive Suite is available if you would like it."

"Absolutely!" we replied. I could not believe it. Lisa had done this so many times during our marriage that I lost track of the official count. As we walked to the Executive Suite with one of the young women, we both looked at each other and could not believe it was happening again. As we approached the room, we realized we hit the jackpot this time. The suite was at least 1500 square feet with two bedrooms, two baths, a huge living area, and a kitchen. It had its own separate balcony and outside jacuzzi—Lisa's magic dust had worked again! Why? Because she had the courage to ask.

My wife and I have always been deal hunters. We are frugal to the point of being fanatical. We love nice things, but only for the right price. We are always looking to save money or find a better deal. It does not matter if we are negotiating a new car, upgrade for a hotel, a warranty issue with a product, or using two in-store coupons at the same time. We are always on the hunt to get more for our money.

We have hundreds of stories like the one above. You can have the magic dust, too; you just have to be willing to ask and be persistent in challenging the listed price. Our batting average is probably in the 60% to 70% range. We have saved a tremendous amount of money over the years as well as getting things we absolutely never anticipated, like the Executive Suite in Santorini.

When trying to stretch your dollars, be willing to ask for just a little bit more. They may say no. So, what. They might say yes. You never know what you could have received if you don't have the courage to ask.

———————•●•———————

IT IS ONLY $10,000

It was 2002, and Michaels was rolling. The company had made a successful turnaround from financially troubled to a profitable company by just scratching the surface of its potential. The biggest was that the company was no longer fighting for its life. It had put that phase behind them in 1999 and early 2000, and they were now able to make investments in people, technology, stores, and distribution centers, to name a few things.

Even though things were getting better financially, the CEO, CFO, and I were extremely strict with expense management and capital investments. My focus was on all the strategic investments we were making and planning to implement over the next five years. As part of that focus, I was a member of the IT Steering Committee.

The role of the IT "Steering" Committee was precisely as it sounds: to steer them to get the most of our limited resources—money, time, and people. To do this, the business and the IT teams had to work together to prioritize both the tactical and strategic initiatives.

As we discussed a couple of smaller projects, one of the IT directors presented a project to upgrade one of our systems to help the division that made all the custom picture frames for Michaels Stores. When he finished, the big question remained: What was the cost? His response, "It is only $10,000."

I could not believe my ears. When does anyone used "only" and "$10,000" in the same sentence? Apparently, when they think corporate money is different than personal money. Over the last 25 years, I have held or been a part of many financial-related meetings. You would be surprised how many individuals don't realize how a company actually makes money. It is not something that many companies teach employees. There is an expectation that they should know, but many do not.

You would also be surprised at how many people would come to me for business advice, and I would find out how terrible they were at managing their personal financial situation. My favorite line was one associate who said he had saved $500 on a purchase. I asked what he paid for the item. He said, "Only $2,500."

Whether it is company funds or personal, you need to understand the value of money. Spending too much, saving too little, and living beyond your means all add up to poor money management and can lead to disastrous circumstances. Take a class, find videos on YouTube, or read a book. Learn how to improve your skills at managing money and never use "only" and even $100 in the same sentence. Your savings account will thank you.

DON'T JUST SHOW THEM, LET THEM

I was about 7 or 8 years old when my dad asked me if I wanted to help him change an electrical outlet in my bedroom. I loved doing things with my dad, so I was all in. He was an incredible handyman. He could fix just about anything around the house or garage.

The first thing we did was go to the hardware store to get a replacement socket. We entered the store and walked to the electrical aisle. There were many varieties of outlets. I asked dad how he knew which one to choose. He selected a few different outlets and explained the difference between them, then he chose the one for my bedroom and explained why this one would work.

When we went to the counter to pay, dad let me hand the money to the clerk, and he told me how much change we were supposed to get in return. The clerk handed me the money, and I gave the change to my dad. He handed me a penny and told me to get myself a piece of bubble gum.

When we returned home, dad said we first needed to turn off the electricity. As we walked to the basement, he explained why this was the most important step in the process. At the fuse box (we had twist-in fuses, not an on/off circuit breaker like most homes have today), he held me in his arms so I could open the door. Then he took my hand in his and helped me unscrew the fuse.

We went back up to the second-floor bedroom, and he handed me a screwdriver and instructed me how to take the faceplate off. Then he told me how to take the outlet screws out. He then guided me with his hand and pulled the outlet from the wall. We followed the same process to unscrew the old outlet wires, attached the wires to the new outlet, screw the new outlet in place, screw the faceplate back on and then walk back downstairs to screw the fuse back into the circuit board. The final step was to go back upstairs and see if each socket worked, and they did. Yet another item checked off what dad called his "Honey Do List."

Dad did this process with me with just about every project he undertook. Painting, changing a tire, changing the oil in the car, cutting wood, fixing a clogged sink, etc. You name it; I was by his side. Dad didn't just show me what to do; he let me do it. He let me gain experience not by watching but by getting my hands dirty. Because of my dad's training process, I am a pretty decent handyman myself.

This principle is key when coaching, mentoring, or training someone. I see so many managers and parents tell the person *how* to do a task, but they don't let the employee or child actually do the task. When I ask why, the answer 95% of the time is they wanted it done correctly. The other 5% of the time they say, it would take too long if they let the other person do it. I ask, "But how is that person ever going to learn if you do not let them try?"

The usual answer is, "Maybe next time."

I know it took so much longer for dad to do these chores when he let me do most of the tasks. He knew this was the best way to train me, so he took that extra time needed to help my knowledge and experience grow. Do you do this? **When you transfer your knowledge and skills by helping someone learn through hands-on experience, you make a major difference in their life—just like my dad did for me.**

———— •●• ————

MY FIRST TASTE OF LEADERSHIP

At 17, I became the coach of our church softball team. My dad had managed the team for years but retired a few years before. The team was highly successful, but most of the players (like my dad) were getting older. After he retired, the team struggled to be successful, and some of the better players decided not to play at all. The previous season before I took over as coach, the team went 2 – 12.

We were a small church, and the council of church leaders was discussing not funding the team anymore. My dad had taught me a lot about playing and coaching, and I told him I thought I could get some of the better players to come back and play. If the church could give us one more year, I would put a winning team on the field that would make the church proud. Luckily for me, they agreed.

At the first practice, I was shocked. About 30 players showed up. Some were really good, others were pretty good, and some were not so good. I could not have been more pleased with the turnout. However, the practice was horrible. We only had the practice field for an hour. Not everybody had a chance to take batting practice. When we tried to have a short infield/outfield session, it was a horror show. One thing was crystal clear—the difference between the talent of the players. I had to make a quick leadership decision on how to reduce the size of the team immediately.

I had told the participants that I would not make any cuts to the team until after our third and final practice. However, I knew I had to make cuts right then and there, or I would lose all the better players. I pulled the team around home plate and gave my first Vince Lombardi-like speech: "The only reason we are able to play is because I told the council we would be competitive. If we are not competitive, they will not give us the money to play. I want the best 14 guys (and everybody on that field knew who they were) to stay and play. I need everyone else to come and support us, but we are going to win!"

The next week only 14 guys showed up—all the best players. We went 12 – 2 that season and 11 – 3 the next year and finished in first place both years. All the other players came to our games and cheered us on during the season. It was a fantastic success. It was my first taste of leadership. I was by far the youngest coach in that league by 20 or 30 years, and we beat them all.

It taught me that if you can recognize great talent and put the best people in the right positions, you can win. I also knew that I did not know everything. I had to depend on some of the older players to help with things I did not know or making some difficult decisions. And of course, I always had my mentor (my dad) there whenever I needed a helping hand.

LEADERSHIP IS ABOUT SURROUNDING YOURSELF WITH GREAT PEOPLE. LET THEM EXCEL AND RIDE THE WAVE OF SUCCESS WITH THEM.

I now knew that I could persuade people who had more experience than me, manage people, make tough decisions, get help from others when I sincerely asked and be successful doing it, but I wanted more. The seed of leadership was planted, but it would need a lot of tender loving care. Leadership is about surrounding yourself with great people. Let them excel and ride the wave of success with them.

JENNA

Jenna came into my office one day and asked if she could talk to me about something. At first, I thought maybe she was going to tell me she had found another job. Her current role of Marketing/ Merchandising Support was stretched to not only support the Senior Executives in those divisions but also to support me in my role as SVP of Supply Chain for Tuesday Morning stores.

She was so talented that I really believed she could do anything she wanted. I always worried that she would find a position where she could use all of her skills, and Tuesday Morning would lose a valuable young individual. My philosophy is if the current company can help you reach your goals, give them everything you've got. If they cannot, look for a company or an opportunity that can. I never wanted to selfishly hinder someone's growth.

I was pleasantly surprised that Jenna did not want to talk about leaving (at least not at this moment) but wanted advice concerning her next career move. She said that she knew I was busy but that she valued my opinion and was having a difficult time determining which path to take. No matter how successful I was at helping companies as a manager or Senior Executive, I received the most joy and satisfaction when I could mentor and coach someone.

My first taste was at 17 when I coached a church softball team to achieve back-to-back championships. Since that moment, I have loved the idea of helping others reach their potential as an individual and help a team or organization be successful. Steven Spielberg once said, "The delicate balance of mentoring someone is not creating them in your own image but giving them the opportunity to create themselves."

I say, "My dreams are your dreams." That is where I began with Jenna, and after multiple discussions over a month or so, she decided she wanted to try to make it in the merchandising side of retail. Since then, she progressed from the support position to a buyer at Tuesday Morning, then moved to At Home, where she is currently an associate buyer.

I saw her promotion on LinkedIn, and I wrote her a note. I had not talked to nor seen her for over five years, so I did not know if she would reply. I was extremely excited when she responded. Here are a couple of sentences from her reply, "I still think back to the times working with you and how much I learned. Thank you for taking the time with me and kick-starting my career as a buyer."

I always hope that my mentoring impacts the person I am trying to help, but how can you not get fired up about an unsolicited comment like Jenna's kind words? Winston Churchill is credited with saying, **"We make a living by what we get; we make a life by what we give."** Regardless of who said it, the quote beautifully reminds us that we all need to think about what we leave behind once we are gone. Is it material possessions, awards, or accolades of our business success? Or is it the legacy of a positive influence we have had on a family member, co-worker, friend, or an entire generation (and possibly the generation after that)?

There is nothing wrong with becoming the best professional you can be and all the hard work and dedication it takes to do that. Along the way, take a moment or two to see if you can help someone else. I have had the great fortune of having many mentors during my journey. I would not be here without them.

There is no better feeling in the world than knowing you have had a positive influence on someone's life. Give it a try. Maybe you can help someone achieve their dreams.

———————•●•———————

SO, I GAVE HIM HIS BOOK BACK

Losing my biggest account for Haggar Apparel in Arizona, I found myself living in Dallas once again. My Buick Century was running on its last legs—I needed a new car desperately.

I bought a two-door Acura Legend, and I loved it. It had a sporty flair to it, and it was fun to drive. It was so unlike the two four-door sedans I had driven to date. Unfortunately, I got into a minor accident in less than a year when a small delivery truck just kissed my right front quarter panel. I could not believe it.

I went through the usual process of getting my claim approved. Then, based on my insurance agent's recommendations, I used my car dealer for the repairs, but the car was never the same. When the truck hit me, it shifted the frame on the car. The dealer knew it but said they could do nothing about it. After going 15 rounds with them, I decided I needed to get a different car.

Lexus had been introduced to the United States, and a few of the Haggar executives had bought and loved them. I decided I would give them a try. There was a Carl Sewell Lexus dealership about a half-mile from the office. Carl Sewell was then and is to this day a legend in the car dealership business.

I purchased an ES250 Lexus. It was their introductory model. When I picked up the car, on the front passenger seat was an autographed copy of Carl Sewell's new book, *Customers for Life: How to Turn That One-Time Buyer Into a Lifetime Customer.* I loved reading books about successful people, and I thought it was a nice touch to have this in the car.

After two months of driving the car, I had unfortunately purchased a Lexus lemon. I had it in for service six or seven times within the first two months of owning the car. Engine troubles, part issues, window rattles, etc. After the seventh or so time, I had enough. I set up a meeting with the sales manager.

I figured that with all the stories Carl had written in his book, his dealership would certainly treat me differently. How wrong I was. Even though the manager admitted that my problems were unusual for a Lexus, he could not do anything more than just continue fixing the car. I mentioned the ideals that Mr. Sewell stated in his book. He answered, "That is a book; this is reality."

Well, that did not sit well with me. At home that night, I typed a long letter to Mr. Sewell. I explained in detail what happened and that I believed, based on his writings, that his dealership would be different. I signed the letter and put it in a big envelope along with his book. I put a handwritten note in the book that read, "I believe your people need this book more than I do." I drove to the dealership and gave it to the receptionist the next day.

About an hour later, I received a call from the sales manager saying he would like me to come back to the dealership and he would take care of my issue. They took my car back and renegotiated the entire deal, upgrading me to the ES300. When I picked up the car the next day, there on the front seat was my signed copy of Mr. Sewell's book. A note attached to the book said, "I thought you might want this back."

> **INTEGRITY DEMANDS THAT YOU DELIVER ON THE EXPECTATIONS YOU SET.**

Integrity demands that you deliver on the expectations you set. So many companies and people set expectations, and then they never deliver. All talk and no results. Oversell and under deliver. If you set an expectation with your friends, spouse, company, or customer, DELIVER! It took a while, but in the end, Mr. Sewell delivered.

———•●•———

MANAGING EXPECTATIONS

It was a working session with about seven or eight other consultants preparing for my first consulting engagement with a client. I had been in three months of training classes, and now I was getting my first taste of this new industry I had just joined.

We were going through the project plan, scope, deliverables, client details, and more. It was the standard project preparation meeting, but it was all new to me. I wanted this career change from an apparel sales representative to a management consultant, and I wanted to make a big first impression with the management of EDS. I carefully listened to see if there was any additional role I could play to add extra value to impress the new team and company.

Then the opportunity came. The budget was very tight, and the profitability was pretty low on the bid we made to this client, so they were looking to cut any expenses they could. The target was PowerPoint skills. They had money in the budget for someone to develop all the presentation slides. They asked if anyone could add this to their other duties.

I had just taken five hours of training on basic PowerPoint skills, but I thought I was an expert. So, I raised my hand. Without hesitation, the project lead said, "Awesome, Jeff is now our PowerPoint guru." I knew this was going to be so good for me. What a great way to make a first impression!

How wrong I was. On a scale of 1 to 10, I was a 3 in PowerPoint skills. The person they were going to hire from the corporate office was a 10 out of 10. I was so lost and confused about the basic skills to do the things they wanted. Add to that all the constant changes everybody was making, and I was drowning in trying to keep up.

This was my very first consulting project, and I had to learn how to be a consultant. What a fool I was. Luckily, my wife also worked at EDS and knew some incredibly talented individuals who helped me with the presentation. They really saved me from a very embarrassing situation.

About halfway through the project, we had a team meeting. The partner on the project used a phrase that I had not heard before. He said, "We must be careful to manage the client's expectations. We don't want to say we can do things we cannot do now, don't have the skills to do as a company, or have not put in the scope of the project." I was thinking, *Why did he not say this before I stupidly raised my hand about being able to the PowerPoint slides!*

From that point forward, this simple phrase, "Manage Expectations," has been ingrained into my brain. Sometimes it is hard because your boss, client, family member, friend, or spouse is pushing you to do more. Always work hard, but when pressured to commit to more than you can reasonably do, don't promise things beyond what you can deliver with excellence. It is better to under-promise and over-deliver. My wife's friend saved me; you might not be so lucky.

DON'T PROMISE THINGS BEYOND WHAT YOU CAN DELIVER WITH EXCELLENCE.

---·•·---

EVERYONE IS A SALESPERSON

I graduated from the University of Wisconsin Milwaukee with a BBA in Marketing. I spent four years getting drilled into my head by the business school that marketing is the sales, branding, and communication part of a company. At the time, I thought that the only people that sell are sales or marketing people.

There is no doubt there is a unique skill to be a great salesperson—a splash of bravado, gift of gab, engaging personality, and a lot of B.S. One of my bosses at Haggar once said that either you have it or you don't. He said not everyone can be a salesperson, let alone a great salesperson.

At the time, I thought he was correct. I worked with some of the greatest salespeople God ever created. In the 1940s and 50s, these people were knocking on any door that could possibly be opened to sell Haggar products. They literally could sell ice to an Inuit.

Then I started to change my view. In 1987, I met with the Information Technology Vice President (we called it Data Processing department back then). He presented something called EDI (Electronic Data Interchange) and how he wanted the sales team to begin discussing the benefits of EDI with their retail accounts and how they needed to invest in this new technology.

As the presentation went on, I realized this man who had 20 years of technology experience was selling this idea to us. He was using all the skills I saw from the apparel sales team, but he was from IT. After the meeting, I asked him if he had any sales training in his background. He told me that everyone must sell at some point in their life. Whether business or personal, you will be asked to sell something at some point in your life. He was right. Everyone must be a salesperson.

A person is selling themselves when they want a new job. A CFO is selling Wall Street on a new IPO (Initial Public Offering). A lawyer is selling their case to the jury. A person is selling themselves to a potential spouse. A tree trimming service is selling you on cutting your trees. A plumber is selling you on his services. A politician is selling themselves to get elected. A mom is selling their kids on the idea of how great broccoli is. A person sells altruism to raise donations for a charity.

You get my point. **We all have or will sell something at some time in our life. It might be a product, a company, an idea, or maybe ourselves. My guidance is no matter what your background, experience, or profession, learn how to sell. It is a skill everyone needs to have.**

PRACTICE MAKES PERFECT

At Michaels, we had an annual vendor conference meeting. We would invite hundreds of vendors and close to 1,000 people to spend a day and a half with us to build our relationships, negotiate marketing contracts, and most importantly of all, to tell them where Michaels was headed into the future. We wanted them to know what we were doing, why we were going in this direction, and what we expected of them to continue selling us their incredible merchandise.

Each Executive Committee member would have a section of the speech. Merchandise, Marketing, Finance, Real Estate, Strategy, Supply Chain, etc., would all give an update on the progress they made since last year and what to expect over the coming 2 to 3 years. We worked incredibly hard on writing the speeches, and then we would have 5 or 6 practice sessions in preparation for the actual presentation.

The practice sessions were not the only time I would practice. I would take my presentation into one of the bathrooms in our house and practice my speech repeatedly. I wanted to get to the point that I could almost give it without notes. I wanted it to flow like I was having a conversation with the audience, not reading from a binder. I wanted people to listen to my words, not my actions fumbling through the notes or constantly having to look down to find the correct words to say.

When the big day came, I was ready. Many of the other executives were not. You would see them paging through their notes just minutes before they would have to go on stage. My success rate with the effectiveness of those vendor speeches was not perfect, but it was pretty high from the compliments I would receive from my boss and audience attendees.

This "practice makes perfect" attitude goes back to when I was a young boy trying to become the best baseball player I could be. I was an okay hitter, but I knew if I could play an excellent shortstop or second base, I would have a chance to make a team. My dad would hit me hundreds of ground balls. Man, I was battered and bruised, but I did get better, and my fielding skills were the main reason I played on the teams I did over the years.

I used this same attitude throughout my career to practice many aspects of my job to get as good as I possibly could. I would practice speeches for every type of meeting (board, vendor conference, internal, etc.), phone conversations, interviews, question and answer sessions after a presentation, human resource reviews, headcount discussions, and more. If it meant trying to convince someone of something, I would practice it.

Always be prepared. To be successful, practice things until you are as good as you can possibly be. You will be amazed at how much more successful you will be.

IT IS NOT WHAT YOU KNOW, BUT WHO

"It is not what you know; it is who you know." This saying sometimes refers to getting to know people to get ahead. Relationships do matter, and who you know can help you open doors, introduce you to new opportunities, and help you out of difficult situations.

At 22, I had a college degree, and I thought that piece of paper would help me get to the top of the corporate ladder. I was the first person in my family to get a degree, and I thought it was a big deal. How naïve I was.

When I was ready to leave my first post-college job, this reality hit me. In most of the interviews, they never asked me about my education. They still had specific job requirements that included a college degree, but our discussions only focused on my work experience, future goals, strengths, weaknesses, etc. I was shocked by this. None of these items were ever mentioned in any of my college or high school classes.

I also realized that I was competing with many others who had degrees and work experience just like me. I was one of many, not the one. I was striking out a lot and getting very frustrated. How could I differentiate myself from the crowd?

The answer was to build a huge network of friends, colleagues, and other business professionals (doctors, lawyers, investment people, plumbers, etc.). Looking back, every job I had opened to me was because of someone I knew. Here is the history:

- Gimbels: The career counselor from UW-Milwaukee recommended me.

- Haggar: Dave Lazovik, the General Merchandise Manager at Gimbels, was friends with the President of Haggar.

- Electronic Data Systems: My wife, Lisa, passed my resume around EDS.

- Computer Sciences Corporation: A headhunter I had known for a few years introduced me to a partner at CSC.

- Michaels: The company was my client while at CSC. When I decided to leave CSC for more time with my newborn son, the CEO and CFO asked me to join Michaels.

- Fossil: Jeff Boyer was a great friend and business associate at Michaels and was a Board Member at Fossil.

- Tuesday Morning: Michael Rouleau was my CEO and friend at Michaels. He asked me to join him at a small internet lumber company for a short while and later to join the management team at Tuesday Morning.

- RENI Analytics: David Toth was a friend and colleague at CSC who introduced me to Sam Vahie at RENI Analytics.

- Advatix Consulting: Sam Vahie introduced me to Manish Kapoor, who started Advatix Consulting.

I am grateful for each of the people on this list who helped me progress through my career. My network also helped me in more ways than just getting new jobs. It helped me with leads for new clients, gave me opinions on third-party companies to use for strategic initiatives, references for potential new hires, finding a new eye doctor, giving me guidance on managing my career and life, and much more. My network was a two-way street. I would try and help people whenever they would reach out to me as well.

Starting out, I did not realize the power of a great network. I do now. It is much easier to build a network today with companies like LinkedIn. **Begin building your network early and continue to grow it throughout your life.** Teachers, professors, parents, friends, counselors, classmates, etc. Then continue to expand it throughout your career and personal life. Add value wherever you can as you connect with people. **Relationships are one of the biggest assets you will ever have and worthy of meaningful investment.**

I DON'T GET IT

In 1988, Tom Hanks starred in *Big,* a movie about a 12-year-old boy (Josh) who turns into a 30-year-old man after making a wish. The challenge is he still has his 12-year-old mind. He gets a job at a toy company, and one day he is invited to a presentation for the CEO and company executives by a marketing whiz to pitch a new line of toys. The toy is a building that turns into a bug.

After the whiz finishes the presentation, everybody in the room claps. "Any questions?" he asks, knowing the yes people in the room will not say a word. Nobody raises their hands, except Josh. When the whiz asks what his question is, Josh says simply, "I don't get it."

The whiz is now very irritated. "What don't you get?" Josh proceeds to explain his issues with the product but then offers a solution. The executives who did not say a word after the presentation are now engaging with Josh's solution to the problem he raised. The CEO is incredibly pleased, and the whiz kid is very perturbed.

I love that scene. I have been in so many meetings where a presenter finishes, and nobody asks any probing questions. These meetings would be discussing major decisions that included capital investment, dedicated personnel for the project, new headcount, contractors, and additional expenses. Nobody would say a word.

Afterward, those in the room would complain about how that project received funding. I would ask them why they did not ask these questions or raise objections in the meeting. The excuses would just roll off their tongues, "I don't want to rock the boat. I want my project funded next month. Nobody would listen to me anyway. Blah, blah, blah."

I was the guy who asked the "I don't get it" question. Not on every subject, but I dared to ask questions to make sure we were making the right decision. In my early career, I would carefully pick and choose the places to interject my questions. I did homework on the subject, so I was incredibly informed. Complainers and naysayers rarely have an alternative solution. Picking things apart is easy. Unimaginative. But just like Josh, I would always have a creative solution or two to discuss as a counter-argument.

As my success rate grew, so did my confidence to challenge more topics. I knew the executives or other attendees were interested in hearing my perspective because I would challenge the status quo when they would not be willing to do so. My "I don't get it" questions were now expected.

It takes courage to do what Josh did. **Do your homework on a particular meeting subject matter and choose your challenges wisely at first. Never be known as a naysayer but build a reputation as one who adds value by asking insightful questions and offering positive solutions.** Then slowly broaden your focus to other topics as reputation builds. You might just impress the boss like Josh.

———— • ● • ————

YOU CAN TEACH AN OLD DOG NEW TRICKS

Wherever you go, you hear people complain about their jobs. It is exhausting to listen to them "Why not leave? Why not find another job?" Then the excuses come. "I am too old. I am not smart enough. I have my kid's college education to pay for. I will have to move my family. I ..." There will always be 1001 reasons why, but it is all BULL$#%$@! Here are two examples of why:

The first example is my dad. For years he was a truck driver. He drove a flatbed tractor-trailer for the Georgia-Pacific Lumber Company. He had learned how to drive trucks while he was in the Army. It was a tough job, but he liked it, and it took care of his family. Then he had a disagreement with a tree. It was the middle of winter in Wisconsin, and the roads were receiving a light but slippery coating of snow and ice. He was fully loaded with lumber as he reached the crest of a small hill on a two-lane highway. As he peered over the hill, he saw a school bus that had for some reason moved over into his lane.

He was trapped. If he hit the brakes, he would lose the back of the truck and probably hit the bus. He could stay in his lane and hope the bus could get over in the other lane. Or he could put the truck into the ditch and guarantee the bus and the kids would be safe. He took the ditch and hit the only tree for miles head-on.

He survived, but my mom, "Your driving days are over." He was 51 years old. Now what? The branch manager asked my dad if he wanted to become the warehouse supervisor. He knew that he could do most of the job but was concerned that it required more writing skills than he thought he had. After a lot of thought and prayers, he accepted the position.

He had never held a management position. He had only a GED and had to bury his pride many times to call his son to ask him how to spell a word or understand some of the language on a report he needed to fill out. Yet, he still took the leap to this new position at 51. He held that position until the day he retired.

The second example is my brother-in-law. He has worked in and around the manufacturing business most of his life. He found his sweet spot working for a company that makes CNC machine tools. For example, they made machines for which John Deere would manufacture parts for their farm tractors. He built, installed, and maintained these machines. Then things started to shift as manufacturing began moving out of Wisconsin. He knew he had to do something different, but what?

He chose to be an entrepreneur. He, along with two friends, started their own company. Tri-Star CNC Services, LLC was born. He was 46 at the time. It is a true American success story, and he did it with his own money, a high school education, and a tremendous amount of hard work and determination. He is now 18 years into running this business and still going strong.

So please, spare me your excuses. These two men took a chance later in life to start a new career. It was not easy, but they persevered against many odds. **Excuses are not reasons. If you desire a change, just do it. You will be glad you took the leap.**

CAN YOU MOVE THE NEEDLE?

Michaels Stores was my consulting client. CEO Michael Rouleau was hired to help turn a sinking ship around a couple of years earlier, and he and the team had made tremendous progress. I met with him to discuss Human Resources. At the beginning of the turnaround, it was hard to keep people around because they did not know if the company would become another gravestone in the retail cemetery.

Fast forward two years, and now instead of working on how to keep the company afloat, we were discussing where we could add more people to the organization and begin to upgrade the talent across all divisions. As part of our Human Resources deliverable presentation, I showed Michael organization charts, job descriptions, pay scales, etc.

Michael was not a patient man, and after working with him for two years, I knew that my slides were not hitting the mark. He stopped the conversation and asked me, "What do you think the number one quality of any new hire or any current employee needs to be?" I fumbled through a litany of qualities. Experience, team player, willing to learn, can handle change, and a few more.

"I am not looking for a laundry list of items; I asked you for the number one item," he responded.

Michael loved short sayings to make his point, so I was quickly going through my "Michael sayings" index cards in my brain as he was talking. I knew that he had to have said the answer to me already. I just had to find it somewhere in my memory bank.

Aha! my brain said, "They have to be able to move the needle!" I told Michael.

"Correct!" he smiled. "I want results. I do not need superstars in every position; we can't afford that. I need people who can get results every day in every position in the company—constantly, consistently moving us forward. If we have 100% of the team moving the needle every day, we will be unstoppable. If they can't produce, then we don't need them."

This speech was blunt talk but gave crystal-clear expectations. Results-driven people move the needle every day by incrementally and consistently moving things forward. Are you making a difference? Can you move the needle every single day? Are you results-oriented? It does not matter if it is management, family, friends, or any group you are a part of; can you get results that will move the needle? If not, you need to figure out how to become a results-oriented person.

RESULTS-DRIVEN PEOPLE MOVE THE NEEDLE EVERY DAY BY INCREMENTALLY AND CONSISTENTLY MOVING THINGS FORWARD.

I SUCK AT OFFICE POLITICS

I have been blessed with a variety of skills. Playing the game of office politics is not one of them. It exhausts me. It is such a waste of time. Just like the real world of politics, the game is coldblooded and brutal. My two big problems with office politics; (1) I am too honest and (2) I am too honest.

In 1990, the film *Hunt for Red October* came out. The premise is a Soviet Captain wants to defect to the U.S. and give us a brand-new secret technology submarine. Early in the movie, the main character, CIA analyst Jack Ryan, is asked by the Deputy Director of Intelligence to brief the National Security Advisor and most of the Joint Chiefs of Staff.

Jack is surprised to hear he is the one giving the briefing. His boss says, "You are liable to get some direct questions. Give them direct answers. Tell them what you think." During the presentation, Jack is challenged by one of the members of the Joint Chiefs. Without hesitation, being direct and honest, he blasts away at the general. As Jack is pounding away, his boss slowly places his hand on Jack's arm. A cue to back off a little.

After the presentation, the National Security Advisor asks Jack to stay behind. Jack's boss leans over and says, "I told you to be honest, but holy cow, Jack!" That scene describes 95% of my career, especially as I moved up the rungs of the corporate ladder. I am blunt and honest to a fault. Just like Jack did in this scene, I do my homework before I get into a discussion.

I know I went too far on some occasions, and as I grew older, my self-filter did get better. In my opinion, it takes so much more effort watching your words, couching your statements, and finding the politically correct thing to say than just being able to be honest. It is exhausting.

I wish I had a magic wand that could get all the office politics out of the business world or out of any organization bigger than one person. It is a reality we all must face. My guidance is to make sure that you are aware that it does exist. Understand who can and cannot take your honest opinions.

To help me, I drew an office politics organizational chart of the key people in the company. I added notes on where they stood on the key topics we were discussing at the time. It was kind of like being the majority whip in Congress trying to find out the caucuses' opinion or how they would vote on a bill. I used it to better prepare for meetings or discussions. I wanted to know where everybody stood.

I realize this is a lot of effort just to play the game, but it is a necessary evil. **To get ahead and stay out of trouble will require you to navigate office politics. You don't have to sell your soul. Be honest and direct but learn to do this with prudence.** The effort will be rewarded.

UNKNOWN OPTIMISM TO KNOWN PESSIMISM

In 1997, I was interviewed by five or six principals and partners for the Computer Sciences Corporation (CSC). The division's main focus was on supply chain, but they also worked on process improvement, strategy, and technology implementations. All were outstanding, but practice leader Fred Crawford sold me on joining the company. A rising star in CSC, he was smart, personable, and confident.

After my interviews, CSC extended me an offer to join the firm. The day before flying to Cleveland for initial training, I received a call from Steve Biciocchi, partner for my division. He said, "Jeff, I've got some news I want you to hear from me first."

My heart sank. I thought he was about to tell me they could not hire me. Instead, he dropped another bomb. Fred Crawford had resigned. I was crushed. I could not believe it. How could he have talked to me the way he did during my interview? He had to know that he was leaving. I still thought the entire division was outstanding, and all the other associates I spoke with were great but shaken by the news, I was unsure of what to do.

On the phone, Steve was reassuring. "Jeff, CSC wants you badly. We don't want to lose you, and if you join the company, things will turn out great. Listen, this division is more than Fred Crawford, and I think this will turn out to be a positive move for you." These were incredible words, and I was sold again.

Steve continued, "With most new jobs, there is a transition from 'unknown optimism, to known pessimism.' It always happens. It is just how long it takes. You just had it happen before you started with the company."

He was exactly right. In all my jobs throughout my career, there is that moment where the wave of reality hit me. At Gimbels, it was counting thousands of leather jackets in a hot warehouse; at Haggar, it was driving people around like a chauffeur; at EDS, it was the consulting division I joined had very little power over the old established technology divisions; and finally, at Fossil, I realized that they really did not want to make the changes they talked about in my interview.

In every new job, a moment happens that takes the wind out of your sails with the company. Don't panic; it's normal. Assess if the company will still help you meet your goals. If yes, stick with them. If no, give them your all while beginning a search for something new.

As a side note, CSC led me to meet Michael Rouleau, CEO of Michaels Stores. That introduction was the most important single event in my career.

CORPORATE LIFE IS RUTHLESS

J C Penney was going through one of their many restructurings in 2012. It was yet another challenge for the once-great company. One of my directors at Tuesday Morning was a Director of Planning and Allocation. She was part of the management team working on a downsizing plan—who would stay and who would go.

These are always horrible discussions. You are glad that you are staying, but it is horrible to know that good people are going to get fired. After working on her area of responsibility she turned in her documents and waited for the downsizing day to come. A short time later, she received an email asking her to come to the auditorium.

When she walked in, she realized that she had been duped. Everybody in the room were people she knew were on the cut list. That meant she was on the cut list as well. As she was working on her list, someone was working on a list that included her. RUTHLESS!

When I first joined the corporate world, I was a starry-eyed 22-year-old. I thought if you worked hard and played by the rules, the company would take care of you for a long time. How wrong was I? One of my bosses used to have a saying for this, "Eat or be eaten."

He was right. Office politics. Horrible management decisions. Terrible bosses. Corporate raiders. Private equity companies. Management consultants. All of these and more make corporate life a game of survival of the fittest. It was eye-opening to realize this fact.

The sooner you realize this, the better. You can't ignore it. It will not go away. It does not mean that you must become one of the many SOBs that work in the corporate world, and it also doesn't mean that the Doctor of Pink Slips won't find you. It *does* mean you have to be proactive to understand how you navigate around these obstacles.

Keep your resume and LinkedIn profile updated. Have an exit strategy. Take calls from headhunters and recruiters—even when you love your job and think everyone likes you. **Never get complacent about managing your career. You can be an optimist, a pessimist, or a realist. The corporate world requires realism. They will not take care of you; you must do this for yourself.**

———————•●•———————

ROME WAS NOT BUILT IN A DAY

It was the opening night dinner of the National Sales Meeting for Haggar Company. Even though I was doing very well in my sales territory, I still felt intimidated by almost everyone in the room. I was the youngest salesmen there, and I really felt like it. Most of the sales force and the management team were between 15 - 20 years my senior.

Moving around the lobby, I stopped to greet people and listen to their stories of things that happened to them while working for Haggar in 1970, when I was ten years old, or when they began at Haggar 20 years ago. I heard stories about trips they had taken to different countries or the beautiful resorts in places like Hawaii. They also talked about all the people they knew in the industry. Someone would ask, "What happen to the DMM at the May Company store in St. Louis?" Then a few different people would chime in with the answer.

It was so frustrating. They had so much more experience and knowledge than I did. They had so many more experiences than I had, and they knew so many more people than I ever thought possible to know. Even though my confidence in myself was off the charts, these meetings would always bring me down to earth.

After dinner, Larry Tolini (one of the newest members of the Haggar team) saw me standing by myself, waiting to get a glass of water. Larry was always there to offer me advice like I needed on this night. He asked me how I was doing. I told him okay. He said, "Okay? That does not sound like the brimming-with-confidence Jeff Wellen that I know."

"It is intimidating and frustrating to be so inexperienced compared to everyone else in the room. I wish I had ..."

I only got a few words out before he started to laugh. It was not the reaction I expected.

"Take a breath and listen, Jeff. There is not a person in the room who doesn't remember being in the same exact position you are today. We all were a little green behind the ears at your age, and that is okay." He continued, "We all wanted to have more knowledge, more experience, or to know more people when we were 26, too. We all felt intimated by older individuals in a room, and we all wanted the answers to every life question before we ever knew what we really wanted to do in our lives. When we were 18, we wanted to be 21. When we were 21, we wanted to be 30. And when we turned 40 ... we wanted to be 21 again!"

I laughed with him, my tension relieved. "Do not wish your life away," he continued. "Just live each day to its fullest, and before you know it, you will be the old, experienced guy in the room."

"ROME WAS NOT BUILT IN A DAY." WELL, NEITHER IS YOUR LIFE. EVERY DAY IS A BUILDING BLOCK OF LIFE LESSONS. THAT IS HOW YOU GAIN EXPERIENCE AND KNOWLEDGE.

It was some of the best advice I ever received. There is an old saying, "Rome was not built in a day." Well, neither is your life. Every day is a building block of life lessons. That is how you gain experience and knowledge. It includes family, friends, mentors and foes, high highs and low lows, wonderful successes, and horrible failures that take place in both your personal and professional life.

There is no shortcut I know of for experience, so don't sweat it. Do not! I repeat, do not wish your life away or be challenged that you don't have all the answers at 22, 32, 42, or whenever! Just live each and every day to its fullest by continuing to add life's building blocks to your shining city on a hill. The more you experience and the more knowledge you gain, the more the city will take shape. Then one day, you will be like me, celebrating your sixtieth birthday as I write this story and looking out over my still growing metropolis and wondering where the heck did the time go!

LONG AND WINDING ROAD

Even though I had set my goals at 24 years old, my path to get there was not a straight line. I knew I wanted to be a Senior Executive or run a company, but what kind of company? What industry? A senior leader in sales, marketing, or finance? I knew what I wanted to be, but my plan on how to get there was very sketchy.

Here is my career in a nutshell: I started as an assistant buyer and group sales manager, then became a sales representative, a failure at being an entrepreneur, a junior consultant for retail and apparel, a senior consultant and principle for a supply chain practice for any industry, a senior vice president (SVP) of strategy for a retailer, a SVP of strategy for a men's and women's accessory company, a SVP of inventory management and supply chain for a retailer, a partner in a startup analytics company, a SVP of operations for a startup supply chain company and finally back to being an entrepreneur.

I have many friends who had a more direct career path: Get a degree in finance. Work for an audit firm. Get hired as a financial analyst. Then move up to comptroller. Then VP of finance. Then CFO. Then president of a company. That is the more traditional straight-line career path. Mine was a little less direct, yet successful nonetheless.

Your first job after school does not have to be your job for the next 40 years. It is a stepping stone along the way. Do not get hung up thinking that you cannot make a course correction with your career position or your company.

Some people completely change their careers with a full stop on one thing and start another. Here are a few examples:

- Jeff Bezos had a lucrative career in computer science on Wall Street and then took on various roles at financial firms before launching Amazon at the age of 31.
- Vera Wang was a figure skater and journalist before entering the fashion industry at age 40.
- Harrison Ford, after being frustrated with the acting roles he was receiving, became a self-taught carpenter for 15 years until he got his acting break in the 1973 movie *American Graffiti* at 31.
- Colonel Sanders (of Kentucky Fried Chicken fame) held a variety of jobs throughout his career before he first started cooking chicken in his roadside Shell Service Station in 1930 at 40 years old.

Everybody's path to success is different, so set your goals but be flexible enough to adapt to the changing environment, fluctuating opportunities, and evolving attitudes. When an opportunity knocks, open the door. It may well lead you to a place you never planned on going. Enjoy the journey. Always move forward even if the path is a long and winding road to success.

CHAPTER 2

STARTING MY FIRST
REAL-WORLD JOB

I went from a nine-month-a-year student (with three months of breaks and vacations) to a full-time worker for the Gimbels Midwest Department Store company in a split second. The management had this crazy idea that just because they were paying me, they expected me to change my priorities. They actually expected me to be a working professional on day one! They watched everything I did to ensure they made a good investment in me.

If they decided I was not ready for prime time, I would be shown the door, and someone would be there to replace me in a second. I was the low person on the Totem Pole after thinking I was the big person on campus just a few short weeks ago.

I also realized that my first job did not have to define my entire career. It was a starting point for me to learn, grow, and begin the journey towards finding what I truly wanted to do.

I wish someone would have told me a few stories about what I should expect before I started my first real-world job. This section does just that.

THEY WERE WATCHING ME EAT

When I began interviewing for jobs during my senior year in college, I used the college placement office to help me as much as they could. In 1982 there was no LinkedIn, Indeed, or Monster. You had to check a job posting board 3 to 5 times a day to see if there were any new opportunities. When it came to preparing for actual interviews, the college had a couple of pamphlets you could read, and you could talk with one of the counselors.

The tips were extremely basic: have a firm handshake, look people in the eye, sit up straight, give direct and honest answers, know your strengths and weaknesses, and thank them for the interview. But there was one thing that they did not tell me.

I was interviewing with Kohl's Department Stores, a completely different company today than it was in 1982. Back then they were a 10 to 15 store chain with most stores located in Wisconsin. They were positioned between department stores like K-Mart and Wal-Mart. They sold apparel, sporting goods, car supplies, and candy.

Kohl's brought in about a dozen applicants, and we all had a rapid-fire interview process. We met with various people in the morning before they brought the entire group back together for lunch. They served fried chicken, coleslaw, and a roll complete with the standard-issue plastic knife, fork, and napkin.

As we began eating, everyone was struggling to get the knife to cut through the chicken. It was a challenge not to make a mess because we were all dressed up for our interviews. The skin on the chicken was tough, and the knife was not working. I was hungry, and I didn't really want to work at Kohl's, so I dug right into the chicken with both hands.

When I got home, I told my parents I thought the interview portion went well, but I probably lost out because of the way I ate my meal. A week or so later, I received a call from Kohl's—to offer me a job! The person said, "The people you interviewed with thought that you would be a great fit for Kohl's." I was stunned.

I had just received and accepted an offer from Gimbels a day or two before this, so I answered, "I appreciate the chance to work with Kohl's, but I will have to pass on the offer." She said she understood, and then I said, "I can't help it, I have to ask this. I used my hands to eat that fried chicken when all the other candidates were meticulous with their knives and forks. How did that not blow the interview?"

She laughed and said, "In fact, that was a factor in them offering you the job. You showed a creative problem-solving streak and did not conform to what was expected. They like that in a potential merchant." She continued, "In our interviews, we watch everything you do—not just how you answer questions, but how you interact with other applicants, the receptionist ... everything."

Well, my college counselor never told me about *that* when I talked to her about the interview process. **When preparing for an interview, learn what companies look for beyond the resume. Do a little homework on soft skills, too: body language, people skills, and other character traits the message boards say a company likes. Be as prepared as you can for those unexpected questions.** And *always* eat fried chicken with your fingers!

———————•●•———————

IF IT IS IN YOUR BLOOD

In our first session with the Executive Team of Gimbels, there were about 15 members of this year's class of executive trainees. A standard among all department stores, the Executive Training Program started with a 2 to 3-month introduction to all parts of the organization, including the buying office, sales floor, distribution center, accounting, finance, and customer service.

After the program, you were either put in a buying office as an assistant buyer or placed in one of the stores as a group sales manager. After 12 – 18 months, you flipped roles. Assistant buyers went to the stores, and the sales managers became assistant buyers. The goal was to get one of the highly coveted buyer positions after no more than three years.

This meeting with the executives was to give us a flavor of what the road ahead would be like for the next three years. Our CEO, Tom Grimes, was the first speaker. In a few short sentences, he gave us the most straightforward reality check I have ever received about a new job. He said, "Retail sucks." Then he paused dramatically, letting that statement sit in our minds for what seemed like an hour.

You could hear a pin drop. We all had just joined Gimbels; now the CEO said our future career sucks. "But," he continued, "if retail is in your blood, you will have a wonderfully long and successful career in this industry. If it is not, you will know quickly, and we will wish you the best of luck in your future. Now look around the room; more than half of you will leave within the first three years."

Talk about a cold splash of reality! I didn't even have a chance to process his last statement before he continued, "Retail can be an incredibly challenging career. Fashions change like the wind, customer behavior changes, it's hot when you needed it to be cold, cold when you needed it to be hot, and countless other things that affect what and when someone will buy something in our stores. But for those who love this industry and love the challenge of that fight, you will be successful."

After an almost 38-year career, Mr. Grimes was absolutely right. Every time I tried to get away from the retail business, I got tugged back into it. Retail is in my blood, and I love it, but it took me a while to realize it. He was also right about half our training class leaving Gimbels before they finished their third year ... including yours truly.

Young consultants may find they do not like their projects or the travel. Young engineers discover they do not like that 90% of their activities are not designing anything. Young accountants realize that a life with numbers is not for them. It is all a natural step in finding what they genuinely love to do. Sometimes it takes a little time before you hit gold.

The one thing that I know now that I did not know then is this: **Regardless of the industry, there is generally a high turnover in many introductory positions. Keep digging for that career until you discover what is in your blood. When you do that, it will no longer be a job for a paycheck but a career full of satisfaction.**

DID I GO TO COLLEGE TO DO THIS?

After the Executive Training Program at Gimbels, I was promoted to Assistant Buyer for Men's Outerwear, Rainwear, and Suits. I was so excited and ready to sink my teeth into my first real job after college.

With all the boring and tedious training completed, I thought, *now I will really get to use my college degree!* At 23, I was ready to conquer the world.

Then reality hit me. I *expected* to meet with vendors to select the new line of products for next year or travel to New York to go to a fashion show or conduct focus group studies on where the fashion trends were heading. But no. My first task was to go to our distribution center and count and sort thousands of leather jackets purchased on consignment. We only had to pay for the jackets customers bought in our stores; the rest we could send back to the vendor. There were four or five colors, four or five styles, and four sizes. They were all in shipping crates, and I had to pull each jacket out to count and sort by size, color, and style, then fill out all the paperwork to process the return to the vendor.

It was a one-person show with no help. It took me a week to get this done, and every moment of every day, I kept asking myself why I went to school to get a four-year degree in marketing to do this! Anyone could do this. I thought the task was beneath me. After all, I had this piece of paper that said I was a college graduate, not a stock-room worker.

I didn't know then, but I now know that this is part of being a buyer and a retailer. This was the job. It was not all glamour and fun traveling the world for new fashions. Retail is detail. Doing these things well would determine whether or not I would eventually get promoted to the next level.

I had to understand the entirety of the job. Return to vendors was part of the job, as was working on the sales floor, moving clothing racks around, signing advertising copy, etc. It was the first of many waves of reality that hit me. My first job had particularly good and fun moments, but the foundation was hard work on all the little details that made the difference between being successful or not.

Had I known this back then, I would have spent less time being mad and used that energy to learn more about all the nuances of my job. These lessons learned were invaluable as a broader knowledge base throughout my career and personal life.

When you first enter the workforce, you will do things that challenge you to your core. No matter how high you climb, every job has its moments when you will question why you must do this. Focus your energy on doing the absolute best job you can, not on the

negative of a particular task. Excellence in learning the details of a position will pay huge dividends in your success.

————— • ● • —————

CAN YOU MAKE MONEY PLAYING SOFTBALL?

After settling into my new assistant buyer role, I thought everything was going great. My boss was great, and I was learning a lot. He was giving me more and more responsibilities, and I had just received a small raise. Life was good.

Then Don Franklin, the head of personnel, wanted to see me. Don was a great guy and had been awesome during the recruiting phase. I did not know why he wanted to see me but assumed it was about how well things were going.

I entered his office, and he told me to sit down. For the first few minutes, it was small talk about my new position and how I liked working at Gimbels. Then he asked me one of the most direct and sledgehammer questions I have ever been asked, "Jeff, can you make money playing softball?"

Caught completely off guard, I thought, *where is this coming from?* I didn't answer right away because I was trying to figure out where the conversation was going. So he asked again, "Can you make money playing softball?"

"Well, sir, I love playing softball, but, no, I am not good enough to make any money at it."

"How many nights a week do you play softball?"

"Four. I also play tournaments on weekends, and I play hardball with a team on Sunday nights."

"That's a lot of softball," he said. I agreed, nodding my head, but I still did not know where he was going.

"Jeff," he cut to the chase, "I like you. Your buyer likes you. Your General Merchandise manager likes you. Heck, everybody likes you. You have a chance at a great career here at Gimbels, but you must decide if you are willing to realize that you are now part of the working world.

Your priorities must shift to how you are going to make money and have a successful career."

My stomach sank as I realized as he was giving me the "you are not in college anymore" speech. He was correct. It was the sledgehammer to the head I needed. I had not made Gimbels and my career a priority even though they were paying me. I was still playing sports and going out with my friends at the same pace I did when I was in college.

He complimented my skills and said, "You can be anything you want to be. But you must put a greater effort into your career than you are doing."

From that moment on, I realized if I wanted to be great at my job, I needed to shift my priorities. It happened that day. This may have been the most important conversation in my early career. Years later, I asked him if he would have fired me if I did not change. He answered indirectly, but I knew the answer was yes.

There is a healthy balance to find between work and play. But unless you can make money at your extracurricular activities, you need to focus on your job and have fun in your spare time.

THE DEVIL IS IN THE DETAILS

During many of Gimbels' training sessions, they drilled, "Retail is Detail." I had heard it so many times; I was going to make *sure* I would get into the details of my new position. I was on the job for about three weeks, when I had to go on the sales floor to check in some new merchandise.

We had just purchased an expensive leather jacket with the softest leather you ever felt. We only bought a few for the downtown store to test that type of jacket and the higher price point. I was on the floor with a seasoned sales floor manager. We were focused on getting these jackets out because we had to put a locking system on each jacket because we did not want them to be stolen.

We were unaware that the CEO, Tom Grimes, was walking our section of the sales floor. As we were locking up the last of the jackets, a voice asked, "How many of those jackets did you buy?" We both looked up, startled. I had heard he walked the floor to quiz buyers and associates about their business, and it was now my turn.

The more I answered, the more detailed his questions. The more detailed the questions, the more I did not have answers. Not one of the questions was out of line. I should have known every answer. Five minutes of this felt like five hours. Then he stopped and gave me a challenge. "The next time I see you, I want you to be able to answer *all* my questions."

A few weeks later, I saw him on the sales floor. Instead of hiding or hoping he would not stop, I approached him. "I'm ready for your challenge." I passed with flying colors. The term "Retail is Detail" is true about any business. You need to know your business better than anyone else. To succeed, you must get intimate with the details. I learned this to be true whether I was an assistant buyer at Gimbels, a sales representative at Haggar, or a Senior Executive at Michaels.

YOU NEED TO KNOW YOUR BUSINESS BETTER THAN ANYONE ELSE. TO SUCCEED, YOU MUST GET INTIMATE WITH THE DETAILS.

Could you pass the Tom Grimes challenge for your job? If not, get into the details. Don't be embarrassed about what you don't know; show them what you do know.

———— • • • ————

IF YOU CAN'T HANDLE YOUR OWN MONEY ...

One of the biggest perks executive trainees received at Gimbels was a 40% discount on all purchases, including sale items. It was significant for many reasons. First, we were recent college graduates, and most of us did not have a proper business wardrobe. Back in the 80s, you had to be in business attire all the time. There were no casual dress days.

Second, you had to furnish a new apartment since most new hires were from out of state and had to find new living arrangements. Finally, our starting salary was only $15,000 per year (the equivalent to $40,000 per year now). That's a decent starting salary, but when you add up rent, insurance, a new wardrobe, car payments, etc., making ends meet was a challenge.

The discount was a Godsend that helped stretch our wages. Unless, of course, you could not control your spending. Then things could get out of hand not only from a personal finance standpoint but from a career perspective.

Don Franklin, the head of personnel, told me a story about a trainee who used the Gimbels' credit card and their discount to build up quite the bill for shoes, clothing, apartment accessories, and more. The person was deeply in debt within the first four months of joining the company. I asked, "What happened to them?"

"We called them into a meeting and told them that management was tracking their credit card problems and was concerned about their spending habits. We told them if they could not get control of their personal finances, they would not be promoted to the buyer level in the future. It is hard for management to believe that you can steward millions of dollars of open to buy company money when you can't handle your own finances."

I had never put the two together, but Gimbels' management had, as do most of the companies I have worked for. For example, as a consultant, I would monitor the expenses other consultants turned in during their projects. I always challenged them about why they spent so much money on meals or hotel rooms when the project was to help the company save money.

HOW YOU DO ANYTHING IS HOW YOU DO EVERYTHING. MANAGING YOUR MONEY WELL IS CRITICAL FOR YOU AND YOUR FAMILY. MANAGING THE COMPANY'S MONEY WELL CAN BE CRITICAL FOR YOUR CAREER.

Just because it is company money does not mean you should not try to spend it wisely. How you do anything is how you do everything. Managing your money well is critical for you and your family. Managing the company's money well can be critical for your career.

IN CHARGE AT 24

One reason I chose to work for Gimbels was the opportunity to run my own business within a business at an incredibly young age. I had visions of running a company early in my career, and this idea of running a piece of Gimbels' business was too intriguing to pass up.

My first taste of this came when my buyer, Dave Levey, got promoted from men's clothing to the hot young men's category, which needed a more experienced buyer due to the ever-changing customer desires. Dave wanted an experienced assistant, and we worked well together, so he asked me to join him to tackle this new challenge.

One advantage of this move was Dave giving me the responsibility of running the jean department. I was off the charts excited! The buyer and their assistant had to do everything related to their departments— shop the market, negotiate with vendors, write purchase orders, develop and manage their merchandise plans and open to buy dollars, manage inventory, allocate quantities to the correct stores, reconcile inventories, write ad copy, return goods to vendors, monitor inbound freight to the distribution center, monitor freight shipping to the stores, and so much more. At 24, I was responsible for everything related to the success of the young men's jean department.

After about a year, I was promoted to Group Sales Manager in one of our stores. Now that I learned the ins and outs of the buying office, Gimbels wanted me to learn how to run a small section of a mall-based store. I was moved to the Southridge store where I managed 23 people, wrote weekly labor schedules, managed 15 or so men's departments, handled incoming freight, built fixtures, folded clothes, constantly remerchandised the sales floor, set up the store for big sales, built merchandise displays, conducted physical inventories, and most importantly, help take care of our customers.

Both positions exposed me to all aspects of the retail business. It was a perfect stepping stone for my goal of being a senior leader, either running a company or being on the management team that ran a company. I could have made more money at first if I had accepted one of the sales representative jobs I was offered after college. Financially, I would have been much better off.

I chose a position early in my career not for money but for knowledge. You can manage your career for short-term financial gain, but that may sacrifice a longer-term plan. Think about where you want to be 10 or 15 years down the road and choose wisely with the big picture in mind.

———— • ● • ————

MY FIRST BITE OF THE BIG APPLE

One of the best things about being a buyer was going to markets around the United States and the world. It was a chance to meet with all your accounts, see all the new fashions, place purchase orders, and see new vendors that could have the next greatest product. You would also get wined and dined by vendors, which was an especially nice perk.

I wanted to go on a buying trip to New York, but there was a problem. I was an assistant buyer, and assistant buyers did not travel to New York. You could drive to the apparel mart in Chicago, but they only allowed buyers to travel to other cities. I had been in my position for about a year, and I thought it would dramatically improve my learning curve for getting promoted to a buyer if I could go to a New York market week. I had to figure out a way.

Even though I knew the company policy, I still asked my buyer and my SVP. They both reiterated the company policy, but I was not deterred. I talked with my parents about the situation, and they asked why I could not go. "Because the company does not pay for assistants to travel to cities like New York," I explained.

"What would happen if you paid for it? Can you take your own vacation time and pay for the market trip like it was any other vacation location?"

Genius! The next day I went to the SVP and proposed, "If I took a weeks' vacation and paid my own way to New York, could I tag along with my buyer?" I had him stumped.

"To my recollection, no one has ever asked this before. Wow, if you are willing to use your own time and money to learn more about the buying position, and if your buyer is okay with that, then so am I!" My buyer agreed.

It was one of the greatest learning experiences in my career. I had never been to New York, so I learned about a place I would travel to more than 75 times throughout my career. It was my first exposure to the product development cycle from the vendor side of the equation. Some of these vendors were looking out two to three years in the future, which was a valuable lesson when I went to work for an apparel company.

It was my first exposure to meeting with associates of our other Gimbels divisions and how they handled the complexities of a differing customer base than the one we had in Milwaukee. A valuable lesson was that each city and each store within a city has a unique customer base. I also learned how to walk fast, safely walk against a red light, and stand back from the curb after it rained or risk getting splashed by a puddle and spoil the rest of your day! Valuable lessons for all future trips to the Big Apple.

I learned much during that trip—an invaluable experience. It was an investment in me. **How can you invest in yourself? Take a class. Get a new certification. Learn a new skill. Find a way to improve yourself. Investing in yourself will give you the greatest return on any investment you will ever make.**

TOO BIG FOR YOUR BRITCHES

Young Men's was a hot category. No longer just smaller sizes of the major men's vendors; the merchandise was now a fashion-forward category constantly changing and on-trend. You pick a winner, and you were a hero. Miss the trend, and you had huge markdowns for the next buyer and assistant buyer to clean up your mess.

It was a major boost of confidence to be asked to move to this area. Buying for my previous department was basically a reorder business. The raincoats, blazers, pinstripe suits, etc., did not change that drastically so you were just refilling sizes. That was not the case with the Young Men's area. You needed to constantly look for the new "it" products, then turn the merchandise floor as fast as you could with new looks. It was risky, and if you made a wrong call, hopefully, it wouldn't cost you an arm a leg to get out of the product and move on to the next buy.

We hit the ground running, and our business was on fire. We were helped by new vendors entering the marketplace to support this ever-growing trend. Levi's 501 Jeans caught fire as well. Backed by a huge marketing campaign for the 1984 Olympics in Los Angeles, you literally could not get enough stock. Plus, there was a price war between retailers because Levi's was such a draw to the store that we were selling them for nearly our costs. It seemed like we could not make a mistake with what we were buying.

Then we bought *Ghostbusters* outfits. Yes, you read that correctly. The 1984 movie was a smash hit, and we thought how great it would be to sell the outfits from the movie in our trendy department. Each outfit cost about $75, and we priced them at $150. The average cost of items in our department was around $13 - $18, so a $75 price tag was a gamble.

I believe we bought twelve. That was twelve too many. We marked down eleven to a ridiculously low price, and one was stolen. Was there a marketing benefit to show we were on the cutting edge of fashion? Sure, but we were so far over our heads that there was no way to make lemonade out of this lemon. It was definitely a shock to our egos.

Some people never get on a roll and get to ride a wave like we had in that area. The stars aligned for us, and my buyer and I were pretty good at what we did, so we took full advantage of trends in the industry.

But just when you think you are invincible, a brick wall of reality hits you. Is there something coming around the corner? I don't care if it is in business, personal life, investing, or snow skiing. When things are going great, step back and ask yourself what you are missing. Ride the wave but keep your eyes open for the unexpected and never get too big for your britches.

WHEN THINGS ARE GOING GREAT, STEP BACK AND ASK YOURSELF WHAT YOU ARE MISSING. RIDE THE WAVE BUT KEEP YOUR EYES OPEN FOR THE UNEXPECTED AND NEVER GET TOO BIG FOR YOUR BRITCHES.

POTTY BREAKS, FIRST DATE, AND WHY I'M LATE

After working for a time as an assistant buyer, I was given the opportunity to explore a new role as a Gimbels Group Sales Manager. I managed 23 people and 15 different men's departments—one of the company's highest sales volume areas.

Life in the stores is dramatically different than the rhythm of the buying offices. Open seven days a week with extended hours; I worked at least 60+ hours each week. I was responsible for making sure my departments were clean and merchandised correctly, making my sales numbers, staying on or below your headcount budget, handling customer service ... and *managing people*!

Nervous and excited, I arrived early for my first day on the job. I went to my little office area in a back stockroom and was doing some paperwork when an area manager dropped by to congratulate me on my new position. I had known him as an assistant buyer, but now I was his boss, and his welcome and promise to help me succeed was a great start to the day.

Then my first curveball came. "I just had surgery," he said, "and I am on some medication that affects urinary function, so for the next several weeks, I'll need you to come to the floor often and spell me when I need to use the restroom."

"No problem, I understand," I told him. "I hope you are back at full health soon!"

Sixty seconds later, a young female employee entered my office. "Hello, Mr. Wellen, do you have a minute to talk?" "My door is always open," I smiled. After she congratulated me on my new position, she threw me curveball number two.

"I am going to need you to switch my hours around. I'm scheduled for Friday night, but I can't come in that day."

"Can you tell me why?" I asked.

"Well, Billy asked me out," she beamed. "Oh? Who's Billy?" I ventured. "He's this *really* cute guy I've wanted to date since the beginning of the school year. I just *have* to go out with him!" she pleaded.

In a true rookie move, I asked, "Can I change the work schedule for you?"

"Of course you can! You're the boss!" she stated.

"Okay, I just need to check on how to adjust the schedules, but if you come back and see me before the end of the day, I'll see what I can do for you."

As she was leaving my office, in walked curveball number three. "Mr. Wellen," she came in, breathless. "I'm so sorry I was late for work today, but I have a very good reason."

"Oh? I did not realize you were late," I responded." I was starting to feel more like a counselor than a manager.

"You see, I breastfeed my baby, and this morning, it just took a little longer than usual," she replied.

In my mind, I was thinking, *What a trifecta—urinating, dating, and now breastfeeding!* I had *no* idea what to say. I was only 24 years old, and even in 1985, there were landmines of political correctness I had no interest in stepping on. I took a deep breath, searching for how to answer her, but she spoke up before I had the chance.

"... I'm working on pumping more breast milk. That way, my mom can feed the baby in the future. I won't be late again, I promise!" "That ... that seems like a good solution," I said cautiously.

"Thank you for your understanding," she replied and left the room.

I looked at my watch. After coming in half an hour early, I was officially now three minutes into my role. "I'm exhausted!" I said to myself, "Why don't they teach you any of this stuff in the training class?" I had received no instruction for how to navigate the human resource side of managing people. All the focus had been on hitting numbers and meeting sales goals. We drilled down on inventory, payroll, customer service, and promotions, not post-surgery issues or dating desires.

The incident underlined how high my employers' expectations were for me so early in my career. I quickly realized that **part of being a great manager is understanding all the things people have to deal with in their lives. It is much more than just the hours they are at work with you.**

As a manager, there is a line to walk between pushing people to perform and mastering the human factor. Those you manage need a healthy work/life balance, and it is up to you to lead the way in understanding and by example.

REALIZED I DID NOT HAVE
THE "IT" FACTOR

My buyer and I met with one of our many vendors who showed us a new, extremely fashion-forward line of tops and bottoms for the fall selling season. The styles, colors, and silhouettes were changing rapidly. It was always a balancing act as a buyer to make sure you were right on-trend. Too early, and the customer is not ready, resulting in massive markdowns and a missed season or two. Too late, and the customer has already bought it someplace else, resulting in massive markdowns and a missed season or two. The next buyer then has to fix what you broke.

The positive side of the equation is if you are trend right, you get to ride that wave as long as possible. Then you have to do it again and again. It was and still is one of the hardest parts of the retail business and their vendor counterparts. To be a great buyer, you have to have the "it" factor. You have to be able to see where the customer is going or else move the customer in the direction of the trend. It is much more art than science.

In the heyday of department stores, recruiting and training the next generation of buyers was critical for the company's success. In my training class, the college degree earned varied greatly. Most of my training class had merchandise degrees, one person had a degree in finance, I was the only business major, and we had one or two with degrees in psychology. It was a shock to me at first, but the more I learned about the buyer position, the more I understood how knowing the psychology of the customers was extremely important.

As I first contemplated leaving Gimbels, one reason was I realized I did not feel I had that "it" factor. I am a very analytical person. I am good with numbers and analysis, but the critical softer side of predicting what a customer would or would not like was in noticeably short supply for me. I had to be honest with myself. To move up the corporate ladder in the retail of the 1980s, you had to be a really successful merchant. I probably could have held my own, but I did not think at the time I could excel.

I realized that I needed a different path up the corporate ladder. Hence my move into sales and then consulting, where my analytical skills and gift of gab were a perfect fit. Those moves were critical to my path to a senior leadership position.

Constantly do a self-evaluation. Ask if you are in a position you are not incredibly happy with and are just okay at. Are you in a position that maximizes your skills? Can you make a good living if you used these other skills you have? Would you be happier if you worked in a position that leverages your best attributes? If so, it might be a time for a change.

It is much more fun and exhilarating to use your best skills and talents instead of struggling to master skills less enjoyable to you. Challenge yourself to find a position that is fulfilling, not just functional.

O-FER

In the Urban Dictionary, the definition for "O-fer" is to repeatedly try and fail. An example is if a batter in baseball gets zero hits in four at-bats, he can say he had an O-fer for the game. When I was thinking about leaving Gimbels, my thoughts turned to what I would like to do for my next position. I loved sports. I always have. Played them, watched them, read books about my teams and my favorite players. I thought how great it would be to work for a sports team. It would blend my passion for sports with a career.

I decided to write to as many sports organizations as possible to see if I could work somewhere in their organization. This was before the internet, so I could not do a quick search on LinkedIn or the team's home page. I had to go to the library and do extensive research to find the names and addresses of all the organizations. I focused on the big four professional sports: baseball, basketball, football, and hockey. I also researched the athletic programs for hundreds of colleges in the Midwest. Big school or small school, I did not care.

After a month and a half of research, I was ready to go. I got out our electric typewriter and began typing. I would sit at our exceedingly small desk with my name and address list and type the same letter over and over again. I had no computer or word processor to just change the name and address and a few things specific to that team. I had to type each and every cover letter separately. I wrote to hundreds of organizations and included a copy of my resume.

Now you email or upload your resume, but back then, it was a major process to select the correct paper stock and find a quality print store. I selected an off-white paper with a slightly textured finish to it. The envelope was the same stock. I was told that changing the color and texture would cause my letter to stick out from all the other mail.

My mom and I stuffed all the envelopes, and then I took a couple of boxes full of letters to the post office. I don't remember the entire cost of this endeavor, but it was not cheap. I put all the letters in the mail and went home and waited with what assuredly would be a multitude of callbacks and interviews.

Of the hundreds of letters I sent out, I think I might have received letters back from 10. All rejections. After all the time, effort, and money, I had hit a big O-fer. It was so disappointing. I was crushed. How could not one of these organizations not want to hire me? Rejection is painful.

I was upset, but I decided to say screw them all. They are the ones missing out. I did not need hundreds to like me; I just needed one. And that is exactly what happened. A few months later, I accepted a new job. This job did not hit my passion for sports, but it did use my sales and marketing passions and my desire to move to a different city.

I know it can get discouraging when you get rejection letters. It is a definite energy drain. Keep trying. Keep putting your name out there. Don't Quit! Use rejection as fuel in your belly to keep looking for your dream job. Something good will happen if you keep looking. You only need one to say yes.

HORRIBLE BOSSES

"People Don't Leave Bad Jobs; They Leave Bad Bosses." This was the headline of a 2019 article in *Forbes* magazine. A 2017 Gallup poll of more than one million employed workers in the US found that the number one reason for quitting your job was a bad boss or immediate supervisor. The report concluded that 75% of workers who voluntarily left their jobs did so because of their boss.

I can thank Jane Doe for forcing my decision to leave my first job after college. I use Jane Doe because I don't want to use her real name. My Gimbels promotion was quite a vote of confidence from the corporate office management team. Then I met my new boss. I knew her from my store visits as an assistant buyer. Though her reputation proceeded her, my interactions did not indicate how she would treat me as my direct report.

From the very first day, it was hell on wheels. I really think she thought her job was to break me instead of training me. The new position was stressful enough, but the constant belittling grew tiresome. She would tell me that I would never make anything of myself. It was the exact opposite of the support and mentoring I received in my previous years at Gimbels. I was a highly thought of assistant buyer, but now I felt like the worst employee that ever existed. As the criticism mounted, I realized that I could not put up with this person another day, let alone another year.

When I added up my initial thoughts about leaving my job due to wanting to leverage other skills and this horrible boss situation, I knew my days at Gimbels were numbered. I spoke with my parents and told them I needed a change. They did not like the fact I was thinking of leaving a job without a job but said they would support me in any decision I made. After six months of hell, I wrote a resignation letter and quit my first real job. I did not quit my dream of trying to become a CEO. One of the main reasons I left because my boss was not helping me learn, grow, and prosper as I worked my way toward that dream.

Though leaving a job without having another one to go to was a very risky move, it was the best decision for me personally. I did not want to have one person tear me down during the early stages of my career to the point that I might not be able to recover. It was also one of the best decisions I made professionally. Within three weeks, I had accepted a new position and was soon driving to Dallas, Texas, to start my new job.

My timing ended up being very advantageous. Gimbels went out of business one year later, and unfortunately, everybody was fired. No one saw that coming, but I am sure glad I jumped before I got caught up in the scramble for jobs when the company closed its doors.

I learned two great lessons from my time at Gimbels. First, **your first real job is only a stepping stone and not a career-defining position.**

Your first job helps you get going in the business world and begin the process of learning what you really want to do.

Second, it is a sad commentary on the corporate world that there are so many Jane Does out there. **Horrible bosses are a reality. You can often fight through it, but if it negatively affects you personally and professionally, start looking for a new position.** If it gets as bad as my situation, you might have to take the risky move to leave the situation behind even without another position.

When a situation happens that you are dealing with a horrible boss or realize this job is not what you really want to do, it is not the end of the world. These challenges might just be the push you need to find that position you absolutely love. It did for me.

———— • • ————

SIGNIFICANT EMOTIONAL EVENTS

Dr. Morris Massey was one of the most influential workplace experts. One of his areas of focus was significant emotional events. He defines a Significant Emotional Event as:

> **"An experience that is so mentally arresting that it becomes a catalyst for you to consider, examine, and possibly change your initial values or value system."**

In 1985, I had a significant emotional event. My father suffered a heart attack and a stroke. It shook me to my core. My dad was my hero, the toughest person I knew. I remember going to see him at the hospital. All these tubes that they had in him—I just could not believe this could have happened to him. I was lost.

They performed open-heart surgery and found problems in many arteries, but the doctors believed it was plaque from his carotid artery that caused his stroke. The surgery went great, but the stroke had caused some significant damage. The left side of his face drooped a little, and his speech was affected. This tough man was in tough shape. Over the next six months or so, he worked his butt off to get his speech about 99% back to normal, and he was able to go back to work as the warehouse supervisor for the Georgia-Pacific Lumber Company.

As dad recovered, I was thinking about my life and my future. I had lived in West Allis my entire life, and I was still living at home and saving money when this happened. Dad's situation started me thinking that I needed to change my life.

First, I now realized that there were heart problems in my family. My dad's mom died of a heart attack at 63. His dad died at 53 of emphysema, but he also had heart issues. So, I started eating differently and began working out to help my heart hopefully fight against my genes. As of now, I am 60 years old—so far, so good.

Second, with this knowledge that life can change in an instant, I realized I needed to make a significant change in my life. I needed to challenge myself to make the biggest, boldest move now, or I would never do it. I started with quitting my job and leaving Wisconsin.

I hated leaving my family, friends, and everything I knew about life. But dad's heart attack made me realize that life is temperamental. You never know when something will happen. I did not want that "something" to happen without me exploring the world and living life to its fullest. I have lived a full life to date. One I don't believe I could have imagined if I did not make a move to Dallas. And still, I have so many things I want to accomplish.

Most of us will encounter a significant emotional event. Live life to the fullest every single moment. Take chances. Have Fun. Have no regrets. If you fail, pick yourself up and start over.

———•—

THINGS WILL WORK OUT

In June of 1985, I had had enough. My boss was horrible; I realized that I might not have the skillsets to be incredibly successful in my current role, my dad had just recovered from a stroke and heart attack, and I had struck out on getting a new job after sending out hundreds of resumes. I was losing weight (which I couldn't afford to lose) and not sleeping at night. I was 24 and had a few bucks in the bank. So, I had flexibility. I needed a change. I needed to make a bold move.

Bold it was. I moved across the country. It was the height of a building boom in Texas and an exodus of people from the north were moving south. I thought I had enough money to last for about six months in Dallas and look for a job. I knew I could work part-time at a retailer to make a few bucks and pay some bills.

My parents thought I was nuts. They tried to talk me out of it and told me to just keep looking for a job in Milwaukee or maybe Chicago, Madison, or Minneapolis. I wanted to get out of the cold weather, and those cities were still too cold for me. In the end, they did not like it, but they supported my decision.

I typed a resignation letter and gave it to the store manager that afternoon. He tried to talk me out of it using all the same things my mom and dad had said. He knew I had a problem with my boss and said he could make some managerial adjustments for me. I told him I appreciated everything he was trying to do, but I had made up my mind that I needed a change. He asked me not to make it official until I talked with the personnel director.

Like the leaks you read about in politics, by the time I drove to the downtown office about an hour later, everybody knew I had resigned. The Gimbels rumor mill was better than Twitter. I walked through security and ran into a group of people standing at the elevator. The group included an assistant buyer in the men's area and three individuals from the Haggar Apparel Company—the local sales representative, the regional vice president, and the national sales manager.

The assistant buyer already knew I had resigned. On the way up in the elevator, the Haggar sales representative (who I had worked with when I was an assistant buyer) asked me what I was going to do. I told them my plan to move to Dallas and look for a job.

"Have you ever thought about working for Haggar?"

"Of course!" I answered, and the rest is history. I interviewed with the national sales manager a couple of hours later on the sales floor. A visit to Chicago, a trip to Dallas, and six weeks later, I was their newest sales trainee, living in Texas.

Sometimes you need to take bold action to get out of a challenging situation. I did not quit and then decide what to do. I had a plan, but God expedited my move by meeting the Haggar folks at the elevator. I am not suggesting that you quit your job without a job. **If you believe in yourself and that you will get a lot of assistance from above, you can get yourself out of difficult and challenging situations. Faith and a helping hand from God will show the way.**

CHAPTER   3

WHEN

MAKING A SIGNIFICANT LIFE AND CAREER CHANGE

Almost everyone I knew had done things the same way. After high school or college, you got a job, found a place to live within 15 miles or so of where you were born, got married in your early 20s, started having kids a couple of years after that, and took the typical Wisconsin vacation by going "up north" to stay for a week or two at a lake house. It was right out of a picture-perfect Norman Rockwell painting.

At 24, I was not ready for that life just yet. In 1985, against every bit of advice I received from family and friends, I decided to quit my job and move to Dallas, TX.

This section discusses the courage required to take risks, experience new things, meet new people, take on new responsibilities, take *more* risks, and grow as a person. It will encourage you to leave your current comfort zone and challenge the status quo. In the end, the only way to truly know what you are capable of is to **try**.

WILL THE "BIG D" BE TOO BIG FOR ME?

I resigned from my first "real" job at Gimbels Department Stores, and I accepted a job as a sales trainee with Haggar Apparel Company. Six weeks later, I was preparing to drive 1000 miles to Dallas to begin my new job. I was running on pure adrenaline. I did not take the time to understand what I was really doing—all I knew was that I left a job I did not like. I had an off-the-charts level of confidence that I could tackle the world, and Texas was going to me my new home.

After shedding more than a few tears saying goodbye to my family and friends, I got in my Oldsmobile Cutlass Ciera and began my 18-hour drive to Dallas. The farthest I had ever driven by myself was to Chicago, which was about 95 miles south of Milwaukee. This trip would be a test of stamina and awareness to make sure I made it safe and sound to the "Big D."

The first three hours were an easy drive. I was making fairly good time, and everything was going according to plan. I was south of Springfield, Illinois, when I picked up the St. Cardinal baseball game. I was not a fan of the Cardinals, but the talking helped keep me awake. As I approached St. Louis, a commercial came on the radio advertising ticket sales for the Cardinals. The tag line was something to the effect of, "Bring your family and friends to a ballgame."

I was now 400 miles away from home, and it hit me like a brick wall. My family and friends. I just left all of them behind. The adrenaline rush I was on instantly evaporated, and I said to myself, "What the hell am I doing?" I had never lived anywhere except with my parents. I could not afford to go away to college, so I went to UW—Milwaukee. I lived at home during my three years at Gimbels to save some money. Now I was moving 1,000 miles away with no support system.

The DFW Metroplex population was about four times bigger than Milwaukee County, and each year added almost twice the population of my hometown! The distance from one side of the metroplex to the other was almost 65 miles—almost the entire drive from my home to Madison, Wisconsin. For the first time, I asked myself, "Why Dallas? Will this entire experience be too big for me?"

The tears began to pour down my face. I pulled off I-44 and found a truck stop to get myself back together. It did not help. Luckily, no one saw me, or they might have called the highway patrol. I sat there for about an hour. I cried and prayed and then cried and prayed some more. I cried so much that I finally just put my head back and fell asleep.

When I woke up, something was different. I felt refreshed for the 10 hours or so I had remaining to drive, not only physically but also mentally. This move is what I wanted, and I was not going to fail. I would be alone and scared, but I had to persevere. I could not quit after only five hours into this new journey in my life.

It was a big step for me. I knew things would not be easy, but I had to toughen up and grow up fast if I was going to survive. My confidence meter was going back up again. I was not going to fail—no matter what was thrown at me, my faith and abilities were going to overcome any challenge or setback.

The rest of my drive went by like a breeze. As I approached downtown Dallas, I was humming at the top of my lungs the theme song from the hit TV show *Dallas*. I was ready, though I knew there would be more troubles ahead. **When you take chances in life, do not lose confidence at the first sign of trouble. Adjust accordingly and keep moving forward. Each step forward is a step closer to your dream.**

———————•●•———————

YOU CAN'T DO IT ALONE

As I began my new adventure in Dallas, I knew that I was going to be alone. I would have no family or friends in Dallas to support me; they were all 1,000 miles away in Wisconsin. It would be only my faith, myself, and my newfound confidence to get through this new journey. After my first two weeks working with Haggar, I found out I was 100% wrong. I was not alone; I became an adopted member of the Haggar company family.

Haggar was one of the biggest apparel brands in America, but that is not what made it a great place to work—it was the people who worked there, including the Haggar Family themselves. It was a perfectly timed gift from above for a green, naïve young man from West Allis, Wisconsin, to go to work in a new city after leaving everything behind. God knew I needed this tender loving care and support, and He put not just one but a multitude of motherly, fatherly, and kind people in my life.

First, let me tell you about the wonderful ladies of Haggar. I went from having one wonderful mom to many maternal figures. Bobby Bodmer, Donna Harrington, Gracie Thomas, Bobbie Schmidt, and Opal Roberts are just a few who provided me with guidance, support, and most importantly, ears to listen to a sometimes scared young man.

Equally as important was the assistance and mentoring I received from the great men of Haggar. I was not only new to Texas but also to the profession of selling. I needed a lot of help understanding this new world of selling apparel, and I received it from some of the best gentlemen you will ever meet. Men like Jimmy Palasota, Steve Carter, Jim Herman, Corbett Howard, James Thompson, and Tim Lyons. I was a fish out of water, and they were the perfect blend of friend, father figure, and mentor I needed.

I was never alone. I had God looking over me from above, and everywhere I turned in my first eleven months at my new job in my new city, there were always incredibly kind, generous, and authentic people. At that truck stop outside of St. Louis, crying my eyes out, I asked God many times, "*How* am I going to do this?"

He answered by putting all these people and more in my life, which taught me a great lesson. You are not alone unless you choose to be. You cannot fight the world on your own. If you have wonderful people in your life, continue to grow those relationships. If not, find a place where you can get positive assistance in your life—a church, social organization, work, friends, and of course, family. And always ask for some help from above; God's gifts will help you get through difficult times.

POSITIVE PEOPLE ARE A BLESSING, AND THEIR INFLUENCE HELPS YOU BE SUCCESSFUL. TAKE FULL ADVANTAGE OF THE OPPORTUNITY TO LEARN FROM THEM.

The people from Haggar were willing to help me in part because I was open to listening to them. I respected them, and they knew it. Positive people are a blessing, and their influence helps you be successful. Take full advantage of the opportunity to learn from them.

DRIVING MISS DAISY

When I began working at the Haggar Apparel Company, I was supposed to train in Dallas for about six months before management would move me to a sales territory where I would begin my new career as a sales representative. I was told the training would include hands-on experience with other sales representatives, customer service representatives, tours of our factories, product development processes, piece goods discussions, etc. Exposure to all these was an outstanding foundation when I did get to move to my territory.

But there was one thing they did not tell me. I also had to be a chauffeur! I did not realize at the time that this was part of my training. I felt it was like pledging to the Haggar Fraternity, and at the beginning, I hated every minute of it. I thought it demeaning to have to do this. I was supposed to be this new hot-shot salesperson, not a chauffeur to be on call 24/7.

I did not realize at the start the incredible people I would be driving around Dallas and the tremendous knowledge, friendships, and future relationships that I could leverage that I was gaining by doing this.

For example, let us start with the man himself, Mr. JM Haggar, the 93-year-old founder of Haggar Apparel Company. He was a Lebanese immigrant who founded the Haggar Apparel Co. in 1926, and it was the nation's largest manufacturer of men's slacks, sport coats, and suits. A short time before I arrived in Dallas, Mr. Haggar either was in a car accident or nearly caused one, and the family said he could not drive anymore. He hated the idea of losing his independence, but he gradually conceded when someone was always there to drive him around. Hence the reference to the 1989 movie, *Driving Miss Daisy.*

Mr. Haggar was still coming to work almost every day, and he was still as sharp as a tack. His assistant would drive him to work and run other errands with him. When she was not available, they called on me. When they first asked me to drive Mr. Haggar to get a haircut and then take him home, I was, to say the least, not pleased. Instead of saying, "What a great opportunity to be with this legend of the apparel industry!" I was pissed off. Then I remembered an earlier experience at Gimbels counting thousands of leather jackets and changed my tune.

I am glad I did. I drove Mr. Haggar around about 25 times during my initial time in Dallas. Some people were at Haggar longer than I was alive and never had that kind of access to this special man. Every ride, I would learn something. You cannot put a value on those 25 rides. Even though this was not part of the job description, I would not have traded these experiences and lessons learned.

Over those 11 months, I drove so many people around, and each taught me something or impacted my life in a way that I could not imagine. **Every job has its challenges and situations that you might literally hate doing, especially early in your career. Before you react too negatively, allow for something positive to come from it. Learn and grow.** I turned a lemon into lemonade by realizing this demeaning task was, in fact, a tremendous learning experience. You can do the same.

———————— • ● • ————————

IT STARTS AT THE TOP

It was an early Sunday morning within the first month I had been in Dallas when my phone rang. I first thought something must have happened back home because my family was the only one with my home phone number. I answered said with a cautious tone, "Hello."

On the other end of the line, I heard a voice ask, "Is this Jeff Wellen?"

I did not recognize the voice at first, but I answered, "Yes, this is Jeff."

" Jeff, this is Joe Haggar, the third."

Joe Haggar III (Joe 3 for short) was the President of the Menswear Division of Haggar and the founder's grandson. I had met him on several occasions during my orientation, but I had no idea he had my phone number. He apologized for calling me so early on a Sunday but wondered if I would join him for a round of golf. He needed a fourth player and knew I played. Since I was new to town, he thought I might be available.

Before I could even ask, Joe III said, "Don't worry about paying for anything; you are my guest today."

I jumped at the opportunity! We would be playing with his dad, Joe Haggar Jr. (President and CEO of Haggar Company), and his cousin Jimmy Haggar (a lead designer) at Preston Trail Golf Club, arguably the most exclusive country club in Dallas in 1985. My golf experience to date was playing county or municipal courses back home. I had never sniffed the grounds of a country club, let alone one that had only about 200 members. The member's list included the who's who of the wealthy in Dallas, and Joe III had just asked me to play there with him.

It was an incredible day. The golf course was immaculate, and the competition was fantastic. I actually played pretty well once I got over the case of nerves. Joe III and I were a team against his dad and cousin. We won on the last hole. Throughout the entire day, the three members of the Haggar family never once treated me like a new trainee. They treated me as a person, and I got to know these three men in a different light than what could be seen at work.

Two weeks later, Mr. Joe Jr. came by my cubical and said he had an extra ticket to the Dallas Cowboys game and wanted to know if I would like to join him in the Haggar box at Texas Stadium. I jumped at the opportunity.

This was not the Haggar company box in the end zone; this was the Haggar family box on the 45-yard line. Of course, I accepted the offer and had another fantastic day based on the hospitality of the Haggar family.

I began to realize the reason the Haggar company was such a special place. It was six short letters. H-a-g-g-a-r. Even though they were a remarkably successful family and had more money than I could ever imagine having at the time, it was their kindness and genuineness that showed me **a company's culture starts at the top—how you treat your people.**

Joe Jr. and Joe III did not have to invite me to play golf or go to a Cowboys game. Haggar's great ladies and gentlemen did not have to take me under their wing to give me the guidance I so desperately needed at the time. They did it because it was embedded in the culture from the top. **Wherever leadership genuinely cares about the people who make it all happen, a healthy culture flourishes, allowing people to thrive.**

FIX'N TO HAVE SOME
CHICKEN FRIED STEAK

On my first day, Bobby Bodmer (in charge of my training) said, "Jeff, a few of us are going upstairs to eat lunch in the cafeteria. You are welcome to join us."

I gratefully accepted, and when we got upstairs, there were about ten people in line ahead of us. A couple of people were discussing what they were going to have for lunch. "I'm fix'n to have some chicken fried steak and peach cobbler for lunch. What'r y'all havin'?"

Without a doubt, this confirmed I was no longer in Wisconsin! I am sure my face must have had a strange look on it because Bobby started laughing. She said, "You don't talk like that in Wisconsin?"

"No," I shook my head, "we don't talk *or* eat like that in Wisconsin!" And now everybody in line was laughing.

"There's a lot to unpack here," I addressed the crowd. "Fix'n and y'all are one thing, but what the heck is chicken fried steak? I have had fried chicken, and I have had steak, but I have never heard of chicken fried steak!"

For the rest of lunch, I received many more lessons on being a Texan and living in the south. I was fascinated as we compared stories about the differences between Dallas and Milwaukee. Bratwurst vs. chicken fried steak. Yous guys vs. y'all. A cream puff vs. peach cobbler. You-betcha vs. fix'n. I also told them that their southern accents would take some time for me to get used to.

"Our accents," they exclaimed, "what about yours?" Then Bobby asked me to pronounce Wisconsin.

So, I did, "Wee-sscooon-sin." It includes the heavy nasal tone from back home. I never realized it before, but I do say Wisconsin kind of funny.

After living there for 25 years, this was one of the many reasons I left. I wanted to see the world, gain new experiences, and meet different people. Dallas was my first step. I have since been able to travel to about 42 states and 29 different countries. Do yourself a favor. Get out and see the world. It doesn't mean you need to move like I did, but you can travel to different places and experience different cultures from around the world.

It makes this big world just a little smaller when you see and experience it for yourself. **Traveling forces you to appreciate the diversity of other cultures and grants you the incredible gift of a broader perspective. You quickly realize that though we are all quite different, we are also remarkably similar.**

———•●•———

DRUG DEALERS, STRIP CLUB DANCERS, AND GUN SHOTS

When I first arrived in Dallas, I went straight to my apartment complex. There were no online search engines, no Airbnbs, etc., to help with finding accommodations. So, I took the recommendation of the head of sales training for Haggar. Unfortunately, I don't think she realized the neighborhood had changed just a little.

The apartments themselves were nice, and they were just one mile from the office, but I soon realized that this neighborhood was in a challenging area of the city. While moving in, I met the person who lived next door to me. He was a really nice guy, and we began a friendship. One day around my second week of living there, I came home from work, and my new friend was standing just outside my door talking to a couple of individuals.

When I walked up to them, my neighbor introduced me to his friends. We talked for a while. When I was ready to leave and go inside, he looked at his two friends and said, "Hey, this is his apartment. Please tell everybody he is a good guy and leave it alone."

Taken back by the comment, I just left and made a mental note to ask him what that meant later.

About 20 minutes later, I heard through my door that the conversation was over, so I went to ask my neighbor what that statement was about. "Oh," he said, "those guys know everything that goes on around this area, and sometimes they get into some bad stuff. I told him that you were a good guy and to leave your apartment alone and to tell anyone else that might think of doing something to leave you alone."

Remember, two weeks earlier, I was living with my parents in a typical suburban middle-class neighborhood. Now I was on my own and being told that my apartment was safe because this person told two guys not to touch it. So much for my new life!

Later, I found out a strip club dancer was living across the hall from me. I met a guy at the pool one weekend who was a small-time drug dealer. There were gun shots every couple of weeks. I did not know what to do. I was naïve and scared, and I knew if I told my parents or sister that they would probably come and get me and tell me that I made a huge mistake moving to Dallas.

I could not fail. I really like working at Haggar. I also knew that I could not afford to move because I would have to pay to move my furniture and the rent was too high in the nicer places. I knew that I would be moving in a short time to a territory, and I realized I just had to make the best of it.

While I lived there, I never had my place broken into, and my neighbors always had my back. I traveled a lot during my training period, and they would always watch my car for me. I was slowly learning to make it on my own, and I quickly realized that my new world was definitely different from my Norman Rockwell painting-type life in Milwaukee.

Those eleven months in Dallas opened my eyes to the reality of the world I lived in. It was baby steps in my early years away from Wisconsin to help me see the world differently. **Sometimes you need to get out of your comfort zone and maybe even your neighborhood to see how the rest of the world lives.** I received a quick baptism under fire and duress, but I am a much better person for it. You will be too.

———— • ● • ————

5,000 DAMN TURKEYS

One day while working in my cube unit, Mr. J.M. Haggar came by and asked if I could drive him to a couple of places and then drive him home. I said, "Of course," and we proceeded to the car and began our drive. As usually happened, Mr. Haggar began the drive with something that was happening at the office that day. It was about mid-October, and from my understanding, they discussed Christmas bonuses and other things related to the holiday season.

He said, "Young man," (that is what he always called me. I do not know if he ever knew my name, but he knew me) "before you ever start something that you think is a good deal for the people remember that it will set a precedent that you will never be able to change."

Not fully understanding, I asked, "Can you give me an example?"

"Yes," he nodded, "in the early days of Haggar, I thought it would be a great idea to give everybody a turkey for Christmas. This was especially popular during the Depression days of the thirties. It started out with 25 or 30 turkeys. As the company grew, so did the number of turkeys." His voice deepened, and he asked me, "Do you know how many turkeys we give away now?"

There was a hesitation after he asked me the question, but I knew he did not want me to answer. "5000 damn turkeys!" he thundered. "And now, if we ever want to stop giving away the turkeys, I will get blasted for being a bad person. **Always be careful when you are starting something you think is a good thing. Try and imagine how the idea or program could grow to a point it might not be sustainable or financially doable anymore.**"

Mr. Haggar was a great salesman, so I always wondered if he was stretching the truth just a little, but he made his point. I remembered the same thing happened when I was at Michaels. In the early days of the turnaround (1997-98), the company was teetering on going out of business. They could not afford much in those days. The first Christmas party they had was a potluck where everybody brought something. It was fantastic.

Then as things started to roll in the early 2000s, things were looking up, so the human resource folks asked the Executive Committee if we could have a bigger Christmas party where we would rent a hall, invite a guest to join the employee, etc. After some discussion, I remembered the 5,000 damn turkeys story. I thought the party was a good idea, but I mentioned we must put some guardrails around this event, or it could get out of hand quickly.

Well, we did not listen to the advice of Mr. Haggar. Every year the Christmas party grew bigger and became more and more expensive. Bigger halls, better food, better bands, etc. We always had to top last year. Then in the mid-2000s, we were trying to cut money from our budget. The Christmas party was an unfortunate prime candidate.

We surveyed the employees, and Mr. Haggar was correct. Everybody hated us.

Be careful when you are thinking of doing something new for the organization, a friend, or even a family member that could set a precedent you will regret. There is an old saying—no good deed goes unpunished. For me, it is easier to say, "5,000 damn turkeys!"

———•●•———

MARIJUANA JOINTS AND BALLOONS

When I first moved to Dallas, I knew only one person. I will call her Jessica. I had stood up with her at one of my best friends' weddings, and I knew her all of about 36 hours. When I got settled in a little, I gave her a call. She told me the some of her friends were having a party at her apartment complex and I should come by. Many of her friends were Cheeseheads from Wisconsin or recent transplants from the Midwest, so I thought this would be a perfect way to make new friends in my new city.

The party was fantastic. There were about 20 or so people at the party, all of them in their mid-20s, and most had moved to Dallas within the last year. Like most gatherings of this nature, a few partygoers had a little too much to drink but coming from a beer-drinking state; it was no problem. Plus, I had my first chicken fajita.

As I drove home, I thought things just got significantly better. The party was exactly what the doctor ordered. A group of people my age, struggling with trying to make it in the "Big D." Life was looking up.

Later that week, Jessica called again, inviting me to another party with the same group of people, this time in Arlington, a suburb between Dallas and Fort Worth. She gave me the address and time, and because I lived closer to Arlington, she said that I should just meet her there.

When I arrived, the place was packed, and I had to park about three blocks away. As I entered, it was as if they were trying to set the world record for how many people you could fit in one house, and what seemed like hundreds of balloons were hanging from anything and everything. As I was wandering around, I kept looking at the balloons, noticing they seemed to have something at the bottom of each balloon. It seemed very odd.

I finally ran into Jessica and her friends, and over the loud noise, I asked, "What the heck is in the balloons?"

One of Jessica's friends laughed and pointed to a balloon and said, "THAT is a little after 11:00 surprise. THAT is when the party really starts!"

"What does that mean?" I shrugged.

"Those are joints," he shouted over the music, "at 11:00, people will start popping the balloons and get high!"

I soon learned there were other more powerful drugs in some of the back bedrooms. I could hear my dad's voice in my head saying, *"Show me who your friends are, and I'll tell you who you are."* I desperately wanted some people to hang out with in my new city, but not people who behaved like this, so I left the party immediately, and that was the last time I ever saw Jessica and her friends.

I do not claim any moral superiority, but I have never associated with people who did hard drugs, and I was not about to start. I could not imagine what would have happened if the police would have raided the house—try explaining that to my new boss, the Haggar family, and my mom and dad!

I was a little down on my way home, thinking it might be a lonely time in Dallas. Then James Thompson, the National Sales Manager at Haggar, invited me to his church. He told me they had a huge singles organization, and I might meet some great people. He was right. I hooked up with about 15 guys who played softball and needed a short stop. All were my age and the kind of people I wanted to be around. It was a match made in heaven.

Choose your friends and acquaintances wisely. Find those with great values and a solid moral compass. They don't have to be perfect, just good and principled. Avoid people who will bring you in harm's way.

CHOOSE FRIENDS AND ACQUAINTANCES WITH GREAT VALUES AND A SOLID MORAL COMPASS. THEY DON'T HAVE TO BE PERFECT, BUT PRINCIPLED AND WHO WILL NOT BRING YOU IN HARM'S WAY.

DON'T TRUST VPs, SVPs, OR EVPs

One day I was asked to drive Mr. J.M. Haggar home. It was about a 20-minute ride. When he got in the car, I could see he was agitated. Before I could ask him, he started telling me why he was upset. He had just gotten out of a meeting with management and said, "If I could fire all the VPs and SVPs, I would do it today!" I knew he had a reputation for firing people and then saying, never mind, but he was worked up. Before he went any further, he asked me what I wanted to be 25 years from now.

I told him, "I would like to see if I could work my way up that ladder to run a company someday."

"Young man, if you ever *do* run a company, don't ever trust VPs or SVPs," he declared.

Taken back because some of the best people at Haggar had these titles, I asked, "Why shouldn't I trust these people?"

He answered, "Do not get me wrong. They are exceptionally good people, but they tend not to tell me the truth about what is going on with some things within the company. They hide things because they do not want it to affect their future promotion. A VP is now proper management and can taste the next level. So instead of remembering the hard work and success that got them there, they all become politicians trying to get to the SVP level. As for SVP's, they are even worse. They can smell the EVP level and all its perks. They focus more time on what is right for them than what is right for the company. Those on the EVP level know they have arrived, and so they just fight to keep their stature."

AS A LEADER, GET TO KNOW THE PEOPLE WHO ACTUALLY DO THE WORK. YOU WILL BE AMAZED AT WHAT YOU LEARN.

I considered his words carefully, then stated the nugget that has stuck with me to this day. "If you really want to know the truth about what is happening, get up and walk around the office, distribution center, or a factory and talk to the people. Get to know the people who actually do the work. Get to know something about them, so they begin to trust you—not as the CEO or management—but as a person. Ask them about what is going on. You will be amazed at what you learn!" His eyes twinkled, and he chuckled, "When management sees me walking around, they get nervous because I always find *something* they are hiding or uncover an issue that can be resolved quickly."

As we pulled up to his house, he looked at me and thanked me (as he always did), and said, "When you become a leader of a company, don't ever forget where you came from and the people who really make the difference between success and failure. The people on the front lines."

In 1982, Tom Peters and Robert H. Waterman wrote a book called *In Search of Excellence, Lessons from America's Best-Run Companies,* in which they used the term management by walking around. Mr. Haggar had been doing that since 1926.

After dropping Mr. Haggar off, I drove to the end of the block and pulled to the side of the road. I thought about his use of the word "when" I become a leader of a company. It was so inspirational and gave me about 1,000 hops in my step over this great man and the confidence in what he saw in me to use that term. When I finally made it to the VP and SVP levels, I never forgot those powerful words Mr. Haggar said to me when I was just 25 years old.

Never forget where you come from, and always make sure to engage the people on the frontlines who actually do all the heavy lifting.

YOU KNOW, YOU CAN GO FASTER THAN 35 MPH

Shortly after lunch one day, I was asked to take Mr. J.M. Haggar to Preston Trail Golf Club. I said, "Absolutely." I was no longer chafing at being used as a chauffeur; I now looked forward to my drives with Mr. Haggar. I always learned something new, and this time would not be any different.

I drove him in a Lincoln Continental Mark VII, one of the Vice President's cars. It had some of the newest technology available in 1985, including power seats, keyless entry, a digital instrument panel, and an onboard computer message center. When I started the car, I could not believe the instrument panel—it was like something out of Star Trek. Especially striking was the large digital speedometer. No one in the car could miss how fast you were going.

Mr. Haggar got into the car and, as always, thanked me for driving him. "Do you know the directions to the club? If not, I can tell you the way there."

"I am getting to know Dallas pretty well now, so I think I will be okay," I smiled, and we proceeded out of the parking lot and headed east on Lemmon Avenue to Wycliff Avenue. I took a left at Wycliff and headed east towards Preston Road. As I was driving, we were having a nice conversation, but I noticed that he was leaning more to his left in the seat. I thought he was just trying to get comfortable, so I did not say anything.

I turned north on Preston Road, and it was now about a 30-minute ride to the club. We still were enjoying a nice talk when I realized that Mr. Haggar was now *really* leaning to his left. Before I could say a word, he gave me the reason. "Young man, you know you can go faster than 35 miles per hour!"

Now it made sense. He was leaning over to see what speed I was going because of the large glowing digital display. I had been told that he liked to drive fast, but he was not driving I was. I replied, "I am going the speed limit, and I do not want to get a ticket. Much more importantly," I continued, "I have valuable cargo I need to deliver safely to his destination." He chuckled about being called valuable cargo, then returned to the topic of the speed I was driving.

"Sometimes, you must put the gas pedal down just a little more if you are going to accomplish everything you want. While others are driving the speed limit, that little extra gas will move you ahead of everybody. If you went about 42 miles per hour, you could make a few more of the stoplights." He was right on both counts.

After dropping him off at the club, I started my drive back to the office, thinking about what he had just told me. Here was a man that came to America as an immigrant and built Haggar into one of the dominant players in the apparel industry. He did not do it by going the speed limit. This story was a metaphor for what he had to do to become successful.

If you want to change things up a little in your life, give it a little more gas. Take chances. Push through trouble. Outwork the competition, and put a little more pressure on the accelerator.

———— • ● • ————

FRUGAL? CHEAP? OR A BILLIONAIRE?

I was days away from driving to my new territory when I got one last bit of advice from one of the sales representatives who told me a story I would like to share with you:

Sam Walton and Mr. Joe Haggar, Jr. were going out to West Texas to bird hunt. The men were dressed in hunting outfits and had their bird dogs in the back of a pickup truck. They were in their late fifties or early sixties at the time, and to anyone on the street, they looked like two older gentlemen out for a day of hunting. They did not look like the richest men in America and one of the wealthiest men in Dallas.

They pulled into a gas station, and while Joe filled up the gas tank, Sam went into the small convenience store. While inside, Sam saw a newspaper stand and picked up a copy of yesterday's news. He took the paper and his other items to the counter, and the clerk rang up everything.

Sam asked the man, "What would you charge me for the newspaper?"

The man behind the counter said, "Fifty cents."

"But, it is yesterday's news. How can you charge me full price for something that is out of date?"

The man seemed stumped at the question, and after a little haggling, he charged Sam twenty-five cents. Sam walked out of the store and told Joe the story. Joe went inside to pay the man for the gas and asked him about the newspaper incident.

The man answered, "No one has ever asked me about selling old newspapers at a discount. After a couple of days, we throw them out, so I figured I would get something for it."

"Do you know who that man was that bought that newspaper?" Joe asked.

The man behind the counter shook his head no.

"That is Sam Walton of Wal-Mart stores. He loves to negotiate *everything*."

"Do you mean to tell me that Sam Walton, the billionaire, just negotiated something that saved him only twenty-five cents?"

Mr. Joe replied, "Why do you think he is a billionaire?"

I could never independently verify this story, but after reading Sam Walton's book and reading why Wal-Mart was growing like crazy, it sure sounded like something he would do. It was the perfect story to take with me to my new territory. I was going to be a straight commission sales representative, and I had to pay all my own expenses.

I always have been frugal, known the value of money, and loved to save it. I had never been an exceptionally good negotiator, but that changed after this story. I added negotiating to my list of skills as it related to managing my finances. **Making money is hard; managing money is even harder. Earn, save, negotiate, invest wisely, and you can build your net worth.** If a billionaire does it, you should do it too.

———•◉•———

BY THE TIME I GET TO PHOENIX

As my Dallas training came to an end, Haggar assigned me my new sales territory in Phoenix, Arizona. It included about 75 small mom and pop accounts, four AAFES (Army Air Force Exchange Stores), and a nine-store chain called Goldwater's.

I was excited and scared at the same time. I had waited eleven long months for this day to arrive, and now many emotions were surfacing. I was taking another big risk, moving to a place I had never been to before, starting a job I had never done before. I was also now a straight commission salesman; no more salary for me. It was a chance to make a lot of money for someone my age. There was one simple rule; sell you eat, don't sell, you don't eat.

I was concerned about was my age. Though I was 25, I still looked like I was about 16. Everybody I met since I moved to Dallas mentioned this to me, and I wondered if people would buy from someone so young and inexperienced. Then I started thinking about all that I had learned in the last 11 months and how fortunate I was to have learned from the legends of Haggar. The list included the founder of the company, his two sons who helped build the company, his grandson, and about 15 of the best sales representatives Haggar had ever produced.

With all this going on in my head, I went to the AAA building and mapped out my trip to Phoenix—there were no Google maps or cell phone apps in 1986. The drive was about the same distance as it was from Milwaukee to Dallas, roughly 1,000 miles. This time, however, there was no stopping, and crying my eyes out, wondering if I was doing the right thing. I knew I was ready. This is what I wanted, and now it was time to put everything I had learned to good use.

Just like my move to Dallas, God put another great person in my life to help me with my move to Phoenix and my start as a new salesman— Jim Herman. Jim was based in Phoenix and sold to the two other department store chains in the area (Dillards and The Broadway). As with all the other Haggar salesmen, he invited me into his home and took me under his wing.

He had a wonderful family. Three beautiful daughters (Michelle, Kathy, and Lisa) and a young son named Matthew. His parents lived in Phoenix as well, and Jim's entire family basically adopted me. Their support and guidance made my stay in Phoenix extra special. We became so close that Jim was a groomsman in my wedding.

This next chapter in my life began as my first. The Lord put another great mentor and friend in my life to help me navigate this new environment. As in Dallas, I needed to believe in myself—especially when taking chances and risks. It was a risk moving to Dallas, and it was an even bigger risk moving to this new sales territory in Phoenix.

Because I had survived and even thrived in Dallas, I had more confidence than ever to make it in Phoenix. I knew it wasn't going to be all smooth sailing, but I knew with God's help and the knowledge that He would keep surrounding me with great people, I would be successful.

Football coaches like to say they want their teams to stack successes on top of each other to help reach their full potential. The same is true for you. **Stack successes, no matter how small, to build your confidence to take on bigger and bigger goals. Winning breeds more confidence, and when you are confident, the sky is the limit for you to take on the world.**

———————— • ● • ————————

SELL WITH THE HIGHEST LEVEL OF INTEGRITY

On my first sales trip, I visited stores in Lake Havasu City, Bull Head City, Kingman, and Wickenberg. These were all small towns in the northwest part of Arizona. I called all the accounts and introduced myself. I asked them if I could make an appointment to visit their store the following week, then I mapped out the drive, made my hotel reservations, packed my samples, a cooler full of food, and headed off.

My first stop was a small men's store in Lake Havasu City. This is a beautiful area of the state that sat right across from California on the Colorado River. I unpacked my car and put all my five sample bags on a rolling rack. Each bag had about 20 or so items. I took a deep breath and said a quick prayer and rolled the rack down the sidewalk to the front door of the store. The women who ran the store saw me coming and came out to meet me. As I entered, she commented that I was as young as she had heard. I remembered what Mr. Ed Haggar had told me, "The Haggar name will get you in the store; the rest is up to you." Well, I was in the store, now what?

The first thing on my list was to count (this was before technology took over this function years later) the basic pants she had in stock. Haggar sold a variety of everyday pants, and I took a count and filled in the sizes that were missing. I then looked at her remaining displays of men's products and took an inventory of what she had on the floor to determine what she had sold based on her invoices. When I was finished, I asked her if she was ready to see the new spring clothing line. She answered, "Before we look at anything new, there is more product in the back-stock room you need to inventory."

I could not believe my eyes when I walked to the back room. It was loaded with boxes of Haggar product that had not even been opened yet. As I counted the product from the packing slips, I knew it would be difficult to sell her anything more, but I needed to sell to eat. After I finished, I began showing her the line for the following season. I steered away from what she already had and sold her on some new fabrics and colors. She was hesitant but agreed that the new looks would sell better than what she had in the back. I wrote up the order, and she agreed with the styles, quantities, and sizes. I told her I would enter the orders later that night and send her the copies as soon as I received them.

I packed the car and drove to my next account. As I drove up AZ-95, I could not get what just happened out of my mind. Advice given to me by the president of a major retailer while I drove him around Dallas came to mind. He told me, "Always sell with the highest level of integrity. Sales can be a tough profession but work on getting a reputation that you will work with the client to make both of you successful, not just sell them more and more stuff. If you get a reputation as a person of integrity that will help you no matter what your career."

That night I called the woman back and told her I sold her too much. I told her I would work with her to sell what she had in the back by getting her some marketing materials and ideas about setting up a sale that I learned at Gimbels. The only order I placed was the fill-in order and a couple of at once orders for shorts. She was incredibly grateful. I did not make any money on the account that day, but I did the right thing.

IF YOU GET A REPUTATION AS A PERSON WITH INTEGRITY, IT WILL HELP YOU NO MATTER WHAT YOUR CAREER. SOMETIMES IT IS HARD TO DO THE RIGHT THING; MY EXPERIENCE IS THAT IT PAYS OFF IN THE LONG RUN.

As I continued covering my territory the first time, word had gotten around about me. One was that I looked awfully young for my age. The other was that I was a young man with integrity. I more than made up for the orders I did not enter for that first account with business I gained from other accounts. I have tried to do this same thing with every account or client I have ever sold products or consulting services to. Sometimes it is hard to do the right thing; my experience is that it pays off in the long run.

"BOY, I DID NOT COME OUT HERE TO TAKE A SCENIC DRIVE"

My first two weeks of my inaugural selling season had gone well. The people I met were great—patient with the new guy and placed some genuinely nice orders. The third week would be dramatically different. My regional manager Jerry was going to be traveling with me the entire week. He was a former professional football player who played in the late 50s and early 60s. Jerry had joined Haggar shortly after his playing days were over.

We were headed to the northeastern part of Arizona. Account locations included the cities of Apache Junction, the mining towns of Superior, Miami, and Globe, and finishing off with the small resort towns of Show Low and Pinetop. As with the previous two weeks, I used my trusty AAA paper maps to chart my course.

The first three stops went beautifully. Jerry was very complimentary of how I handled the accounts and also gave me some pointers on things I could improve. I thought to myself that things could not be going any better. Then we left Globe for Show Low. The map indicated it was approximately 90 miles, so I had planned about two hours for travel time, just in case. How wrong I was!

I did not realize from the map that we were about to drive the most hair-raising, scary, exhilarating, and beautiful drive I have ever been on in my life. The drive starts at an elevation of 3,500 feet in Globe and rises to about 6,000 in the first 30 miles. Then you descend about 2,000 feet with multiple hairpin turns into the Salt River Canyon (also known as the Little Grand Canyon) before ascending back to about 6,000 feet over the next 30 miles or so. The last leg is the easiest stretch, but there were still several ascents and descents that challenged my little 4-cylinder engine.

You then add that I got trapped behind a semi-trailer truck or slow-moving cars on more than one occasion, and there was no way I was going to make my next appointment. The final straw was Jerry, with all his football-related aches and pains, was having a difficult time staying comfortable in my car while we were going around all those crazy 25 mph hairpin turns. We arrived in Show Low about 45 minutes late, and I called the account. They were genuinely nice and rescheduled for the next morning. They also apologized for not telling me about this drive. My paper maps were deceiving!

I got back into the car and told Jerry that the account would reschedule so I would not miss them on this trip. I also said something to the effect of at least it was a scenic drive. Jerry responded in a not so pleasant tone, "Boy, I did not come here to take a scenic drive." Lesson learned. That night I called the former salesman in the territory and asked him about every trip I was going on over the next six weeks.

I never made that mistake again. I also learned that even though I thought I was prepared, there was so much more I needed to know about my territory and being a salesman. I spent that next weekend talking to my friends Greg and Chip. They had been through one selling season and had learned from their mistakes. I figured why not eliminate as many potential mistakes as possible by learning from them.

This was a great lesson for the rest of my career. The consulting term for this is "best practices." **Find someone who has done things successfully before you and learn from their mistakes. Discover what they know so you can eliminate mistakes, perform better, and beat your competition. Are you inquisitive? Do you try to learn from others? If not, start. You may be able to avoid mistakes like the ones I made on this trip.**

———————— • ● • ————————

SUPER BOWL XXI

I was watching an NFL playoff game in early 1987 when I had an idea. *Could I check off a big bucket list item by going to a Super Bowl?* The game was being played in a few weeks in Pasadena, California. Haggar was a big advertiser with the NFL, and I thought someone might be able to get me a couple of tickets. That, someone, was Joe Haggar, III (President of Haggar Menswear).

I got to know Joe III well when I lived in Dallas, and he had always been very nice to me. We had played golf at his country club on a few occasions and frequently talked at the office. I called Joe the next day and asked him if he could possibly get me a couple of tickets for the big game. He said it might be a challenge at this late date, but he would give it a try. I thanked him and then waited to see if he could work a little magic to get me those tickets.

It was the Tuesday before the Super Bowl when I received a phone call from Joe III. He said that he had two tickets for me if I still wanted them. I could not believe it. "How much?" I asked.

"$75," he replied, "the tickets are in an endzone corner about halfway up the bowl of the stadium."

I did not care where they were; I was going to a Super Bowl! He told me he would send the tickets by express mail and I should have them by Friday.

I was ecstatic. I immediately called Jim Herman, the other salesman in town, to see if he would like to go. He said he'd love to but had a commitment. I called a friend from high school living in the Phoenix area, but he also had a commitment. Finally, I asked my upstairs neighbor, Rocky. He said, "Absolutely!"

Unlike my other trips, I did not have time to plan anything. On Saturday morning, Rocky and I packed the car and headed west on I-10 towards LA. It was about a 6-hour drive, and we arrived in the midafternoon. With no Expedia or Trivago apps yet invented, we started looking for a place to stay, but anything close to the Pasadena area was packed. We ended up in a hotel in Costa Mesa, about 50 miles from the stadium, but we enjoyed a great night around the Newport Beach area.

On Sunday morning, we drove to Pasadena and found a gas station to fill up our car for the ride home after the game. While we were standing at the pump, a couple of guys asked if we had tickets. We said yes, and they offered us $800 per ticket. They had traveled from New York to see their Giants, and they *had* to see the game. It was a lot of money, but I said no. I don't regret it one bit.

The Rose Bowl was an incredible stadium. The atmosphere was electric. The game was great. The Giants beat the Broncos 39 -20. The game was over at about 7:30 local time. By the time we got to the car and found our way to the expressway home, it was around 9:00 pm, and we arrived back in Phoenix at about 4:00 am. What a 48-hour whirlwind!

This whole experience was so unlike me. I like to have everything planned out with every "i" dotted and "t" crossed. We had none of that for this trip, and everything still worked out. It taught me that I could do something spontaneously. I did not need to always have everything planned out. I also got to check a big item off my bucket list at only 26 years old. **Every once in a while, do something spontaneous. Fun is good for the spirit and the soul!**

$25,000 IN DEBT

One of the reasons I wanted to become a sales representative for Haggar was the chance to make a lot more money than I was making at Gimbels. At Gimbels, I was a salaried employee. In 1983 I started out making $15,000. By the time I left three years later, I was making approximately $19,000. This was a decent increase for the time, but I thought I could do better as a sales rep.

At Haggar, I was paid on straight commission. I made 5% on first quality product and 2.5% on closeouts. One major challenge was that I had to pay for all my own expenses. Everything—including hotels, gas, entertainment with clients, meals when I was on the road, car repairs, office supplies, phone bill, etc. All of it was out of my pocket. In addition, Haggar billed us every month for things such as samples ($250) and a computer ($125). I averaged about $450 a month of deductions from the corporate office.

All these expenses were not even the biggest issue I faced during the first year of my sales career. My biggest challenge was debt. We had two main selling seasons in the men's apparel business: the fall selling season (January to March for shipments August through January) and the spring selling season (July to August for shipments in February to July). There were nuances for each season, but these are the basic parameters.

"At once" orders helped tremendously, but the major money-makers were orders shipped for the new spring or fall product lines. This meant I was not going to be making any real money for a while.

Haggar knew this was the case for all new sales representatives. To help, they put you a "draw towards commissions." They gave you a monthly stipend to get you by until the commissions started to come in. It was basically a loan that you had to pay back out of your checks until you were out of debt. At my peak about 12 months into my tenure,

I owed the company $25,000. This included not only my draw but all the expenses (samples and computer) that I had not yet paid back from previous months. I had never been in debt like this in my life. I hated it. Plus, I did not want to look bad to the Haggar management, so I wanted this debt gone.

I worked my butt off, and after 18 months, I was debt-free with Haggar and living off my monthly commission checks. I continued managing every penny, whether personal or business expenses and saved a good deal of money. In 1987 I made 2.5 times the money I made at Gimbels.

I hear a lot of stories about debt (especially student loan debt). This draw debt was like my student loan. I had to pay it back, or I would have been fired. **Debt can be a heavy burden and a heck of a challenge to eliminate, but remember that you accepted the terms of the arrangement when you accepted the funds. A deal is a deal.**

HALF OF SOMETHING IS BETTER THAN ALL OF NOTHING

I was in my new territory for about two months when I received a phone call from my regional manager, Jerry. We were talking about business and how things were going when he asked a very blunt question. "Why haven't you sold any closeouts?"

Closeouts were a combination of things in the Haggar vocabulary. The term mostly covered individual styles that we had leftovers of colors, certain sizes, or both. Sometimes it could include products with defects like a missing belt loop, a side seam sewn incorrectly, or a dye lot mistake. These items still had a cost associated with them, and Haggar wanted to get whatever they could to get them off the shelves and get a little cash in the bank.

There were a couple of challenges to selling closeouts. Not all customers liked them. They wanted only the colors and sizes that they knew would sell. Another problem was it could, and many times did, take money out of an account's budget to buy these. That meant they could not buy other first-quality items.

However, the biggest problem with selling closeouts was they were only half commission, and they were also discounted off the regular price. We made 5% commissions on all first quality goods. We made 2.5% on closeouts. A first quality pant might cost $10.00, and a closeout of the same would cost $6.75. I just did not like the math.

I gave Jerry a couple of reasons, but they were not very persuasive. He responded by saying, "Boy, half of something is better than all of nothing. This time of the year (end of summer) is a perfect time to sell these goods. Retailers are looking to clear the summer lines, and they need to discount their remaining stock. You add some good closeout buys, and they reduce their overall costs, then they can make just a little more money clearing their racks."

He had a point. We did this a couple of times at Gimbels, but the quality of the closeouts is what made the difference. I did end up selling closeout goods during my time at Haggar, and even though I only made half commission, they did help my customers. It also gave me a tremendous knowledge-base to leverage when I joined Tuesday Morning stores years later. They were predominatley a closeout business.

"Half of something is better than all of nothing." I love this quote, not because of half-commission apparel items. I love it because of how you can look at it within the context of a discussion, an argument, or a business decision. Sometimes it is better to get something instead of losing completely. **You will not win all the battles you will face in life, sometimes if it is better to take a little win or small amount of progress compared to a total and complete loss.** You can use this little win as progress toward the ultimate goal.

---•◦•---

MARVALEE AND THE MAY COMPANY MATRIX

In October 1986, everything changed for me and my territory. First, May Department Store Company purchased Associated Dry Goods, the owner of Goldwater's. At the time, it was one of the largest retail mergers in history ($2.7 billion). Second, at about the same time, a new buyer, Marvalee Nakata, took over the men's pant business reins. These two changes rocked my early career like a 7.5 magnitude earthquake.

Let's start with Marvalee. She was slightly older than I was and had a wonderful personality. We hit it off from the first day we met. I can't remember exactly why, but we struck up quite a friendship as well as a great business relationship. We worked well together, and I felt that we both knew that we could help make each other successful.

The transition to Goldwater's being a May Company store was an incredible break for me. The old corporate office (Associated Dry Goods) had an okay relationship with Haggar. It was extremely hard to get a lot of Haggar business because of the roadblocks put up by the corporate directions. That all changed dramatically after October 1986.

May Company loved Haggar. We were a major part of what was called the May Company Matrix. The Matrix was a list of products by vendor that you could buy within your departments. If you weren't on the list, you were in trouble. The change almost tripled the amount of Haggar items Goldwater's could now buy from Haggar. It was not a guarantee that I would get the business, but it meant I could at least have a chance to sell Marvalee.

With Marvalee as my buyer and the Matrix in place, my business started taking off like a rocket ship. I was not only adding significantly more quantities to my current products; Marvalee was giving me programs previously given to the Farah or Levi representatives. In addition, with the higher level of purchases, we had more advertising dollars to market more Haggar products to the Goldwater's customer than ever before. The stars were aligning.

With my retail background, I knew the things could get a buyer in trouble with a fast-growing department. I learned my lessons with the young men's division at Gimbels, so I stayed on top of the business from every angle. I was in stores constantly talking with customers and sales associates. I wanted to know what was working and what was not. If we needed to adjust sizes or colors, I was on it. Marvalee was doing the same. We were proactive in managing the business, not just watching the numbers grow.

In a year, my business tripled with Goldwater's, and there was more growth to come. It was fun seeing my name at the top of the rankings in my region and company. We were on a roll. Who knew how long it would last, but we were going to enjoy the ride!

Sometimes in life, the stars align. When they do, work your butt off to take advantage of it. That is the time to push harder on the accelerator—not the time to relax and coast.

————— • ● • —————

TOO SUCCESSFUL TOO FAST

My business was rolling. I was only in my territory for a year, and my numbers were off the charts. My relationship with the buyer of my biggest account, Marvalee, was great. I was getting along very well with the Goldwater's management team. Haggar was shipping my orders on time, and the product was selling well in the stores. I was also getting comfortable living in Phoenix. I had a rhythm established with my business, but I was also having fun on a personal level. Life was great.

Then one day, someone tried to throw cold water on my success. My boss was in town to see Jim Herman (the other salesman in town) and me. He had spent a day or so with Jim, and now it was my turn to take him to see the Goldwater's Buying Team. I picked him up at his hotel, and we were driving up Scottsdale Road when he asked me about my business.

"It is on fire, and I am working hard to keep it that way!" I said proudly.

His next statement blew me away. "Jeff, I am concerned that you have become too successful too fast. You have not paid your dues enough yet."

I don't remember what he said after that because I was hot. I could not believe what I was hearing. I gathered my thoughts, and when he was finished, I responded. "Why would you say that? I completely understand the May Company buyout was a gift from God, as was Marvalee, but I was not just sitting in my house taking orders. I took complete advantage of the opportunity. I was constantly at Goldwater's either in stores or in the buying office. The Matrix also had Farrah and Levi items on it, but I got the orders. Business is up in my other accounts as well, and that has nothing to do with May Company. If I continue this trend with all my business, I could very well be the salesman of the year next year."

Before I could continue, Jerry cut me off, realizing the line he crossed. He apologized and said, "You did take advantage of a great opportunity. I am just concerned that you might not keep working hard because this happened so early in your career."

"I completely understand your concern," I answered. "I promise that I appreciated this gift and thanked God for it every day. If you ever think for an instant that I am slacking off, you can let me have it with both barrels!" We agreed, and our conversation turned back to how to get more business out of Goldwater's.

Two things happened after this conversation. First, this added more fuel to my belly to not stop at anything to reach my goals. I knew there would be many hurdles to overcome on my journey, but negative words would not slow me down. Second, as I got older and began to manage individuals younger than me, I made a concerted effort not to use negative language or words that could break their spirits. I could still get my points across during those teachable moments without hurting their feelings.

Mentoring and coaching are a little bit art and a little bit science. Use language that can support a person without being demeaning. Make your point without having to cut someone down first. Help people grow instead of cutting off their wings. Then, you can then watch them soar to new heights.

I NEED $3,000 ASAP

The good news about being a sales representative on straight commission is that you can make a particularly good income; the bad news is that the income flow is inconsistent month to month. If you do not watch things closely, you can be underwater in a hurry.

Most of our orders shipped during a 6- or 7-month period. For the fall season, the majority of the orders shipped from August through October. In the spring season, most orders shipped from January through March. The remaining months were fill-in orders on the basic items or maybe a closeout or two. I would make about 65% of my income in those 6 or 7 months. The other months could sometimes be very lean.

I was in one of those lean periods. I knew my future orders were significant because of a change in ownership at Goldwater's and the new buyer now working in the men's pant area, but those orders and the subsequent commission checks were months away. I knew once I got over this hurdle, I was home-free. But where could I get about $3000 ASAP?

I thought about asking for more money from Haggar, but I was just a month or two away from paying off my debt to them. I also did not want to give them any reason to doubt my abilities seeing I was still relatively new to the position. I decided I would call one of my mentors, Jimmy Palasota.

Jimmy listened to my situation and had a quick comeback. "Go get yourself a short-term small business loan. This will do two things for you: get you over this hurdle, and help your build up your credit history. If you ever want to buy a house or another car without someone having to co-sign for you, you need to increase your credit score."

I had never even thought about my credit rating before this conversation. Jimmy walked me through getting the loan and helped me every step of the way until I received my cash.

The loan helped me get over my financial challenge and build up my credit history. If my memory serves me right, I paid back the loan earlier than the due date. Had I not gotten this loan, I know I would not have been able to buy my first house in Phoenix when I did a short time later.

So many young adults don't understand the need to build their credit history. Many of them use a credit card in their parents' names, and then when they want to buy a car or borrow money of any kind, they need a co-signature. When my son was 18, he signed up for his own credit card. We did not co-sign. He had to use his own money as collateral for the first year until he built up his credit history.

My parents and mentors like Jimmy helped me to understand how to manage my money at a very young age. **Understanding personal finance is critical at any age, but especially when you are young. You can build up some bad habits without proper guidance. Seek counsel from people you know or from money management books. Take great notes and put yourself in a much better financial situation.**

OPTIONALITY

It was late 1987, and the residential and commercial real estate markets in Arizona were as hot as a July summer day. People were moving to Arizona to escape the cold weather in the Midwest and Northeast. In fact, the reason I was sent to Phoenix was that the former representative had left to sell real estate. He thought he could make more money selling real estate than pants.

A woman in my apartment complex was also in the real estate business, and we talked all the time about me getting a real estate license. She said, "It doesn't cost much, you will learn a lot, and maybe you might want to change careers. A lot more millionaires are made buying and selling real estate than you might imagine."

She shared a famous quote from Andrew Carnegie, the billionaire industrialist, "Ninety percent of all millionaires become so through owning real estate. More money has been made in real estate than in all industrial investments combined. The wise young man or wage earner of today invests his money in real estate."

So, I entered a night real estate license training class, took the real estate license test, and passed with flying colors. I could now sell real estate in Arizona.

This might seem odd to you when my Haggar business was doing so well, but I love learning something new. I wanted to stretch my knowledge on as many topics as my brain could absorb. I never wanted to stop learning. Even though things were going great with my Haggar business, I started to get a little antsy. I had been through my third selling season, and I was beginning to ask if I could see myself doing this job 15 years from now—selling black, navy, brown, and grey pants. I also started to ask myself how I could move up in the ranks at Haggar. All the management positions were held by people in their 40s, and they were not going anywhere for the next 15 or 20 years.

I was looking for options because you never know what might happen. My friend, Jeff Boyer, uses the phrase, "You need to have optionality." That is what I was doing by taking those classes. I learned a tremendous amount, and I met some wonderful people. I also had a new path available to me if I chose to do something different.

Always give your current position 100% effort, but keep your options open. Just when you think you are comfortable, life can switch things up on you in a moment's notice. Optionality can be an exceptionally good friend.

———•●•———

ARE YOU A DRUG DEALER?

With my real estate license in hand, my first transaction was to buy my first house. Even though I was getting a little antsy about Haggar and selling pants for the rest of my career, I loved the Phoenix area. I thought I would buy a house in a nice area and live in it for a couple of years and then rent it out and buy another home. No matter what I was doing, I believed I could make money in real estate.

I purchased a house in East Mesa with a beautiful view of the Superstition Mountains. It was three bedrooms, two baths, a two-car garage, and a nice big backyard for a swimming pool. The house sold for $105,000, which is equivalent to about $250,000 today. It was a nice starter home for a young guy who had lived in an apartment complex with drug dealers and gun shots going off just two years before. The neighborhood was 99.9% young families or retirees. The 0.1% was me, a 26-year-old single pant salesman.

I became the talk of the neighborhood. I befriended a young boy about ten years old who lived next door. There were not too many kids his age in the neighborhood, so I would play catch with him in the street or shoot baskets with him in his driveway. I had been living in the house for about five months when he asked me an interesting question, "Are you a drug dealer?"

I was taken off guard by the question. I thought, *where the heck is this coming from?* I said, "No, of course not! Why would you ask me a question like that?"

"People are wondering how someone so young can afford a house like this," he answered, "they don't believe you can make that much money selling pants. You are gone for weeks at a time, and you told my mom that you travel to the Mexican border once a month ... so everybody thinks you are selling drugs."

I was flabbergasted! I did not know if I should overreact because he was only ten, but if he was correct, I needed to change their thinking before they called the cops on me! But then I thought, *why would his mom let me play catch with him if she thought I was selling drugs.* I asked him if he could get his mom to come out and talk to me.

His mom came to the front yard and told me, "It's okay; many of the neighbors do, in fact, ask these questions, but I tell them the truth about what you do. All the neighbors think it is amazing that a young man could be doing well enough to buy a house at such a young age." What a wonderful compliment. My confidence meter was on overload after she said that!

They did not realize it took every penny I had to buy that house. I did not have enough money for a washing machine or dryer, landscaping, or furniture in the living room. As commission checks came in, I eventually checked those items off the "to buy" list. It is funny now, but it taught me a lesson about the difference between what you think compared to what you know and how easily someone can form an opinion based on rumors or incorrect information.

Get the facts before you judge something or someone. Don't form an opinion based on hearsay, rumors, or, God forbid, Twitter. Never judge people by the way they look. Get to know them before you form an opinion.

DON'T BUY THE CAR; PLEASE CALL ME FIRST

I was in the waiting area of a new car dealership waiting to get the final numbers on a new car I was about to buy. The Buick Century I bought when I first moved to Phoenix was close to its end due to the roads of Arizona taking their toll. The salesman walked by and said he needed about 15 more minutes. I asked him if I could use his phone to call my answering machine.

One message changed my life forever. The new buyer at Goldwater's was just a few months into her job, and her message was short and had panic in her voice. "Don't buy the car; please call me first."

My heart was racing, and my mind went into overdrive. *Why the panic in her voice? Why would she tell me not to buy a car? What the heck was happening?*

I called her right away. Her voice changed from panic to tearful. "What's going on?" I asked.

Then she dropped the nuclear bomb. "May Company has decided to merge Goldwater's with a couple of other May Company divisions, and they are closing this buying office. All the buyers were getting fired, the DCs are closing, and all back-office functions are being eliminated."

My mouth went dry. Adrenalin rose. I could not believe it. In a matter of two short years, May Company had helped put me on the map and now had just eliminated 75% of my income. They also eliminated hundreds of jobs for all the great people who worked at Goldwater's.

We talked for a little while to help each other process this news. She asked if I had bought the car. I said, "No, not yet, thanks to your phone call."

Within a few months, Goldwater's office transitioned to the new division, and I was looking for something new to do.

Just when you think you have an open road ahead, life can give you a crazy turn of events. I did not know what was going to happen. But I knew after the success I had at Gimbels and now Haggar, the positive transition to living on my own, moving to two different cities, and thriving in both locations that I could tackle anything. I did not fear the unknown. I was willing to accept the new challenge with the knowledge that I could be successful again.

No matter what life throws at you, you can overcome anything if you have the right mindset. Doubt will always try to enter your mind—keep pushing it to the side. Keep moving forward each day, even if it is just an inch. You can conquer this challenge.

YOU CAN OVERCOME ANYTHING LIFE THROWS AT YOU IF YOU HAVE THE RIGHT MINDSET. THOUGH DOUBT WILL TRY TO ENTER YOUR MIND, KEEP PUSHING IT ASIDE. KEEP MOVING FORWARD EACH DAY, EVEN IF JUST AN INCH. YOU CAN CONQUER THIS CHALLENGE.

DON'T WORRY ABOUT ANYTHING; WE WILL TAKE CARE OF YOU

I was sitting in my car in the dealership parking lot, and I told the salesman I could not finish the deal because I just lost 75% of my income. He was shocked at what I just stated. He wished me good luck and said he would pray that things would work out for me.

There were no cell phones in those days, so I could not call anybody from the car. I started my car and figured I would drive back to my house ... "Holy crap, my house!" I had been in my house for less than a year. *How the heck am I going to pay my mortgage? Add that to the list of things I need to take care of!* My mind was reeling.

When I got home, there were two new messages on my answering machine. The first was from Frank Bracken, the EVP of Haggar, who had hired me. It was short and to the point. "Jeff, I just heard about what happened with Goldwater's, don't worry about anything; we will take care of you. Give me a call when you get this message."

What a powerful message. It was just what the doctor ordered. The Haggar company had been so good to me, and now, after hearing this horrible news, one of the top executives in the company just told me to, "RELAX!" Haggar company had my back.

The second message came from another Haggar executive, Milton Hickman, who ran the Reed St. James division. "I would like to talk to you about an opportunity I am working on to add another person to my division. I think you might be a good fit for our team. Give me a call when you get a chance."

I called Frank first, and he reiterated his message not to worry about anything. He reassured me that though it might take him a while to find the right territory for me, he would find one. "In the meantime," he counseled, "finish any loose ends with Goldwater's, sell your house, and keep in touch with me as often as you like."

"Frank," I hated to ask, "what about my income?"

He said, "Don't worry, we will cover you as a salaried employee when your commission checks run out."

"You are going to pay me to wait for a territory?" I marveled.

"Yes, and at your current income level," he assured. I could not believe it. I thanked him 20 times over.

I called Milton next. Another great southern gentleman from the Haggar family, he asked me how I was doing, and I told him much better after Frank's call. He said, "You have done a heck of a job in your short time in Phoenix, and we need to keep you with the company." Then he told me about the opportunity he was working on and how it might be a perfect fit for me. "Give me some time, and I will get back to you," he encouraged.

Wow, in a matter of 60 minutes, I almost bought a new car, I lost my sales territory and the lion's share of my income, and I had heard from two executives at Haggar to tell me that I had options. **The twists and turns in life can be nauseating. Just keep the faith that things will work out.** They might not happen in 60 minutes, but they will happen.

———•●•————

WHO IS REED ST. JAMES?

It had been about four months since the announcement was made about Goldwater's merge, and I still had not received a firm commitment from Frank Bracken about a new Haggar territory. I knew he was struggling because this decision by May Company had repercussions in other parts of the country as well. Because of this, I shifted my attention to my conversations with Milton Hickman, the SVP of the Reed St. James division.

We had several conversations about the division, his plans, and my role. After each conversation, I became more and more intrigued by this opportunity. The strategy for this division was to get the best names in the men's apparel industry to make product underneath the Reed St. James (Reed) label and sell these products to the mass merchant retailers. By doing this, these vendors could get a foothold in the growing discount store market without cannibalizing their department store business. Other vendors included Jockey and Levi.

This division had only six dedicated associates; Milton, three salesmen, one product development person, one manufacturing/sourcing person, and an administrative assistant. I would be employee number seven.

Each person in the division had to be a jack of all trades. We were to leverage Haggar's back-end divisions, including Data Processing, Distribution, Piece Goods, etc.

Milton's pitch was that I could learn everything about running a small apparel company by joining this division. If I stayed with the Haggar label division, I would get another territory just like I had in Phoenix. I would get a new product line every six months, sell as much as possible, and then do it again in six months. I would never be exposed to every aspect from product development to the sale of products on the retail sales floor.

This opportunity was perfect—exactly what I wanted. I could learn so much about the entire business and feed my goal of running a business someday. I was already getting antsy in Phoenix doing the same thing every six months, and his pitch to me hit home.

The last selling point was that I would be working with three of the best Haggar salesmen ever: Ted Demerle, Clay Huston, and Corbett Howard. Ted worked in the northeast. Clay was in Chicago and helped start Reed. Corbett was the person who first sold Reed product to Wal-Mart a few years ago. Ted and Clay were getting close to retirement, so I would take over their territories and get to support Corbett with his Wal-Mart duties.

Reed was checking all the boxes. Great people to learn from, being exposed to the entire life cycle of the business, including back-office functions, back in Dallas so I would not have to learn a new city, getting to work with Wal-Mart and their growing influence over the retail industry. I would be salaried plus expenses and could still make more money than I did in Phoenix. I was sold.

It took a little convincing for Frank to accept my decision. He had invested a lot in me, and now I was moving to another division. It was a great compliment from him to not just let me go without a fight. I was taking a chance by moving to this much smaller, basically startup division, but the risk was worth it. The decision was perfect, and the people were the best. Over the next three years or so, I was exposed to 100 times more than I ever could have imagined.

As you can tell by now, I am not risk adverse. **You must take some chances in life if you want to reach your true potential. You cannot fear failure; it is just part of life's lessons. Don't just touch your toe in the water, take a risk every once in a while, and jump right in.**

CLAY AS IN MUD, HUSTON AS IN TEXAS

I was standing in the waiting area of Shopko corporate offices in Green Bay, Wisconsin, to be introduced as the new sales director for Reed St. James. The salesman I was replacing was winding down a tremendous career selling Haggar label product and then helping to start the Reed division. We went to the reception area to sign in and ask our buyer to come and get us.

The receptionist asked for our names and our company name. In a bold and confident voice, the former salesman said, "My name is Clay Huston. That is Clay as in mud, Huston as in Texas." I heard him say this 100 times, and it never got old. It was such a great way to introduce himself. If there was any apprehension that someone might have about meeting Clay, it was instantly gone.

Clay was one of a kind. A quote from a 2008 article written in the *Chicago Tribune* after his death said, "Clay D. Huston's unflagging enthusiasm for people and apparel, along with a street-smart grasp of the psychology, produced stellar sales out of Chicago for Haggar Clothing Co. for 37 years." It was the perfect description of Clay.

He dropped out of High School to join the Navy in 1945 and then worked at various jobs selling apparel before joining Haggar in 1959. Clay reminded me a lot of my dad, who did not finish high school and received his GED with the Army. Both men would not be considered by some as "Ivy League smart," but they more than made up for it with common sense, street smarts, and an uncanny ability to get along with everybody.

On this trip, Clay would take me around to stores in Wisconsin, Illinois, and Michigan. We would be based out of his apartment overlooking Lake Michigan and Lake Shore Drive—not a bad location for a high school dropout! He and his lovely wife had invited me to stay at their home. When he picked me up at O'Hare Airport, he said he would give me an equivalent of a Master's in business, psychology, and life during the next two weeks.

He was not lying. We put on about 2,000 miles during those two weeks, so we spent a lot of time in the car together. I wish it would have been longer. For every new lesson he would tell me about, I would ask him 20 questions. Watching him with customers was like watching a concert pianist play each key with purpose and commitment. I took many mental notes so I could ask him about each little nuance when we got back in the car.

We also laughed our you-know-whats off. Clay could tell some of the greatest stories ever. There was more than one occasion I thought we were going to get in an accident because we were laughing so hard. Clay's teaching did not stop after this trip. He continued to provide me with guidance and mentoring throughout my three years or so with the Reed division.

Many times, we judge people based on their degrees, the college they went to, or what side of the city they came from. In my life, I have learned just as much or more from people with a GED than a degree from Harvard. There has never been a person in my life with more knowledge than Clay Huston about life, personal and business relationships, how to interact with people, and how to use every ounce of your skills to succeed. Look around; there are Clay Huston's everywhere. Find them and learn everything you can from them. No master's program will help you more.

I WANTED TO SEE HOW IT ALL FIT TOGETHER

I wanted to join the Reed division to learn as much as I could about what it takes to run a company. As a sales representative, you came to Dallas twice a year to get your new clothing line, price list, and samples. Haggar gave you all the tools you needed to sell in your territory. It was as if they were giving you a new cake to eat, but I had limited knowledge about how the entire cake was made. I wanted to know.

Many sales representatives did not care, but I did. My goals were crystal clear—learn everything I could about running a company so that maybe one day in the future, I could do just that. I wanted to know what ingredients were used, how long the cake needed to bake, and how you determined the cost of the finished product. In the new world of Reed St. James, I was exposed to all of this. From the initial idea during the product development phase to the new technology needed to analyze the business and replenish orders. I was getting a hands-on MBA courtesy of Haggar.

Here are a few highlights:

- **Product Development** – I was now involved with the initial generation of ideas for the new lines not only six months from now but two years from now: piece goods selection, costing, models of the garment, size range, silhouette, and sample development.

- **Sourcing** – I worked directly with our head of production to source where in the world we were going to make the product. This included not only a potential location but factory standards, quality and assurance metrics, costing, lead times, in-line inspections, transportation costs, product and carton labeling, just to name a few items. We were also the first part of Haggar to source in China and the Far East. Talk about night and day differences than dealing with a plant in south Texas.

- **Forecasting** – As a Haggar salesman, we were responsible for giving our forecast monthly to assist the corporate office with the rollup of the entire company-wide numbers. After I sent in my numbers, I was done. Now I had to not only generate a forecast but also work with product development, piece goods, and sourcing departments to ensure that we could make the product to meet our ship windows.

- **Technology** – Because the retailers we were now selling to had so many stores in so many states, it was impossible to physically count the stores as I did in Arizona. We had to leverage technology, and luckily, Haggar was at the forefront of Electronic Data Interchange (EDI) and Quick Response (Replenishment Processes).

- **Selling** – Even though I was part of all these functions and many more, my main job was to sell and market our products. If I could not sell the product, all the other efforts would have been wasted.

My boss had absolutely fulfilled his commitment. I was part of everything that went into making the wonderfully delicious cake (apparel product) and analyzing if the customer liked it or not. Then we did the entire process over again. Without these three years, I know that my career goals would have been much harder to achieve. Even though many people said I made a mistake going to this smaller division, they did not understand why I did it. I was managing my career, not having someone manage it for me.

Do not depend on your company, boss, or peers to dictate what you can and cannot do. Take control of your career. Only you know what your dreams and aspirations are. So, put on an apron and start mixing up some new ingredients and see if you can make a wonderful new cake/career path. Mine ended up with a nice cherry on top; hopefully, yours will too.

— • ● • —

THE TECHNOLOGY TRAIN IS COMING

During my time selling in Arizona, one of my main ways to make money was taking physical inventory counts once a month and sending what we called fill-in orders to the Dallas distribution center. A fill-in order literally filled in the sizes and colors that had sold out during the previous month, plus prepared for an increase on what you *thought* might sell until the next inventory.

It was incredibly inefficient. There could be weeks that a store was out of what we called the "gut" sizes. These were the 5 to 6 sizes that sold, sometimes up to 65% of all sales. It also could cause a glut of excess inventory. If you misjudged the customer, you might load a store or the entire chain with six months of supply.

This caused havoc with the entire supply chain for a vendor. How much piece goods do you need? What sizes do you make? How much inventory do you have in your distribution center? How do you keep maximum efficiency in your manufacturing process? Then you factor in the lead time necessary for all these steps, and you have a nightmare situation. The answer was, "Just-in-Case Inventory."

Neither the retailer nor the vendor wanted to miss sales, especially on basic items items, so they purposefully kept excess inventory. Something had to change. The answer was technology, and Haggar had been at the forefront of technology during my entire tenure with the company.

It was called Quick Response. The vision was to use technology to enhance the inventory management processes to enable quicker deliveries, reduce excess inventories, increase day-to-day in-stock positions and provide enormous amounts of new data on customer buying habits.

Haggar was one of the first apparel companies to barcode products. They started with barcoding fabric to help with the dye lots and with cutting and producing certain products. They then moved to bar code all their apparel products years before retailers had the technology to read the label. The last step was to bar code cartons. We were one of the first, if not the first, to scan each item into a carton and then scan the carton label that then generated an electronic invoice. All this is second nature now, but this was revolutionary in the late 80s and early 90s.

During my initial sales training with Haggar, I would spend a lot of time with the technology folks. I could see the future, but I could not use it in my territory due to the lack of capabilities of my accounts. Now three years later, I was in a division that had to use technology to support the size of the retail chains we were selling to. You could not sell to Wal-Mart or Target without having these capabilities.

You had to be blind not to see what technology was doing and going to do to our industry. Many stuck their heads in the sand—like Blockbuster watching Netflix emerge—believing that this would not impact them. I talked to many of my Haggar friends in sales and told them, "You better keep your eye on what is happening with technology. It is going to make the sell and repent (oversell so much you ask God forgiveness), and make the monthly count sales representative obsolete." It fell on deaf ears.

With the dramatic increase in retail consolidations and the implementation of new technology, the Haggar salesforce saw a dramatic downsizing over the coming years. Many had been with Haggar for over 20 years and were only in their late 40s or early 50s. They were caught off guard by what was happening around them, and I did not like to see this happening to these great people.

Do not get caught off guard by the winds of change that are swirling around you. It is much better to be a little early in finding something new than too late. Always stay abreast of what is happening within your industry. You always have to stay ahead of the technology train, or you are going to get run over by it.

THE BIG APPLE BITES BACK

It was the first time I traveled to see my new accounts with Ted Demerle, our salesman in the country's northeast area. Like Clay Huston, Ted was a legend at Haggar and was winding down a highly successful career. He was going to help me transition all his accounts to me.

On this trip, we would see Bradlees (Braintree, MA), Hills (Canton, MA), Ames (Rocky Hill, CT), and Caldor (Norwalk, CT). I was then scheduled to take a train from Connecticut to New York City to spend a couple of days seeing additional accounts. It was going to be one heck of a week and a half.

Ted was a tremendous teacher throughout the entire time. We drove in a two-door Mercedes convertible around the backroads of two states I had never been to in my life. Just like my trip with Clay, we spent as much time laughing as we did discussing his sales accounts. He could really tell some funny stories. As with all the other Haggar salesman I traveled with, he was kind enough to invite me to stay at his home.

With the combination of a trade show in Las Vegas, traveling with Clay, and now this trip with Ted, I was getting really comfortable with my new territory. These trips also helped me get over any anxiety I had about traveling the country instead of just driving around one state. I was enjoying not only seeing different parts of this beautiful nation but also meeting new people. It was just what I wanted when I left Wisconsin. I was experiencing the entire country, and my next stop was the Big Apple, New York City.

I had visited New York as an assistant buyer when I was with Gimbels, but on this trip, I would be on my own. The last time I just followed my buyer around. I learned some things, but I was still naïve to the rhythms and rules of the city.

Ted dropped me off at the train station in Connecticut. It was scheduled to leave at about 6:45 am and get into Grand Central Station at about 8:30 am. I had never taken a train into New York, but Ted talked me through it. I was fascinated that people did this ride every day. We arrived on time, and I grabbed my two suitcases (one with samples and one with my clothes) and exited the train. It was my first time in Grand Central Station—an amazing structure and busy as heck.

Ted had told me what exit to take and how to locate a taxi stand, but I got turned around in this massive building and exited at the wrong place. The people were moving so fast that I could not get anyone's attention. I looked for a taxi stand, but there was not one in sight. I remember how my buyer Dave Levey would hail down a taxi, but I sucked at it. People were jumping in front of me left and right.

Then a guy came up and asked me if I needed a cab. I said I sure did. He said, "Give me ten bucks, and I will get you a cab."

Naïve Jeff believed him. I gave him $10, and he ran away. A lady standing next to me saw what happened and asked me if I was new to the city. I was now apprehensive about talking to anyone. She could see it in my eyes. She did not wait for an answer; instead, she walked out into the street and hailed a cab. She called me over and said, "Hurry up; this one is for you." I got into the cab and thanked her profusely. Her last words were, "Take some time to learn the city, or it will definitely bite you!"

Lesson learned. Within two minutes, a jerk stole money from me, and a wonderfully nice lady got me a cab. Just like my early mistakes traveling some of the crazy roads in Arizona, I knew that I had to learn about all the new places I was traveling. **Not everything in life goes according to plan. You must be flexible to shift and, yes, even make mistakes to learn and grow as an individual.** The Big Apple took a little bite out of me that day, but it never happened again.

———— • ● • ————

1991 – OUTSTANDING SALES AWARD GOES TO ...?

Before I lost my biggest account in my Arizona territory, I was on a roll. My numbers were outstanding, and I was in the running for salesman of the year at the tender age of 28. I will never know if I would have been able to bring the trophy home, but I know I wanted to see if I could get my new territory on a similar roll.

This time, I would not benefit from a corporate buyout with a company that valued the Haggar brand to jump-start my business or be blessed with a new buyer close to my age that I immediately built a strong partnership with. In my Reed territory, these were all very experienced buyers—often in the business longer than I had been alive. I would have to use all my skills from Gimbels and my first few years at Haggar to survive this new environment and thrive.

The salesmen I was replacing had laid a fantastic foundation, but I needed to take it to the next level. The first season I was the new guy, and these veteran merchants were going to test me every step of the way. I held my ground and showed them I knew what I was doing. My numbers were okay but nothing to write home about. Still, I earned my buyer's respect, and it set the stage for my second year in the territory.

During my second year with a new line of causal bottoms called Loafers, I caught fire. The line was very well received, and the orders started coming in. I also convinced many of the accounts to adjust some of the size ranges we were carrying in stores based on the numbers I saw from our business with Wal-Mart. For example, stores we thought should have more 38-inch waist pants actually needed more 32-inch waist pants. The shift seemed minor, but sales started rising.

Corbett (the other Sales Director) and I were locked at the hip with David Barber, our head of operations, to make sure our forecasts were as accurate as possible. We were constantly analyzing anything that changed with any of our accounts. This scrutiny enabled David to better plan pieced goods buys and set up the manufacturing lines more efficiently.

We were tracking our numbers until the last cutoff day for the sales year. When the final numbers came in, I received the 1991 Award of Excellence—Outstanding Sales! It was such an incredible feeling getting this award. It validated that my performance in Arizona was not a fluke. It also validated in my mind that I was good at what I did. Finally, it solidified that I had the power to persuade people. In this case, it was to buy a product, but it would be about selling ideas in the not-so-distant future.

I know we have built a culture of giving everybody awards. I am not a fan. If Haggar would have handed out 125 trophies, why would you try to get better? **Always strive for excellence and get the most out of your God-given talents. Push, sweat, and struggle to be the best you can be. Sometimes you win an award, and sometimes you don't. The question is this: are you giving it your all? If you are, then you are the best you can be. That is what matters.**

THE YELLOW LEGAL PAD

Technology and operational efficiency were key to Wal-Mart's early growth and dominance. However, there was another major reason for Sam Walton's success—his yellow legal pad. Sam never knew when he would discover a new idea or have a thought on how to make Wal-Mart better. He always wanted to have something to write these new inspirational thoughts on.

Here are a few quotes from Sam's book, *Made in America*:

"Great ideas come from everywhere if you just listen and look for them. You never know who's going to have a great idea."

"Wal-Mart was built almost entirely off of other retailers' good ideas."

"Most everything I've done I've copied from someone else."

I know some people will say that copying is a bad thing, but I disagree when it is done the way Sam did it. He was like a football coach watching another team have success with certain passing plays. Everybody who was watching could see them; they were not patented or hidden in a locked safe. Sam did the same thing. Almost all his ideas were in plain sight if you were willing to get out of your ivory tower and look for them. You also had to be willing to admit that someone else was doing something better. Then, you take the best ideas you find and make them better and implement them with lightning speed. That is how you leapfrog and then put laps around the competition.

Most retail CEOs then (and some today) were unwilling to look under every rock or talk for hours to a person who worked in the stock room about their ideas of how to make a process better. Sam was a man of the people. Just like Mr. J.M. Haggar told me years before, "If you want the truth, ask the workers or ask the customer." Both Mr. Haggar and Sam Walton did not care where an idea came from. If it was a good idea and could help the company, they wanted to know about it.

There were many stories about how Sam would visit competition with members of his management team in the early days of Wal-Mart. After the visit, they would discuss in the parking lot what they saw. Many times, there was nothing but negative comments spoken about one thing or another. Then Sam would say something about a marketing sign topper he saw in the sporting goods area. A month later, they had either copied it or made it better, and it was in all his stores.

Tom Grimes, my CEO at Gimbels, said, "Retail is detail." Well, Mr. Sam Walton never missed one detail. Whether that was in his stores or operations or his competitors. He was inquisitive and was not afraid to ask questions. He knew a minor change here or there could generate more sales or save the company money. He was not too proud to say the idea came from someone else.

In life or business, you need to continually strive to get better. Why not investigate how others have become a success? Take the best ideas that fit your situation, tweak them if needed, and then implement them. Don't be too proud to learn from others. If it worked for the man who built the largest retailer in the world, it sure can work for you.

BONEFISH LAMB

After I left Wisconsin, I made it a top priority to travel and experience as many things as possible. My dad's philosophy taught me to put experiences and memories above material possessions. While living in Arizona, I had visited San Diego, seen a Super Bowl in Los Angeles, traveled to Savanah, Georgia, and famous Tybee Island, and went on a cruise to St. Thomas, Puerto Rico, and St. Marteen.

When I moved back to Dallas, I did not stop. My friend Chip Humphrey and I traveled to Paradise Island in the Bahamas to go to a Club Med. We were both single at the time, and they were known for an exclusive experience for young adults. We met people from France, Australia, Germany, Spain, and Britain as well from all over the United States. It was a blast and amazing meeting people from all over the world.

We had so much fun that two years later, we vacationed at another Club Med. This time on the Turks and Caicos Islands. Resorts are so awesome that you don't need to leave the property, but these islands were known to have great fishing for something called a bonefish.

Chip told me that bonefish were bottom-feeders that swim in shallow waters—not the best to eat but a fun adventure to catch! It would cost about $250 for a three-hour finishing trip. I was not immediately sold on this idea since my fishing experience to date had been such a waste of time casting and reeling for hours and never getting a bite, let alone catch anything. But I told him I would think about it.

When I went to work the next day, I asked some of the people in the office if they had heard of bonefishing. At least five people warned me that they are exceedingly difficult to catch, and if you were not knowledgeable about their habits, you might be wasting your money. Still, it was something I had never done before, and it would be with one of my best friends, so I called Chip and said, "Let's go!"

We arrived at the pier and met our guide. "I'm Bonefish Lamb," he said, "and we are going to catch some bone today!"

I looked at Chip and said, "Well, at least we have a confident guide." But all I kept thinking about how difficult they told me bonefishing was at the office. All the way out to our fishing spot, Bonefish Lamb told us stories about all the "bones" his guest would catch and that he is the best guide in all the Caribbean. My confidence was rising.

We stopped in an area where the water was about one foot or less deep and was clear as the water in your bathtub. Bonefish was baiting my line when he looked over to a spot about 20 feet from the boat. He let out a soft scream and said, "Boys, we are going to be catching some bone today!" and he gave me my fly-fishing rod and pointed to an area where the water changed colors. He said the "bone" are right over there. I cast the first time and missed his spot. I reeled in the line and cast one more time. I had a bite!

After a fight of about 5 minutes, I pulled in a bonefish. Chip and I could not believe it. We were high-fiving and searching the boat for our camera. Before we could find it, we heard a splash. We looked up and Bonefish and had thrown our bonefish back into the water. We went crazy. We told him no one would believe us that we caught a bonefish. He looked at us both and said, don't worry, boys, there will be lots of bone today. He was right—we caught five bonefish that day and have pictures to prove it.

It was an amazing day, and 30 years later, Chip and I continue to reminisce about our three-hour excursion with Bonefish Lamb. These memories are priceless. It is so easy to talk yourself out of doing something adventurous. You might miss the next great Netflix series or the next level of Candy Crush. **There is so much to see and do in this world. So put down the remote or your cell phone and get out there and experience it!**

THE TIME I MET A FUTURE PRESIDENT

My friend Corbett Howard asked me if I wanted to meet someone special. I said, "Of course," but I did not have a clue who I was going to meet. You see, Corbett seemed to know everybody. He was always having people come by the office and get some Haggar pants. This day was no different. Corbett told me to go to one of our sample rooms and make sure it is cleaned up, and he would bring the person back to meet me and select some apparel items.

I finished cleaning the room when Corbett walked in with his guest. He looked at me and said, "Jeff, I would like you to meet George W. Bush."

Mr. Bush walked up to me, shook my hand, and said, "It is very nice to meet you, Jeff. Corbett here tells me you are one heck of a young man." I thanked him and told him it was a pleasure to meet him as well.

At the time, Mr. Bush was the managing partner of the Texas Rangers baseball team, and of course, the son of the current president of the United States, George H.W. Bush. I was struck that there was no sense of arrogance or conceit about him—just a regular guy.

Before discussing what types of apparel he wanted, he said he had to show Corbett his new cowboy boots. He lifted his leg, perched it on the big showroom table, and lifted his pant leg to reveal custom-made boots with the Texas Ranger colors and logo. I am not a Cowboy boot fan, but they were gorgeous. I spent the next 45 minutes listening to Corbett and Mr. Bush tell stories and laugh while we selected a few items that he wanted to order.

When we were finished, Corbett had to go to another appointment, and he asked me if I would walk Mr. Bush out. As we walked, Mr. Bush thanked me for helping him with the apparel order, said again that it was a pleasure to meet me, and he wished me well with my job at Haggar. "You work for a great family and company," he nodded.

"I definitely know that," I answered, and I wished him and the Texas Rangers good luck. I had no idea that four years later, he would become the Governor of Texas and later serve as President of the United States. I wish I had taken a picture with him and gotten his autograph, not because of politics, but because he was an interesting man. That was a good day. The son of a sitting President and owner of a major league baseball team made me feel important. **You never know who will cross your path. Treat them with respect. Be the same person when the spotlight is on as you are when you think no one will notice.**

————— • ● • —————

THE WINDS OF CHANGE WERE SWIRLING AROUND

I was asked to take on more responsibility selling private label product about a year after joining the Reed division. In the early 1990s, retailers began to source more of their products for themselves, trying to cut out the middleman (Haggar) and keep more of the profit margin. They also saw it as a differentiator and a chance to get away from the price competition wars with brands like Haggar and Levi. They would develop a label and market it as a brand name, but it was their brand.

Haggar wanted a piece of that growing business. This would expand their offering to include the Haggar label for department stores, Reed St. James for the mass merchants, and the private label division who could sell any account if we could meet the cost guidelines for the retailer. I accepted this new challenge and added the private label business card to my portfolio.

One of our biggest goals in the division was to sell Target. Target was growing significantly and was trying to position itself between the department stores and the discount chains. They would have loved the Haggar label, but we would not sell that to them, and they did not want the Reed label because it was in Wal-Mart. Like Wal-Mart, to even get an appointment with them, you must have EDI, bar-coded carton labels, etc. We met all the requirements and could sell them a private label product, so it was time to give them a call.

Jerry Dejulius (VP of the Private Label) and I made a phone call to the buyer. We discussed a variety of options and determined it was worth a trip to Minneapolis. The buyer informed us that we would need to bring other people to make sure that we could comply with all their vendor requirements. A sales call that included other divisions of the company was a first for me. I can't recall everybody that went, but I believe we took a person from EDI, accounts payable, and operations.

When we arrived at the Target offices, Jerry and I went to work with the Buying Team, and the rest of our group headed off to meet with their counterparts. Jerry and I were about to be the first people in the history of Haggar to get an order from Target, but it was dependent on what happened with our colleagues. It was a strange experience. The buyer did not have total control of the decision whether we made it to the store or not. This was a company-to-company sale, not a salesman-to-buyer sale, and this lesson would be of great assistance when I began working with Michaels in 1997.

All our colleagues met with the buyer and explained that Haggar passed all requirements with flying colors. We sold Target a men's elastic waist pant for an entire spring season. Unfortunately, we had some major challenges with the on-time delivery of the product and lost the program the next year. It was very disappointing, but I had learned a tremendous amount from this experience.

First, retailers were no longer dependent on major apparel companies—a warning to suppliers, and second, as retailers embraced technology, suppliers needed to be ahead of the curve, not behind. The world was changing. Retailers expected much more than just products. You had to deliver on all their expectations or they would find a way to do it themselves.

Business evolves, and this is a harsh reality. You can be surprised by the changes or get in front of them and adapt. Be proactive and move before you get moved.

FRIDAY NIGHT LIGHTS

It was about 7:00 one morning, and I was waiting outside Corbett Howard's house. Ever since I moved back to Dallas and worked for the Reed division, we carpooled whenever we were both in town, and it was my turn to drive. Corbett was his usual jovial self when he got in the car, said hello, and asked me, "What are you doing next weekend?"

"I don't think I have any plans."

"Well, you do now! I am taking you out to a small town in West Texas to experience a high school football game and go dove hunting."

I looked at him and said, "What the heck are you talking about?"

"You tell me all the time about wanting to experience as many new things as you can," he said. "Well, how about experiencing how people live outside the big city of Dallas? One of my best friends lives out there and has invited us to stay with him. We'll go to the game Friday night, then go dove hunting early Saturday morning." I was all in.

I had heard many stories about life in small-town Texas and what high school football meant to the community. It was the real *Friday Night Lights,* and now I was going to experience it. We rolled into town about 4 pm, and the city was already abuzz for a game that would not start for three and a half hours. Signs were up, people were walking around with the school colors, and you could just feel the energy in the air.

We dropped off our things at Corbett's friend's house, then went to a local diner for a meal, and everybody there was dressed in the school colors, too. When we got to the stadium at about 7:00 pm, the place was already filling up. You could feel the pride and knew that everyone knew everybody. There were about 15 buses for the opposing team and their fans. When people say that the town closes to watch the game, they were not kidding!

During the game, the commentary was fascinating. "Look at that great tackle. You know that is Jenny's boy; his brother plays at A&M," or "Great catch. He is much better than his brother," or "Did you hear Joe is going to sell his tractor? I might put a bid in on it." I don't remember who won the game, but I *do* remember all the people and how genuine they were and how a football game brought an entire community together.

The next morning, we got up at about 4:00 am to take the long drive to go hunting. We wanted to get there before sunrise. I was sure this property was not on any map. You could see every star in the sky because you were so far away from any city lights. After about an hour, we turned off the paved road and onto a dirt road and headed for the house.

When we got there, we were met by his friends' two cousins, and his aunt. The house looked like it had been built 100 years ago— like something out of a movie. It had a dusty porch with old beat-up furniture on it. The roof was sagging and looked like if the wind blew too hard, it would fly right off, but they did not care. It was their home. As the sun rose, we started the hunt. I had not shot a gun in 20 years, but I actually hit a few birds.

When we were done, Corbett's friend gave all the birds to his relatives. While we were visiting with the family, the aunt went inside the house and brought out a big bowl and a wastebasket, and she (with her hands) beheaded and cleaned each bird. Without batting an eye, she asked if we wanted to stay for some dove soup. We thanked her but said we had to get on the road back to Dallas that afternoon, so we needed to get going. What an experience! It just added to all the new memories I was making.

The world is made up of so many different and wonderful people. Get out and meet some of them. Interacting with those who live differently than you will broaden your perspective on life and give you memories to draw from for years.

---•●•---

THE PERSON DOESN'T WORK HERE ANYMORE

In 1984, Gimbels informed us they were bringing in consultants to improve our business. The consultants came and interviewed people from all parts of the organization. They took notes and then gave us a recommendation on a new direction we should take. It was a program called CARE (Customers Are Really Everything). I was fascinated that management gave them the ability to investigate many of the issues we as employees were thinking had to change, and I wanted to know more about this profession.

I began a decade-long education about the major players, companies, and techniques used by this industry. W. Edward Deming began to get recognized for his work with the Japanese Government in the Post World War II era. In the late 1970s, Japan had transformed from a war-torn country to a producer of high-quality, competitive products. The United States and Western Europe were facing stiff competition from Japan and looking for answers. In 1980, NBC News ran a segment titled

"If Japan Can … Why Can't We?" Some of the biggest corporations began seeking out Deming and others to help them become more efficient and raise quality across their organizations.

Besides Deming, I read books about Peter Drucker, Michael Porter, Michael Hammer, Tom Peters, Harvey Mackay, and Robert Krigel, to name a few. Their books include *Swimming with the Sharks, In Search of Excellence, Out of Crisis, If it Ain't Broke, Break It,* and *Competitive Advantage.* New terms were being used like Total Quality Management and Business Process Reengineering. After reading each book, I thought how great it would be to go into a company to find out how to make them better.

In early 1990, I got another chance to put these ideas into practice. Haggar brought in someone to corporate headquarters to help us implement Quality Management (QM) standards and practices. Again, I was intrigued that this QM process could look under every rock, talk to people across different divisions and make recommendations that impacted not just one area but many. So many of the ideas people who worked at the company for years were complaining about, but now management seemed open to making the changes.

One early example of what they found sticks out to me. At the time, almost all reports were printed on 11' x 14" green and white bar paper printed on dot-matrix printers. You could go through a forest full of trees in a day. We were asked to challenge why we printed reports and did everyone use the reports? If you ever saw the movie *Office Space*, we were looking for our own version of the TPS report. Everyone wanted one, but nobody used it.

As with every company, we found many reports that fell under this category. One report was about 50 pages, and we ran something like 30 copies every week. A person had to separate and deliver each copy. The whole process took a couple of hours each Monday morning. When someone went around and asked if it was being used, all 30 people said they never looked at it. In fact, one person said that the report was originally generated for a person who left the company five years ago.

In the consulting world, this is what you call low-hanging fruit. In a blink of an eye, you save 2 hours' worth of labor and 1,500 pages of paper a week. I was hooked. The more I read about consulting; I learned many Senior Executives of companies were former consultants. They used their consulting engagements to learn every aspect of how a company works, how it can be improved, and how to implement change. I thought this might be my next career move.

> **MAKE SURE YOUR CAREER PATH REMAINS ALIGNED WITH YOUR GOALS. GIVE YOUR CURRENT JOB YOUR BEST, BUT IT IS OKAY TO INVESTIGATE OTHER AVENUES. YOU DON'T HAVE TO SETTLE.**

Even though I loved working for the Reed division, I still wasn't sure if this path could get me to my goals. I gave 100% to Reed, but in my spare time, I was starting to investigate how I might transition to the world of consulting. Make sure your career path remains aligned with your goals. Give your current job your best, but it is okay to investigate other avenues. You don't have to settle.

WALK IN MY SHOES

My boss Milton Hickman asked if he could see me for a minute. He had something he wanted to discuss with me. When I sat down, Milton said, "You might not like what I am about to tell you, but it will be really good for you." I did not know what to think about what was coming next.

Milton said, "As part of the Quality Management program, everyone was being asked to 'walk in the shoes' of a person from another part of the company. Seeing that you have such an extensive training period during your initial stay in Dallas, it was hard to find someone you have not worked with." Right then and there, I knew who he was talking about, but I waited for him to tell me. "The only area you seemed to have missed is working at our distribution center (DC) with the manager." (I will call her Jane.)

I actually had been to the DC on several occasions as a trainee, but times had changed. Jane and I were now having a few problems with shipping errors causing chargebacks from my accounts. Our conversations sometimes were challenging, so I would say we were not big fans of each other. Milton continued telling me I needed to spend a week working the DC's hours and directly with Jane. "What about my regular day job?" I asked.

"Unfortunately, you need to make sure nothing falls between the cracks with those responsibilities." The hits just kept on coming.

I left his office and called Jane as instructed to make the arrangements. Her tone told me that she was as happy about this as I was. I tried to keep an open mind that this would be good for me—more experience—so I tried my best to have a positive attitude.

I showed up early Monday morning and met Jane in her office. There was a definite chill in the room, but we kept things cordial. She told me she wanted me to follow the ten or so processes in the building for an hour or two each day: receiving, put-away, picking, packing, shipping, returns, defective products, etc. I responded, "Sure, I will also need to make some phone calls and check things on the computer throughout the day, and you can look over my shoulder."

My first few hours were eye-opening. I could not believe all the literal crap she had to deal with. Shipping errors from our factories, late orders, mismarked cartons, constant order changes coming from corporate via the salesman, requests for proof of delivery from salesman via retailers, and so much more. I never knew what she really had to deal with each day.

Then she sat in on a couple of calls with my accounts. She heard them berate me for late orders or a carton that the label peeled off. She noted the discussions about how my future orders would be in jeopardy if we could not get our act together and so much more. She never knew what I had to deal with each day either.

By the end of the week, I had an immense appreciation for her role and her challenges, and she had the same for me and my role as a sales director. Because of that week, I became a smarter salesperson, businessperson, and person in general. **We are quick to criticize someone for actions they take or maybe did not take. But maybe— just _maybe_—if we could walk in their shoes, we would see things differently. The harshness of our criticisms would swiftly change to understanding and caring.** I am so glad Milton made me do this. Try it yourself.

THE DAY OUR WORLD CHANGED

We had prepared for weeks for this presentation. The Wal-Mart team was coming to the Haggar offices to review our business and see our new product line. Corbett Howard, our sales director for the Wal-Mart account, and Donna Harrington, our product development director, would lead the meeting. I would be there along with Milton, our boss, and David Barber, our head of operations, for support and to answer any questions that Corbett or Donna needed assistance with.

Wal-Mart was a huge part of our business, and we needed to do everything to keep them happy with great product, great prices, and great support in areas like Vendor Managed Inventory. We could not afford to lose any programs or store count. We had to put on a good presentation, and Corbett and Donna were ready. Or so I thought.

When the Wal-Mart team arrived, there was an additional person I did not know. The buyer and the assistant buyer were there, but the new person introduced himself as being in the sourcing area for Wal-Mart. I looked at David Barber, our sourcing guy, and whispered, "I don't like the sound of his role." We had been concerned for years that retailers would begin to do their own sourcing, and Wal-Mart pushed harder every day to get their prices lower and lower. Cutting out the middleman was a company mission if it could save money.

The meeting began with Corbett going over all the numbers. He did not even need the reports. He knew his business backward and forward. Store count, sell-through, margin, tops, bottoms, sizes, geographic differentiation, etc., Corbett had it down. As always, Wal-Mart had their own numbers, but at the end of this part of the conversation, we both agreed Reed was doing very well in their stores.

Then Donna got up to begin the presentation. She started with our men's bottoms business. She started showing our basic polyester pant and a couple of new colors when the person from their sourcing area started asking questions we had never heard before. "What plant are you making that in? How many total piece goods do you use a year? What do you pay per yard for the fabric?"

We were a branded company and never shared the type of information. If we did, the retailer could determine our profit margins, and the negotiations would become harder. Well, that is exactly what Wal-Mart was doing. They wanted to account for every extra penny we were making compared to what they could make it for.

That is the day the world changed for us. After the meeting ended, we regrouped as a team. Milton asked what we all thought of the meeting. I was the first to speak, "We all better update our resumes. If Wal-Mart determines that they can make the same product, with the same piece goods at the same or similar plant, why do they need us? The Reed name is okay, but we have nowhere near the presence yet of brands such as Hanes, Dickies, or Wrangler."

Milton was always the positive person in the room, but unfortunately, we all knew that I was right. We had to become more competitive in the new world of retailers doing it independently, especially in the discount store industry. If we could not, we were in big trouble.

This is another example of how you must keep your eyes and ears open to the realities around you. Do the best you can to not be surprised when something happens in your company or industry. **You cannot put your head in the sand and hope things will just get better. Read the signs and be proactive to adapt to keep your company competitive. Otherwise, you will join the companies in the cemetery that could not adjust to the changing environment.**

———— • ● • ————

TREE HUGGER

The retail business was evolving rapidly, and as I was contemplating what I was going to do, the Reed division was invited to the Haggar Brand National Sales meeting. It was great to see all my Haggar friends. Joe Haggar III was one of the first speakers on the opening night, and his speech helped me make my decision.

Joe talked about how everybody has a comfort zone, and most people never want to leave that zone. It is like a security blanket they can't or won't let go of no matter what is happening around them. He said, "I call those people 'Tree Huggers.' When change is all around you, that's when you need to let go and accept change. You have to let go of the current tree and find a new comfort zone with another."

I never asked him why he gave this speech, but I believe he was telling the entire company the world was changing. Technology was becoming a major factor for every company. EDI and quick response were taking away 50% of what a salesman did. Why pay a person all that money for doing half the job? Also, retail consolidation, which happened to me in Arizona, was picking up steam, and buying offices were closing all over the country. Finally, there was the Wal-Mart ripple effect, and you had to find ways to become as efficient as you could and lower your costs of doing business.

I don't remember much of what he said after that because my mind started to wonder about my situation. He was right. So many people are afraid to let go of their tree. They make so many excuses about why they can't change. Change is hard. Finding a new job is hard. Moving to a new city is hard. Leaving your friends and family behind is hard. Some people are not willing to take the risk because it is the fear of the unknown. They are also afraid they might fail. Then what?

I am not one of those people. I am not afraid to fail. I am not afraid to take risks. I had taken big risks in the past, and I knew I could do it again. Every job I had done to date was dramatically different than the previous one, and I was successful at each and every one—including winning the award for the best salesperson.

I determined that night that Haggar had taken me as far toward my ultimate goals as they could. I got everything I could out of that company, and they got everything of out me. I had tried for almost a year to find something else, but I had the label of a "rag" salesman, and people would not give me credit for any of my other abilities. I was stuck.

I needed to shake that label, but how? I loved everything I knew about consulting, but even those companies did not give me a callback. I had been thinking about some new ideas I saw in marketing areas that I thought were interesting. Then it hit me. *What if I tried to do something on my own? What if I would try and hang my own shingle and help companies improve with my help?*

That is what I did. After a couple of months of putting some plans together, I resigned from Haggar. Everybody was shocked—especially because I was going to try it on my own. I was 32 and had a lot of money in the bank for just this scenario, and I had loads of confidence to succeed at whatever I tried. **Don't be a Tree Hugger! Be willing to take a chance. Get out of your comfort zone. You might fail, but you just might succeed.** Remember my favorite saying? "Success and failure are judged only by those willing to try." TRY!

DO ALL THE RICH PEOPLE ON YOUR BLOCK WORK FOR HAGGAR?

My resignation in 1993 did not go over very well with the management of Haggar, Reed, or the Private Label Division. Just like when I resigned at Gimbels, it was a compliment that people tried to talk me out of making this move. I had a heck of a run at Haggar, and people could not understand why I would want to leave, especially to go out on my own. A quote from one executive was, "Why would you throw it all away?"

I had a meeting with all the major players in the company, but I continued to tell them that I just believed that I had run out of room to grow and needed to find a different path to meet my goals. I knew people that were getting promoted to management positions in their early to mid-thirties, and I would not have that opportunity for many years if I stayed with Haggar. All the executives were in their late forties or early fifties. Also, with all the consolidation and change happening in the retail industry, I told them that they might not need all the executives they already had. They were all listening to me, but they were not *hearing* me.

The last person I talked with about my resignation was Mr. Ed Haggar. He was now the Chairman Emeritus of the Board. He had been in my corner my entire career. When I went into his office, I knew this was going to be a difficult conversation. Haggar Company and the Haggar family had been so good to me I wanted Mr. Ed to know that and know for me it was time to move on.

When I walked into his office, he looked up at me and said, "Jefferson, what the heck are you doing?" He always had called me Jefferson. He continued, "Haggar has taken care of its employees for years, and you have a home here. I *know* you will have a successful career here for the next 25 years."

When he was done, I took a breath and made my case. "This company, the Haggar family, and you specifically are the reason I am making this move. I have learned more in the past eight years than I ever could possibly have imagined. You all trained me so well; I just believe there is something bigger and better I need to chase now. The world of apparel and retail is not the same as they were 20 years ago when a person at Haggar was almost guaranteed a 35 to 40-year career." I let out a sigh and said, "In my opinion, those days are gone. The retail consolidation of department stores is only going to continue to accelerate. Wal-Mart and Target are going to continue to steal market share and push many retailers to close. Retailers will dramatically increase their capabilities to source their own products, and all of this will put pressure on the company."

Everything I told him did, in fact, happen. The Reed division was closed about a year or so after I quit. The salesforce continued to shrink, and many department stores and discount chains closed or were merged into bigger chains.

Mr. Haggar said something to the effect, "After eight years doing this job; you might not be able to find something better." This is not an exact quote, but it echoed what the CEO of Gimbels had said to me when I resigned there. I did not take offense to his comment. I knew he thought highly of me and was pulling every trick in the book to get me to stay.

I leaned forward in my chair and asked Mr. Ed, "Do all the rich people who live on your block work for Haggar?"

He said, "Of course not."

"So ... there are *other* ways to become wealthy and successful?"

"Of course ... " then he realized what had just happened. "Jefferson, you got me!" He stood up, shook my hand, and said, "I wish you luck, and if you ever need anything, let me know."

My time at Haggar had come to an end. I was about to go on a new journey with my faith, skills, and drive to find that one *something* that would propel me to a leadership role at a company or lead a company. The road would not be easy, but I did the right thing. I hope you are blessed one day to work for a company and family as incredible as the Haggar company. If you are fortunate to work for a great organization with outstanding leadership, cherish every moment—even if you decide to leave it one day, the memories, friendships, and lessons learned will last a lifetime.

IF YOU ARE FORTUNATE ENOUGH TO WORK FOR A GREAT ORGANIZATION WITH OUTSTANDING LEADERSHIP LIKE HAGGAR, CHERISH EVERY MOMENT—EVEN IF YOU DECIDE TO LEAVE IT ONE DAY, THE MEMORIES, FRIENDSHIPS, AND LESSONS LEARNED WILL LAST A LIFETIME.

TRYING IT ON MY OWN

Could I reach my career goals by staying with my current company? That is the question I kept asking myself the last couple of years I was with Haggar. The answer was no. So, the next question was what should I do about it?

After months of thought and prayer, my choice was not to try and get there by taking another corporate job and hoping it would lead me in the right direction. I decided to venture out on my own.

These stories talk about this brief test of my entrepreneurial skills. They show how even in failure, you can find a path to succeed. Even at my lowest moment ever, my faith led me to the real dream of my life and a new path to my career goals.

10,000 WAYS THAT WON'T WORK

For the first time in almost eleven years of working, I was on my own. Before I left Haggar, I tried for about a year to find a traditional job. I found many companies or positions I liked and sent my resume to all of them. I did not want another job selling apparel. I wanted to find a position that would get me closer to my goal of running a company or being a senior leader of a company.

My major issue was everybody I interviewed with did not give credit for all the things I had done in my career. All they saw was a "rag" salesman. I needed to change that perspective of myself, so I decided to do that by being an entrepreneur. Below is a sampling of what I tried to do after I left Haggar.

- **Consultant**—My initial focus was trying to transition into a role as a consultant. I targeted two areas:

  - First, I wanted to help other vendors understand and learn how to handle big accounts like Wal-Mart and Target. They had so many requirements besides just buying product. After spending three years dealing with all these requirements, I thought other suppliers could use my assistance.

  - Second, I tried to sell the use of database marketing (DM) to retailers in the Dallas/Texas area. During my time with Reed St. James, I learned about DM, and I was fascinated about how you could use statistics and analytics to better help a retailer understand customer behavior.

- **Cord Minder**—The Cord Minder was a retractable telephone cord. Back in the 1990s, the landline phone was still the prominent way to make a phone call. A couple of friends and I were trying to get the commitment from the inventor to be able to sell the product in a few southwestern states.

- **Jeff's Mobile Catalog (JMC)**—A friend put together a plan to purchase buses and drive to office complexes around the country to sell men's clothing. The idea was to have swatches and samples that men could try on at lunch breaks, and then we would custom make the clothing and mail them to the customer.

- **Electromagnetic Waves**—I worked with a company that was researching to see if electromagnetic waves could cause health issues for people and how to reduce them in everyday consumer products. For example, a microwave oven uses a form of electromagnetic radiation.

- **Copper Health**—This same company was also researching whether copper could provide health benefits for pain, arthritis, etc. It is like what is being sold by Copper Fit today.

Thomas Edison was asked how many times he failed at producing a light bulb. His reply, "I have not failed 10,000 times; I've successfully found 10,000 ways that will not work." After a little over a year, my friends and family were telling me I was failing. I told them, "I'm not failing; I have just found about six different ways how not to move my career forward."

Even though I struggled mightily during this time, I never gave up. After being so successful for the last nine years or so, I could not recapture that same magic formula no matter what I tried. I did, however, learn a lot about myself, and I was proud of myself for trying. I realized that I was blessed with many skills but being an entrepreneur was not one of them (yet). It is harder than you think. To this day, I am so impressed with people who can grow something out of nothing.

The time on my own also helped me settle on wanting to be a consultant. I knew I could not do this independently, so I began reaching out to consulting companies. About six months later, I started working for EDS Management Consulting Services (MCS) in Plano, Texas. This move would propel me to reaching my career goals five short years later. Sometimes the path to your greatest achievements is not a straight line up. There are many dips and valleys, some of which can cause you to have doubts. Keep the faith that God has a plan, and do not quit on yourself.

SOMETIMES THE PATH TO YOUR GREATEST ACHIEVEMENTS IS NOT A STRAIGHT LINE UP. THERE ARE MANY DIPS AND VALLEYS. KEEP THE FAITH THAT GOD HAS A PLAN, AND DO NOT QUIT ON YOURSELF.

I KEPT MY ROUTINE

After it became apparent that my entrepreneurial skills were not ready for prime time, I turned my attention back to looking for a job in the corporate world. It was back to researching companies, looking at the job postings in the newspaper (there was no Indeed or LinkedIn available in 1994), sending out resumes, and networking. It was my job now to find a job.

When you are out of a job, the easiest thing to do is get out of your routine. It is so easy to think this is a vacation or just some time off. That is the furthest thing from the truth. It is a full-time job to find a job, and you have to build a daily routine so you never lose that focus, no matter how frustrating this process can be.

Every day when I was looking for a job, I treated it like I was going to an office. I would be at my home office working by 8:00 am. I would complete any open issues from the previous day, do any networking or make any follow-up calls that I needed to complete, finish any paperwork/resumes and cover letters from the previous day and get those letters ready to take to the post office.

That would take me on most days to about 11:00 am. That was the perfect time to go to the library. There was no Internet to do job searches on, so I went to the library to get the local newspapers from around the US. I would first check the job advertisements to see if there was anything new. Then I would read the front page and business sections. Besides *The Dallas Morning News*, I read the Wall Street Journal, New York Times, Washington Post, Houston Chronicle, etc.

I would also read the latest edition of any local or national business-related weekly or monthly publication. I wanted to stay as informed as I could about what was happening in the business world. If there was anything of interest, whether that be a job posting or an article, I would pay $.03 a copy to take it home with me. This would usually take me a couple of hours, and then I would head home for lunch.

If there were any new opportunities, I would begin a process to determine if I needed more information that I could research the next day at the library or if I could just begin typing a new cover letter and resume to send out the next day. This would take me until about 4:00 pm. Almost a full day.

Half of my days were like this, but the other half, I was done with the entire process by lunchtime. Then my other routine kicked in. I wanted to continue to stay busy, so I began to ride a bike or play basketball at the church across the street for an hour or more a day. I would go to the movies or find a mall (especially during the winter months) to walk around. I would play golf or meet a friend for lunch.

One of the other tricks I played during the slow times was always looking forward to something. Maybe it was a Packers' football game, a movie release, a birthday, or a holiday. It gave me something to look forward to, like a to-do list I would always have when I was working.

Even though there were some extremely low days, I did not want depression or doubt to take over my life. I did not want to sleep my way through this challenging time. I wanted to keep my mind and body sharp and focused on the task at hand and not lose sight of the goal of getting back in the game.

Throughout my life, I have heard so many horror stories of individuals who did not have a focused and positive routine when they were out of work and looking for a new job. They got caught in a terrible downward spiral because they let their mind and body atrophy. **If you are ever in a situation where you are out of work, don't lose the mind and muscle memory of working. This is not a time for a vacation. Keep busy, keep moving forward, keep believing, and keep the faith!**

LIFE WILL BEAT YOU TO YOUR KNEES

I was in Denver, Colorado staying with a friend, Larry Tolini. Larry, Tim Lyons (another friend), and I were working on a proposal to present to the company that owned the rights to sell a product called the Cord Minder. It was a retractable phone cord, and we were trying to solidify a territory in the Southwest where we would be the sole company licensed to sell their product.

It was late at night, and I was downstairs watching TV by myself when the phone rang. Even though I had given Larry's number to my girlfriend in Dallas and my family back in Milwaukee, I never thought anyone would need to call me there, but Larry called out that the phone call was for me. The look in his eyes told me something was seriously wrong.

It was my sister Diane, and she was crying. My adrenalin pumped as I asked, "What's wrong?"

She said, "Dad just died of a heart attack," and my heart sank as she told me how it happened. I asked about mom, but I knew she was devasted. I don't remember much else about the call other than telling Diane I would make reservations to get back to Milwaukee as fast as I could. "I love you. Tell mom I love her so much," and I hung up, numb.

After I hung up, Larry asked me if I was okay. "I just lost my hero, and mom just lost the love of her life," I said, and then I started crying. Uncontrollably crying. I could not believe it. Even though my dad had suffered a heart attack ten years earlier, he had been given a clean bill of health ever since. He had just retired three months earlier—busted his butt for 40 years to take care of mom, Diane, and me—and now he would not have a chance to enjoy his golden years. It was just not fair.

After I stopped crying, Larry helped me make reservations to leave the next morning. I stayed up most of the night talking to God. I was really struggling with my career since I left Haggar. Strikeout after strikeout with everything I was trying and now this. Talk about a valley. This was about as low as you could go.

In 2006, Rocky VI came out. There is a scene where an older Rocky is talking to his son about some of his challenges. Rocky said, "The world ain't all sunshine and rainbows. It is a very mean and nasty place, and I don't care how tough you are; it will beat you to your knees and keep you there permanently if you let it. You, me, or nobody is gonna hit as hard as life. But it ain't how hard you hit; it's about how hard you can get hit and keep moving forward. How much you can take and keep moving forward. That's how winning is done. Now, if you know what you're worth, then go out and get what you're worth. But you gotta be willing to take the hit, and not pointing fingers saying you ain't where you are because of him, or her, or anybody."

This movie came out 12 years after my dad died, but it was a powerful reminder of what I was going through at the time. Life was hitting me pretty damn hard. Even when the lows were really low, I knew that with my talent and confidence and with God's will, I could get out of this situation. It was not easy then, and it is not easy to this day. This is the hardest story to write thus far, and I find myself crying as I write it.

It is a reminder of how blessed I was to have two wonderful parents and how much I miss my dad.

I could not let life keep me down. Even at the low point of my young life, I knew I had to get back up and keep fighting. I clung tightly to God and those who loved me, and I never quit. **Life will beat you to your knees if you let it. Don't let it!**

———— • • ————

SHE STILL MARRIED ME

The year 1993 started out as an awfully bad year for me. My career was in a self-imposed nosedive, and my dad had just died. I spent about a month with my mom and family getting things in order after his death. My mom was doing okay, but you knew she was in a tremendous amount of pain. Our extended family and friends were such an incredible support network for my mom. Three simple words got us through this horrible time. Faith, family, and friends.

My rock was my girlfriend, Lisa. We had met on a blind date three years earlier, and we each had a streak of independence that was getting in the way of making the ultimate commitment to each other. If I had any doubts remaining that she was the right person for me, they all disappeared during this challenging time. When I left my job without a job, she could have said, "See you later," but she did not. She knew that I would find that path I was searching for, and she never doubted my abilities and potential.

When dad died, she was there by my side. She flew up to Milwaukee to spend time with mom and me before the funeral. She helped us with getting things coordinated and stood right by my side at the wake. Every time she saw me struggling, she would squeeze my hand to give me that little burst of energy to continue to talk with those in attendance. She did the same the next day at the funeral.

After I completed helping my sister and mom get everything in the best order we could, I flew back to Denver because my car was still at my friend's house where I was staying when I received the call about dad's death. The business deal I had been working on with them fell through while I was in Milwaukee. My life was a mess, and Lisa was that one shining light.

When I got back to Dallas, I decided to ask Lisa to marry me. I was jobless, struggling, and my heart was ripped apart by grief. I knew I needed her more than ever, and I took the risk to see if she would marry me. I bought a ring, and on what was going to be a casual night out, I asked her to marry me. She said yes.

Six months later, in front of family and friends and her dad and my dad watching from heaven, we exchanged vows. We spoke the traditional lines, "To have and to hold, from this day forward, for better, for worse, for richer, for poorer, in sickness and in health, until death do us part." Just think about it. How many people start their marriage off with one unemployed, no real prospects in the pipeline, and grappling with loss?

We did. Sometimes those vows are challenged, and when times get tough, people leave each other. Not in my case. Times were tough when we started, but she still married me. As I write this, we are fast approaching our twenty-eighth wedding anniversary. Lisa is still the fiercely independent, strong-willed Irish-Italian woman I first met, and I still have my own streak of independence as well.

Those characteristics have helped us deal with all that life has thrown at us over the years—the good, the bad, and the ugly. I know it can be a struggle to find that one person to spend the rest of your life with, especially in the crazy world we live in today. **When you do find that special someone to love and who will support you truly for better or worse, marry them.**

FROM RAG SALESMEN TO INDUSTRY EXPERT

After about a year or so of trying to make it on my own, I realized that things were just not going to work out. I decided that the way I could get back on track was to pick a lane and find a company to join. I picked consulting. I still loved what I saw consultants do at both Gimbels and Haggar, and I wanted to be a part of it. I had read so many stories of consultants getting hired into senior management positions that I thought this could be my ticket to a leadership role or maybe even the top job.

I needed to find a consulting company that thought I could be a part of their team. The consulting industry in the mid-90s was getting some pushback from clients. Most firms were hiring extremely smart and talented young adults from the best MBA programs in America. Harvard, Wharton, Kellogg, Stanford, and MIT, to name a few. The problem was that many of the new consultants did not have experience in the specific industry. The clients did not like to pay the exorbitant hourly fees to teach these people their business. They wanted a blend of MBAs and industry experts.

Consulting firms began to add SMEs or Subject Matter Experts to work on projects. These SMEs had experience in a specific discipline (ex. Supply Chain) or a specific industry (Pharmaceuticals). That seemed to work for a while, but then companies started asking for a blend of the two. The SME many times did not do that actual project work. They were there to show the client that the consulting firm had expertise, but the MBAs still did most of the project work.

Clients wanted hands-on consultants that had this expertise. This desire was timed perfectly for my decision to start sending resumes to the top consulting companies. Even though I did not have an MBA, I had a wealth of industry knowledge in retail and wholesale. I started to get a few calls, but nothing ever materialized. Then I got a call from Electronic Data Systems (EDS).

EDS was one of the largest information technology companies in the world at the time. They had close to $10 billion in sales, 1000s of clients, and over 100,000 employees. Lisa, my soon-to-be wife, had worked for EDS for about ten years and told me that the company was starting a new consulting practice. She sent my resume to a couple of different areas of this new division. Their vision was to blend the current consulting teams within EDS with partner-level talent from other major firms, MBAs from the top schools, and hands-on industry experts to form an unbeatable team.

You then add their technology engine, and it seemed like a winning combination. I had seen the growing impact of technology during my time at Haggar and dealing with companies like Wal-Mart and Target. Companies were going to have to catch the wave or get run over by it. I wanted to be part of that wave in helping companies implement strategies, processes, and technologies to improve their business.

In mid-1994, EDS offered me a job as a management consultant. I struggled for almost a year and a half trying to do something on my own, but I just could not make it work. Now I was back on my feet, working in a new division of a $10 billion company. There was one very ironic thing about this new position. During the last year at Haggar and on many occasions during my attempt at being a solo entrepreneur, I would hear the comment, "You are just a rag salesman." They never wanted to look at or listen to all the experiences I had besides selling apparel.

OPPORTUNITIES COME WHEN YOU HAVE PREPARED YOURSELF TO MEET THEM. THEY WON'T JUST MAGICALLY SHOW UP IF YOU ARE SITTING ON YOUR SOFA WATCHING NETFLIX. YOU HAVE TO BE WILLING TO PUT YOURSELF IN THE ARENA AND TAKE A RISK.

On my first consulting engagement with EDS two months after joining the company, I was the industry expert on the project, and I was being billed out at about $200 per hour. From rag salesman to an industry expert in a snap of your fingers. No matter how many doors were slammed in my face, I kept on going. Even in my struggles, I learned a great deal about myself, and as Rocky said, "The world ain't all sunshine and rainbows." I persevered, and so can you. Opportunities come when you have prepared yourself to meet them. They won't just magically show up if you are sitting on your sofa watching Netflix. You have to be willing to put yourself in the arena and take a risk. Have faith in God and faith in yourself, and never quit. Grey skies will clear up.

CHAPTER 5

MAKING A DRAMATIC CAREER CHANGE IN MID-STREAM

Even after failing at every attempt to be a successful entrepreneur, I never lost focus on my career goals. I realized if I wanted to reach those goals, I had to swallow my pride and return to knocking on doors from the corporate world I left a year and a half earlier.

One of those doors opened for me in 1994. At 33, I joined the world of consulting, a 180° turn from anything I had ever done before, and a move many friends and colleagues told me was a terrible decision.

These stories discuss my fear of wondering if I belonged in this new consulting world, the challenges of joining yet another new company, the struggles to understand how to sell ideas instead of products, and how I dramatically expanded my knowledge of how an entire company operates. Ten years into my career, I realized I could make a successful mid-stream change.

AN ENTIRELY DIFFERENT WORLD

After about a year and a half of struggling to find a position that could advance my career goals after leaving Haggar, I finally found a great new role. I was a management consultant for the Consumer Products and Retail Practice for Electronic Data Systems (EDS) Management Consulting Services (MSC). That is a mouthful!

The company was trying to walk a tight rope with keeping "EDS" in the name of the new division. EDS management wanted to continue selling consulting services to the thousands of technology customers they had as well as open up new companies in new industries. They wanted to be able to compete with the big consulting firms of the day, even if it meant that no technology solution was part of the project. It was a very delicate balancing act of internal politics that had to be overcome every day for every client.

At the time I joined the company, I did not care. It was a new beginning for me, and I was going to work as hard as I could to become the best consultant and, in so doing, learn more about how to be a leader of an organization. Even with my struggles being an entrepreneur, I had not forgotten that I needed to control my career as much as possible. Consulting was an entirely different world that I had just joined compared to my industry positions at Gimbels and Haggar. My focus was to listen, ask questions, learn, and repeat.

The Partner in charge of the Consumer Products and Retail practice was named Charles Jones. As with most of the partners in the new MCS division, he had been hired from one of the big consulting firms. When I interviewed with him, he assured me that a successful career in consulting could definitely be a precursor to a senior role with a company.

"Many of my friends have done just that," he said. "The consulting business is vastly different from holding an industry position. We are brought in as outsiders so we can weed through all the office politics, data, and internal challenges to recommend solutions for companies. We are not selling products like a pair of pants, but an idea backed up with facts on how they can improve their business."

Selling ideas was new. I needed to totally retrain my mind to be successful in this new world. My knowledge of the retail and wholesale industry would only get me so far. Experts were a dime of dozen. I needed to put the same energy and drive into learning every angle of this new profession as I did when I was a newbie at Gimbels and Haggar. My track record of success in those positions gave me the confidence I could do it here as well.

Many people told me this was a mistake. They said things like, "You cannot become a consultant at your age. You needed to get your MBA and start as a junior consultant in your mid to late twenties to do this. This mid-career change will destroy your dream of being a CEO or a leader of a company." One said, "Jeff, you are throwing the first ten years of your career down the toilet!" Not exactly motivational.

It is amazing how many people can only see the reasons why you *can't* do something and not the reasons why you can. As before, I used their negative energy to fuel my drive to excel at another position, even though it was a completely different role for me. I knew this new journey would help me attain my career goals, and I would not be denied—especially by naysayers!

It doesn't matter your age; you can make a career change if you are willing to take the risk, expend the necessary energy to become successful, and not listen to all the negative comments. I found over the years that many pessimists would love to take the chance of doing something different; they just don't have the courage at that moment to try. **Have that courage and make that change, no matter what age you are.**

———•●•———

BEAUTIFUL ANALYSIS, BUT CAN YOU IMPLEMENT?

Just like I did at both Gimbels and Haggar, I took part in a training program at EDS/MCS. I was put in the group of brand-new consultants. This group consisted of newly graduated MBAs and a couple of industry experts like me. When I read the biographies of the individuals in my group, for the first time in my career, I began to wonder if I belonged here.

I was especially focused on the group that had MBAs. They graduated from the best schools—Harvard, Wharton, Stanford, Kellogg, etc. They also had been to some of the best schools for their undergrad education—Princeton, Brown, Northwestern, and Georgetown. Many had interned on Wall Street or for some of the best consumer products companies in the country.

Here I was with my marketing degree from the University of Milwaukee-Wisconsin along with my work at a retailer and an apparel company. A little demon was on my right shoulder, whispering in my ear, "You are just a rag salesman; you don't belong here." Luckily, there was a little angel on the other shoulder telling the demon to mind his own business! It was, however, a tug of war going on in my mind. That war ended about four weeks later.

The last part of the training class was a hands-on case study. We were broken up into groups of five consultants and a four-week assessment with a fictional company. We were to conduct interviews, analyze the company financials and other metrics, and then recommend additional project work with the company. They tried to get it as close to a real simulation of a consulting engagement as they possibly could.

If I remember correctly, the company was in the beer distribution business, and we were assessing their logistic numbers compared to best practices from their industry. We separated the duties. I was asked to be the project lead because of my experience working with CEOs and senior management. Three people were to run the numbers, and the final person was to coordinate all the interview questions and notes.

We were doing a particularly good job for the first three weeks. The training staff gave us high marks on how we conducted the interviews, the relationship we were building with the senior leadership, and the numbers we were producing showed some real opportunity for savings. Then the final crunch week came. We had to make our final recommendations supported by the data. We hit the proverbial wall.

All the cooperation and partnership of the team was being put to the test. The numbers just did not add up. On paper, everything looked fabulous. My concern was that no one could ever implement what the numbers were recommending. After struggling for a couple of days, we asked our project partner for assistance. After listening to both sides, he agreed with my position. He said, "Clients don't want an MBA analysis; they want something that is possible to implement; otherwise, the project is a waste."

The angel and demon war was over. I belonged. I could not then or can not to this day run analysis like those incredibly talented teammates. But they did not yet have my experience in the real world. It was a beautiful match of skills. We tweaked our numbers, gave our final presentation as a team, and ended up winning the add-on business from the fictional client. The reason: our recommendations could be implemented.

It was a tremendous feeling knowing I belonged. I knew that I could learn from all the talented people at EDS/MCS, but I had something to offer them as well. **It sucks when you don't think you belong. It can put doubts in your mind. Be confident that you can bring something positive to the table. If you still have a demon on your shoulder feeding your doubt, sharpen a particular skill that the team might be lacking, or make sure people know a special skill you have. Don't stop until the angel on your shoulder wins.**

UP OR OUT

It was going to be another all-nighter, so we ordered pizza. During our short dinner break, we began discussing why we wanted to be consultants. A couple of people mentioned the money and the ability to travel on the client's dime. A few others talked about being exposed to a variety of areas in a company and different industries. They did not want to be stuck in a position they hated until they figured out what they really wanted to do.

We all talked about wanting to help a company solve its problems. Some, like me, were looking for a faster route to a leadership position either in consulting or back in an industry position. All of these were good reasons to choose consulting. Then someone said, "These are all wonderful reasons—*if* you can survive."

"What are you talking about?" I asked.

He answered me with three simple words, "Up or out." I had never heard those words used like that before, so I pressed him about what he meant. He said, "The consulting firm will watch your performance like a hawk. Perform exceptionally well, and you will continue to move up the corporate ladder. If they get a brief sniff that you cannot continue to progress, you are out."

Well, that was a cold splash of water in the face. In my other companies, there was always pressure to continue to perform well. Sometimes that meant you could earn a promotion. If you did not get promoted, it did not mean you would lose your job if you were still performing well. For example, in retail, you could have a great career as a buyer even if you never had any aspirations of getting promoted to divisional merchandising manager. If you hit your numbers, you did not have to worry about getting shown the door just because you did not move up the corporate ladder.

Consulting was different. Many consulting firms managed their teams under the policy that you are expected to progress through the different layers to reach the partnership level. There was a predetermined pace over a certain number of years that you were expected to hit each level. If you hit all the metrics, goals, and timelines, you would continue to rise.

Typical consulting firms had about five levels: Consultant, Senior Consultant, Manager or Principle, and then Partner. The rationale was you were keeping only the best of the best, making your team stronger from top to bottom. The pressure to advance was enormous. Long hours, crazy travel schedules, all-nighters, and building relationships with the people who made the decisions about who was up and who was out were all part of this new role.

I loved it, and I also liked the pressure. What a great challenge. I am a *tad* bit competitive. I love to win. After this conversation, I went to work, understanding what it took to advance. I wanted to know what made a successful consultant and the factors that could cause you to be asked to leave.

The world is a competitive place. Even the best companies to work for have some type of employee turnover parameters. It might not be as challenging as consulting, but they are there. Don't be naïve to think Human Resources and management are not taking notes on what you are doing. They are always watching. **Before you take a position, get an understanding of what drives employee turnover.** Don't be surprised like I was about the "up and out" policy. **It could be the difference between joining the company or not.**

THE ANSWER IS IN A MANILLA FOLDER

After my training period was over, I was assigned for my first official consulting project. I was ecstatic, to say the least. Ten years after my first encounter with consultants as a young assistant buyer at Gimbels, I was now joining the ranks of management consulting. I remember how I felt when they handed me my business cards, and I opened them and saw the words, Jeffrey L. Wellen – Management Consultant. It was a great day.

My first assignment was with a client based in New York City (I will call the company Acme). It was a women's consumer products company that was moving into a different line of business (apparel), and they needed help integrating these new products into the company. The scope of the project was supply chain, distribution, and forecasting. We had experts that would focus on supply chain and distribution, while my focus would be on forecasting. I was also the SME (Subject Matter Expert) on the project because of my background in the apparel industry. This project was scheduled to last about six months.

After the project kickoff meetings, we began the assessment phase, where we conducted interviews with the appropriate person to get as much information as fast as we could about the current situation. We began to accumulate any reports or raw data we could use to help solve their issues. I had scheduled about 15 interviews over two weeks based on the recommendations by the Acme project team.

After my first four or five interviews, each person mentioned a person's name, not on my list of people to interview. I asked my project manager about this situation, and I received his blessing to schedule an appointment.

The person had a Ph.D. in mathematics. He was brilliant. I told him, "Everybody I talked to told me I needed to talk with you about the forecasting challenge." Without hesitation, he went into a drawer in his desk and pulled out a manilla folder. It was about a quarter-inch thick and was filled with letters.

He opened the folder and handed me a letter addressed to one of our Acme project sponsors. As I read it, I could not believe it. This was the answer to the forecasting problem. Before I responded to him about the letter, I asked him about the other letters in the folder. He told me they were similar but written to different people. "Why didn't they listen?" I asked.

"In my experience, companies would rather pay a consulting firm hundreds of thousands of dollars to get an answer rather than listen to someone in their company," he shrugged.

I shook my head, puzzled, "Why? That doesn't make any sense!"

"Well," he responded, "then if it doesn't work, you can always blame the consultant. You guys are the third consulting firm to be asked to look at this issue, and each has a different Acme sponsor. It was like a revolving door and a large amount of consulting dollars for each firm. A huge wave of reality was hitting me. I was receiving my first lesson in consulting. I have always been enamored with consultants, so I did not take the time to understand what people within the company thought about our work. In many cases, we were not considered the knight in shining armor like I thought.

After the meeting, I talked with the project manager and our analytics team, and they agreed that what we found in the letter was, in fact, the answer. In the assessment presentation we made a couple of weeks later, we were not only able to update the Acme project team on our initial thoughts, but we also presented them with a solution. It earned us high praise to have a solution so early in the project. We gave all the credit to my new Ph.D. friend.

This situation reminded me of what Mr. J.M. Haggar told me—**Find the answer by talking with the people who do the hands-on work. They will not B.S. you; they just want the problem fixed. You just have to be open to listening.** An outside perspective can help resolve a problem within a company. However, sometimes the answer is sitting in a manilla folder in one of your co-worker's desks.

NEW YORK STATE OF MIND

If you are a consultant, get used to traveling. I mean a *lot* of traveling. You can often continue to live in your home city and just travel each week to the client site, but in my experience, it is very unusual to get a hometown client. My consulting days were pre-Zoom, so I was a road warrior. Mondays through Fridays (sometimes Sundays through Fridays I was at the client site.

Though I had traveled extensively in my last three years working for the Reed St. James division at Haggar, consulting was different. At Haggar, I was in a different city almost every day. In consulting, I basically lived in the city with my client for the length of the project. It was a shift I was going to have to get used to.

My first client was based in Manhattan, just a couple of blocks south of Central Park. One of the project sponsors had been a former consultant and knew the rigors of the job. He wanted to make sure we were comfortable during our time in New York so we could be more focused on giving Acme a great deliverable.

His assistant worked out a deal at The Dorsett Hotel, giving us a dedicated room for the entire project. This meant we could leave some things behind and travel with little luggage. Most of the project team declined the offer because they wanted to get their hotel points, but another team member and I wanted the added convenience more than the points. We were booked in a two-bedroom flat on one of the top floors of the hotel.

The Dorsett Hotel was located about three blocks from the client's office. It was not the most beautiful hotel, but it was in a great location. The suite had a small kitchen and two bedrooms with a huge living area that separated the rooms and a stairway with a door that led to the roof. It was like I had just moved to New York and had my own place! The building had about ten floors, so we were a couple hundred feet above the ground. It was like a scene out of a TV show or movie.

This was not my first time in New York, but this would be the longest stay I ever had living in the city. For the next six months, I spent 142 days out of a possible 175 in New York. I had to get to know the city. I learned the ins and outs of the subway system, could now hail a cab with the best of them, bought groceries and lugged them back to the hotel, and even learned to walk at the pace of a New Yorker.

My wife came to visit one weekend, and we had a great time seeing the sights. I came to appreciate the people who lived here 365 days a year. Billy Joel (my personal favorite) wrote a song called *New York State of Mind*. He was born in New York but left for a few years to live in Los Angeles. He moved back to New York and wrote this song about his pride in being from New York. I could see why.

I loved it and found that I could handle the rhythm of the city and I kind of liked it. I was no longer intimidated by New York. I was also no longer that naïve guy who got robbed on one of my early trips, which was another confidence boost for me. I couldn't help but hum, "If I can make it there, I'll make it anywhere," while I walked the city. I was proud to be a truck driver's kid from a town with 60,000 people now living and working in a city with 7.5 million!

After my first few trips to New York, I never thought I could actually become comfortable living in a big (really big) city. **You never know what you can do unless you try. Many people make excuses about why they can't do something. Put the excuses off to the side and take a chance. You might find you really like it.**

<hr/>

WORK WITH YOU? I'VE NEVER MET YOU

I first met my teammates on my Acme Company project in New York a few days before the project was to start. We met in Boston at one of the EDS office buildings to get a few things done before showing up at the client site. We gave a brief introduction of ourselves to the attendees. The partner who sold this project gave an overview of the scope, timeline, budget, and expected deliverables. The project manager gave the ground rules for how he was going to manage the project and gave us our assignments and duties.

As I was sitting in the room listening, I could not get my arms around the fact we were about to hit the ground running at a client site when half of us had never met each other before. How the heck was this going to work? In my jobs at Gimbels and Haggar, except for new employees, you knew almost all the top 200 people in each company. You knew their strengths and weaknesses. You even knew their families, interests, likes, and dislikes. You had months or years to get to know them.

Not in consulting. In my first four or five projects, I never worked with the same team member twice. Consultants often work on a team with people you have never met. You have to get to know these people in a matter of days and solidify a strong enough relationship to deliver the project work.

The same scenario happened with all the client personnel. Clients were paying a lot of money for these projects, and you had to make a good first impression. You also had to learn as much as you could about the lay of the land within each client as fast as possible. Who were the decision-makers? Who really had control of the project? Who could make or break your project? Who were the one or two individuals that could help sell your work inside the company?

Luckily for me, I had some experience getting to know someone new and then building a great working relationship quickly. At Haggar, I had to meet all my new accounts for the first time. I had to make a positive impression on them so they would be confident enough to buy something from me. I also would have to get to know each person (buyer, assistant buyer, Vice President, CEO, or owner) of the account I was selling. First impressions do matter. They help plant a positive relationship seed that can grow over time.

You also had to try and uncover those one or two things that each person likes and dislikes. For example, one of my first clients had about 20 pictures of family vacations in his office. I asked him about one of the pictures, and we began to compare notes on our trips. I had him. Then I found out from one of the project sponsors that he did not like slick consulting presentations. Before each update meeting, I would just give him a bullet point overview of what we were going to be discussing. Nothing slick, just the facts. He loved it. I had him again.

This may sound devious, but to do my job (whether selling clothes or selling ideas), I had to get to know what made each person tick while letting them know I was a good guy and could help them with their business. It is relationship-building 101. Getting to know who you are working with can be an art form. It is a skill I did not have when I was young, mainly because I was too naïve to understand the importance of this skill. I also believed that everybody had my best interest in mind. That changed after my first run-in with a boss at Gimbels.

Developing people skills is a must in the business world. I put it in the top two reasons that I have had a fairly successful career. I was good at it because I worked at it. I read books about it; I asked people who were great at it for tips and practiced it all the time. **I don't care whether you are a consultant, a plumber, or a doctor; you have to have people skills. Study how to get better and practice, practice, practice.**

YOU MAY BE HEARING ME, BUT ARE YOU LISTENING?

O ne of the best skills you can have as a consultant is interviewing and talking to clients. You were often only given 30 minutes to an hour to talk with some of the company's principals. You have no time to waste. You must dig as deep as you can as fast as you can to find that golden nugget or two that could make the project a success.

One of the areas stressed during our training classes was how to write an interview guide. Out of the six to eight weeks of training, we spent about 20% of the time talking about the interview process. The key was not just asking questions or pushing a preordained direction for the project but also learning how to listen. In my opinion, this was the biggest difference between my days selling pants and my new role as a consultant.

"A good salesperson takes the oxygen out of the room. A good consultant lets the client take the oxygen out of the room."

This is not a famous quote from a historical figure; it is something I said to one of my clients when he asked me what makes a good consultant. In the movie *Wolf of Wall Street*, there is a scene where Leo DiCaprio's character is selling penny stocks. In about two minutes, he makes $2,000. He never stopped talking until he got the answer he was looking for. The rest of his co-workers were amazed at what he had just done.

That is not consulting. Because you have such a short time to get to know the lay of the land, your interview questions need to allow the client to speak. You need to ask truly short probing questions and then sit back and listen and take great notes. You are not only listening for the direct answer but for something else the client might say. Your internal radar, sonar, or whatever senses you have need to be on maximum range.

The biggest mistake a consultant can make is going into an interview with the sole objective of getting all the interview questions completed. That is not the point of the interview. The objective of the interview is to gather as much information as possible to help with the ultimate deliverables. I have walked out of interviews where I was just the note taker and realized the client answered all the questions, but we learned nothing. I have also led interviews where I did not get to 25% of the questions, but I still found a golden nugget.

Listening is a skill many of us don't have. There is also a difference between listening and hearing. Humorist and cartoonist Frank Tyger once said, "Hearing is one of the body's five senses, but listening is an art." He is absolutely correct. Listening takes practice, discipline, and the ability to not reply after every opening within a conversation.

Whether you are a consultant on a project, a father talking to his son, a husband to a wife, a repairman talking to a homeowner, or the CEO of a company, you need to be able to listen. If we could all turn into better listeners and actually hear what the other person is saying, I think our workplace, home, and our world would be better.

———— • ● • ————

DID MY WORK REALLY MAKE A DIFFERENCE?

There were many differences between delivering a consulting project and delivering a product. A product you can touch, feel, and put to the test for yourself. Whether it is a pair of pants, a car, a new golf club, or a paintbrush, you can easily determine if it meets your satisfaction. If it did not meet your standards, then you could take the product back or never buy it again. The almost instant knowledge of someone liking my product gave me a level of satisfaction that I was selling and delivering something of quality and value to a customer.

Consulting is different. In consulting, I could work on a project for four to six months and deliver the infamous binder or set of binders at the end of a project. These would contain an overview of the project scope and deliverables, what we had learned on the project, and recommendations for the client to implement. Sometimes we would find a nugget or two that we could implement during the project and see the results of our work. However, in my first few projects, we were not asked to help implement our recommendations, and I always wondered if the client got their money's worth.

The client would spend all this money, time, and resources on having us come in with no commitment to implementing the project results.

You would leave without seeing the problems you identified fixed. This was my biggest challenge with my new career. Did my work make a difference?

My father raised me to be a hands-on doer. Find a project that needed doing, investigate what needed to be done and how you would do it. Buy the necessary supplies and roll up your sleeves to fix that problem. When you were done, you could look at the finished project with a sense of pride. Whether painting a room, fixing a leaky faucet, installing a new ceiling fan, or cutting the grass, I like seeing a job done to the completion.

I talked with our practice leader about this, and he told me that if I completed the work the client asks of me, I did a good job. I replied, "I have clients show me binders from other consulting firms full of recommendations they never followed. I am sure those consultants felt good about their work, but it was now collecting dust on a shelf. Am I really making a difference with my clients?"

"Your job," he stressed, "is to convince the client to not only make the recommendations but to let us implement them." I took this statement to heart.

His goal was to help the client but also to get more consulting fees out of the client. My goal was to find a client that would let my consulting team and me not only make the recommendations but also implement the necessary changes. I wanted to see the results of our work, from recommendation to implementation. I wanted to make a difference for the client, not just complete a project. Early in my career, I reduced one of my retail account's orders because I had sold her too much product. I wanted to sell with integrity.

I felt the same way about consulting. I did not want to just take my client's money; I wanted to really help them—not just give them another binder for their collection. I eventually found that client, and it turned into the most satisfying ten years of my career.

It takes two to tango. If the client (or your current company) keeps asking for ideas and never implements the recommendations, then management has a problem. **Give people the best quality work you can with the highest level of integrity possible. If you always use a filter of honesty and integrity with your work and your relationships, it will pay off in the long run. You will make a difference.**

THE PAPER IS STILL WARM

It was 10:00 pm. Our first major presentation to Acme Consumer Products company was at 8:00 am the next morning, and we were nowhere close to being finished. We had just received some final edits from one of the partners and were trying to complete a few slides with graphs and charts. We knew we were going to have to pull another all-nighter. The project team wanted to show everybody the great work we had done to date, and we would now need a few more hours to make the presentation as perfect as possible.

There was one problem. Where could we make copies of the presentation once it was complete? A teammate remembered that Kinko's had several places in the city that were open 24 hours. After a few phone calls, we hit the jackpot. There was a Kinko's a few doors down from the client's office building. The store manager said if we brought the presentation before 6:00 am, he could make copies and bind them in plenty of time before our meeting.

We finished up about 5:00 am and handed it off to the Kinko's manager by 5:15. At 7:30 am, the presentations were not done. There was a problem with the color printer, and they were still finishing our job. About 7:45, we were handed two boxes of freshly copied documents. We put them on a little two-wheeled dolly and sprinted to the meeting.

Luckily not everybody was in the room yet, so we thought we were in the clear. We were wrong. One of the project sponsors (I will call him Harry) was already sitting in the conference room. We placed the presentations in front of each chair. As I handed one to Harry, he gave me a strange look, placing the still-warm presentation next to his cheek. He looked at me and said, "All Nighter?" with this wily smile on his face.

"Unfortunately, yes," I answered, "but the results are fantastic!"

He laughed and said, "I have been there." A former McKinsey consultant, he could feel our pain.

The presentation went well, and all the client sponsors liked the direction we were going. After the meeting, I went to Harry's office and asked him if he had a moment. "Why did you mention the presentations being warm? I feel like you were sending a bigger message."

He gave me some excellent advice, "As a former consultant, I know everything you are going through. The consulting game will be challenging for you every step of the way. Other members of my team do not think the same as I do, and some of them might not have been as understanding of you walking in five minutes before the meeting. One of my biggest mistakes in my early consulting career was not learning more about the client leadership and sponsors. Do you know the backgrounds of everybody in the room? Have you researched every member of our team? Who did they work for before they came here? Have they used consultants before? Do they like consultants? What makes them tick? Most consultants look at someone's biography and think they know the person—dig deeper. Your research could be the difference between a project being successful or a failure."

> **DO YOU KNOW ENOUGH ABOUT YOUR COMPANY'S LEADERSHIP—THE CEO, THE SVP OF YOUR AREA, OR THE CURRENT MANAGER YOU ARE WORKING FOR? IF NOT, DIG DEEP. THE MORE YOU KNOW, THE BETTER.**

From that day forward, I always worked with my project and sales teams to understand the client personnel as much as I could. The lessons learned were invaluable to my success with clients. You don't have to be a consultant to research management or leadership. Do you know enough about your company's leadership—the CEO, the SVP of your area, or the current manager you are working for? If not, dig deep. The more you know, the better.

———————•●•———————

WRITING FROM THE BACK FORWARD

As a sales representative, I rarely wrote detailed presentations. The major tools in my toolbox were product samples, swatches of the different color offerings, our price list, shipping periods, marketing collateral, and financial reports discussing historical and future sales. In consulting the written word and the use of PowerPoint was king.

This consisted of written notes from interviews or meetings with clients, initial sales presentations, project work updates and finally presentations, along with any supporting data or charts. It was a new world for me. The last time I wrote this much was ten years earlier when I was in college taking exams in "blue books." I had to go to several consulting 101 writing classes to learn professional writing so I could be successful in my new role.

During one of those classes, the trainer said, "The easiest way to think about writing in consulting is from the back forward. Quite simply, you want to know that the Butler did it and spend the preceding pages proving he did." The concept was not novel to me but hearing her describe it so simply left this concept etched in stone in my brain. The concept was easy for me to understand but exceedingly difficult to execute.

I had been a salesman so long that my verbal skills way outpaced my writing skills. When I first started consulting, if someone asked me for a verbal update, I could give them the "elevator answer." Short, sweet, and to the point. My brain had a problem taking the spoken word and writing it down in clear, concise points.

Other guidelines gave me even more headaches. Examples include having only five to six bullets on a page, six words for each bullet, only a certain font size so people in the back of a presentation room could read the slide, limited animation, no more than five words in a header, and no more than two indentations on a slide.

The final challenge was that each presentation had to be timed. For example, let's say we were given sixty minutes to make a presentation. You needed to leave ten minutes for questions at the end, and there were always interruptions, so subtract another five minutes off the total time. Then you add three to five minutes for initial comments, introductions, and general small talk, and now you had only forty minutes for your presentation. The final rule was that no slide should take longer than a minute, so you have a grand total of about twenty-five slides.

Now take two months of project work and put it on twenty-five slides that will take no longer than forty minutes to present. I thought I was screwed. If you could see some of my first attempts at writing, you would laugh your you-know-what off. I was horrible, but I kept after it. I was lucky to have a couple of partners on my first few projects who were very patient with me. Fellow trainees having more formal training during their MBA days were also extremely helpful. Even to this day, my writing skills are a work in progress. However, I am light years ahead of where I was back then.

Even in today's Twitter, text, and emoji world, we still need to be able to write clearly and succinctly. Whether you are communicating via Slack, Email, Word, or PowerPoint, writing skills are still particularly important. In my son's first job, he had to create three or four PowerPoint presentations within his first couple of months. Luckily, we had emphasized writing skills at a young age. He is so much better than me and even had a paper from a college writing course published in a book about how to write—impressive!

If you don't have tremendous writing skills, learn. Take a class and practice. If you do have writing skills, keep honing them. You can always get better. Writing is still a valuable skill in today's business world, and I believe it always will be.

———•●•———

IT IS AN ITERATIVE PROCESS

We were preparing the final presentation for Acme Consumer Products company. It was the all-important final deliverable—the accumulation of six months' worth of interviews, meetings, analysis, and relationship building. The presentation had two main objectives. The first was to present the final information related to the completed project, and the second was to sell them on additional consulting work.

All the formal presentations received partner-level scrutiny, but this one was off the charts. I was right in the middle of all the changes because I had naively volunteered to be the PowerPoint expert. I thought I would get some kudos for offering my services. What a mistake! I was not good enough at PowerPoint to handle the responsibility, but once I opened my mouth, I had to become a PowerPoint guru.

My biggest challenge was how to get all the power brokers on the project to agree on each word, each sentence, and each page of the document. I grew increasingly frustrated because every time I believed we were done, another partner would want to read and edit the document again. I expressed my frustration to the project manager, and he said, "You must get used to the 'Iterative Process' of completing a presentation. Each partner wants to put his stamp of approval on the document, even if it is only a minor change."

I had never heard of the word *iterative used* before, let alone an *iterative process.* According to *Webster's Dictionary,* it means "involving repetition or utilizing the repetition of a sequence of operations or procedures." A couple of synonyms are incessant, constant, and ceaseless. All of those were accurate!

I had to get used to the fact that the only thing that stopped more changes was the actual time of the presentation. If we did not have that hard stop, we would still be tweaking the document today, and 75% of the changes were useless—they did not improve the document. However, 25% of the changes were spot on. They made the final document dramatically better.

Even though I truly despised this process, I am glad I learned how to manage it during my time at EDS. Fast forward about three years or so, and I am now working with a CEO that was the King of Edits. He loved to edit documents. I called him a wordsmithing god. He loved the English language and would change one word twenty times if he thought it made the point better.

If I had not lived through six years of partners doing the same thing, I would have never understood this CEO's passion. It is one of the many reasons he and I got along so well during his time as my client and my six years working for him when I joined the Michaels' team.

Even though my initial reaction to the phrase "iterative process" was one of disdain, it became one of the most important tools in my toolbox. After that first project, I bought myself a *Webster's Dictionary,* all 720 pages, and 170,000 words. This was before Microsoft Spellcheck, Grammarly, or Microsoft Editor.

A simple change here or a tweak there can significantly improve a point you are trying to make. Words matter. Learn how to use the written language, and don't be afraid to use the iterative process to improve whatever project you undertake.

HIRED US AND THEN FIRED MOST OF US 1 ½ YEARS LATER

I was working on a project proposal in the Plano, TX offices of EDS/MCS when the news broke—EDS had just bought AT Kearney, the global strategy consulting firm, for almost $600 million. AT Kearney was going to be merged with the Management Consulting Services (MCS) division to form one of the world's largest consulting firms at the time. It would result in a consulting firm with more than 2,300 consultants in 40 countries.

After the announcement, the EDS corporate headquarters was a buzz. They were already dealing with a massive culture clash after they formed the MCS division in 1993. Current employees were extremely upset with the salaries they were throwing at individuals who joined MCS. EDS raided competing consulting firms to get talent quickly and heavily recruited from the most prestigious business schools.

Those who had worked 25 years for the company and could not get a sniff of the salaries being handed out to the newly-formed consulting team were understandably upset. There were numerous other challenges between the traditional EDS technology team and the MCS consulting team, such as who owned the client? How did you compensate each group for client work? Who controlled the resources put on projects? Who made the final call on client proposals? I could go on.

Now EDS was bringing in over 1,000 more consultants from an established firm with a 60-year history of consulting success. As I walked around the office, it seemed no one was happy. Partners hired a little over a year before wondered if they would be leading a practice or would their Kearney counterpart be in charge. All the MBAs wondered what it meant for them because many had spurned offers from firms like Kearney to join EDS/MCS.

Then there were individuals like me—Industry experts without MBAs that EDS wanted as a core to their new consulting group. I had heard the Kearney did not have a history of hiring people who did not have an MBA. What a mess! I spent a few days talking with as many people as I could to assess the situation. It was my own little consulting project.

I recommended to myself to find myself a new home within EDS as fast as I could. AT Kearney and their partners were going to be running the show and anyone who was hired into the MCS division was at their mercy. I was not going to wait. I immediately called a couple of people I had worked with on proposals and asked if they would like a new employee. They said they needed to see how things played out, but I would be at the top of their list if they could hire me.

It took a couple of months for EDS to tell us the inevitable. AT Kearney would no longer need our services. EDS had formed a new business unit (MCS), heavily recruited close to 1,000 people, and basically said, "See you later," all within a year and a half. Great strategic planning! When the announcement was made, I called the head of the Textile and Apparel division of EDS and was offered a position to join their team. I was safe for the moment, but I began to wonder if EDS's management knew what they were doing after the moves made over the last 24 months. It was a huge disruption to the company, the culture, and the employees.

I really liked working for EDS, and I had learned a tremendous amount, but I knew I needed to keep my options open just in case another shoe dropped. Never get too comfortable in today's business world because you never know when the next headline will affect your career. **Always give 100% to your current job, but never stop looking for an escape hatch. Always try to have options available if one is needed. Keep your resume updated, and be proactive. Your future might depend on it.**

---•●•---

LEMONS INTO LEMONADE

I was sitting in my first meeting with my new team at EDS, in my new role as a consultant for the Textile and Apparel Division of the Manufacturing Strategic Business Unit (SBU). You had to hand it to EDS; they liked l-o-n-g names on their business cards. After the merger with AT Kearney Consulting, many had to look for other positions.

AT Kearney had made it be known who they wanted and who they did not want after the transaction. I was one of those who missed their cut. Luckily, the traditional EDS divisions could hire anyone from the

MCS group they wanted to add to their teams. My background in the textile and apparel industries, coupled with my time at both Gimbels and Haggar, was a nice match for both parties.

I had done some proposal work for this team, so I knew most of the players. They were based in Detroit, so if I was not on a project, then Monday through Friday, I would be in Detroit. It just added to my "Road Warrior" status.

One of the topics of discussion was the sales pipeline. Every firm had a pipeline report. There are some differences, but it is basically a hierarchy framework on the status of all current sales efforts. A typical pipeline could have categories that include prospecting, leads, qualified leads, proposals, negotiations, contracts, delivery, and payments. There was also a sales category section to fill out what we were selling or proposing to sell to a client.

As I was listening, I realized that I had not only moved to a different division of EDS, but an entirely new world. When we discussed our pipeline in the Management Consulting Division, the sales category was filled with strategic plans, business process improvement, change management, supply chain assessment, and customer analysis. About 20% of the time, there was consulting support for a systems project.

In my new division, the sales category used words like systems outsourcing, systems integration, systems development, systems maintenance, and systems implementation. I think you get my point— they made their money selling systems. Any consulting help they needed was to sell a systems solution. At this time, I was exactly where I wanted to be.

I learned a tremendous amount about management consulting from the MCS division, but I had seen what technology was doing for companies like Wal-Mart, Target, and Haggar. The problem was I was on the periphery. The technology wave was gaining steam and getting bigger by the day, and I believed to reach my goal of leading a company or being part of the leadership team, I had to learn as much as I could about the ins and outs of technology. I needed to be riding this wave, not watching from the beach. I was in the right spot to do that.

Life can be a tad bit crazy at times. Just when a situation looks bleak, a gift from God appears. Just like when I left Gimbels and ran into the National Sales Manager for Haggar on my way to do an exit interview.

Or when I lost my biggest account and then joined a division that expanded my knowledge base exponentially. Here was another example of turning a lemon into lemonade. If I had not lost my position after the AT Kearney acquisition, I most assuredly would not have been exposed to the technology wave as I was in my new division.

DON'T GIVE UP WHEN THINGS SEEM LOST. THE NEXT DOOR YOU MAY OPEN COULD BE THE CHANGE OR INSPIRATION YOU ARE LOOKING FOR. JUST KEEP KNOCKING ON DOORS.

I live in Texas, and the weatherman will say if you don't like the weather wait an hour. That is exactly like life. My situation looked horrible for about 60 days; then the seas calmed, and I was in a great new situation. Don't give up when things seem lost. The next door you may open could be the change or inspiration you are looking for. Just keep knocking on doors.

ONLY USE THE TOOL FOR WHAT IT WAS DESIGNED FOR

When I was a young boy, my dad always had me by his side when working on a project. This particular time we were in our basement, and dad was building something for my mom. He had me sit on the high metal stool so I could watch him work on his workbench. To my young eyes, he had every tool you could possibly imagine. Sometimes to keep me preoccupied, he would give me a tool to practice with.

This time he put about five small nails in a piece of scrap wood. He just got the nails started, and then he handed me a hammer to start practicing nailing them all completely into the wood. Even though the hammer was the smallest one he had, it was still a little heavy for me. I tried my hardest, but I could not finish the job. I got frustrated and put the hammer down, and grabbed a screwdriver. It was lighter, and I could grab the metal end much easier than the hammer. I got in a good three or four whacks before my dad could stop me, but the damage was done.

I had taken a couple of nice chunks out of the plastic handle on the screwdriver. I gave dad the screwdriver, and as he inspected the damage, he asked, Why did you hit the nail with a screwdriver?"

"I didn't think it made a difference what tool I used," I answered.

"Son, each tool is designed for a specific purpose. Even if you think it can be used for something else, you see the damage it can do to the tool. Only use the tool for what it was designed for. If I have a problem and do not have the correct tool, then I buy or borrow one. If you use the correct tool, the job will be done correctly."

I never forgot that lesson.

Fast forward, and I am sitting in my first meeting with my new textile and apparel team; I was getting a little concerned. Even though I loved the idea of working with a group that stressed technology's ability to help a company, I wondered if their viewpoint was too myopic. Was their answer to anything ailing a company to offer a technology solution? Did they have only one tool in their toolbox?

The analogy I make is that no matter what the client's issues were, the answer seemed to always use a hammer (technology). Leaky faucet, I got a hammer. Need a new light socket? I got another hammer for that. How about we need to cut the lawn? I have an extra special hammer for that. They had those five systems offerings (outsourcing, integration, development, maintenance, and implementation). Were they just five different hammers probing a client to eventually find a problem to solve?

What about if the client needed help with their strategic direction? What if the client needed help with reorganization? What if the client needed to determine where their new distribution centers should be located? What if they needed a technology strategy? Each one of those needed a different tool to solve.

After the meeting, I met with the division head. I thanked him again for bringing me on board. We discussed the meeting and where he wanted me to start focusing my efforts. When we finished that conversation, I expressed my concerns to him about possibly being too myopic. I mentioned my analogy. He laughed and said, "Before EDS jumped into the management consulting business, technology was all they had to sell." Even though EDS was one of the biggest Information Technology companies globally, they needed more tools in their toolbox.

Just as in business, you need more than just one tool to get through life. **When I was 22, I had about two tools at my disposal, now that I am just a little bit older, my toolbox is full, but I am always looking for another if the situation arises. Expand your toolbox of knowledge throughout your life so you can meet challenges armed with the right devices to solve each situation. Life will be a whole lot easier.**

———— • ● • ————

PEOPLE, PROCESS, AND TECHNOLOGY

During my first week on the job with my new division, they gave me binders full of documentation to read through. It included old presentations, project proposals, project deliverables, client lists, examples of each systems solution, technology sales training, and finally, white papers on how to successfully implement technology solutions.

All the material was a little bit of a fire hose in the mouth, but it provided a great foundation. The white papers really piqued my interest, and after reading all the materials, I asked one of my new teammates (I will call him Rick) if I could ask him some questions. He went into a conference room, and I started asking him questions in a rapid-fire manner. It was great. He answered every single one.

Then I asked Rick, "What makes a successful technology implementation?"

He replied, "First, organizations need to realize technology is an enabler and not the answer by itself. The use of technology is accelerating exponentially, but to make any technology solution operate effectively, you need three things working together. People, Process, and Technology."

He was right then, and he is still right now. Here's why:

- **People** – Includes executive buy-in and sponsorship, organization changes, clearly defined roles and responsibilities, goals, objectives, change management, training, crystal clear communication, and culture.

- **Process** – Includes mapping the current environment, identifying areas of opportunity, mapping the new environment, time studies, implementation, and continuous improvement.

- **Technology** – Includes mapping current technology, identifying gaps, hardware architecture, the definition of systems solution, software investigation, testing, implementation, and maintenance.

I have been part of successful projects focused on organizational change (people) or process improvement that did not include technology. I have never been a part of or seen a successful technology project that did not include people and process.

I have seen too many system/technology projects that an organization just puts in with a crowbar and never looks at how the new solution impacts the people and processes. They magically think technology alone can fix all the issues. When everything begins to break down, management wants to know why it is failing or completely fails. To implement and use technology properly, you need to have a blend of people, process, and technology.

> **TO IMPLEMENT AND USE TECHNOLOGY PROPERLY, YOU NEED TO HAVE A BLEND OF PEOPLE, PROCESS, AND TECHNOLOGY.**

I read recent articles that said the people, process, and technology framework is a thing of the past. I call B.S. Just because you put a system in the cloud or are now using artificial intelligence does not mean you don't have to determine the impact on the organization, processes, employees, customers, and vendor partners.

Do you work for or lead an organization that struggles to successfully implement technology projects? You might want to think about expanding the project scope to include people and process. I guarantee you that it will go much smoother.

A GOLD BENTLEY

My first project with my new division of EDS was for a client I will call Sam's Shirt Company. They were a division of a bigger corporation. We had been trying to sell the bigger corporation on outsourcing all their technologies and a couple of other technology solutions for quite a while. I was never told for a fact, but I viewed working with this smaller division as a test drive with EDS.

Sam's was based in Hong Kong and had manufacturing operations in China and Sri Lanka. They made men's shirts for a variety of name brands. Our scope was twofold; first, we were to assess their current business processes and organization, and second, we were to analyze where technology could be used to assist their business. To do this, we were going to have to travel to their overseas facilities.

I had never been to the far east before, and this trip would take us first to Hong Kong, then southern China, followed by a trip to Sri Lanka and then home. The entire trip was about two weeks. I was excited and apprehensive, but when I left Milwaukee years earlier, one of my goals was to see the world. I was literally going to fly around the world (22,000 miles) during this trip. How many people have done that?

The first leg of the trip would take about 25 hours, with layovers in Los Angeles and Narita, Japan. I was traveling with two other associates, and when we arrived at the Hong Kong airport, we were walking zombies. We checked through customs, picked up our luggage, then we met our driver. The client had arranged for us to stay at one of the best hotels in the city, and a driver was part of their service.

As we left the terminal, we walked past a couple of big sedans that I thought might be our car, but our driver kept walking. Then he stopped at a solid gold four-door Bentley S-Series Standard Saloon. I had to look up the name. I could not believe it. I am not sure what it cost in 1996, but today the range is between $175,000 to $300,000. We got in the back, and our driver had hot washcloths for us and a variety of beverages to choose from. I was living the high life!

When we arrived at the Regent Hotel, about ten other Bentleys were lined up in a row. The hotel was gorgeous. It sits on Kowloon Bay's waterfront right across from the beautiful skyline of Hong Kong Island. Everything was five-star plus. We had arrived a couple of days early to work with the SVP for Sam's. He wanted to make sure we were on the same page with our activities for the week, and he also knew this was the first time in Hong Kong for the three of us, and he wanted us to see the sights of the city and surrounding areas. He was an incredible client.

We took a couple of tours over the weekend, and it was fascinating. Before the trip, I read some books about Hong Kong, China, Buddhism, etc., so I wasn't a totally naïve westerner, but the books did not do justice to what we experienced. Hong Kong was so diverse with so much history. The SVP took us to some fabulous restaurants, and yes, he made me eat the local cuisine. His suggestion to arrive early to get our bodies adjusted to the time change and see the sights was a perfect recommendation.

If you had asked me when I was 22 if I believed I would have taken a trip like this, I would have said you were crazy. Yet here I was on the other side of the world and enjoying every minute of it. This trip stretched my comfort zone, but once I returned to the States, I had a whole new set of experiences to fall back on in the future.

Continue to stretch yourself outside of your comfort zone, and one of the best ways to do that is to travel. Experience other cultures and explore beautiful sites. The world becomes just a little smaller, and your perspective grows just a little broader when you do.

JUST WHAT THE DOCTOR ORDERED ... BUT

Gimbels and Haggar gave me an incredible foundation, and I only left Haggar because I could not see how I could reach my goals staying with the company. After struggling on my own for a couple of years, EDS gave me new life. It got me off the streets and into the heart of the world of consulting and technology.

EDS provided the opportunity to add critical skills and knowledge I could not have received if I had stayed with either of those companies. These included being exposed to:

- How different companies operate strategically and tactically.

- Different industries.

- How governments can shift/control how an industry can operate in different countries.

- How important business processes are to an organization.

- Every single discipline within a company.

- Being able to quickly identify the key issues and put together a total solution to fix and prevent the problems in the future.

- Transitioning from selling products to selling ideas on how to improve their company.

- How to persuade executives, executive teams, and project teams.

- All facets of the information technology world.

- Traveling the world and learning about different cultures, different business practices, and different business rules and laws.

The bottom line is this was just what the doctor ordered. I would never in a million years have learned all of this at Gimbels or Haggar, and I learned all of this in three short years. There were so many naysayers telling me I was making a major career mistake shifting trying to be a consultant at 33. How wrong they all were! Friends and colleagues continued to underestimate my work ethic, desire, and my willingness to take risks to achieve my career goals.

But now, things were not all well with EDS. The once-powerful industry leader had started to struggle with poor management decisions, bloated bureaucracy, and money-losing contracts. It had ballooned to something like 50 different business units, and there was a general feeling that this was a gigantic rudderless ship. It felt like EDS management was on cruise control. I don't like cruise control, and unfortunately, I was correct about EDS being in big trouble. After a series of management changes and acquisitions, within ten years or so, EDS did not exist anymore. A once-great company was now a historical anecdote.

Because I saw this coming in late 1997, I knew that I needed to find another company to continue my learning curve and help propel me

EVEN IF YOU LOVE YOUR JOB, THE CULTURE, AND THE PEOPLE; EVEN IF YOU ARE LEARNING AND MOVING FORWARD IN YOUR CAREER GOALS; IF THE COMPANY (OR INDUSTRY) IS IN TROUBLE, YOU BETTER BE WORKING ON AN OPTION TO GET OUT.

closer to my goals. I accepted a position with one of their biggest competitors.

I know change can be hard. You must protect yourself and your family. The last thing you want is for the company to tell you that you are gone before you have a chance to actively find something else. Even if you love your job, the culture, and the people; even if you are learning and moving forward your career goals; if the company (or industry) is in trouble, you better be working on an option to get out. You might be better off taking a risk and jumping before you are pushed.

.

C H A P T E R 6

YOU HAVE A FRONT ROW
SEAT TO THE C-SUITE

About fifteen years into my career, with all its ups and downs, the stars finally aligned. I connected with the perfect client at the perfect location with the perfect leader at the perfect time working for the perfect company.

These stories discuss how I won over the leader and took advantage of an opportunity to learn from an incredibly successful CEO of a company that is a household name. I'll talk about how he turned around this challenged company and share insights gained as I built a reputation for taking on and solving significant issues to support the rebuilding of the organization. Some of my most fulfilling moments came when I realized the position I had worked for throughout my entire career was at last within reach!

WHY DON'T YOU MEET THE MICHAELS' TEAM?

It was early June 1997, and I was the newest Senior Consultant for my new company, Computer Sciences Corporation (CSC). At the end of my weeklong orientation, I met with my partner (Steve Biciocchi) to discuss potential projects I could soon be assigned to. No projects were immediately available, so Steve suggested I go to a current project site with a local client in Dallas.

He told me the client was Michaels Stores. They were in the process of a major turnaround. Through acquisitions over the last ten years or so, they had grown to around 430 stores and were doing $1.4B in sales. However, they had lost $31M in 1996 and were hemorrhaging cash. To help fix the problems and turn the ship around, they named a new CEO—Michael Rouleau. He was a veteran of Target, Shopko, and Lowe's with broad expertise in merchandising, store operations, logistics, and real estate.

"The situation is a mess," Steve said, "and will need years to fix. Literally, everything in the company has to be addressed. Michael Rouleau (note, he is not the founder of the company, it is just a coincidence that his name is the same as the company name) has been dealing with bankers, lawyers, vendors, and also trying to run the company." Steve continued, "Michael will need a lot of help, and if we can complete the current quick-hit projects successfully, there should be much more work for us in the future."

I was intrigued by a few things. First, a company in distress can be an incredible opportunity for a consultant. There have not been too many tremendously successful turnarounds. What I mean by "truly successful" is that many turnarounds are just smoke and mirrors. A new CEO comes in and cuts expenses to the bone, runs some slick new marketing campaign, talks a good game on Wall Street, and everything looks fine for the first few years. Then the balloon pops because fundamental changes that caused the company to be in distress were never addressed because they may take too long, and Wall Street and the Board run out of patience.

Second, Steve shared that Rouleau was the type of leader who would not skip steps in turning Michaels around, and the Board seemed to agree with this philosophy. Third, Mr. Rouleau reminded me of Mr. J.M. Haggar and the stories I heard about Sam Walton—all tough and disciplined leaders. The more Steve kept talking about the new CEO, the more I wanted to meet him and hopefully work with him.

Finally, Michaels was located 20 miles from my house. No planes, hotels, airports, rental cars, or restaurant food. My wife and I had just been blessed with our son Zachary in February, and it would be awesome to be able to be home every night instead of some hotel room somewhere in the world.

After my meeting, I prayed that this might be the break I had been working for my entire career. I prayed that if this were God's plan, I would give CSC and Michaels and Michael Rouleau everything I had. I knew this was a long-shot prayer. I had no idea what was happening at the account or if I would even be officially assigned to Michaels, but I did not care. I felt this was a perfect situation, and I left it in God's hands.

From mid-June 1997 (except for a three-month project elsewhere), I was associated with Michaels first as a consultant and then as an employee until January 2008. It was a career-defining ten-year period. **Setting crystal clear goals, a willingness to take risks, working your butt off, and help from God can lead to incredible career fulfillment. Some think prayers are crazy and worthless—I disagree. Maybe if you start believing in yourself and the power of prayer, great things can happen for you too!**

YOU WILL NEED TO STAY UNTIL WE ACCEPT THE DELIVERABLE

I met the CSC team at a nearby Hilton Garden Inn. They had scheduled an early morning breakfast meeting to discuss the deliverables for the week and introduce me as the newest member of the broader CSC team. All welcomed me with open arms, which gave me a boost of energy. My boss told me the week before in Cleveland that the project was winding down, so the discussion was about getting Michaels to sign off on the remaining projects and continue laying seeds for future projects.

Joe McKinney, one of the partners on the project, gave me three things to focus on. First, get up to speed on every project background, work product, and deliverable. Second, since I was a local resource, meet as many Michaels' people as I could in the hopes of maintaining contact in the event we did not get any immediate add-on work. And finally, help present the final deliverable for one of the "Quick Hits" to the Michaels' team.

The first two objectives were easy. The CSC team had a great central location for all documentation, and if I had any questions, I could just ask the team leaders for the answers. And because the team leaders took me around to their meetings, they could introduce me around the office. By the end of the second week, I was up to speed on every project.

The final request was going to be a little more difficult. Joe was going to present the final deliverable to the Store Ordering Quick Hit. Its focus was to help the stores more efficiently order the correct quantities of products for their stores. This was before Michaels had corporate-driven automatic replenishment, so every store ordered for themselves. It was an inventory management nightmare, but automatic replenishment was still years away, and you had to make any improvements you could as fast as you could.

The presentation was to the head of stores and the head of IT (Information Technology) and a few of their lieutenants, along with a couple of other project team members from Michaels. As the presentation went on, there seemed to be too many questions being asked for a final deliverable. In my experience, you walked the final deliverable around to the key players and got their comments and buy-in, so the final presentation was a *fait accompli*. Duane Hiemenz, SVP of Store Operations, said, "This project still needs work." Unfortunately, the entire Michaels' team agreed, and he continued, "You will need to stay until we accept the deliverable."

Those are not the words you want to hear from a client! The CEO brought Duane over with him from Lowe's, and we did NOT want him to tell the boss, or there could go any future work. We had to fix this, but how? The project's primary consultant was already working with another client.

Joe answered, "Jeff and I will fix this, and you will get the deliverable you deserve." For the next several weeks, Joe and I worked through every issue the team had raised. I walked the changes around to every team member, and if there was conflict, I brought all parties together and got it resolved. I was constantly in Duane's office giving him a status report. The final presentation took about five minutes because I had gotten everybody on board before the meeting. We had fixed the project and recovered what could have been a real problem with this client.

This effort helped me earn a reputation within Michaels that I could fix things. After 15 years in the workforce, I finally found my calling: to quickly identify and permanently fix company problems. This reputation would stick throughout my entire relationship with the company and the remainder of my career. **Sometimes it takes a while to find that one thing you really love to do and are exceptionally good at performing. Keep searching until you find it because when you do, it is an amazing feeling.**

————— • ● • —————

GETTING READY TO MEET THE BOSS

After we successfully redid the "Quick Hit" project the SVP of stores had declined to accept; we wanted to discuss more consulting projects with the CEO. Michael was concerned about starting any new projects because his team needed time to absorb the recently completed "Quick Hit" projects. My boss then offered to do an in-depth strategic analysis of Michaels for free. All we needed from the company was data and people's time for interviews or project validation discussions. The CEO agreed.

It was a big commitment from CSC management to do pro bono work, but they felt that this account and the relationship they had built with Rouleau made the investment worthwhile. Joe McKinney, Cheryl Doggett, a principal out of the Dallas CSC office, and I were chosen to lead the project. Our objective was to: *Create a framework to identify strategic options to enable Michaels to meet or exceed its growth target of $6 Billion by the year 2005.*

Rouleau's goal was to have a thousand stores doing a profitable $6M per store. It was definitely a stretch goal, but it was easy to understand. The challenge was a far cry from the current statistics. At the end of 1996, Michaels had sales of $1.4B, 453 stores doing $3.1M per store, and had lost $31.2M. We knew Rouleau was focused on putting out about 100 fires a day, with one or two more starting every day. He had inherited an absolute mess and needed his full attention on survival, so if he could live to fight another day, that was a winning day.

We thought we would look towards the future. Our management believed Rouleau would right this ship and would be ready at the right time to turn his attention towards the future. We wanted to lay the seeds of what needed to happen over the next 3 to 5 years and how we could help. We spent the next five weeks putting together a detailed financial, operational, competitive, strategic, and retail industry analysis. It is one of the best work products I have ever worked on.

During this same time, I was doing another research project. A client sponsor from my first EDS consulting project taught me a lesson about doing homework on everybody—getting to know them better than they knew themselves. Whenever I went back to the Michaels' office, I would always ask whoever I met with about Rouleau. What was he like? What are his do's and don'ts? What makes him tick?

I also spent a lot of time with Duane Hiemenz because he had worked with Rouleau at Lowe's. I gained a great deal of insight about the leader of this company—a man we needed to persuade to get more consulting work. The bottom line is Rouleau had an incredible amount of retail experience. Before joining Michaels, there was no retail position that he had not held except for CEO. He was one of the original 25 or so people who started Target stores in 1962. You could not B.S. him. He would sniff you out from a mile away. A few people used the name General Patton to describe him. He was a tough, disciplined, no-nonsense leader.

He also was born and raised in the Midwest. Duluth, Minnesota, to be exact, and he loved people who had that Midwestern work ethic. Most importantly, you could not outwork the man. He wanted you to speak the truth, but sometimes it was how you delivered that truth that mattered. If you made it seem like it was his idea, you had a winner. If you made it seem like the truth took a shot at him personally, you had better duck. The presentation was ready, and so was I.

I had used everything I had learned at EDS to prepare myself for what I thought could be the biggest meeting of my entire career. This presentation had to be great, and I had to know the intricate details of the man I was about to meet. Doing your homework is something your parents tell you to do all the time. It is a lesson you need to follow your entire life. Being great at something is hard; that doesn't happen by chance. It takes time and a commitment to become better at something than anyone else.

BEING GREAT DOESN'T HAPPEN BY CHANCE. IT TAKES TIME AND A COMMITMENT TO BECOME BETTER AT SOMETHING THAN ANYONE ELSE.

"HELLO MICHAEL, MY NAME IS JEFF WELLEN"

On September 15, 1997, Cheryl Doggett, Joe McKinney, and I presented a strategic framework document to Michael Rouleau. After six weeks of research, analysis, internal discussions, and interviews with Michaels' associates, we were ready. I had not met Rouleau before this meeting, but I had learned a tremendous amount about him. I wanted to see if what I learned about him was a myth or real.

We entered the Michaels' offices, signed in at the front desk, proceeded upstairs, then into the office complex's northwest wing, and walked down the long hallway to the corner office. When we reached the end of the hallway, Joe introduced Cheryl and me to Rouleau's Executive Assistant, Debi Mitchell. Debi's desk sat outside Rouleau's office. Debi told us to take a seat, and we would be able to go in to see Michael shortly. This was the first time I met Debi, but she and I became best friends during my time with Michaels Stores.

As we sat outside Rouleau's office, I was excited, anxious, and nervous all at the same time. Then we heard Michael's voice, "Debi, I am ready." Joe walked in first, followed by Cheryl and then me. Joe knew Michael from the previous "Quick Hit" project work and from crossing paths at Target. They shook hands and exchanged pleasantries, then Michael said hello to Cheryl before turning to me. I reached out my hand and said, "Hello Michael, my name is Jeff Wellen, and it is a pleasure to meet you."

Michael looked at Joe and said, "Is this the guy Duane told me about?"

"If you mean the guy who helped rework the Quick Hit project, then yes; this is the guy," Joe said.

Michael said, "I heard you helped fix that project."

"Joe and I did the work together, but I do like fixing things," I replied.

"Well, there are a lot of things to fix here," he shook my hand firmly. My confidence was exploding.

The presentation was very casual. We did not go to a conference room, just stayed in Michael's office. He had a couch and a couple of chairs, and we talked through the printed copies of the presentation. The document was about 60 pages long, and we were told we had two hours with the boss. From the first page, everything people had told me about him was spot on. He cut through all the consulting B.S. and wanted to get to the facts. He asked probing questions, and sometimes the answers were difficult because we did not want to come across as challenging Michael personally.

For example, when discussing recommendations we had for the future, we emphasized that we knew Rome is burning, and his focus must be there first. He challenged us on some of our numbers (which was my section), and I did not back down. I stood my ground and underscored I was the messenger because these were industry numbers. As the meeting went on, I felt he liked our honesty and appreciated our approach. It was a helping hand we offered him, not a document to criticize his leadership to date.

I still have the notes from that meeting where I jotted down, "Michael commented continuously throughout the meeting that we had, in fact, raised issues that he had not thought about. He said, 'You now have given me ten more things I have to worry about.'" The next line in the notes to my management said, "The overall results of this project were a complete success." We did a great job.

I also believe that I personally made a positive impression on Michael. He asked me as we were getting ready to leave, "Are you a local guy?"

I said, "Yes, I'm from the Dallas area."

"Well," he said, "I hope you are available if we do some more work together in the future."

"That would be great!" I said, and I'm sure my smile matched my mood. The stars were aligning. Five years after I left Haggar to try it on my own, I had been given a golden ticket. **It can be a crazy risk to leave a successful company and a career to chase a dream, but sometimes you must take a risk if you want that dream to come true.** Mine was about to pay off. Big time!

———•●•———

KEEPING ALL THE PLATES SPINNING

When I got home from my first meeting with Michael Rouleau, my wife wanted to know everything about it. She was so excited that I had this big opportunity to make a presentation to the CEO of a billion-dollar company. She had supported me through a lot of crazy times, but it seemed like things were starting to look a little more positive.

I told her I was scared to death when I finally met him. I had heard so much about him and done so much research about what a formidable reputation he had that I was just a little intimated. Mr. J.M. Haggar told me one time that some people feared him, and he liked it. He told me never to show fear to someone like him, and he said, "Stand your ground. Don't pick a fight, but make sure they know you are not going to be a pushover."

I told Lisa that I did not back down. I respectfully disagreed on occasion and followed it up with a fact. I had heard Michael like to use catchphrases. One of them was, "Tell me what you know, not what you think," so I never said, "I think this, or I think that." It would have been a death sentence. I did not want him to sniff any fear from me. To this day, I believe if he had, he would not have asked for me to work on future projects. Years later, Michael paid me a huge compliment when he said that I was one of the most fearless people he had ever met.

Lisa asked me what else happened, and I told her about how well the presentation went and that he commented about working with him on future projects. Then I said, "I got a firsthand look at the realities of a CEO. Not just any CEO, but one trying to turn a company around that was an absolute mess. He had a yellow legal pad with pages and pages of notes on things he had to do yesterday, and he talked about having to deal with board members, Wall Street, bankers, lenders, and vendors, all making demands of him and his time daily."

Michael told us about a meeting he had with a small group of vendors who were basically begging to keep shipping products to him even though he did not know how he would pay them. He shared concerns some of the employees would start jumping ship if they thought he might not be able to get things going in the right direction and how every day, a board member would call with a new idea on what to do.

It was crazy. All of that had nothing to do with running a 450-store retail chain but were challenges he faced. He told us stories about things he found out that the stores were doing just because they could—ordering anything they want from whoever would sell to them. He said, "As I sit here today, I cannot tell you what each store has in inventory and what they are selling by item."

I could go on. Though I knew the CEO of Gimbels and all the senior management at Haggar, I never sat in any management meetings. At EDS, the executives were on a separate floor that you had to have permission to access, and at CSC, all the Senior Executives were in California. I had dreamed of the day that I could be in those meetings and working through all the issues they must deal with.

After listening to Michael, I had second thoughts for a moment. I realized a CEO's job is like the person in a variety show that must keep ten plates all spinning on top of a stick without letting any of them fall. At the same time, you have hundreds of people pulling and pushing you around. It is one heck of a balancing act. Even with all these challenges, I wanted to learn more.

SPEND A DAY WALKING IN A CEO'S SHOES AND YOU WILL THINK DIFFERENTLY ABOUT WHAT YOU SAY REGARDING THAT POSITION AND PERSON.

I really don't believe most people have a clue what a CEO deals with every day. The stress of running a company is tremendous. If people could spend one day walking in a CEO's shoes, I believe they would think differently about what they say about that position and person.

I WANT THE LOCAL GUY

In January 1998, we were waiting to hear back from Michael about a couple of proposals we made to him for additional work at Michaels' stores. After our tremendous meeting at the end of September, Michael wanted to wait until after the all-important holiday selling season before starting another project. He had inherited a mess, but in a little over a year, you could see signs that his leadership was impacting Michaels' business results, the organization, and the entire Arts & Crafts Industry. The year-over-year results were quite impressive:

	1996	1997
Year End Sales	$1.378 Billion	$1.57 Billion
Year End Net Income	$(31.2) Million	$30.1 Million
Earnings Per Share	$(1.34)	$0.52
# of Michaels Stores	453	452

Even with these results, Michaels was nowhere near out of the woods. They were still 25 to 30 years behind modern retail companies like Wal-Mart and Target. However, the early success did buy time for Michael to continue to build a rock-solid foundation the right way. No shortcuts, no slick ad campaigns, and no smoke and mirrors.

I received a call in late January from Steve Biciocchi, my partner. He told me that Rouleau had called him and wanted to do so more process improvement work. He also told me, Rouleau said, "I want the local guy that made that presentation to me last fall." Steve told him I was available and would be at the Michaels' offices tomorrow to discuss the details of the project. The next day I went to meet with Michael to scope out the project. It was my first time to go one-on-one with him, and it would not be my last. It was the beginning of an incredible 18-year working relationship.

On this day, Michael wanted to focus on three critical processes that were a mess. Here are a couple of highlights of why these were an issue:

- **Ad Process** – Michaels spent millions of dollars each week on ads, and upwards of 40% of the items run in the ads were out of stock the day the ad ran.

- **Order Writing Process** – It could take a buyer upwards of 17 days to get their orders signed and entered into the system and another 17 days to get them into the stores.

- **RF Store Ordering** – Stores had an in-stock position of anywhere between 65% to 80%, and at the same time, the company was over inventoried by hundreds of millions of dollars.

Can you imagine being part of a retail company that had such horrible inventory management issues? During the entire conversation, Michael could not have stressed more the need to have solid processes built first or built in tandem with technology. He was speaking my language. He told me, "Don't ever try to sell me a technology solution if we don't look at the processes and organization first. We will not skip steps to please Wall Street and the Board only to have the technology project fail because we did not do it right." Then he told me a story about Target in the 1960s when the situation went off the rails. He learned his lesson.

Michael had so much experience I realized that I had just entered a Ph.D. program in retail, business, leadership, and life. Michael loved to tell stories to make his point. They were powerful testimonies as to his thinking and how to make sure you don't make the same mistakes he lived through. The impact his stories had on me is one reason I wrote this book the way I did. **Some people might not want to listen to some older person's stories, but if you take the time to listen, you can earn your own Ph.D. to navigate your life and career.**

————— • • • —————

WHAC-A-MOLE

At CSC, I attended a seminar on establishing strategic plans, setting key initiatives, and other topics related to long-term planning. Most of the speakers did a decent job, but their comments were pretty boilerplate, to say the least. Then one gentleman left an impression that sticks with me to this very day.

He talked about the need to focus. To be successful meant you had to focus like a laser beam on those initiatives that could really move the needle. His true message was that if you could focus on a few things, your chances of success went up significantly.

To demonstrate this, he rolled out a Whac-a-Mole arcade game. Yes, the game where the little moles pop up and down randomly, and you use a mallet to hit them. The more moles you hit, the more you score. For this presentation, he changed the scoring to the percent of moles hit, not just the total score. He asked three people from the audience to help him with his theory.

He asked each to take a shot at seeing how many moles they could hit (percentage to total) in a one-minute time frame. There were ten moles that you could whack. The scores after the first round ranged from about 35% hit to 45% hit.

Then he grabbed a piece of plywood that had a hole cut into it. He placed the piece of wood over the top of the game. It perfectly covered up three of the moles. Now only seven moles could pop up and down. The scores after the second round ranged from about 60% to 75%. This demonstrated that by being more focused, the success rate went up.

Finally, he replaced that board with a different board. This one only allowed four moles to pop up and down. The scores ranged from about 85% to 100%. The simple message was **focus**.

The other message was to have the **"courage"** to ignore the other moles (initiatives in this case) that were still trying to pop up and distract you from the initiatives that really matter. The constant noise of the moles hitting the wood was incredibly distracting. It seemed like they were screaming at you to be let loose.

Many organizations don't seem to have the ability to focus and lack the courage to say no, not now. Wall Street, board members, senior leadership team, customers, etc., are all pushing organizations in so many different directions that it is easy to get distracted and put too much on an organization's plate. The result is inevitable, all the initiatives and projects fail, or there are delays, overruns on budgets, etc.

Do you have the courage to say no? Are your priorities based on the Whac-a-Mole arcade game? Swinging at all ten moles, hoping you hit one? **Don't have too many concurrent strategic initiatives. It is better to focus on a select few initiatives that you can successfully execute than it is to focus on too many initiatives at once and fail at all of them. Have the courage to focus.**

WHY WOULD A BALDING MAN NEGOTIATE THE PRICE OF HIS HAIRCUT?

I had just entered Michael's office to get him to sign a few invoices. He had me wait until he completed writing a note on his yellow legal pad. We were about ¾ of the way through our current project, and I wanted to get the invoices signed and checked off my to-do list.

When Michael was finished, we exchanged a little small talk about the project and how things were going with all the other issues he was dealing with. "The biggest problem with Michaels," he said, "is that we have so many issues to deal with at the same time." I told him about my plate spinning analogy, and he said, "That is exactly the case, except a few more plates are added every day. It is hard to fix an issue because everything is broken."

He continued, "That is the problem, but the blessing is everything that is wrong with Michaels can be fixed. If we stay focused, choose the priorities wisely, and don't get distracted by all the noise around us, we will turn this thing around." I mentioned the Whac-a-Mole seminar I went to, and he loved it. When we were finished with our small talk, I handed him the invoices to sign.

He took them from me and laid them on his desk. He leaned back in his chair and started telling me a story. "I went to my barber, and I was perturbed that I had to pay the same amount of money for my haircut as a man with a full head of hair." Michael was bald on top with hair on the sides. He ran his hand over the bald section and said, "How can he charge me when there is nothing to cut!"

I had no idea where he was going with this story, but I knew he had a point, so I listened attentively. He continued, "I told my barber, 'If I come in for a haircut every four weeks instead of every six weeks guaranteed, I will pay you half the current price.' After some haggling back and forth, we came to an agreement, and I saved myself about $50 a year."

As I sat there, I realized he was sending me a compelling message early in our relationship. Money matters. Every penny, every nickel, and every dime. They all add up. He was telling me to watch our billable hours and watch our expenses on the projects. It was his way of telling me he was watching me, and if $50 a year mattered to him for his haircut, so would tens of thousands of dollars for consulting costs.

It reminded me of the story about Sam Walton negotiating the price of a day-old newspaper to save $0.25. I heard Michaels' message loud and clear. His short story was a more powerful reminder of managing expenses instead of just hounding me about them instead. I was beginning to develop a secret decoder capability with Michael. There was meaning to everything he said; you just had to know how to decipher the message.

Telling stories can provide a more powerful message to your audience. In this case, it shows yet another successful leader who knows how to watch company funds and their personal funds. It is one of the many reasons they are successful and wealthy. **Managing your money and watching your expenses is a necessity. Be a stickler for every penny, and your wealth will continue to grow. Spend foolishly, and you will always be running to find a way to stay ahead of the bill collector.**

———•●•———

WE HAVE ALWAYS DONE IT THAT WAY

I was in the Michaels' auditorium leading a cross-functional team on developing a current (as is) process flow map for the advertising process. Our scope for the project changed because one of the original assumptions that the problem with the process was mainly in the marketing and advertising areas. After a few weeks of interviews and discussions, the root causes were much further back in the process. In some cases, it went as far back as the buyer and vendor initial negotiations.

Due to this new information, we added people from the Buying Team, Vendor Community, Order Writing, Distribution, Logistics, Finance, Inventory Management, Information Technology, Store Planning, Human Resources, and Store Operations. It was an entire Michaels' organization effort.

We were creating a step-by-step plan, organized by person and division responsible, date, and a countdown calendar. It was about a hundred steps that coordinated that the product and the marketing materials all showed up in the stores at least a week before the advertisement would run. We also coordinated the store labor hours needed to set the ad, the physical location of the ad items in the stores, and fixture changes needed. It was a thing of beauty when it was completed.

Getting to the result was a long and sometimes tedious process. Each organization represented had to offer reasons why this step needed to be added or why it needed to be completed a week earlier. Every change caused three other issues to fix. There were a couple of new people in the room for this meeting that had been recently added to the team. They were doing their best to get up to speed with the rest of the group and with my facilitation style.

Learning how to facilitate a meeting successfully is a definite art form. You are making statements, asking questions, or in some cases, sitting back and listening to try and get the group to make progress in resolving issues. Part of my style is to ask why? Like a five-year-old kid asking his parents a hundred questions about why does the sun rise, or why is the sky blue? I did the same thing. I wanted to challenge the group to dig as deep as necessary as to why something was done a certain way to get to the root cause of the issue. I did not want superficial change; I wanted the problem never to happen again.

I asked another "why" probing question, and one of the new people in the room said arguably my most disliked seven words a company or person can say, "We have always done it that way." There was a gasp in the room because all the other attendees knew this was on my Mount Rushmore of statements I did not like.

This attitude is one of the reasons companies can fail. They stop asking why and settle for, "That is just the way it has always been." In my opinion, this is such a lazy and cowardly way out of trying to find a better way to do something or to fix something that is broken. I know that person meant no harm, but that attitude and mentality had to change if Michaels was going to get out of the mess they were in.

DON'T BE LAZY ABOUT ANY LIFE OR WORK SITUATION AND SAY THERE IS NOTHING YOU CAN DO BECAUSE THAT IS HOW IT HAS ALWAYS BEEN. EVERYTHING CAN CHANGE, AND IT STARTS WITH SHIFTING YOUR ATTITUDE TO "I WILL FIND A BETTER WAY."

Don't be lazy about a situation in life or at work and say there is nothing you can do because that is the way it has always been. Everything can change, and it starts with shifting your attitude to "I will find a better way."

BAD PROCESSES MAKE GOOD
PEOPLE DO BAD THINGS

I was in my office when one of the ad process team members came to see me. He asked me if I had a few moments to talk. The person (I will call him Tim) wanted to speak to me about the advertising process we had been working on for about two months. I thought he wanted to give me some insight on an area to improve the process or comment about the meetings. Instead, he hit me with a curveball. He said, "Some of the team members are feeling a little dejected. We just continue to show how screwed up things are at every meeting, and some team members feel like it is their fault. They have been here for years, and they are blaming themselves for all the problems."

This was not the first time that a Michaels' associate talked to me in confidence. I had built a reputation very early on that you could tell me anything, and I would then figure out how to deal with that information. I would never let anyone know who told me, but I would take time to make sure it was truthful and not just a "sky is falling" comment. People knew me as someone who could get things done, which might have been the single most significant factor in my success at Michaels.

I told Tim I would take care of it during the next meeting, which was in a couple of days. I spent those days walking around the office talking with other team members. I wanted to see if I could verify what Tim had told me. He was spot on. With that verification, I was prepared to talk to the team at the next meeting.

I did not change the agenda to speak on this topic specifically but maneuvered the conversation to see if someone would bring it up. About a third of the way through, it happened. We all realized that if we made a couple of changes to the process, we could eliminate about 20 other steps. One person interjected, "Every time we find something like this, it makes me feel so stupid." I had my opening.

I told everybody, "Take a break for a second. No one here is stupid. No one walked into the office today and said, 'I am purposely going to do a bunch of dumb things to hurt Michaels.' The one simple truth is this: *'Bad processes make good people do bad things.'* After I said it, I did not say a word for about 10 seconds. I wanted to let it sink in. It did.

For a while, it began like a rallying cry to finish the ad process and begin implementing the changes.

I told the boss during an update meeting a short time later about the situation. I did not tell him how I found out it was an issue; I mentioned only the "stupid" comment made in the meeting. I also asked him if he would come to the next meeting to tell everyone from the CEO's mouth that he appreciated their hard work and could not wait to see the new process implemented. You cannot believe the impact it had on the team to hear from the boss.

This was the first time I had gone to Michael to advise a situation. It would happen countless times over the next eight years. Our relationship was building. He told me that he liked that I was a doer, not a talker and that I produced results. It also showed that Michael was exactly right to focus on process work before all the glitzy things the Street and the Board wanted him to do. The foundation he was laying was going to pay off when the company started investing hundreds of millions of dollars in the next few years.

Why do process improvement projects fail or are never looked at as a solution to many of a company's ills? They are tedious, non-sexy projects that don't get leadership many headlines. They take time and 100% commitment and ownership from the top. That means the CEO. **If your processes and procedures suck, it is not a reflection on your people; it is a reflection on leadership that ignores the actual root cause. They would rather find the next shiny objective to distract everyone than get a little dirty working in the trenches. Get a little dirty!**

IT'S NOT MY JOB

I was getting ready for a conference call with one of the ad process team members (I will call her Sandy). We were going to introduce some of the changes to a few store managers. We wanted their feedback, so Sandy could write up the new best practices documents for all stores and some talking points for the SVP of stores to deliver on his next conference call.

It amazes me how many touch points you must cover when rolling out something new in an organization. I was quickly becoming a change management expert. I was always expected to step back and make sure we had all the bases covered. Everybody else had a day job, but this was my one and only focus—to help change the company. This focus would become even more important as I became a full-time consultant on the Michaels' account, then later when I joined the company.

We decided to let Sandy lead the discussion. Once everybody was on the call and introduced themselves, she gave an overview of the project objectives and then dove into the team's changes to the process. The biggest impact for the stores was that we would be getting them the ad product and marketing materials at least a week in advance. They had such a problem with out of stocks for ad items we wanted to put a little cushion in the process until they got better.

We wanted the stores to make space in their backrooms to stage the goods so they could put all the advertised products out Saturday night before the ad broke Sunday morning. This meant the stores would have saleable product that they would have to hold for an ad. However, Michaels had been so poor at managing inventory that many managers would put ad goods out early to cover their every day out of stocks. They were just trying to make their daily numbers, but it created havoc with customers on Sunday mornings.

One of the managers quipped, "It is not my job to hold goods in the backroom for a week because the corporate office can't do their jobs. It is your job to ship it to me the week of the ad so I can get it right to the floor." I just cannot stand the phrase, "not my job." It stops me in my tracks every time I hear it and is another phrase on my Mount Rushmore of things I don't like. It is selfish for anyone part of a team to say anything is "not my job."

I took a deep breath and waited for Sandy to respond. "This was not a request," she began, "this is not a could-you-please-do-this?" This directive is from the CEO, the entire Executive Committee, and the SVP of stores. We know this is not the ultimate process. Our goal is to do exactly what you said, but we are not ready for that yet. This process will ensure that we have ad goods to sell for the millions we spend on ads. This is the right thing to do for the company, and it will help your store in the long run."

The store manager backed down. She spoke to his frustration with out of stocks in a way that helped him understand what was best for the company. It is hard when you have goals and targets to meet, and you are now being asked to do something that could affect that. Sandy did not tear into this person but told him the future vision. By doing this, she persuaded him to give this a chance. We needed their long-term buy-in, and she got it.

It is so easy to say this is not my job. On hundreds or maybe thousands of occasions, I have felt that way. What I try to do is put myself in the shoes of the person who is asking. Why are they asking me to do this? Does it have to be done now? Will it really help the company, division, etc.?

Don't be a "Not my Job" employee. Find a way to work together as a team to find the solution that will benefit the entire company and all parties involved. Be part of the solution, not part of the problem.

THRIVING ON CHAOS

I had never been associated with a turnaround before. All the companies I had worked for or consulted with were never in such a challenging spot when I was associated with them. Michaels was my first turnaround, and let me tell you a little secret—turnarounds are hard. Really hard!

So much is broken it is hard to determine where to start. The usual scenario goes the company has lost its way, so sales are down, profits are down, they are bleeding cash, suppliers are concerned, lenders are concerned, and investors have the stock at all-time lows and going lower. Finally, board members get re-engaged, and customers don't know if they can trust the company to continue operations, so they look for alternatives. Employees also begin to look for a lifeboat to jump to safety from a sinking ship.

For years, the board has allowed a CEO and the management team to run the company into the ground. A company does not go south in a couple of days; it builds up over years. Lack of a clear strategy, lack of adequately investing in the right initiatives, failure to implement key initiatives successfully, executives making tactical decisions to save a penny here or make a penny there just to improve the next quarterly earnings report, and an executive's unwillingness to make the difficult decisions are a few of the many reasons companies begin to fail.

Then after years of neglect, the board searches for the next new CEO savior and expects them to turn around the failing company. This is the situation Michael Rouleau inherited in 1996, and one I joined in 1997 and worked as a consultant for three years.

You want to fix all the broken systems, processes, customer attitudes, etc., right away, but there are so many things wrong. Where do you start? You must tackle fixing some of the problems while keeping the company operations going. You still have to generate sales, and in this case, operate almost 500 stores, buy merchandise, pay bills, and try to preserve as much cash as possible to keep fighting another day. You must be on guard as the competition will take advantage of you in your weakened state. Finally, you must keep the workforce engaged and content enough that they don't all jump ship.

In 1987, Tom Peters wrote a book called *Thriving on Chaos*. One review had this quote about the book, "He predicts this rapidly changing world—fueled by new technology—will be unpredictable, so companies must learn how to 'thrive on chaos' to survive the turbulent times ahead." The urban dictionary puts it more succinctly; "**to thrive amid disorder**: to prosper, to do well when surrounded by chaos or mayhem." There is a reason many turnarounds don't work or last more than three years. It is incredibly difficult.

It takes a special person with unique skills to work in a turnaround environment. It takes an extraordinary leader even to want to do this, let alone be able to handle the chaos and be successful in the end. Rouleau was that leader, and he had done just that with his team. He was steady, focused, disciplined, passionate but not emotional, was able to bob and weave like a fighter avoiding the knockout punch, and he had the endurance of a marathon runner.

Fortunately for me, because Michael allowed me to participate in many of the discussions and decisions he had to make, I learned all of these critical elements to thrive in a turnaround environment. I also realized that I could thrive in the crazy chaotic atmosphere. I was finding my niche, and I loved it.

> **LEARN TO KEEP YOUR WITS ABOUT YOU, STAY FOCUSED, AND NEVER STOP FIGHTING, AND YOU WILL BE ABLE TO THRIVE WITHIN ALL THE CHAOS THAT IS AROUND YOU.**

There is a famous poem by Rudyard Kipling called "If." The first line of the poem reads, "If you can keep your head when all about you are losing theirs ..." That is a perfect description of working in a turnaround. Life, like business, can be incredibly chaotic. Learn to keep your wits about you, stay focused, never stop fighting, and you to will be able to thrive within all the chaos that is around you.

———•●•———

COPY, COPY, COPY

By mid-year 1998, I prepared to present an update on the Ad Process Project to the Monday sales and operations committee meeting. In the meeting, the leaders of the merchandise, store operations, marketing, inventory management, distribution, and finance areas would all give updates on the day-to-day operations for the last week. Issues still needed to be fixed, but running the business was still the number one priority.

One of the merchandise managers was presenting their numbers, and they were not particularly good. Half of the departments he was responsible for were going up, and half were going down, so basically, his businesses were running flat to last year. Michael Rouleau was hot. He had been working with the merchants for over a year to turn their businesses around, but he was frustrated it was going so slowly. Then he did something I had heard about but had not yet witnessed. He became Preacher Michael, not CEO Michael. For the next 15 minutes, he began one of the many sermons I would hear him give from the pulpit of the boardroom.

He usually started with a story. He said, "In the late sixties, I was running Target's operations, and I was in an airport when I ran into Sam Walton. Sam and I struck up a conversation, and we talked for a short while. I was cautious about talking to him because we all knew that he was getting ahead by copying other companies' ideas. After the conversation was over, no matter how hard I tried, I knew I had just told him about a new system Target was putting in. A year later, Wal-Mart was doing the same thing, and it was better than Target's way!"

He continued, "If the richest man in the world got that way by copying, why can't you? Are you too proud? AC Moore, one of our regional competitors in the Northeast, does $6.6M per store. We do about half that per store. I don't know if you know this, but I just hired a couple of new people in the store operations area from AC Moore. They told us that they are doing four times the business per square foot than we are in our stores. Why the heck is that?"

He did not want an answer from us and continued, "Because, at this moment, AC Moore is a better merchant than we are. We will get there, but I can't wait years. I want you to get on a plane right after this meeting and get up to an AC Moore store and copy their assortment and don't come back until you do." He finished by saying, "... and that goes for the rest of the merchants and everyone in this room. If someone is doing something better than us, copy it!"

It was a trademark of Sam and Michael. Copy, copy, and copy some more. You take the best of the competition and the best of your company and blend it together, and you will become the best in the industry. It was one reason Michaels had made up so much ground in sales and profitability in the early days of the turnaround. It was also a reason they were able to catch up and, in some cases, pass other retailers by the early 2000s. Because we were 25 years behind Wal-Mart and Target, we could use their playbook for success.

I know some people will say that copying is wrong. In this case, I disagree. For example, if we knew in 1983, Wal-Mart put point of sale cash registers in their stores and began scanning bar codes for more efficiency, and Michaels did not have either of those capabilities, should we not copy that? As for the merchants, fast forward a couple of years, and Michael organized an annual trip to the Northeast to visit AC Moore stores and other competitors in the area. They would find out we were coming, and, in some cases, they would meet us at some of the stores. By 2003 we had passed them in merchandise assortment quality. Guess what? They started to copy us!

If someone is doing something better than you, don't be shy. Copy it.

WHAT GETS MEASURED GETS DONE

I received a call from Debi Mitchell that Michael wanted to see me. As our time working together continued, Michael would consistently call me into his office to ask my opinion of something he was working on or to give me another lesson at the "Ph.D. School of Rouleau." Today I was going to class.

He first asked me to read a memo he was writing to our project team, and he wanted to get the wording correct. He was a stickler for wordsmithing. He wanted it the best he could make it. After we had finished with the memo, he called out to Debi and asked her to get Duane, the SVP of Store Operations, to come to his office. He then looked at me and said, "Don't say a word, just listen."

Duane walked in and sat next to me in front of Michael's desk. Michael handed Duane what looked like a report. I did not get a copy, so I just sat and continued to listen. Michael said, "This is a new report I've been working on measuring a variety of store labor and expense metrics. Duane, the field must get a handle on their labor and expense costs. I want to use some of the savings to make some desperately needed investments."

Duane asked a couple of questions about how to read the report and when the field would be able to see it. Michael responded, "This is an ad hoc report I worked on with IT. It will be a while before I can give it to the field. For now, only me, you, and the zone vice presidents could get a copy."

Duane asked a few more questions, then he got up and left the office. Michael looked at me and said, "You mark your calendar and come see me about this topic in a month, and you will see what I just did." That was it. He said nothing else. Michael loved reports. He loved digging into the details of every area of the company. He never wanted one of his direct reports to know more about the business than he did. But for the life of me, I could not figure out what he was doing.

One month to the day later, I called Debi and asked if I could see Michael. She said, "Come on down; he has a few minutes." I walked down the hallway, and I ran into Duane because Debi had asked him to join us. We walked into Michael's office and sat down by his desk. He gave both of us an updated copy of his report. In the month since he first showed this to Duane, it had gone through 50 iterations. Michael then proceeded to tell Duane that the numbers that were supposed to go down were and the numbers or percentages that were supposed to go up were, in fact, going up.

Michael agreed that the stores *were* doing a great job, but he thought they could do even better. He was never satisfied. If you gave him $2 in savings, he wanted $3. Duane and Michael continued their conversation for a few more minutes, and then Duane left the room. Michael looked at me and said, "Do you see what happened here?"

"The numbers on the report show the stores did a great job," I offered.

Michael shook his head, "That is not it. Some executives would have paid millions in consulting to get the results I just got. It is a simple phrase, 'What gets measured get done!' All I did was make the stores aware I was looking and care about store labor and expense management. I did not need a new labor management system or a new HR bonus program. I just created a simple report and told them I would be watching them like a hawk."

In one month, every major metric dramatically improved. No big initiative. No memo. It was pure genius!

If you want to get people to respond, just make sure they know you are watching. Let them know you care about the improvement you want them to make and applaud them for their efforts. What gets measured truly gets done.

PUSH IN HERE, AND SOMETHING COMES OUT THE OTHER END

Amir Hoda (a fellow CSC consultant) and I worked on several inventory management-related projects at Michaels. We were putting the finishing touches on a presentation to use for Michaels Executive Team strategy session. It was the kind of slide that gave me a great deal of heartburn and anxiety when showing a client.

The slide depicted a five-year historical overview of the distribution center (DC) fill rate. Fill rate is a calculation used to measure how many units were ordered to be shipped from the DC to the stores compared to how many were actually shipped. It looked like an electrocardiography (EKG) heart monitor of a patient that occasionally went into cardiac arrest. The blue line had dramatic swings up and down each year, but at the end of 1996, 1997, and in 1998, it dropped precipitously.

My apprehension was because a management decision caused the drop. The chart highlighted that in '96 and '97, there was a management directive to cut the end-of-year inventory. In '98, there was a management decision to have "hard limits" on open to buy (a retail term used in inventory management discussions). My high anxiety level in presenting these facts came into play because these decisions were made by Michael Rouleau himself, the CEO of Michaels.

In Michael's defense, the company was hemorrhaging cash in 1996 and needed every penny just to stay afloat. In '97 and '98, he was trying to manage inventory with spreadsheets, band-aids, and duct tape. Everyone knew this, but the slide still showed the dramatic drop-in fill rates and store in-stocks regardless of the good intentions. When I showed the slide in the strategy meeting, Michael said, "I guess this is a perfect example of what I have been saying to all of you. When you push in here, something is bound to come out the other end. With everything so broken around here, we need to understand the consequences of our actions."

In 1983 my dad suffered his first heart attack. I was 23 years old and wanted to do everything I could to try to avoid having one myself. My dad's doctor told me to exercise more and watch my fat and cholesterol intake. I changed my diet dramatically. I started eating no fat or low-fat products. My cholesterol numbers got markedly better, but something else happened, my sugar numbers were going up. All the low-fat things I was eating were loaded with sugar to make them taste better. You push in here, and something comes out the other end.

Sir Isaac Newton, widely considered the Father of Physics, developed the three laws of motion. The third law states, "For every action, there is an equal and opposite reaction." What Michael applied to business, Newton had developed in 1686. These laws work not only in the physical world but also in life, business, politics, sports, etc. We can have the best intentions but still not be aware of or even try to understand the consequences of our actions.

Before you make a decision, take a step back and contemplate what could happen if you make that decision. You can't be paralyzed to the point you don't do anything, but you will be better informed about the consequences when the decision is made.

---·●·---

PROGRESS NOT PERFECTION

From 1967 to 1991, my beloved Green Bay Packers had a record of 152-208. They had only four winning seasons during that time. This was a far cry from five World Championships and two Superbowls in nine seasons like they had in the 1960s. In 1991, the Packers hired Ron Wolf as General Manager to turn around the perennial losing franchise. In 1992, Ron hired Mike Holmgren to be the new head coach. He started drafting better players, traded for Hall of Fame quarterback Brett Farve, and signed one of the greatest defensive players in NFL history, Reggie White, to a free-agent contract.

Wolf's goal was to bring a Super Bowl Championship back to Green Bay. He knew the mess he inherited could not be changed overnight. There was no magic dust to sprinkle on the field to turn a broken franchise into an instant winner. He needed to make progress every year. Build one success on top of another as each success bred a new desire for more. The bar could then be raised. The attitude of just hoping not to embarrass ourselves changes to let's kick everybody's butt every time we step on the field.

From 1992 to 1996, the Packers record was 51 - 29. They had five straight winning years. They went from winning nine games in 1992 to 13 in 1996. They made the playoffs in 1993, the NFC Championship game in 1995, and then won the Super Bowl in 1997. They made consistent and steady progress to get to the ultimate goal of becoming NFL Champions.

As I sat in another Michaels' Executive Committee waiting to present an update on a current project, I was reminded of this sequence of events based on the conversation that was taking place. The discussion centered around the fact that some of the executives did not feel that enough was being done to fix some of the issues in their areas of responsibility. They were pushing Michael Rouleau to spend more money on headcount or invest in a new system now.

Michael listened for a few moments before he stopped the conversation. "I know things are still a mess. I know we are missing many core competencies that other companies have had down for 25 years. We are 25 years behind modern retailers, and we can't make that up in one day or one year. Plus, we are still taking on water in some areas. We put our finger in one hole, and three other holes appear.

"In a turnaround, all we need is progress, not perfection. We need to push hard to continue to move forward on all fronts—no going backward. You make progress, hold that line, and then begin to move forward again. We will learn along the way and be smarter for when bigger decisions are needed. If we do that, we will be in a much better position when we do begin to invest. I want perfection just as much as you do, but for now, we just need progress!"

So many companies and people believe there are shortcuts to success, whether that be a company trying to get to number one in their industry or a person trying to improve their golf swing. **There are no shortcuts in life. The best way to chase your dreams is to consistently make progress, every day, every week, and every year. No going backward. Progress builds confidence. Confidence becomes contagious. Goals can then be raised higher until you reach your ultimate peak.**

———————— • ● • ————————

DO IT RIGHT THE FIRST TIME

CSC had been working on improving processes for Michaels Stores for about a year. The CEO was a process-driven leader, and he wanted Michaels to be a process-driven company. In 1997 and 98, he knew he did not have the money to invest in bigger IT initiatives or equipment, but he knew process changes could be a quick and effective way to improve the company.

Rouleau also knew that if the processes were already improved, technology implementations would be much easier. But Michaels was not a process-driven company. There were ways that things were done, but nothing was written down. Things just happened. When you would ask about a process, someone would say, "I think that Jennifer does it best." It was tribal knowledge, and that is just the way it was done on steroids. For example, in 1997, there were 432 stores, and there were 432 different ways that a store would order product.

Michael Rouleau wanted and needed all that to change. It was one way, the best way, the Michaels' way. It was hard to get an organization to understand how changing a process could fix some of its problems. One of the biggest complaints from Michaels' associates was that they did not have enough time to do their job. When asked why not, their answer was, "We are always fixing problems."

I had an update meeting with Michael and explained to him I thought we needed to **"shock the system."** He liked to use that phrase, and I liked to use his words when trying to make a point or move the company forward. I explained the situation and said, "I need to be a little tougher on the ad process team. We are making progress, but there are still many doubters on the team that changing the process will do anything."

Michael asked what I wanted to do. I told him, and he liked my plan. I put it into action at the very next meeting.

We were in the auditorium and getting ready to start the meeting. Instead of going to the whiteboard and documenting the process, I had the overhead screen down. I lowered the lights and put up one slide. It read, "If you have time to fix the issue, did you not have time to do it right the first time?" I did not say anything for about 15 seconds. Then I began the meeting.

I asked, "Does anyone know how long it actually takes an order entry person to enter an order into the system if all the information is complete and accurate?" I paused, then said, "Between 5 and 7 minutes max. You know the top five reasons it takes longer? The buyers never fill out the entire form with accurate information. Then there is a 14 day back and forth process with the order writing team to get the correct information from the buyer." The room was quiet, and I asked, "How long does it take the buyer to fill out the order form if they have all the accurate information? Fifteen minutes. If the buyer fills out the form correctly the first time, we can cut days out of the process and eliminate hours of back-and-forth headaches that waste everybody's time."

You could now hear a pin drop. After a short pause, I started talking again. "We have so many areas in this company that we can improve if we just give the process of improving processes our 100% commitment." They all accepted the challenge. We finished the process and implemented the changes. The productivity began to increase, people realized they were spending less time putting out fires, and the orders were getting into the system faster, so the goods were arriving in the stores more quickly. Win, Win, Win.

The headline from then on was *"Do it right the first time and every time."* **Think about how much time you complain about wasting time resolving issues. What if you took some time to determine why this was happening and changed the process? You will be surprised how efficient you become and how much time you save.** Give process improvement a try!

TRUST BUT VERIFY

The entire Executive Committee was going to conduct their monthly meeting in one of the stores. Michael Rouleau had a few items on the agenda to talk about while walking the floor of the stores. One was an analysis my team did of the case sizes that Michaels should be ordering in the future to improve their in-stock positions.

The primary assumption was that Michaels was spending too much money on inventory carrying costs, and case quantities had to be reduced. The logic was inventory carrying costs outweighed handling costs throughout the supply chain. Amir Hoda and I had worked on this project for months, and we thought that was crazy. Amir had been a supply chain analyst at Wal-Mart and had seen how they had worked with vendors to find the optimal case configuration to improve in-stocks and improve the total cost of the product throughout the entire supply chain.

We were going to do a little Sam Walton copying and show the Michaels' management team their assumptions were wrong. Amir was so talented. He built a merchandise carton cost model from scratch. He looked at inventory carrying cost versus the cost of store handling and distribution center handling, as well as the fixture or peg that the product would be displayed on in the store. The retail lingo is the "planogram location."

When it was complete, you could put any item into the model, and it would give you a recommended case configuration. The roll-up of the numbers showed that store handling and transportation savings matter more than the inventory carrying costs. Even though we had walked Michael and every member of the Executive Committee through the analysis before this presentation, we knew there was dissension in the ranks.

Amir and I were pummeled with questions, and as Amir was answering one, I noticed Michael was not saying a word. In previous Executive Committee meetings, he was usually the first in line to ask questions or critique a presentation. I was beginning to learn more and more each day about how Michael clicked. Something was up, and I wanted to know what. When Amir finished and before anyone else could ask another question, I looked at Michael and said, "You are awfully quiet for such an important topic."

He said, "I wanted the team to have a chance to fire away at you to see how you handled their questions. We will probably get the same questions from the Board and the Street, so I wanted to hear how you would answer. It was a practice session for me to learn my talking points."

Then he made the killer comment, "After you and Amir walked me through the document, I began calling friends who are experts on this material—guys that built the systems and processes at Target and Lowe's. I told them about your analysis, and they said you were spot on, and that when most companies are in trouble with inventory, they make the mistake of looking at carrying costs more than the other higher supply chain costs."

What a great lesson. It was the old Ronald Reagan line, **"Trust but verify."** Michael trusted us, but there were major implications to what we were recommending. He showed great leadership. First, he had a vast contact list of people who could help him when he did not know the answer or needed validation. Second, he showed us just how hard he worked to make sure he was making the right decisions for the company. There was no stone he would leave unturned.

I realized I was still always one step behind him. He had been in business longer than I had been alive, and no matter how much he taught me, he still had hundreds of other things up his sleeve. **When making big decisions, it is always good to get a second opinion or two. Trust but verify needs to become part of your vocabulary. It will help you make better choices.**

<hr/>

DRIVING MISS DAISY AGAIN

We were nearing the end of a project, and I needed to get Rouleau's agreement about the next steps for our continued consulting work with the company, but it was challenging to find time on his schedule to connect. Even though he worked from 7:00 am to 7:00 pm, his calendar was always stacked. I had to see him before the end of the day, but it was Friday afternoon, and Michael was leaving early to go out of town for the weekend.

I was in constant communication with his Executive Assistant, trying to find five minutes. I told her I would eat lunch with him. That was out. Then I said I could talk with him after a meeting we were both in after lunch. She said that was out because he needed to speak with a board member after the meeting and probably would have to leave early. Then she made what she thought was a funny comment.

She said, "If you want to drive him to the airport, you can get 10 minutes of his undivided attention."

Thank you, Haggar! I had a flashback to the many times I had to chauffeur Mr. Haggar and other executives around Dallas during my sales training period. Initially, I thought it was insulting, but when I realized who I was driving around and how much I could learn from them, I immediately changed my mind.

I told Debi, "I'll do it!"

She laughed and said, "I was just kidding. You don't have to do this. It is kind of demeaning."

I told her a brief story about my time at Haggar and told her, "I will do it. Being a chauffeur is just the cost of doing business with a busy CEO like Michael." We both agreed this was our own little stroke of genius. Debi canceled Michael's car service, so it was me, or he would not be going to the airport.

Debi did not even have time to tell Michael until I showed up at his door about five minutes before his car service was due to arrive. Debi knocked on his door and said, "Your driver is here."

He walked out of his door and saw me standing there and said, "Where is my driver?"

"You're looking at him," I said, "I am your driver. I need to talk with you, and I know my way around the airport better than any car service."

He knew he had been set up. As we walked to my car, he asked, "Which one of you thought of this crazy scheme?"

"If you like it, it was my idea. If you hate it, it was Debi's!" We both laughed. I got him to the airport on time, and I got the answer I needed. As he reached for his luggage, he looked at me and said, "You are one tenacious SOB! I like it; keep it up."

The following week when he returned, Debi called and said Michael wanted to talk with me. I entered his office, and he told me to sit down across from his desk. "I really liked what you did last week with the trip, and it showed a drive to never stop pushing to get the job done. That could be a problem ...."

Confused, I said, "How?"

He chuckled and said, "The more you give me, the more I will expect from you. I will keep raising the bar of my expectation for you."

In my mind, I said, *bring it on*. To Michael, I said, "Challenge accepted."

The stars were aligning. All the lessons and experiences in my 38 years on earth were now helping me get closer and closer to my goals. They were like building blocks. I would have never even thought about driving Rouleau to the airport if I had not had such a great experience at Haggar. I knew that I had still so much to learn, and Michael was willing to teach me and expose me to new things. There was more building to do.

At 22, I thought I knew everything. I had a college degree, and I was on top of the world. The reality is I did not know much at all about the world, business, life, leadership, relationships, etc. **Experience is gained only through the trials and tribulations in life. You must experience life to grow. Each lesson builds character. Character leads to knowledge. Knowledge will eventually lead to wisdom.**

IF YOU DON'T KNOW WHERE YOU ARE GOING, ANY ROAD WILL LEAD YOU THERE

It was mid-year 1999, and CSC was just completing three consulting projects with Michaels. We had been working with the retailer for over two years now, and the company was making tremendous progress in transitioning from a money loser to a profitable enterprise. However, they had squeezed every ounce of productivity increases, sales increases, and cost savings they could without making many major investments.

Michael Rouleau's experience told him that if he could focus on improving key processes, instilling discipline and accountability across the organization, provide tough and honest leadership and hold off the board from making unwise and ill-timed investments, he could give the company a rock-solid foundation. His plan had worked. Now what?

Michael and I were in his office discussing the next steps and whether or not it was time to look beyond day-to-day firefighting and begin developing a proper strategic roadmap. He was big on the correct timing of things, and he wanted to know my opinion if the timing was right.

Over the last year, Michael invited me to his monthly Executive Committee meetings and the weekly Sales and Operations meetings. He wanted me to update the attendees on our project status to keep everyone engaged and bought into our work. He also wanted me to sit in those meetings to listen for new opportunities or issues that might need to be addressed.

He challenged a Merchandise Manager (responsible for 3 to 5 buyers) in one meeting, asking if he had a strategy for his merchandise classifications and how he would meet his sales goals. Michael said, "If you don't know where you are going, any road will lead you there. So where are you going?" Fast forward a couple of months, and I was sitting in his office talking about a shift in focus for the company. I sometimes liked to use Michael's words against him, so I took a shot again.

I said, "Michael, if you want to get to the sales and profitability goals in six years, how are you going to get there? If you don't know where you are going, any road will lead you there, so where are you going?" He chuckled. He knew exactly what I was doing. I continued, "Let's get the entire Executive Committee together for a couple of days for a focused discussion on what is next for Michaels. I will facilitate the meeting, and by the end of those two days, we will have a strategic roadmap. You will also get buy-in from your leadership, and we are off to the races, building the next phase of your turnaround."

As always, he told me he would think about it. A couple of days later, he agreed, and he told me Debi was finding a couple of days to schedule the meeting and asked me to put together a draft agenda. I instantly handed him a two-day off-site agenda before he could finish his thought. We held two all-day strategy sessions on May 3-4, 1997. A month later, we held another half-day session. When we were done, we had a three-year roadmap. It included a view into the future of Michaels Stores in 2002. They now knew where they wanted to go.

People and companies often go about their business not really knowing where they want to end up. It is much easier just to live day-to-day. It is hard to sit down and contemplate what you want for dinner tonight, let alone where you want to be five years from now. **Don't wander aimlessly through life. Pick a path, set some goals, take a risk or two, and be willing to course-correct along the way. When you know where you are going, you have a much better chance to actually get there.**

SELF-FULFILLING PROPHECY

To prepare for our upcoming strategy sessions with Michaels, the CSC team met in Cleveland for a two-day workshop. We brought in several consultants who had worked on the Michaels' account over the last several years. We wanted to brainstorm about what our vision for the company should be and how to facilitate the meeting to get the best results for the Michaels Executive Team.

We had every work deliverable for all our projects, including the strategy document we had shown Michael Rouleau about a year and a half ago. We had facts, talent, and all of us had a little skin in the game because we had done work with this client. We all liked everybody we worked with there and wanted Michaels to be successful. We also obviously wanted to continue working with them for the foreseeable future.

For two days, we went at it, and at the end, we came up with our vision for Michaels. It was a five-year roadmap to dominate the Arts & Crafts Industry and become one of the most profitable retailers in the industry. The focus was to become world-class at managing inventory, supply chain and distribution operations, vendor relations, store operations, and merchandise. It would emphasize investments in people, processes, and technology that supported these categories. The overarching theme was to take Michaels from a decentralized to a centrally driven company.

We all agreed we had one problem. How do we get Michaels' executives to see this vision or any vision for that matter? It was not that the Executive Team was not talented, but they had been focused for the last two years on fire fighting. Could they step back and look out three to five years? Steve Biciocchi, my partner, said, "Why don't we write an article that would be written four or five years from now."

It would be a retrospective of how four years ago, Michaels' management team sat in a room and designed the future Michaels. It would focus on these above categories with interviews of each Senior Executive. Steve said, "People are visual, so let's paint them a picture." It was pure genius!

Steve and I worked on that paper for a couple of weeks and received great edits from our brainstorming team. After the first strategy session, our vision and the vision of Michaels Executive Team were only slightly different. Steve and I tweaked the article, and we handed it out the next day as part of the recap notes. The article was dated June 2, 2003, and the headline read:

RETAIL REPORT—Michaels Stores has come to dominate more than just craft sales—they have become the premier definition of a destination stop for their customers. The result? Booming sales and profits.

One of the sentences in the article read, "Finally, in mid-1999, Michaels' executive management team found the time to sit down together and work through the issues they would face."

It hit home. Michael said it was an incredibly clever way to show what the world could look like in 2003. Fast forward to November 25, 2002, *Forbes* magazine published an article about Michaels' success. It was called "Crafty Fellow." The focus of the article was the management of inventory. Our prophetic article was off by six months. We actually implemented things faster than we thought.

BEING A VISIONARY IS ONE THING; IMPLEMENTING THE VISION IS TOTALLY DIFFERENT. CAN YOUR COMPANY SAY THE SAME THING? IS YOUR PERSONAL VISION FOR YOURSELF HAPPENING, OR ARE YOU ALL TALK?

In 1999, CSC and the Michaels' team laid out a vision and the strategic initiatives roadmap. In 2002, the world was recognizing that we had done one hell of a job. Being a visionary is one thing; implementing the vision is totally different. At Michaels, we did both. Can your company say the same thing? Is your personal vision for yourself happening, or are you all talk? Thomas Edison once said, "Vision without execution is hallucination." Enough said.

———•●•———

I HAD EVERYBODY BUT THE I.T. GUYS

In preparation for a two-day work session, I wanted to ensure that I knew where all the Executive Committee members were coming from. This was the first time this team was ever going to do something like this, and I did not want to have any surprises if I could help it. I wanted to know what they liked, what they disliked, their priorities, and where they saw Michaels five years from now.

Many times, in meetings like this, a few people will dominate the talking time. I wanted to avoid that by having notes from each session to help get someone new into the conversation. It was not to set them up, but the group needed to hear from everybody. Otherwise, you would not get the complete buy-in for the plan. Michael needed this plan to be a company strategic plan not based on one person being the loudest or most talkative person in the room.

I was exceedingly confident that I had everybody on board with the session objectives and knew where everybody stood. There were a few that slanted towards self-interest projects, but nothing that would disrupt the ultimate direction. I did, however, have one exception.

It was with the two leaders of the Information Technology group, the CIO and the Vice President of Systems Development. The CIO had joined the company from Shopko in 1997, and the VP had joined from Caldor in 1998. They were both great guys, but they were concerned that the meeting's outcome would be a ton of new I.T. projects that would get dumped in their laps with no resources or business support.

They were concerned that they were getting set up to fail, afraid to become the scapegoat when everything went south. My experience at EDS and CSC had taught me that they were 100% right. The average length of tenure for a CIO is about three years. A recent headline said it best. "The 'C' in CIO stands for 'C' ya later!" I told them that as long as I was associated with Michaels, they had a person who knew it took more than I.T. to implement projects successfully and that I would always support them even if we disagreed on certain subjects.

Sold. In the meeting, the CIO ended up being one of the best people to help lay out the sequence and timing of our initiatives. I even got him to get up and take my marker and start editing my notes on the whiteboard. After I left Michaels, the VP was nice enough to write a message on my LinkedIn page. Below is part of his comments:

"As a consultant, Jeff was deeply knowledgeable in retail and a very skilled consultant. He always brought the right talent and very talented people to each engagement. I found Jeff to be someone with whom you might disagree, but he was always willing to listen and would work to turn things into a win-win situation."

"When he became an employee of Michaels, I worked directly with him in aligning the corporate strategic initiatives with the I.T. short- and long-range plans. Jeff became one of I.T.'s strongest allies when working with Michaels Senior Executives. He would always challenge I.T. to stretch and flex to 'do the right things,' but he would also push back to the Senior Executives when resource constraints prevented I.T. from 'doing the right things right.' Jeff was a good partner."

Those words meant the world to me. **Many companies throw so much crap at the people in the I.T. department, and then they wonder why projects fail. Most executives don't have a clue about what it takes to implement a full I.T. solution successfully. They just want their new I.T. toy yesterday.**

This was a lesson in walking in someone else's shoes. After my experience at Haggar, I always tried to understand where the other person was coming from. **In business and life, take time to understand the other person's situation before forming an opinion. You both will be better off because of it.**

---·●·---

IF THEY GRAB THE MARKER
YOU GOT THEM

As a young consultant at EDS, I prepared to facilitate my first client meeting. My job was to get the client team members to engage in the conversation fully. I needed them to actively participate and give us their ideas, thoughts, likes, and dislikes to use this information to complete our project deliverables.

One of the project managers did a practice session with me. We worked on things like controlling the room, getting everybody to participate, asking open-ended questions that would lead to more conversation, and successfully bringing the meeting to a close, and making people feel like it was worth their time and effort. Not a small task list.

As we practiced, he kept emphasizing the need to get them engaged. He said, "You must bring ideas out of them. We only have them for an hour and a half." When it was over, I was exhausted, but it was great. It was hard to listen to his critiques, but I was learning a lot about this facilitation artform. As we wrapped up our training session, I asked him, "How do you really know you have their attention and that they are genuinely engaged?"

He said, "If they grab the marker, you got them." When they take action to grab a marker and go to the whiteboard and start writing notes or drawing an image, you know they are engaged and want to be part of the solution." The next day I tried it out.

There were a couple of rough spots in the first 15 minutes until I got my sea legs underneath me, and then things started to click. One attendee started explaining something I was trying to write down. I was not getting her point, and I turned to her and handed her the marker. Without hesitation, she got up, grabbed the marker, and finished writing her statement. I had her and the entire room.

Fast forward a few years as I facilitated a strategy session for Michaels' management team. We were using the boardroom, and I had about 10 of those giant Post-It notes easel pads spread around the room. I had two whiteboards on wheels and a big whiteboard in the front of the room. I was not going to miss any comments. The meeting was going great, but I was having a tough time keeping up with the note-taking. At one point, one of the executives put out his hand and said, "Throw me a marker." He got up and started to take notes on one side of the room. Then another executive did the same on the opposite side of the room. Several times, Michael (CEO) would get up and grab a marker and start drawing on the board.

I had them. All of them. They knew what was at stake, and they wanted to be part of the solution, not the roadblock to their success. It was beautiful to watch and be part of. Another technique to get people engaged is to write ideas on Post-it notes and make them get up and place them on easel pads. You can't just talk with them for an entire hour. You will lose them. Once you lose them, it is extremely hard to get them back.

WHEN ALL PARTIES ARE FULLY ENGAGED, YOU WILL GET A MUCH BETTER SOLUTION TO A PROBLEM OR DIRECTION FOR A COMPANY.

Sometimes it is hard to know if someone else is really paying attention or engaged with you. Hand them a marker, and you will make your conversations more meaningful. When all parties are fully engaged, you will get a much better solution to a problem or direction for a company.

HERDING CATS

The day had finally arrived. Twenty-three months earlier, I showed up at the Michaels' corporate offices to meet a team of CSC associates finishing up five months' worth of consulting projects. That was supposed to be the finish, but through a series of unpredictable events, I was about to lead the Executive Committee of Michaels through a two-day strategic planning session.

After two years of hard work, disciplined focus, and CEO Michael Rouleau's leadership, the company had come out of a challenging corporate turnaround with the wind at its back. All the fires that had been put out and all the selling and persuading of employees, customers, investors, vendors, and the board to be patient had paid off. They were ready to look forward into the future and determine the strategic roadmap that would take them to the top of the retail industry.

I had spent weeks preparing for this meeting. I had worked with the CSC team to put together a strategic framework to help lead the discussions. I had met with each executive member on numerous occasions to make sure I understood where they stood on all of the issues we were going to discuss. Most importantly, Michael Rouleau gave this session his 100% support. It was his meeting that I just happened to facilitate. Without his full-throated commitment, this would have been a waste of time. **That is a lesson for all CEOs. Unless the boss is vocally behind a direction the company is going to take, everybody knows that the project initiative will fail.**

Even with all the preparation and Rouleau's backing, I was scared to death. There would be twelve powerful personalities in the room, and I had to try to manage them, the message, the meeting and the time all at once. The last thing I wanted to hear from anyone, especially the boss, was that this was not going well or we were wasting our time, or I have more important things to do.

Fast forward to January 30, 2000. It was Super Bowl Sunday. The St. Louis Rams were playing the Tennessee Titans. During one of the breaks, one of the greatest commercials ever made aired its debut. It started with a young cowboy showing a picture of his great grandfather and telling the audience that his grandfather was the first cat herder in his family. Behind the young cowboy was a horse and on the saddle was a cat. The rest of the commercial showed various pictures of cowboys trying to herd cats like cattle on the prairie. One of my favorite quotes from the commercial is, "Herding cats. Don't let anyone tell you it is easy."

That is precisely what I was going to be doing during this strategy workshop. For the next two days, the Michaels' management team talked, shouted, agreed, disagreed, took both sides of an issue, laughed, joked, actively participated, complained, and applauded. At the end of the second day, I was exhausted, and so were they. I felt just like the guy at the end of the commercial, "When you bring a herd into town and you ain't lost a one of them, there isn't a feeling like it in the world."

More importantly, that is how the boss felt. There was still more work to be done, but 12 talented people with powerful personalities, egos, and individual points of view, came together to set the direction for Michaels for the next three years.

That commercial is a perfect metaphor for what I did in that meeting and what I did for the next eight years working with Michaels. It sums up the job of every business leader, politician, clergy, coach, and parent. **We each have our own personalities, opinions, backgrounds, and experiences. Bringing all those together to get everybody going in one direction can be just like herding cats. Even when you are successful, you still might have a lot of scratches and scars from the effort, but a job well done is worth it.**

A LONE BABOON IS A DEAD BABOON

I was in Mrs. Schafer's eighth-grade reading class, taking part in a discussion about a short story. The topic was baboons. We discussed the author's writing style, areas where the author could have done things differently, and then described the story's ultimate meaning. This was the typical process we went through for all our reading assignments, but this day was more memorable.

When the discussion turned to the story's meaning, Mrs. Schafer went around the room asking students for the answer. One student explained, and Mrs. Schafer's said, "No, that's not it." Another took a shot, and Mrs. Schafer again said, "Not quite," and made a few comments to hone us in on the correct answer. She called on another student. Same response from Mrs. Schafer. A little agitated, she said, "Think more deeply about how the baboons live, eat, play, and protect themselves."

After a short pause, another student raised their hand and said, "A lone baboon is a dead baboon." Mrs. Schafer applauded and, with her somewhat deep and guttural voice, said, "Yes, Yes, Yes—a lone baboon is a dead baboon on the prairie. Baboons must be in their groups to survive. Even though they are fierce animals, they can lose against a larger predator if they are alone. They use their numbers to deter attackers."

Fast forward to Michaels Stores in 1999. The CEO had a mighty presence about him. He had so much experience, had been through so many battles, and had been extraordinarily successful. It was hard to win a discussion or an argument with him on many topics. He also used a special technique—divide and conquer.

If it seemed like a consensus was building against his current thought process, he would try and separate dissenters so that he could go one-on-one with them. It was not a fair fight. It was like Michael Jordan playing a fifth-grader one-on-one. The longer the match would go on, the remaining dissenters would decide to lay down their arms. Discussion over—Rouleau wins.

Michael was correct on many things but not all things. I remembered Mrs. Schafer's short story, and I told everyone who would listen about not being a lone baboon. If there was a topic that the consensus of executives agreed on, I told each of them that we had to stick together like baboons on the prairie. We used this technique during the May 1999 strategy meeting. The consensus was that we needed a strategy that focused directly on improving the capabilities of the vendor base.

The Arts & Crafts Industry at that time was made up predominately of small independent suppliers. Someone had an idea about a craft product, and they began selling it to anyone who would buy it. That was their skill, and they were spectacularly good at it. The problem was they lacked any real infrastructure, technology, or processes to be able to ship to us consistently as Michaels' store count and sales grew. We could do everything right with implementing our initiatives, but if vendors did not improve their non-product development capabilities, Michaels would never reach the playoffs, let alone their Super Bowl.

When this topic came up in the strategy session, Michael began his divide-and-conquer strategy. Nobody backed down. We had facts to underscore the discussion, comments from presidents of the Vendor Community, and one last thing, we were copying someone else's success. We proposed exactly what Target had done eight years earlier when I was selling products to them while I was at Haggar. Michael thought very highly of his former company, and we were copying one of the best company's ideas.

We won the discussion point with Michael, but the company won in the end. Vendor relations became a key go-forward strategy for Michaels and became a case study at the Kellogg School of Business on dealing with your suppliers.

We all have situations where a domineering person seems to push everybody around, especially if you are one-on-one. Build consensus among peers, address the person directly, select the right time, and don't back down. Remember, a lone baboon is a dead baboon on the prairie.

HOVERING

We were fast approaching the second session with Michaels' Executive Team. The first meeting had been successful, and now we were going to meet again to finalize the strategic initiatives and next steps, but I could not get sign-off on some of the presentation materials from some of the executives. Travel schedules, other deadlines, or just running their day-to-day business—I could not connect with them.

I had for a long time used the Management by Walking Around methodology Mr. J.M Haggar told me about in 1986 to talk to different people inside Michaels' organization to get the truth about projects, but I also used a technique called *"Hovering"* to get the information I needed to continue to move my projects forward. As an outside consultant, many times, people do not consider you a priority. They had businesses to run and a new CEO that they did not want to perturb.

Most people would send an email or two and wait for a reply. One might say "Urgent" in the subject line. Others would call and leave a voice message or two or three. Today someone might send a text or Slack message. What did I do? I would "hover."

I would find out where the executive was located in the building, and I would hunt them down. They might be in a meeting in a conference room. I would get to the meeting room about five minutes before it was scheduled to end, and I would hover. I might talk to someone in the area, or I would just hover outside the door. Then when the door opened, I waited for the executive to come out, and I would pounce.

A typical conversation would go like this.

Jeff: "Bryan, I need your answer on the fiscal year sales number."

Bryan: "How the hell did you know I was here?"

Jeff: "I have my sources; now what is that number?"

Bryan: "I have another meeting to go to."

Jeff: "I will walk with you."

Bryan: "Okay, what is the last number I gave you?"

Jeff: "$3.9B."

Bryan: "I think Chris has a slightly different number now."

Jeff: "Can I get the number from Chris?"

Bryan: "Yes, he's running all the models; just work with him."

Jeff: "Thank you very much, have a nice meeting!"

Bryan: "You know you are a big pain in the #$@&%*!"

Jeff: "Yes, I know, but I needed an answer, and it couldn't wait."

I earned a well-deserved reputation for someone who walked around a lot during my time at Michaels. I also had a well-deserved reputation for getting stuff done. Most people send a text, email, or leave a voicemail and then wait for someone to reply. Not me. I had things to get done, just like when I took the CEO to the airport. I needed an answer, and I could not wait for him to get back with me. I went to him.

Hovering was crucial for helping CSC and Michaels complete our consulting projects successfully. It was one of the key tools in my toolbox to move the company forward when I joined as the Head of Strategic Initiatives. **Everyone is busy today. Their inbound messages are overloaded, and it is hard to keep up. If you need something from someone, try hovering. You will likely get your answer much faster.**

———————•●•———————

PUTTING LIPSTICK ON A PIG

Preparation for the final Executive Strategy meeting was getting a little crazy. I wanted to make sure there was no stone left unturned going into the session so we could finalize all agenda items and begin moving forward. Michaels needed to stop talking and start doing. I did not want to be the reason that they could not start implementing their strategy. One of my final prep meetings was with the Information Technology (IT) leadership and a few key members of the inventory management team.

In the previous strategy session a month earlier, the Executive Team agreed that the number one priority was to invest in dramatically improving inventory management across the entire supply chain. On a scale of one to ten, one being absolutely horrid and ten being best in class, Michaels Stores were a two or maybe a three. Michael Rouleau used to say, "The bad thing is we are only a two or a three; the good thing is we have a lot of areas where we can improve."

Wal-Mart was the best in class in the late '90s in managing vendor relations, logistics, distribution, merchandising, inventory planning, and store operations. They had been investing in people, processes, and technology for the past fifteen to twenty years. They left a roadmap if anyone was interested in following it. The challenge was many people that had worked at Michaels for ten to twenty years had never worked for a great company before. They were great people, but they had not seen best practices like at Wal-Mart or Target. Trying to convince them the current Michaels' way was not the best way could sometimes be challenging.

In this prep meeting, we were facing this challenge. The inventory management area used an Excel spreadsheet-based report called

"Could Have Sold (CHS)" to help manage and allocate inventory to each store. Fellow CSC consultant, Amir Hoda, succinctly assessed the problem with this tool. In a quote from that document, "CHS, in its present format, is a viable tool for predicting lost sales but is inadequate for forecasting demand and allocating units."

The IT executives were pushing to find an accurate allocation and replenishment tool instead of having IT put hundreds of hours into the CHS spreadsheet. At the height of the disagreement, Gale Binder, VP of Systems Development, stopped the discussion in its tracks. He said, "If you continue to invest in that spreadsheet, you are just putting lipstick on a pig." Classic!

I had never heard that statement before. I loved it and have since used it thousands of times. The definition I like the best is, "making superficial or cosmetic changes is a futile attempt to disguise the undesirable nature of an item or thing." That is precisely what we would have been doing had we invested all the required time to try and make CHS a better tool. Instead, we decided that though we needed to keep putting a couple more pieces of duct tape on the tool, we would put 99% of our energy into implementing a much better tool.

Sometimes fixing things with a little cosmetic cover here or a superficial change there may seem like the right thing to do. Be careful; you might just be wasting your time. To make real change happen and last, have the courage to change the root cause of why something is not working correctly.

YOU DON'T BUILD A HOUSE ONE ROOM AT A TIME

In our final push for the next big strategy meeting with Michaels' Executive Committee, our discussion centered on building out an IT strategic roadmap that aligned with its strategic roadmap. Michaels put in a point-of-sale system in the stores in late '96 through early '97, and they were working on implementing an Enterprise Resource Planning system called Retek. The question for the group was, what is the next thing to do?

The business leadership was focused on individual applications to solve one issue or another they were having in their areas of responsibility. They wanted a merchandise planning tool, replenishment system, allocation system, new reporting tool, distribution management system, transportation management system, labor management system, improved radio frequency gun system, and many, many more. As I have written, Michaels needed a lot of systems.

But how do you put all of this together? There were so many complimentary yet disparate systems. All the new applications would have to systematically talk to the new Retek system and maybe talk to each other. The business owners were arguing we just needed to select the systems with the biggest impact. The IT folks asserted that they needed that view of the end state or it would be more costly to implement and maintain every year.

I agreed with the IT leadership; they needed a view of the end state for all the IT strategic initiatives. As the facilitator of the meeting, I was struggling to paint that picture. Then the VP of Systems Development saved the day.

He asked simply, *"Would you build a house one room at a time?"* He did not say another word, and it was such a perfectly timed and delivered question that illustrated the image so beautifully no one could argue with that I let the room stay silent for about five seconds. After a brief moment of silence, I looked at the business leaders and asked, "Any thoughts?"

One of the executives spoke up and said, "It is kind of hard to say anything following that." Everyone else agreed. We spent the rest of the meeting discussing the roadmap notes and timeline from the original executive strategy sessions. This consensus was one of the major reasons Michaels was so successful at implementing initiatives and projects. The business and IT planned and executed everything as a team and always looked three to five years down the road.

Do you do things without a plan or vision of where you are going? It is hard for most people to think beyond what is going on today, let alone five years down the road. Billionaire Warren Buffet once said, "An idiot with a plan can beat a genius without a plan." **If you build your life one room at a time, you will have too many disparate and competing things in your life. Take a little time and write down a** longer-term view of where you are headed (i.e., the entire house you are trying to build). You can make modifications along the way but have a blueprint for your future.

———————— •●• ————————

IT IS NOT WHAT YOU START; BUT WHAT YOU SUCCESSFULLY COMPLETE

Another objective of our next strategic planning meeting was to prioritize the many initiatives introduced during our first meeting. Michaels Stores were missing so much that there was not one area that did not need some type of people, process, or technology investment. It was a little overwhelming.

Michaels did have a couple of positive things going for them in 1999. First, they were now in a much better financial position to make key investments. Second, all the executives were focused on the company's major problem—inventory management.

The biggest challenge was balancing how many initiatives and projects the company could handle at one time without distracting the company from running day-to-day operations. CEO Michael Rouleau had a well-deserved reputation for pushing to get more things done faster, but he also knew there was a line you could cross that would create havoc. I also was concerned that the company had not delivered one single major product on time and on budget in the past few years. So, you had a company that needed to fund and implement a lot of initiatives but thus far had not demonstrated the ability to execute initiatives already defined. Quite the dilemma.

In the second strategy meeting, I made sure all the attendees understood this paradox. I mentioned the many experiences I had with EDS and CSC, where even these world-class technology-driven companies struggled when trying to implement too many things at once. Michael then spoke up and helped guide the rest of the meeting.

Rouleau said that he had been part of companies that started a bunch of initiatives and projects and saw the excitement of individual divisions as they began. They would have big kickoff meetings, and then reality hit. The projects were delayed or never completed because they were just too much on the company's plate. Or the worst situation is when a project was implemented that did not work, and they had to go back and fix the problems. He said, "I will always push to get more things done sooner, but our motto must be, *'It is not what you start; it is what you successfully complete.'*" Point made!

It was the perfect statement for this team, and it had to come from the boss. He set the tone for the six or seven years of investments, push for more, but successfully complete every project. **This is a lesson to all future leaders, take ownership of what your company is working on and make sure everyone knows what success means to you. No ambiguity.**

This lesson also applies to individuals. I have friends who like to tell me all the things they are working on. Then I will talk to them a couple of months later, and they are still "working" on the same projects plus a few more. I laugh because nothing is completed.

How many projects do you have going on in your life? Paint the bedroom, redo the backyard garden, lose a few pounds, change the batteries in the smoke alarms, etc. Are any of them successfully completed? How many projects can you realistically complete and still handle all your day-to-day activities? **Just as with companies, it takes leadership to balance the need to get a lot done with the goal of actually finishing something successfully. Prioritize your life, and you might get a few more things checked off your to-do list.**

--- • ● • ---

A HOT DOG AND A NEW CAR

We scheduled a quick half-day meeting with Michael's Executive Committee as a little buffer between the bigger strategy sessions. Most did not relish the idea of having to spend another five to six hours talking about their investments for the next three to five years. A few of them took a couple of shots at yours truly, saying that CSC should have more than enough information to give their recommendations. "Why do we have to sit here for another half day and talk about the same thing?"

At the time, it was becoming apparent that Michael liked the CSC work, and he especially liked what I was doing. He invited me to many of his meetings, and it got around that he was spending a lot of time with me, but that was not the reason for the complaining. They thought putting out the day-to-day fires was more important than talking about what strategic initiative would happen three years into the future.

That is one of the biggest challenges for most Executive Teams. They are all particularly good at day-to-day operations, and they better be. That is their primary focus. It is easier to think about the tasks to be done over the next week or so, than some initiative that could happen in five years. Plus, as of that moment, all their objectives were operationally focused, so there was a financial and career incentive to make sure they hit their numbers.

Michael Rouleau knew this. He had been talking for six months that now that the company was in a better financial position, they had to start looking at the future. He also explained that to do this, the Executive Team would have to handle double duty. He didn't want the team to miss a beat with running day-to-day operations while still spending time on the future of Michaels.

After a few minutes of back and forth, Michael had enough. He said, *"I love my wife dearly, but you know she spends the same amount of time thinking about buying a hot dog as a new car."* He continued, "You can't do that. You have to put more time into things you are going to spend a lot of money on. There has to be more homework and thoughtful discussions. Then and only then can you make a decision."

He then looked at the CFO and asked him, "How much capital expenditures do you have in your five-year financial plan?"

The CFO answered, "About $50 Million per year, including new stores."

Michael looked at everybody and said, "I think that is a lot of money, don't you?" Point made. We continued the meeting after he made us swear we would not tell his wife about this story. (Hopefully, she won't read this!)

His comment also set the precedent that as long as he was CEO, strategic planning and long-range financial planning would have a dedicated time slot on the company meeting list. He also established that the more the price tag goes up, the more research, discussion, and thought are needed to decide.

I know many people who are particularly good when it comes to money matters. I also know people who don't have a clue. **Learning how to manage money is one of the most important things you can do. A good first step is putting more time and research into spending on things that cost more than a hot dog. Your bank account will love you for it.**

———•◉•———

IF YOUR HOUSE WAS UNDER REPAIR, WOULD YOU INVITE PEOPLE TO A PARTY?

I was sitting in Michael's office discussing the upcoming strategy session. He wanted an update on all my prep meetings to determine if there might be any landmines he needed to know about. He did not want to have any surprises. He wanted to take care of any issues before the meeting or address them in the meeting.

I told him there were two concerns he needed to be aware of. One was that some of the executives were voicing concern about the amount of time we were spending on, and I quote, "Strategy Stuff." Michael said, "Don't worry about that one; I will take care of that. What is the other issue?"

I said, "I believe the Marketing, Merchandising, and Store Operations executives will take another shot at getting more dollars for a bigger marketing campaign." He was not happy.

He said, "How many times do I have to tell these people it's not the right time for that?"

I told him I had an idea how he could paint a visual picture that made the point. Once I told him, he said he liked it and would use it in the meeting.

A few days later, as we neared the end of the meeting, three executives asked for a few minutes to raise one more topic. They talked about starting a dedicated marketing campaign to bring more people into the store for about five minutes. They took a slight shot at Michael and me asking, "How will the company pay for all these initiatives that you and Jeff want us to do without more sales?"

When they were finished, it was Michael's turn to do a little preaching. He asked the entire room, "If your house was under repair, would you invite friends over for a party?" He did not wait for an answer but said, "Of course not. Could you imagine the pool has no water, the guest bathroom is not complete, the kitchen still needs appliances, and the lawn is still dirt? That is Michaels Stores today."

"We are under construction. Our merchandise still needs improvement; we still have as many out of stocks as we do in stocks. We still have many managers that are struggling with our new processes. The good thing is we have many customers who have tolerated us for years, and they are willing—thankfully—to stick with us through our repairs. We cannot spend millions of dollars attracting new customers only to disappoint them, and then they won't want to come back. Then it will take ten times the marketing dollars to convince them when we are ready for them to give us a try."

He finished, "It is all about *sequence and timing.* The initiatives we talked about today are the priorities that will repair our house. We will continue to run millions of dollars of circular advertising, but we will not spend any more money on marketing until our house is in order." Everybody in the room got his point. They did not like it, but they understood what the priorities had to be now.

It takes a lot of courage in a turnaround not to spend money on a slick marketing campaign that will only end up putting lipstick on a pig. You need to focus on the things that caused the company to be in this situation in the first place. The plan we put in place was based on a simple fact: if the company could not efficiently and cost-effectively keep up to 1,100 stores in stock, nothing else matters. Michael Rouleau knew that from the first day he walked into a Michaels during his recruitment to join the company. After two years of righting the ship, he was now going to invest in solving his top priority—world-class inventory management.

Abraham Lincoln once said, "It often requires more courage to dare to do right than to fear to do wrong." Have the courage to make the tough decisions in life and don't take the easy way out.

WHY THE HECK IS THE STOCK DROPPING?

There was a high level of excitement in the CSC offices after we got the word that after all the strategy meetings, Michaels was going forward with our multi-project multi-year proposal. We now had to staff the project, get all the project protocols in place, make travel arrangements, get office space at Michaels' headquarters, and so much more.

I also had to get all the project team members from the Michaels' organization. We were starting with six major projects that quickly expanded to about fifteen. It made more sense to add a few smaller tangential projects that we could complete earlier and feed the larger projects. Also, as Michael began to realize how effective my new role as orchestra conductor over all the projects was working, he asked me to manage some of the other company projects as well.

Everything was getting completed on schedule, and it looked like we could hit the ground running a couple of weeks earlier than scheduled. The final piece of the puzzle was the announcement of the multimillion-dollar deal to the world and, more specifically, Wall Street. I had never been a part of something this big before, and I had never had to concern myself with a press release—incredibly important to so many people (shareholders, board members, employees, vendors, and the media). Thankfully, I had the use of CSC's experts to assist me.

Michaels also had their expert, an investor relations person, used to write all their press releases. I thought this would take a couple of hours max. I was wrong. First, we had two different ideas of what was the objective of the release. Michaels wanted just to state the facts. This is what the project is, how much, and the temporary hit to earnings. CSC wanted to add why Michaels was spending this money and the benefits after the project's completion. We were at an impasse.

I asked my experts why they were so adamant about adding the additional language. They said, "We have made hundreds of these announcements for numbers 100 times larger. If you don't tell Wall Street why you are spending this money and when they will see an increased shareholder value, they will not like it." When I explained that to the Michaels' team, they said they had some pushback internally. I never found out from where, but I assumed it was from the board.

After about a week of back-and-forth, Michaels settled on the announcement. We agreed, but it is not what CSC wanted. The announcement went out. It was such a proud moment for CSC, the Michaels' team, and me. Then the stock ticker started to drop. Michaels' stock was falling, and it was because of the announcement. I just became the most hated person at Michaels and with anybody who owned Michaels' stock. I ran down to the CFOs office, and he waved me into his office.

I did not want to say, "I told you so," but all his calls with investors were, "Why are you spending that amount of money, and what are the benefits of the investment?" We quickly worked on a few talking points. There were two main reasons for the $5M project. First, Michaels would recoup the hundreds of millions of dollars in savings over the next several years. Second, it would help them decide how to spend upwards of $250M to $300M in capital over the next five years. Problem solved. The stock price recovered, and we also addressed all concerns with what we were actually doing with the initiative.

What a lesson! **During my early days in consulting, I did not like the words "wordsmithing" or "iteration." As I gained more experience, I realized the power of the written word and that every word matters. A slight change here or a lack of a word there can impact the entire message.** This situation raised the wordsmithing bar so much higher because of its impact on so many people.

The written word has taken a beating over the last ten years or so. Author Edward Bulwer-Lytton wrote, "The pen is mightier than the sword." After this situation, I agree more than ever.

I BECAME AN ORCHESTRA CONDUCTOR

In the fall of 1997, three consultants from CSC presented Michael Rouleau with a strategic roadmap. It was a bold view into the future of the opportunities and challenges for Michaels to reach the goal of being a $6B company by 2005.

It was also a visionary document to show the possibilities for this company. However, Michael was the new CEO, and he had inherited a hornet's nest of problems, and it seemed like more were found every day. His priority was to eliminate as many of the problems as possible to return the company to profitability. It was hard to look more than one day into the future, let alone five years.

It was now 1999, and with Michael's leadership, the company was in an entirely different position. Sales and profits were up as well as employee, board, investor, vendor, and customer confidence. The management team could now set their sights on the future. The person in charge of completing all the initiatives and projects to build that future was ready to begin the most challenging and influential position he had ever had in his career. That person was me.

CSC and Michaels had recently agreed to a $5M multi-year and multi-project engagement. My new role was the Program Manager Office (PMO). My objective was to direct all resources (people and money) and manage all projects and initiatives, delivering each to a successful conclusion. To this day, people will ask me to give a layman's answer to what I did. I always say I was an orchestra conductor (OC). Here are a few duties of an OC vs. a PMO.

- They keep the orchestra or choir in time and together vs. keeping the projects on time and in sync.
- They serve as a messenger for the composer vs. serves as a messenger for the CEO.
- They manage the tempo at which the music is played vs. managing the tempo of each project.
- They keep the ensemble on cue and working together to convey the musical piece as a unified whole vs. managing each project team to work together for the benefits of the entire company.
- They are teachers, ensuring that everyone is taught how their part should sound vs. being a mentor to each project team member on their roles and responsibilities.
- They inspire the group by giving pep talks or using body language to reassure them that they perform well vs. providing motivation and recognition of a job well done.

The PMO reported directly to the CEO. I led a task force made up of six Executive Committee members. The first phase had six concurrent projects, which expanded to about 15 in a couple of weeks. I had close to 100 people (including CSC, Michaels, and outside vendor associates) reporting up to the PMO. Besides running the day-to-day business, there was nothing else more important to the company's success than the successful delivery of all these projects.

At last, I was on the threshold of my goal of helping lead or being a senior leader of a company. Even though I still worked for CSC, I had as much influence as any other Senior Executive at Michaels. I was edging closer and closer to my goals with every passing day.

Success is never a straight line or easy. If you set a clear goal, work hard, and manage your career without ever taking your eye off the ultimate prize, you can achieve it. You must learn to handle the ups and downs and still move forward. If you can, the sky is the limit for you.

> **SUCCESS IS NEVER A STRAIGHT LINE OR EASY. IF YOU SET A CLEAR GOAL, WORK HARD, AND MANAGE YOUR CAREER, WITHOUT EVER TAKING YOUR EYE OFF THE ULTIMATE PRIZE, YOU CAN ACHIEVE IT.**

———— • • • ————

A THIRD, A THIRD, A THIRD

I had the perfect scenario for a consultant. The boss was the project sponsor. Most CEOs would designate this responsibility, not wanting to take the time to get into the details of the individual project work. It also gave them a scapegoat if the project ran into trouble.

That was not Michael. He owned this project just like he owned every other major decision that impacted that company for the last two and a half years. He had waited a long time for his shot at the top job, and he was not going to let a direct report mess anything up. The buck definitely stopped with him, and he loved it. I respected him a great deal for this.

Our discussion did not center around the projects related to improving inventory management; it focused on the softer side of the project—change management, a consulting buzzword that simply meant ensuring the organization successfully handled the changes from new systems and new processes. So many companies fail to see the importance of training and change management. They wonder why a new software system is failing to get the promised results until they are told they forgot a major driver of successful projects.

Michael knew better. He had been part of big projects like this dating back 30 years, and he knew what success looked like. He asked me about my assessment of the organization. I told him, "You had turned the majority of the company into believers since I first showed up a couple of years ago. They have seen the dramatic change in the day-to-day results, and they are totally on board. As it relates to the new projects, I would say we are 1/3, 1/3, and 1/3."

He looked at me and asked, "What the heck does that mean?"

I answered, "Most people here have never been part of something like this. They had seen the day-to-day success, but as you know, this is an entirely different animal. Right now, 1/3 of the people are pushing the sled in our direction, 1/3 are sitting on top of the sled and going along for the ride, and 1/3 are pushing against the sled. They are the Debbie downers and naysayers."

I continued, "In my opinion, you will always have the people who sit on the sled. They have figured out if they don't raise their hands or don't get involved, they can survive anything. We need to try and get some of those pushing against the sled to start pushing with us. The biggest thing is to get most of the people now pushing against the sled to switch their position and start pushing the sled with us. We need to turn people's opinions about these projects like you turned them about day-to-day operations.

"We need to get them involved with the projects, so they are participants and not spectators, and then we can deliver results. Finally, we should reward the people on the project teams for a job well done. Other associates will take notice, and I bet you ten bucks that we will have volunteers for the second phase of work." That is exactly what happened.

Everybody wants to be part of a winning team. Not everybody is willing to step into the arena to help right away, but when they see success and observe people being rewarded for excellent results, they quickly change their point of view. You will never change

everybody. **Some people will always be spectators or doomsayers. Focus on the people you can change and watch your team succeed.**

---••••---

AN OSCAR-WINNING PERFORMANCE

The time between October and December is critical for every retailer. It can make or break you. Every day is critical because customer traffic levels continue to build and are exponentially higher than any other time of year. In 1999, the retail world was still a store-centric business. Foot traffic meant everything.

I was still a full-time consultant for Michaels, and there was not an area of the company that my projects did not touch. To make sure the entire organization stayed up to speed, Michael wanted me to update the organization continually. I was scheduled to update the Monday sales and operations meeting, and I knew on this occasion there was a possibility that they might not have time for my update.

The reason was because the weekend numbers had not been particularly good. The company had made tremendous progress, and the turnaround was picking up steam, but the world of retail has a way of bringing you back down to earth quickly. Due to my role, I was able to see all day-to-day sales numbers, and they were not very good. It was not a big miss, but it was a miss to the sales goal.

I walked the halls to see how everybody was doing. They were combing through report after report to see if they could determine what happened. But their bigger concern was how Michael was going to react to the miss. Michael had the well-deserved reputation of being a tremendously hard taskmaster. In good times he rode the team hard, and when things went south, he rode the organization even harder.

Everybody just knew this was going to be an awful meeting, expecting three hours in hell. I tried to see Michael before the meeting, but his Executive Assistant said he did not want to be bothered. That was not a good sign. Everyone was seated around the big boardroom table, anxiously awaiting Michael to walk in.

A few moments later, he walked in with a cup of coffee in one hand

and a stack of reports in the other. You could cut the tension with a knife. I had grown to know Michael well after working with him for over two years, and I thought he would take the group to task, judging by his mannerisms. He sat down and calmly asked, "How is everybody this morning?" You could hear a pin drop.

He continued, "I know we had a tough weekend. Let's discuss what happened and what we have to do to fix things, so we still have a great quarter and year." As the meeting continued, key areas were identified that needed to adjust for the rest of the holiday season. I watched Michael closely, noting that though engaged, he did not take over the meeting like he was prone to do. When the meeting was over, I followed Michael to his office and asked his Executive Assistant if I could go in. She said yes.

Immediately, Michael asked me how I thought it went. I said, "Great. Your reaction was very unexpected, but I think it accomplished a lot. May I ask why the different tone?"

"I realize the team has been giving me everything they have," he said, "and it just wasn't the day to take them to task even though I wanted to very badly."

"So, you were acting?" I asked.

A STEADY HAND AT THE WHEEL IS NEEDED IN DIFFICULT TIMES, EVEN IF THIS REQUIRES A BIT OF "HOLLYWOOD-STYLE" ACTING TO BE THE CALMING PRESENCE FOR THE PEOPLE YOU LEAD UNTIL THE STORM PASSES.

"Of course! Sometimes leaders need to be the calming influence in a storm. Even if that means acting a little bit," he smiled.

"Well, you should win an Oscar for your performance!" I quipped.

Michaels finished 1999 with twelve straight quarters of sales and profit increases. It was a great lesson in leadership. A steady hand at the wheel is needed in difficult times, even if this requires a bit of "Hollywood-style" acting to be the calming presence for the people you lead until the storm passes.

HE TOLD EVERYBODY HE OWNED IT

The auditorium was packed. There was a buzz of anticipation in the air for what they were about to hear during the kickoff meeting for the big consulting project at Michaels. All of Michaels' Executive Committee, about 70 or so Michaels' associates ranging from managers to Vice Presidents, my entire CSC project team, and our boss, Steve Biciocchi, were all in attendance. The only person missing was the boss, Michael Rouleau.

Michael had joined the company about three years earlier and had done a tremendous job turning around a sinking ship. He had inherited a mess, and through his skill, experience, discipline, and focus had positioned the company to take a huge step forward. After fixing the things that were broken, Michaels was now ready to invest in building the future capabilities that would enable them to become a dominant retailer. This initiative was the first major investment to accomplish that objective.

The door of the auditorium opened and in walked Michael. He proceeded to the front of the room. The lights dimmed just a little, and the screen lit up with the title page of the presentation. Everybody stopped talking, and Michael began. I was about to bring up the first slide, but Michael said to wait; he wanted to make some opening remarks. For the next few minutes, he spoke from the heart with the passion and conviction of a head coach whose team was about ready to take the field for a big game.

He first spoke about what he had inherited three short years ago. He talked about having to beg vendors to keep shipping and lenders not to cut off the funds and the long hours of wondering if they could last another day. He said, "We have fought, kicked, and scratched our way to being a profitable company with a solid financial foundation. Now is the time to build upon that foundation. That is why all of you are here today."

He surveyed the room and continued, "Management and I have signed an agreement with CSC to help us begin to build our future. We cannot do this ourselves, and most of you have worked on one or more of the projects CSC has done for us in the past. This one, however, is different. It is bigger, more complicated, more expensive, and broader in scope than anything this company has ever done." He paused for emphasis and leaned in, saying, "I need everyone in this room to understand that this is my project. I own it. The person ultimately responsible for its success is me, and that is why Jeff will report directly to me."

He waved for me to join him on stage and said, "I know you all know Jeff. He has been working with us for a long time. I want you to know that Jeff is the most tenacious, persistent, hardworking, results-oriented SOB I have ever met. That is why he is the perfect man to lead this effort. He has my total support. I need all of you now to give me even more than you have given me already. I know you will."

What a project introduction! Michael did something I had never experienced with any of my previous consulting projects—a message from the top that this project was important to him. This was his company, and it was going to rise or fall because of his directions on the important initiatives. He could not have set the table better.

Many leaders delegate things because if something goes wrong, they have someone to blame. **True leadership is taking ownership and leading by example. Sometimes that means getting a little dirty, but I believe it shows the organization that the leader is part of the team, not just someone in the corner office. Lead by example, and you will see how positively people will respond.**

———— • ● • ————

THE POWER OF PERSUASION

I was sitting at the head of a table in a conference room of Michaels Stores about to conduct the first Supply Chain Task Force meeting as part of Phase I of the consulting engagement. The organization chart had all projects and personnel reporting to my role as head of the PMO (Program Manage Office), reporting directly to the CEO. During this first phase, there were about 100 people from CSC and Michaels reporting to the PMO at the peak. That included six members of the Michaels' Executive Team that comprised the Supply Chain Task Force.

Here was the dilemma. All the associates, including the Executive Committee members, reported to the PMO, but they did not report to me—a clear line of delineation. The six Executive Committee members reported to the CEO. He reviewed them, managed them, and could fire them. All the other Michaels' associates working on the projects reported to their Managers, Directors, VP, SVP, or EVP at the company. Their management had the same managerial responsibility for them as the CEO had for the Executive Team.

I was running the most important initiative the company had outside of running the day-to-day business, but without the power to review or fire them. So, how could I get everyone from an IT manager to the company's Chief Operating Officer to listen and respond to me as if I were their manager when they knew I had no direct authority over them? The answer, "The Power of Persuasion."

Even though the CEO had told everybody at the engagement kickoff meeting that I was in charge and had his full support, I could not run around the office saying, "The CEO said to listen to me." That would have lasted about two minutes, tops. I had to earn their respect myself, and that is just what I did.

Over the previous two-and-a-half years, I worked with them on projects and gained a reputation of integrity, honesty, and no BS. They knew I was results-driven, and I had handpicked most of them not only because they were the best for the job, but also because we had developed a great working relationship. I knew what made them tick, and they knew what made me tick—and also what ticked me off!

I was known for letting other people get credit for the results of previous projects and for taking a few incoming arrows if needed to protect an individual. Taking one for the team can build immeasurable respect and rapport. I also had the gift of gab. If necessary, I can sell milk to a dairy farmer. **Part of persuading people is the ability to tell a story or paint a picture of *why* they need to do more, change their attitude, accept a change in direction or be a better teammate.**

The power of persuasion is more important than having the power to review or fire. **In my book, fear is not a great management technique. It is better to persuade than rule with a hammer. Leading with integrity, honesty, being results-driven, no BS, giving others credit, protecting people when needed, having mutual respect, building rapport with a little bit of salesmanship are much better tools than intimidation and anxiety. You get better, longer-lasting results.**

GET TO THE ROOT CAUSE

The Vender Development team, heading up one of the most important projects at the time, was having a heated discussion. I had been given an update that they were having a few problems agreeing on the initial direction, and the CSC lead asked me to sit in on the meeting to see if I could help resolve the situation.

Michaels' Vendor Community was incredibly creative at its core. These companies dreamed up the next new craft item, the next new project, or the next new product that would make the crafter's life a little easier. On a scale of one to ten, they were a ten in product development and had a great understanding of the arts and crafter.

Michaels entire initiative focus was to build a supply chain and inventory management infrastructure and supporting processes to rival that of the best retailers and the best companies around. That meant our vendors would have to begin to follow significantly higher standards for product quality, product packaging, carton packaging, carton labeling, and much more. The problem was 98% of the vendors, on a scale of one to ten, were about a three when it came to meeting these new standards.

We had to get to the bottom of why that was so, which is what caused the disagreement in the meeting. The buyers in the room thought that fining the vendor would cause them to comply with the new standards. The distribution people in the room wanted the buyers to find different vendors. The inventory management people in the room wanted to change every carton quantity to manage inventory better, which would help the vendors ship better.

After listening to this go on, I asked a simple question, "What is the root cause for why the vendors can't or won't comply with our standards?" Everyone had an opinion, but none were even close to the root cause. I asked again, and this time, I led the witness. "Can you show me the document, email, or memo that specifically told vendors what they had to do?" You could hear a pin drop. Maximizing the effect, I said, "I'll wait if you need to go to your desk and get a copy to share with the team." Crickets. No takers.

"So, how can the vendors comply with Michaels' requirements when you have never given them any to follow?" You could see the lights go on. "That is the root cause of the problem. Not fines or the buyers picking different vendors, this team has to put together a vendor manual and tell them what you expect from them."

We rarely get to the root cause of an issue. We keep fixing symptoms without addressing the real reason for the pain. Like a back issue caused by weak hamstrings or a toothache caused by problems with a sinus infection, or fatigue caused by dehydration. **Why do you think duct tape is so valuable? It is an easy fix, but most times, it doesn't even come close to solving the root cause of the problem. Before you spend hours, days, or years trying to resolve an issue, take the time to find that root cause and make the issue go away permanently.**

•————•●•————•

ARE YOU REALLY WORTH $1.1M A YEAR?

It was 7:00 pm, and I was sitting outside of Michael Rouleau's office. I needed him to sign invoices for the consulting engagement I was leading for CSC. We were billing hours against six different projects for each phase of the initiative, and each one had a separate invoice, along with an invoice for my role as PMO.

I enjoyed so many conversations with Michael, but this was not going to be one of them. Suppose you measured Michael on a scale of one to ten, with one being "spend money like it grows on trees" and ten being "Scrooge," Michael was a 25! A couple of years back, Michael told me a story about how he had negotiated getting haircuts with his barber to save about $50 bucks a year. I was about to hand him invoices that totaled somewhere close to $400,000.

Then I heard him call me, "Jeff, I am ready for you." As I walked into his office, he looked at me and said, "No small talk. I know why you are here, and I don't want you to soften me up with some of your stories just so I will sign away all of the company's money without looking at each invoice." We had worked together long enough to know each other very well. I knew most of his secrets tricks, and he knew most of mine. I laughed at his statement and handed him the invoices.

As he paged through them, I could tell his mind was going a hundred miles an hour to try and find the right words to give me a shot for how expensive we were and how I better be getting everything out of the CSC team. Then he got the last page. My invoice. He turned around and grabbed a calculator, and started punching in some numbers. I didn't know where he was going with this action.

He wrote down a couple of numbers and then grabbed what looked like one of the original documents about project costs we showed him when we pitched the project. After what seemed like an hour, he looked up and said, "Are you really worth $1.1M a year?"

I said, "Actually, sir, that is for the entire project, not just one year."

That is not the answer he wanted.

I did not really have an answer for him, so I stalled, trying to think of something to say. Then it came to me. "Sir, I promise I will give you an answer *after* you sign the invoices!"

He laughed and said, "I can't wait to hear this answer." He signed the invoices, and we walked outside his office to the copy machine. As he hit the button to make a copy, he said, "Alright, smart guy, what is your answer?"

I said, "I must be worth it—you just signed the invoices!"

I won't write exactly what his reply was, but we had a nice laugh. Then I told him, "I could tell you that I am worth it because I honestly believe no one has as much knowledge as I do about this company, the strategy, and the current projects. If I walked out the door, you would lose valuable time and have to get two or three people to replace me. So, then yes, I am worth it. But honestly, it is hard to fathom that I am billing you at $350 an hour. All I can do is continue to give you everything I have and make sure every CSC person does the same. Then I believe at the end of all this; you can tell me that we more than delivered value to Michaels."

He liked both answers.

What are you really worth? We all struggle with that. It took me two-and-a-half years to earn the value I believed I was bringing to Michaels. **Make yourself indispensable and outwork everybody else, and your value within your company will continue to rise. If you feel your current situation does not recognize what you believe is your value, test the marketplace. You may find another organization that will**

value you and your skills more. If you find no takers, get back to work and keep building your skill level and value!

———————•●•———————

NEED TO WATCH HOW THE CAKE IS BEING MADE

We were well underway on our huge consulting engagement with Michaels. Part of my role as PMO was to immediately address any issues or risks to the successful delivery of the project. When you are running 15 concurrent projects, you have to worry about a delay in one project that could negatively impact the others.

Every project was interdependent on the others. Not one could be done in a vacuum; they had to work in concert with each other. Nowhere was this more evident than in the Information Technology (IT) area. All had a current or future impact on the hardware architecture, database architecture, or the systems application roadmap.

The IT leadership was adamant that they be well represented on each project team. That is exactly what we did. The manager in charge of store systems was a member of the Store Transformation team. The director of merchandise systems was a member of the Merchandise & Inventory Management Transformation team, and so on.

Everything seemed to be going fine until I got a call from Gale Binder (VP of Systems Development). He said, "Houston, we have a problem, and it needs to be addressed immediately." In 30 minutes, I had Gale, the CIO, and a few other IT managers in my office. Gale had the floor and started to describe a gaping hole in our plans.

Gale said they were discussing all of the projects in their weekly update to the CIO, and each person was describing what was happening with their projects and the impact it could or would have on their group. The problem arose when the managers tried to explain what was going on in the project team meeting to their IT team. Even though they all took good notes, they could not capture more than just the essence of the meeting.

The programmers and the system architecture associates had 100 questions of each manager because they were not in the meeting. Gail said, *"It is like the difference between seeing how the cake is made compared to just buying the finished cake.* We believe we need to have more IT people in the kitchen at this critical stage of the project. We need to be in that room to hear the conversations to get an understanding of how to better and more efficiently scope our work so we can successfully complete all the projects."

So, we began to invite the broader IT group to the project team meetings. By being in the room, they understood what was expected and, more importantly, why a new application or modification was needed. They could not complain about the "damn" businesspeople making unrealistic requests or moan that the business doesn't have a clue about what it takes to do an IT Project. They became part of the discussion and the solution. They had skin in the game.

It was one of the main reasons we successfully implemented all the systems-related projects over the next six years. We had the entire organization from the CEO on down involved every step of the way. We did not allow a spectator to point fingers; everybody was part of the game plan and playing the game.

WHEN MAKING A BIG DECISION THAT IMPACTS MANY, MAKE SURE EVERYONE HAS AN "APRON" ON AND IS ACTIVELY INVOLVED IN DISCUSSING THE INGREDIENTS NEEDED TO "BAKE" THE FINAL OUTCOME. WHEN EVERYONE IS PART OF THE DECISION-MAKING PROCESS, THERE IS BUY-IN, AND YOU WILL GET MUCH BETTER RESULTS.

I remember a friend describing how he got his entire family involved with a decision to move to another city. He had received a new job offer but wanted this to be a family decision, not just by his wife and himself. The decision had a great impact on the entire family, and he wanted them to be "in the kitchen" as the decision was being made. When making a big decision that impacts many, make sure everyone has an "apron" on and is actively involved in discussing the ingredients needed to "bake" the final outcome. When everyone is part of the decision-making process, there is buy-in, and you will get much better results.

WE GRADE EVERY PLAYER AND COACH ON EVERY PLAY

It was Monday afternoon, and the new head coach of my beloved Green Bay Packers was taking part in a weekly press conference. The Packers had won the day before, but the coach did not seem happy. After a couple of opening questions, one reporter asked him why he seemed so grumpy after winning yesterday.

The coach responded, "If you saw what I saw on the tape review of the game, you would not be happy either. As you know, we grade every player and coach on every play, and that includes me. We had way too many missed assignments. I counted 13 missed tackles, and on the one touchdown play, both the quarterback and the wide receiver made errors. Yes, we won, but if we don't clean up these mistakes, we will be in big trouble in future games."

He finished by saying, "We have to be extremely critical of ourselves. We cannot accept just getting by. We need to critique everything we do and take it to the practice field, and then it better show up on the field on Sundays." That is the same attitude Michael brought to his new job in 1996. He joined Michaels when they were a money-losing mess. One of his keys to success was leaving no stone unturned to find some way to improve the company.

At the beginning of the turnaround, it was difficult to do anything other than survive to fight another day. After the organization solidified the foundation, Michael wanted the entire team to be much more critical of everything they did. To do that, he had a process he called "Correction of Errors (COE)." I was not fond of the name, but it was his process for studying the Monday morning game film.

It was one of the first processes he had me help put in place, and I believe it was in the top five more critical processes we ever implemented at Michaels. The premise was after every major event in the company; you had to have correction of errors or lessons learned process. We built a COE process for each ad campaign, planogram set, new store opening, vendor conference, board meeting, budget process, quarterly financial meetings, systems launch, new distribution center opening, benefits enrollment process, etc. Everything was critiqued.

Just like the Packers, we graded every player and every coach. That included the CEO himself. It was very painful for the participants, but it allowed you to see the opportunities that you left on the table. Unlike a football team with another game to play the next week, some of the processes in retail, like Christmas, happen only once a year. If you did not correct your mistakes, you could blow two holiday selling seasons. If that happens, you better update your resume.

Does your company have a COE or post-game film grading process? If not, why not? How about you? Do you critique yourself on decisions you made or did not make, friends you keep or walk away from, your diet or exercise routine, or the way you spend money?

The only way to get better and grow is to have an honest process that can critique and correct mistakes. If done well, incremental improvements can add up to dramatic results.

IN A NEW YORK MINUTE

It was coming close to his three-year anniversary, and Michael and I were having an update meeting on all the projects I was managing. We had made outstanding progress on all projects, and we were beginning to see some dollar savings and a few early signs of efficiency and productivity gains from all the process work we were doing.

The day-to-day business was also continuing to get better. The days of fighting the daily fires in the early stages of the turnaround were over. Things were beginning to look up for the company and its leader. I asked him, "How close was the company to having to file for Chapter 11?"

Michael answered, "It was touch and go for a while. I don't miss those days."

"Can you now definitely see a light at the end of the tunnel?"

His response was classic Michael. "I do, but I just hope it is not a train! The moment you get complacent in this business, it will tear your heart out. The foundation at Michaels is still solidifying, and we have a long way to go to finish all of the projects you are working on. We still have three or four years of heavy lifting to do.

"I cannot and will not let this company get complacent. How many retailers have closed or gone out of business because they did not see Wal-Mart coming? How many did not think the country folks from Bentonville could ever affect their business? They were lazy and forgot they still had work to do to stay competitive, and now they are all looking for jobs. Some of them have called me looking for jobs here!"

It was a great lesson. It is hard to become a great company and even harder to stay there. Here is a fascinating statistic. According to the American Enterprise Institute, only 12.2% of the Fortune 500 companies in 1955 were still on the list 59 years later in 2014, and almost 88% of the companies from 1955 have either gone bankrupt, merged, or still existed but have fallen from the top Fortune 500 companies (ranked by total revenues).

In Don Henley's song, *New York Minute,* there is a line that says, "One day they're here, next day they're gone." The song is about how quickly and drastically life can change. Michael often said he wanted to *make* history, not *be* history. He was going to continue to push for excellence and not let up for a moment. For Michaels to reach its full potential, there was no time to rest on their laurels. You can never get too high or too low in the retail business because it will humble you in a *New York Minute.*

Business is like life. Just when you think everything is going great, something happens. Don't ever get complacent or think the good times will always be here for you. I think the last line of the song says it best: "Everything can change, In a New York Minute."

PUT THEIR HEAD IN A SHELL LIKE A TURTLE

Everyone was seated in the auditorium of Michaels, and we were ready to go, about to kick off the planogram process project. We had about 25 people on the team, comprised of a couple of CSC consultants and Michaels' associates representing just about every discipline in the company.

The planogram process was arguably the most important process in the company. It determined what products made it to the shelves in every store, affected every area of the company, and included all merchandise vendors for Michaels.

If you did it right, your sales should go up. If you did it wrong, you might be looking for a new job. It was critical that this team come together to fix this broken process. Because of its importance, I spent more time on this project than any other project that reported to me. I had spent the last two years consulting for Michaels, so I knew where all the skeletons were.

Many in the room had been on previous projects with me, but I had some new individuals on this team. I gave an opening statement and then fielded questions before diving into the process improvement effort. There were questions about the time commitment, their role, and how we would know when we were done. Then someone hit me with a showstopper. "Can I really be honest in this room? I am concerned if I say something controversial that Rouleau will hear about it."

I knew exactly why she was asking the question. Michael had done a fabulous job leading the company from the abyss over the last several years. He did it with a tough, no-holds-barred, focused, and disciplined approach. He had earned the respect of the Board, Wall Street, and the employees. He did, however, have a well-deserved reputation for taking people to task if he thought they had done something wrong. If you were in his crosshairs, it was not a pleasant experience.

I completely understood her concern but also the importance of everybody being open and honest in these discussions. In 1999 we did not use the term safe space, but that is what I told them these meetings were. I said, "That is the reason I have most of the meetings on the other end of the office complex from Rouleau's office." Within a few seconds after I said that, who walks in the door? Michael Rouleau.

Instantly everyone in the room shrugged their shoulders, and it literally looked like they all put their heads in their shells like a turtle trying to protect themselves. Michael's entrance into the room was innocent, but the reaction from the team was telling. After Michael left the room, I told the group what I saw them do. Some laughed, and others just nodded their heads. We talked it out, and the team proceeded over the next six months to complete the project successfully.

When you manage from a position of fear and intimidation, people will clam up to protect themselves. It is no different than in nature when an animal senses danger. The first order of business is survival.

Using intimidation may seem like the right way to get results, and some may say the means justify the ends. As a leader, you have to have every tool in your tool kit: compassion, respect, kindness, perseverance, focus, and gratitude with an appropriate amount of toughness and discipline.

———————— • ● • ————————

WE HAVE ONLY COMPANY INITIATIVES

We were several months into the engagement, and all our projects were doing quite well, with each team was hitting all of their major milestones. I consistently updated Michael Rouleau on each project's progress. It was tremendous to have this access to the boss because if I needed an answer that only he could give, he was always available.

During one of our updates, I told him about a concern I heard about from all the projects. As an example, I was in discussion with one of the teams investigating all of the requirements to enable Michaels to replenish each stores' inventory automatically. At that time, each store ordered its own products, but one of the key strategies was implementing a sophisticated program that would run from the corporate headquarters instead.

There were hundreds of requirements, but one of my issues was the language used during the discussions. One person would say, "Well, that is an IT project." Another would say, "No, that is a Store Operations project." Yet another would say, "That is a project for Finance."

Before I could finish another word, Michael said, "I will take care of this in the next update meeting."

When we assembled a week later, Michael led off the meeting. "At the start of this initiative, I told all of you that I owned the success of this endeavor. The biggest reason for that is I wanted everybody to understand that this is driven by me and the entire management team. We do not have IT projects, Store Operation projects, or Supply Chain Projects. We have Company initiatives and Company projects.

"For example, when you call it an IT project, you are establishing that if something goes wrong, you can blame IT. We are better than that. It is all for one and one for all. No finger-pointing. No excuses. I am holding every single one of you, the management team, and myself responsible for each and every current project and future project. We don't have time for the blame game; we only have time to do it right and do it right fast."

Just as his comment a couple of months earlier that he owned the entire CSC initiative had set the tone, this directive that he was holding everyone accountable for the success of every project, including himself, adjusted the culture. I had been on too many project teams in the past that struggled because of constant infighting and finger-pointing between divisions. It would have been great if those bosses had cut it off at the pass before it started to fester.

As a leader, you need to ensure that everyone is on the same page. It starts with clearly communicating your expectations of everyone in the organization, including yourself. You need to emphasize this: we will rise and fall together. It is the team working as a unit that will propel them to greatness. No going solo or looking for scapegoats. All for one and one for all!

CAT'S IN THE CRADLE

It was late summer of 2000, and our consulting engagement was coming to an end. After about 16 months of effort, CSC and Michaels had successfully completed approximately 20 projects. As the PMO, I was not only responsible for the successful completion of each project but also for the transition of all the information and recommendations to the Michaels' team.

As the teams were finishing the final deliverables, I sat back and realized three of the best years of my career were coming to an end. I had been working with Michaels since 1997, and this experience had been fantastic for many reasons.

The most important of which is that I got to work with the CEO daily. We had developed a great relationship, and he had taught me so much over the last three years. Because he exposed me to so much during our time together, I felt even more of an obligation to doing everything I could to help his company. Besides this wonderful relationship, there was another reason this account was special. It was located 20 miles from my house.

It is exceedingly rare for a consultant to have a local client. The job description lays out pretty clearly that you will travel at least 95% of the time. So this gig with Michaels was a gift from God—I did not have to travel every week to get to this account. It was especially satisfying because my son Zachary was born in 1997, and I was there for those special early years of a child's life.

Now I had a dilemma. I loved my work at Michaels, but the engagement would be ending soon. I loved working for CSC, and they had just promoted me to Principal a little more than a year ago, so they thought highly of me as well. I loved consulting, but I knew if I continued, I would have to begin traveling again. If I traveled all the time, I had to leave my beautiful wife and young son for extended periods.

I did not know what to do. I prayed a lot and talked to my wife, Lisa, but the answer was pretty simple. All I had to do was watch Lisa and Zachary play together, and I realized I needed to find a job that would not force me to travel too much.

When I was twenty-two, my priority was me. All my decisions were based on how things would impact me and my career. Many conversations would start with "I want this" or "I think I should do that." Things were now dramatically different. I wanted to be with my wife and son as much as my career would allow.

In 1974, Harry Chapin released a song called *Cat's in the Cradle*. It describes a father too busy with work to play with his son. Two lines capture why I wanted off the road.

"But there were planes to catch and bills to pay ... He learned to walk while I was away."

There is a point in everyone's life where you transition from what is important to me to what is important to us. Some still choose their career, money, titles, and fame over family. Survey what is most important to you, but I suggest putting a lot more weight on not missing all of those priceless memories. You won't regret it.

MOVE THE COMPANY FARTHER AND FASTER OR I WILL FIRE YOU

was sitting in the office of CFO, Bryan DeCordova, and we were discussing what I was going to do after the current consulting projects with Michaels ended. "I will definitely get assigned to another client somewhere in the world, but I am actively looking for a job to keep me off the road," I said.

"Are you serious about leaving the consulting business?" he asked.

I nodded, "I love what I do, but I do not want to be away from my wife and three-year-old son."

"Have you discussed this with the management at CSC?"

"I have had a few discussions with my boss, Steve Biciocchi, about staying off the road. He understood and told me it is the number one reason people leave consulting. All he could do was try and get me clients as close to Dallas as possible, but there were no guarantees," I answered.

Then Bryan asked me the million-dollar question. "Have you ever thought about coming to work for Michaels full time?"

"Of course, I have! I spent the last three years of my life here. I love all the people here. Michael has taught me so much, and I think I have accomplished a lot for the company. Plus, all the plans are in place, and things are ready to take off like a rocket ship. However, there are two problems. First, as an outside consultant, I have been given a lot of latitude to push this organization without fear of getting fired. I would lose that autonomy if I joined the company. Second, we have an ironclad non-compete clause in our contract. It could get very ugly if we even tried."

Bryan asked, "If we can overcome those two obstacles would you come to work here?"

Without taking a breath, I said, "Absolutely."

I cannot explain what happened behind the scenes, but Bryan and I met a week later, and he told me both my issues could be worked out. "First," he said, "you need to talk with your boss at CSC and let him know your desire to join Michaels."

So, I left his office and immediately called Steve Biciocchi, who was not surprised by my call. He asked me if I had talked with Rouleau, and I said, "I have not because of the non-compete clause. I felt like I needed your approval first." It took Steve a couple of days to work things through with all the powers that be at CSC, but they agreed to waive the non-compete clause.

Now I needed to talk with Michael. In all of the three years I had been working with him, I had never been that nervous. I sensed he felt the same way. We talked about my desire to get off the road and how this would be a perfect place for me to land. He said that he had invested a lot of time and money in me, and he liked the idea that it was not going to go out the door when the projects ended.

Then he solidified the deal. "If you join the company, it will be for one reason only. You will move this company farther and faster because you are here, or I will fire you. I will give you the cover of my office so you can remain an independent voice of what we need to do. You will not lose your autonomy. I need you to do exactly what you have been doing for the last three years. Can you do that?"

I did not say a word. I got up off my chair reached out my hand to Michael. He stood up and reached his hand to mine, and we shook. "Welcome to Michaels," he said.

On September 11, 2000, I started working for Michaels as a full-time employee. It was yet another gift from God. I could now check one of my major goals off of the list. At 39, I was now one of the Executive Committee members of a major corporation reporting directly to the CEO.

Nothing in life is easy. What is easy is to give up on your dreams when times get tough, or when things don't go your way. If you really want something, fight like hell for it. Don't quit! Don't ever quit! Believe in yourself and believe in God's plan for you. Someday it can come true.

IT IS EASY TO GIVE UP ON YOUR DREAMS WHEN TIMES GET TOUGH, OR THINGS DON'T GO YOUR WAY. FIGHT LIKE HELL FOR WHAT YOU WANT, AND DON'T QUIT! BELIEVE IN YOURSELF AND GOD'S PLAN FOR YOU, AND SOMEDAY IT CAN COME TRUE.

I HAD PREPARED MY ENTIRE CAREER FOR THIS

I was in Michael's office finalizing all the contractual details of joining Michaels. After working as a consultant for the company for the last three years, I became its latest employee. It was not just any position but a position I had dreamed about for most of my career. At 24, I had set the goal to be a CEO or an executive that helped run a company. On this day I was 39, and I was about to do just that.

I became the newest member of the Executive Committee, reporting directly to the CEO. Michael asked me, "How does it feel being a retailer again?"

"I started my career in retail," I answered.

"You know I only know you from your work here; what is your background?"

I laughed and said, "I am glad you asked me that *after* we signed all the paperwork!"

I told him my journey in detail, from Gimbels to Haggar to my entrepreneurial struggles. My transition into technology and consulting working for EDS and CSC. And finally, my time at Michaels, where I was part of rebuilding every major process in the company from the ground up. "I orchestrated 25 projects that are the building blocks to your future," I told him, "and I have been exposed to the Ph.D. School of Michael Rouleau."

Michael said, "I never knew 75% of that. You had to have exposure to almost every area of the company before you ever got here. Now it makes sense why you were able to get so much done."

"I have prepared my entire career for this opportunity. Every decision—good or bad—was made to become an executive someday and help determine a company's future.

There was one other thing I wanted to tell Michael but didn't for fear it might have been a little arrogant. I honestly believe that my diverse background was perfect for the role I was taking at Michaels. I had chosen a different path from other executives. For example, the EVP of Store Operations at Michaels was a 30-year veteran working in the stores, and the CFO spent most of his career in the finance area.

I spent my entire career learning how an entire company operates and how every part of the company must work in concert together to be successful. I could have a detailed conversation with every role in the company and not miss a beat. I was right where I was supposed to be, working for a man who knew how to use my talents.

The best way to describe it was that we were a match made in heaven. God had brought us together at this time to work together. For the next six years, our relationship grew, and so did the sales and profitability of Michaels. It was, without a doubt, the most successful years of my career and the most successful run by any company I ever worked for.

When I tell people my story about how I ended up working at Michaels, some will comment that I must live under a lucky star. I vehemently disagree. **To have great things happen, you have to be willing to take risks, bust your butt, make mistakes, build relationships, and show you can succeed. You can't just sit in your house hoping that things will break your way. If you want to succeed and reach your dreams, roll up your sleeves and get to work.**

BECOMING THE
RIGHT-HAND MAN OF A CEO

made it. I was part of the Executive Team for Michaels Stores. Now, what do I do? My focus had always been very narrow throughout my entire career, limited to the departments I managed at Gimbels, my sales territory at Haggar, and my clients at EDS and CSC. Now I had to think about how my decisions and work ethic could impact millions of customers, thousands of employees, hundreds of vendors, Wall Street, and the Board of Directors—and I relished the challenge.

This was the pinnacle of my career (to date) and yielded some of my most fulfilling and rewarding memories. These stories discuss my journey as the right-hand man of the CEO, the realities of how to change an entire organization and its culture, how you set the strategic direction, determine company priorities, build a company into a retail powerhouse, and create a lasting legacy.

OFFICE OF THE CEO

The EVP of Real Estate had been with Michaels a long time and helped grow the company from 87 stores to over 900 by the time he left the company. He was a really smart guy, but also known as a real smart @$%!. He came into my office with my hiring announcement in his hand and asked, "How the hell did you convince Michael to give you such a crazy title?"

My title was Head of Strategic Planning and Initiatives, Office of the CEO. I reached into one of my file cabinets and pulled out a Harvard Business Review article and said, "The answer is all there."

The title of the article is "The Office of Strategy Management." The two Harvard Business School professors who wrote it did years of research on why there is such a disconnect between strategy, initiative execution and performance. They used a Bain Consulting study that said 90% of 1,854 global companies failed to achieve profitable growth. Here are a few highlights:

- Most organizations do not have a strategy execution process.
- Many organizations have strategic plans but no coherent approach to managing the execution of the projects.
- Many organizations do not have a consistent way even to describe their strategy, other than in a larger strategic binder.
- 60% of typical organizations do not link their strategic priorities to their budget.
- 66% of HR and IT organizations develop strategic plans that are not linked to their strategy.
- 95% of employees in most organizations do not understand their organization's strategy.

Here is a quote from an article written about their white paper by Martha Lagace in 2006.

"An Office of Strategy Management (OSM) is typically a new unit at the corporate level of an organization, overseeing all strategy-related activities—from formulation to execution. It is not intended to perform all of this work, but to facilitate the process so that strategy execution gets accomplished in an integrated fashion across the organization.

Typically, a strategic planning unit has little or no influence over the process of executing the strategy it helped to create. In our view, one unit should facilitate both strategy formulation and execution process, making an enhanced strategic planning unit a natural home for the OSM."

I told the head of real estate, "Michael just paid about $7M to my old company, and all the knowledge is either in those 25 binders over there or in my head. As the Program Manager, I was responsible for developing the strategy and the corresponding initiatives roadmap. The only way to get all of the initiatives implemented was to have an independent role, just like the professors described. It could not just report to the CEO on an organization chart as the professors suggested; I recommended the role actually be driven from the CEO's office. The bottom line is Michael wants all of the initiatives successfully implemented, hence the title and my role in getting all of it done."

Michael's latitude in agreeing with this title and role complimented his willingness to think outside the box. His sole desire was to get all these initiatives in place. I was his man to do it. A recent *Forbes* article says, "The success rate of strategy execution is incredibly low." The same problems exist today that existed 20 years ago. **Strategies and ideas only matter if they can be successfully implemented. As a leader, if you can't execute the idea, get someone who can. Give them the power to execute and watch your ideas and strategies become a reality.**

YOU DON'T REALIZE THE POWER YOU HAVE

It was one of my first meetings as the new Head of Strategy for Michaels, and I ran it as I had the last three years as a consultant. I sent the agenda out a week in advance and talked directly to all on the schedule about what I expected from them during the meeting. Because this was a reoccurring meeting, I also attached meeting notes and a checklist of to-dos.

I have never liked sitting at the head of the table. When consulting, it didn't feel appropriate. As Head of Strategy, I preferred more of a "Knights of the Round Table" approach to foster collaboration than communicating a hierarchy based on who sat where. I wasn't going to let a new title change me, so when someone commented about my choice of chair, I said, "I'll leave that seat open if another Executive Committee member comes in, but I like my seat just fine."

Although this group had been meeting for months, something was different. Instead of freewheeling and open conversations, there was a hesitancy to speak up. They seemed to wait for me to say something before they would speak up. It was like I was a different person. When we finished the meeting, I asked Mary Kuniski to stay behind.

Mary had been with the company a long time and was one of Michaels' most valuable people. Since joining the company, she had played many roles and was critical on many of the consulting projects I led. Mary now reported directly to me in my new position, and she headed up the new Vendor Relations Team. I asked her if she noticed anything different about today's meeting. She said, "Absolutely."

"What the heck is going on?" I asked.

"You are no longer a consultant," she replied, "and even though Michael gave you a lot of power when you were outside, I don't believe you realize the power you now have."

I cocked my head to the side and, with genuine curiosity, asked, "What does that mean?"

"The title of Office of the CEO carries more weight than I think you can ever imagine. The bottom line is now they believe that if something goes wrong, you have the power to get them fired. Your words mean 1,000 times more as an employee than when you were a consultant. They trusted you as a consultant; they are figuring you out as Head of Strategy. You need not be cautious with what you say because that is not your style. You just need to understand the impact of your words is magnified now."

I was grateful and said, "I appreciate your feedback. Do you mind if I ask why you feel you can be so open with me?"

She smiled and said, "Jeff, I know you better than most because of all the time we have spent together. I know that you will listen and take advice to heart."

"Your perspective is valuable; what are your thoughts about how I can get over this hurdle?" I asked.

"Just tell them during the next meeting from your heart that nothing has changed," she offered, "and that you will spend every day proving it to them."

This advice proved to be some of the best I had ever been given. It took me a couple of weeks for all the Michaels' team members to realize that my new title did not change me.

My dad always told me never to forget where I came from. I try every day to remember that. I have seen many people change dramatically when they get a new title or role. The taste of power can be intoxicating. The more you get, the more you want. **No matter what promotions you receive or positions of power you attain, remember what it was like when you were subordinate, and the person in authority over you was a jerk. Be different. Treat people the same as you want to be treated, no matter how high up the ranks you go.**

CHALLENGING THE NEW GUY

During my transition from consultant to employee, I was concerned I would lose my autonomy to speak freely. Michael Rouleau committed to me that he wanted nothing to change. He expected me to be the same honest and blunt person who had been helping him for three years, but my challenge was how other Executive Committee (EC) members would respond to me as their newest member.

We were discussing a five-year timeline calendar to track every initiative and the corresponding sequence and timing. The document had been circulating for a month, and I had spoken with every Executive Committee member before the meeting. I thought this should just be a sign-off, and we could move on to the next agenda item. But one of the EC members threw a wrench into the situation.

Basically, he said that he did not sign off on the timeline, and we needed to have more conversations offline. I was hot. He was lying, and I knew it. He knew it too, but what should I do? As he was speaking, a thousand things went through my head. *Do I call him on it? If I do, will Michael believe me? Would he back down if I called him out in front of the team? If I don't, what the hell am I doing here? If I say nothing, will it get around that I am a pushover since joining the company?*

I had to stand my ground, so I called him on his statement. "Michael, the truth is this person has agreed with everything on the timeline, and I have an email to prove it." The room was electric with the shock that I broke protocol or decorum rules, but I did not care. I knew Michael did not hire me to be another passive employee that just went along with the status quo.

Michael said, "You know you are challenging his integrity?"

"He is challenging mine as well," I said. After an awkward pause, Michael asked for the email. I pulled it out, and as I was handing it to Michael, the person admitted that he had, in fact, agreed. A little discussion about how we got our signals crossed followed, and after things got smoothed out, we finished the meeting. We all decided, "no harm, no foul."

As the meeting concluded, Michael asked me to come to his office and said, "You know you took a hell of a chance in there, but I am glad you did. They are all going to challenge you, Jeff. You are the new guy. They don't really like the role I gave you, and they think you have too much power. They want to see if you have the right stuff. You cannot back down. If you do, they will smell blood in the water, and you will not be effective. If that happens, you will have the shortest career ever at Michaels."

Players on a football team will challenge a new coach. Employees will challenge a new manager. A baseball team will challenge their new high-priced free agent, and members of the Executive Committee will challenge the new person in the room. In all these scenarios, they want to see if you have what it takes. Can you hold your own, or will you be a pushover? If there is even the slightest sense of weakness, it will be a long climb back out of that hole. **When you are the new person, show them you know your stuff and that you belong. Stand your ground. Gain their respect, and you will be on your way to a successful start to your new position.**

A LITTLE BIRD TOLD ME

Shortly after joining the team at Michaels, I talked with Larry Fine, the EVP of merchandising. Larry had been with the company since 1996 and had been an integral player in helping with the successful delivery of many of the consulting projects I had worked on during that period. We had developed an exceptionally good relationship over the years, and we could talk about almost any topic knowing that the conversation would never leave that room.

He quizzed me about how I thought things would change now that I was an employee and not a consultant. He asked me if I was concerned about losing the autonomy to say almost anything, knowing I still had a job with my consulting firm if it wasn't well received.

I told him, "At some level, that will always be a concern, but I am going to continue to do what I always have done. If the CEO continues to let me be me, then all is fine with the world. However, if that changes in the slightest, I will move on to something else."

He then asked me the million-dollar question, "Jeff, how the heck do you always know something about seemingly every issue we have in the company? It's like you have eyes and ears everywhere, like when you knew the stores were not following the new ordering guidelines. No one else on the Executive Committee, including the boss, knew that was going on. You not only knew, but you had a ton of facts to back it up. How do you do that?"

I laughed and told him that was my little secret. He kept pushing, asking me to answer his question, "Seriously, it is uncanny how much you know!"

I lowered my voice and said, "I'll tell you if you promise not to tell anyone else." He nodded his head in agreement, so I leaned in and said, "Little birdies tell me things," and we both laughed. "Seriously, though, since I showed up here in 1997, I have built a network of friends and confidants across the organization. It started out with people who worked on my projects and then expanded when my reputation for listening in confidence to whatever a person wanted to tell me grew across the organization. They could trust me."

"In addition," I continued, "and unbeknownst to our CEO, probably 80% of what I heard we have addressed as a company. I also have a good reputation for fixing the issues that people raise to me. Sometimes I address it immediately, and for others, I would lay seeds in the minds of the Executive Team, and in due time, the seeds bloom, and someone else notices that the issue has to be addressed. It works amazingly well."

Larry chuckled and said, "Here I thought you were some kind of a wizard; I didn't know you had a network of spies!"

"Spies?" I laughed, "No, not spies—I like the term birdies *much* better!"

"How long have you been doing this?"

I thought for a moment and answered, "Well, I first started in 1985 after the 93-year-old founder of Haggar told me that is how he learned secrets about what was really happening in his company. Mr. Haggar was concerned that the executives and managers were not telling him the truth, so he would walk around the company and ask the employees on the front lines. I thought, if it worked for him, I figure it can work for me too."

It is such a simple thing, but many managers and executives seem to forget what it was like when they were working their way up the ladder. **People want you to listen to their concerns. You can't chase every issue raised, but if you gain the reputation of someone who listens, it is amazing what you can find out. The more you learn, the more you can benefit the company. Get up from behind your desk, and walk around the office—you might learn a thing or two!**

———————— • ● • ————————

TEACH THEM HOW TO FISH

Before I joined Michaels, my consulting team helped document all the major operational processes for the company. This enabled Michaels to gain much needed efficiency and find real dollar savings, which helped pay for our entire consulting project. When I joined the company, my focus turned to documenting and improving all processes.

Just like he feared when we began work in 1997 on the operational processes, Michael Rouleau knew the processes were not written down, only one person really knew how things worked, and they were inherently broken. He was right on all three accounts.

I no longer had my consulting team with me to document what turned out to be hundreds of processes in every functional area of the company. My challenge was getting all these completed and in a timely fashion, so I turned about 25 Michaels associates into junior consultants. In a little over a year, they documented every process in the company, including the budget process, board meeting process, health benefits provider selection process, finance end of month closing process, store manager hiring process, etc.

Someone in our Human Resource department specialized in building training material, so I worked with them to create a training document focusing on these four topics:

- Why this was important.
- The definition of process management.
- A how-to guide using a tool to document the process.
- Guidelines for how to improve processes once documented.

Training all of these individuals increased our talent concerning how to initially document and then continually improve our processes, so I was no longer the only person who knew how to do this. As the old saying goes, **"You can hand them a fish, and they will eat for a day. Teach them to fish; they will eat for life."** We taught them to fish. This provided a wealth of talent and leadership to spread the gospel of process management throughout the company.

For the next seven years that I worked at Michaels, it was my responsibility to continually improve every process, but I had a tremendous team to help me with this role. It is incalculable how much money, time, and effort this endeavor saved Michaels. It was not flashy; in fact, it can be boring, tedious work, but necessary to help a company run efficiently and effectively.

In the short term, teaching a person *how* to do things takes longer than just doing it yourself. In the long run, it helps expand the knowledge base and abilities of everyone. I challenge you to add mentoring and coaching to your to-do list. The end results are so fulfilling.

WE COULD NOT WASTE
THAT MUCH TIME

The new countdown calendar for the planogram process was complete in early February 2001. After about six months of effort, the Michaels' team of associates had developed this new process for more efficiently resetting merchandise space in every store. For example, the company wanted to redo a 25-foot section that sold craft paint. The countdown calendar had approximately 200 tasks starting with analyzing the proposed changes, the costs/benefits of the changes, buyers working with vendors on the exciting new product, placing orders, receiving product in the stores, and then the store personnel resetting the space.

This new process was built to eliminate many problems with the old method, such as having more than 25% out of stocks of the new items when the reset took place. Think about that, you spend upwards of nine months on a reset, and then you have 25% of the fixture with no inventory. It is hard to make your sales numbers with no stock, and it just looks horrible to customers who knew we were changing the space so they would get excited about the new product additions, only to find empty pegs or shelves everywhere.

The second major problem was that missing inventory caused the stores to waste millions of payroll dollars, continually going back to the new planogram to adjust due to the out-of-stock units. We wanted them to get all planogram materials upfront and go to this space once to reset, returning only to restock the shelves because of all the sales we received from the new merchandise.

We had one major problem with the new process. It was completed in the middle of the current planogram reset period. In retail, you would reset your stores from late January to late July. Then the stores would turn their attention to all the seasonal merchandise that would be arriving for the fall and holiday selling period. As you entered the most important time of the year for any retailer, you would have great new planograms in spring and summer and exciting new seasonal merchandise in the fall and for the holidays. The goal was to increase sales and profits with all the new merchandise.

Every team member was concerned we would have a major mess on our hands if we started the process now. I told them I understood their concerns, but if we did not begin immediately, we would not be able to learn where adjustments were needed for over a year from now during the 2002 planogram season. We could not waste that much time. We had to start now, learn, make mistakes, adjust, take notes, and redo the process at the end of this season. The 2002 season would be dramatically better. If we waited, we would not know our issues until 2003. That was unacceptable.

We took the new planogram process, and wherever a new reset was on the calendar, we started using the new process. For example, if we were four weeks from the stores' reset date, the team started using the calendar at week four. If it was 12 weeks from the stores' reset date, the team started using the calendar at week 12. If it was 24 weeks from the stores' reset date, the team started using the calendar at week 24. It worked perfectly.

It actually worked better than if we would have started from the beginning. Because we threw so many resets at the process at once, we found where 90% of the holes were. It also gave us a view of how to react to different merchandise categories. For example, some of our categories had a significant amount of imported merchandise. We needed to adjust those areas to give them more time to order their product so we could receive it on time for the reset.

The bottom line is we saved a year by doing it this way. Over the first 18 months of joining Michaels, we documented every process in the company. They all used this implementation technique, even for those done only once a year, like the budget process. If we did not follow this same implementation strategy, we would have to wait a year for results. The CEO was not a patient man, and neither was his new Head of Strategic Planning and Initiatives, and our motto was, "Progress, not perfection." Using this implementing-when-ready technique, we made a ton of progress. We had no time to waste, and we did not waste a second.

Documenting and continually improving processes is vital for long-term, repeatable success. The sooner you analyze, implement, and adjust your processes instead of always chasing the shiny new object, the sooner you will begin to see positive results.

WHAT'S THE PROBLEM?

In the 2011 movie *Moneyball*, Brad Pitt plays a General Manager for the Oakland A's baseball team. In one scene, he discusses how to replace three star players who just left the organization. He is sitting around the table with several 25-year veteran player scouts, who explain to Pitt's character why one player is better than the other. After a short discussion, Pitt's character asked a simple question, "What's the problem we are trying to solve?"

The scouts list off a variety of things they think are the problem. Pitt's character gets increasingly frustrated because they aren't even close to the answer. The problem was that the team had one of the lowest payrolls in baseball and could not afford any of the players being discussed. They had to focus on that problem—how to get the right players for what they could afford—to solve how to be a winning team. Hence the name *Moneyball*.

Michaels was in the same situation when their new CEO showed up in 1996. At the time, Michaels had about 450 stores with sales of around $1.3B but were losing money like crazy. Michael Rouleau told me stories about conversations he would have with vendors, the board, executives, relatives, Wall Street, and even some of his friends about what he should focus on first.

It was exactly the same scenario from the movie. Some would say he needed to spend money on marketing. Others would say they needed to remodel all of their stores. Still, others would say they needed a new branding campaign and a new logo. Michael's response was always the same. "That is not our problem. The problem is we are horrible at managing inventory throughout the entire supply chain. If we can't fix that, then a new logo or a newly remodeled store would be a huge waste of time and precious resources." He was 110% correct.

Michaels has a very unusual inventory situation. Each store carried approximately 35,000 everyday items (in retail, these are called SKUs or stock keeping units). They also carry another 5,000 to 10,000 seasonal SKUs like pumpkins for Halloween. Each SKU needs to be in stock every day in every store because a crafter needs an average of six different SKUs to complete a project. For example, they may need felt, scissors, glue, glitter, paint, and a paintbrush. If any one of those items is out of stock, you could miss an entire sale.

Inventory was the number one problem he had to solve, or the next CEO would be hired in a blink of an eye. It takes experience, knowledge, and courage to identify the real problem facing a troubled organization. Many new CEOs only got a couple of layers deep when digging for the issues. Michael dug down 25 layers before he hit the answer. Once he did, he was laser-focused on fixing this issue.

As we solidified the top multi-year strategies, five of the six focused on dramatically improving inventory management. When we had implemented all the initiatives that supported these strategies, no one in the retail industry could manage inventory like Michaels. If you analyze the company's financial success from 1996 to 2006, it all centers on Michael identifying the real problem that faced the company. No matter how much he was pushed, he never lost sight or shifted his focus from his target.

If you are working for a company that is challenged or even one that is having some success, do you ever wonder if management is discussing the right problem(s)? Do they seem to make knee-jerk decisions, investments, or seemingly shift strategies every year? **To succeed in life, career, or as a leader of an organization, you must be willing and able to identify "What's the Real Problem?" so you can properly focus your attention, energy, and resources on fixing it.**

WE DID NOT WANT TO WIN AN AWARD

In 1998 two colleagues at CSC and I put together a strategic framework for our client, Michaels. As part of my research for this project, I wanted to learn about how other companies built strategic plans. I read hundreds of articles, white papers, and press releases from various companies in a variety of different industries. The first articles I read were when the new strategies were announced to great fanfare by the company, industry insiders, and Wall Street investors.

I then researched the individual strategies to see if there were common themes. Most were very slick documents often produced by the biggest and most expensive consulting firms in the business. McKinsey, Bain Consulting, and Boston Consulting Group, just to name a few.

Then I fast-forwarded a few years to see how successful the companies were at implementing the strategic plan. The results were extremely poor. In my opinion, the bottom line was that most of these documents were meant more to win awards and praise when they were announced rather than executable strategies that would actually improve top and bottom-line performance.

Two years later, Michaels asked me to lead the effort, and along with their management team, put together a five-year strategic plan. When I originally talked with the CEO, we used the term "operational strategy." We wanted to make sure we could operationalize and successfully implement the strategies. At his core, Michael Rouleau was one of the best retail operators in the country. He thrived on execution, and that is exactly the strategic plan that we built.

The main goals were simple:

- Centralize all inventory management functions back to the corporate office to free the store personnel to have more time to spend with customers.

- Implement a framework to inform, educate, and interact with our vendors so they could be able to support our future growth.

- Implement a distribution network and supply chain strategy that focused on servicing the store and dramatically reduce costs.

- Implement new, efficient store routines, so the store personnel had more time to spend with customers.

- When these objectives were met, we could then develop the next generation store and enhance our marketing efforts.

Pretty boring, right? Who cares? Everyone in the organization understood the goals. All our investment in people, process, and technology over the next five years focused on these five simple strategies. As we gained more efficiency, our costs went down, in-stock levels went up, and our sales and profits increased. Then in 2004, we were able to shift to a new strategic direction. It was called the "Pursuit of the Perfect Store," which entailed developing a new store prototype and new marketing and branding efforts—just like we had planned in 2000.

None of my strategic documents would ever win an award. I did not care. I did not want to become a statistic for the next consultant who researched how many company strategies fail. **If more companies focused on executing their strategic plans instead of producing slick binders that eventually just collect dust on a shelf, we would see more successful turnarounds and more profitable companies.**

———————•●•———————

CONCRETE, MERCURY, OR EVER-MOLDABLE CLAY?

It was early 2001, and I was having an update meeting with my new boss. One of the topics was our strategic plan. He was concerned about how we would continue the process going forward. He wanted to get an example of our strategic planning philosophy, so if anyone asked him, he had an easy answer. I replied that our philosophy is quite simple. I break down strategic plans into three distinct categories:

- *The Concrete Strategy* – In this strategy, as the plan is being developed, it can be maneuvered around as you can do with concrete. Concrete has a liquid-like form that can be pushed and pulled within the framework's boundaries that hold the liquid in place. Once the plan is settled, just like concrete, you let it dry, and then it becomes rock solid. The problem is that it is impossible to adjust once it dries. Management is saying this is what we are going to do, period. It is fixed like stone regardless of what is happening around us.

- *Mercury Strategy* – In this strategy, the management continually adjusts based on the next shiny object that comes their way. They are constantly chasing this elusive substance in hopes that they will someday be able to capture it. Their strategy is constantly changing, and the organization is whiplashed back and forth. It also allows management to be a little slippery and hard to nail down exactly where the company is going, just like mercury.

- *Ever-Moldable Clay* – In this strategy, management does all the necessary homework and sets its strategic roadmap. It has form and substance after the first interaction of the process. Then management continually reevaluates all aspects of the environment to see if you need to change the shape of the strategy. The strategy can be remolded with a tweak here or a push of the finger there. At its core, the strategic direction has the same foundation formed originally but can be reshaped. If you decided to blow up the strategy completely, you just get a different piece of clay.

I told Michael our strategy would be the "Ever Moldable Clay." Then I handed him a strategic and financial planning countdown calendar. The CFO and I had built the calendar to consider all the operational processes, the budget process, the new capital committee process, the annual review process, the wage and benefits process, and the new headcount priority process. I told him that all the calendars were now integrated with dates; they would either feed the strategic planning process or get an output from the process.

As part of the strategic planning process, I would continue to analyze the competitive and industry landscape, work with the merchandise and marketing leadership to understand where they saw the consumer trends, coordinate with real estate on any changes or challenges, understand any regulatory or legal issues and coordinate with finance to identify any issues that could impact attaining those goals. I would be looking three to five years into the future compared with the day-to-day operators focused on hitting all the numbers for this fiscal year.

MAKE SURE YOUR STRATEGIC DIRECTION IS NOT SET IN CONCRETE OR AS ELUSIVE AS MERCURY. INSTEAD, MAKE SURE IT IS LIKE A MOLDABLE PIECE OF CLAY, WHICH HAS FORM AND SUBSTANCE BUT CAN BE ADJUSTED IN A CHANGING ENVIRONMENT.

We used this process from 2000 to 2005. We raised sales from $1.9B to $3.6B, store count from 559 to 889, and net income from $62.3M to $219.5M. We were not going to be one of the thousands of companies that never achieved positive financial results from their strategic plans.

To become a powerhouse in your industry, make sure your strategic direction is not set in concrete or as elusive as mercury. Instead, make sure it is like a moldable piece of clay, which has form and substance but can be adjusted in a changing environment.

I DON'T KNOW, THAT IS UP TO ALL OF YOU

It really was beautiful. To build something like this in an Excel spreadsheet was quite an achievement in 1999. You could change a few key inputs, hit the enter button, and out would come an updated version of the plan. You had to applaud the effort to build something like this without a dedicated software tool. What was it? It was the Michaels' five-year strategic financial plan.

The CFO and his team had built this model to run what-if scenarios to see the impact on sales, earnings, net income, stock prices, and more. Inputs included things like the number of stores, comparable store sales increases, capital expenditures, corresponding depreciation schedules, and general selling and administrative expenses. If you wanted to see the impact of opening 50 stores compared to 75, you would just input that into the model, and you could see the effect.

It was not a line-by-line budget tool; it was measured at the 30,000-foot level. When I was a consultant just beginning a project with Michaels to develop a strategic plan, the CFO wanted to show the management team how the model worked. He had three or four scenarios based on certain assumptions, and then he had the corresponding financial outlooks.

Of course, all the scenarios had everything going up that was supposed to go up and everything going down that was supposed to go down. The outputs were tantalizingly impressive. Sales were off the charts, earning per share set records, and best of all, for every member of management, the stock price quadrupled. It was the heyday for management to have a significant portion of their compensation in stock options. Every single one of them had some type of stock option spreadsheet that they could enter a number and see the impact on their net worth.

As impressive as the model was, I had one big issue and raised it during this meeting. I asked the CFO how he planned on Michaels achieving those fantastic results. He said, "I don't know; that is up to all of you to figure out." I realized it was just a spreadsheet exercise.

Many strategic planning organizations report to the CFO. They do research and run models like crazy that can include the current business operations, mergers and acquisitions, or even the sale of the existing company. The outputs are hugely impressive, but the models many times are not connected to the rest of the organization regarding how to get those results. It is like they are built in a vacuum. At Michaels, we were different.

After this meeting, I talked with the CFO and said, "The next time you show that model, we will have the action item plan on how to actually achieve those results." He and I became locked at the hip. As we developed the strategic roadmap and the initiative timelines, he would then take those facts and adjust his model accordingly. If we were planning a new distribution center in two years, he could enter all the upfront capital expenditure, potential savings, and then ongoing expenses once the building became operational.

In 2005, two Harvard professors' research showed that "most organizations do not have a strategy execution process, and many organizations have strategic plans, but no coherent approach to manage the executions of the plans." This is also the major problem when companies hire strategy consulting firms. Are the strategies executable?

In my strategic planning experience, there was one main reason why strategic plans fail. The absolute disconnects between a three to five-year financial plan to any realistic way to deliver on those results. At Michaels, the strategic plan, the five-year financial plan, the strategic initiatives plan, and the day-to-day operations were synchronized together as one cohesive unit. They were not separate or competing processes. Can your company say the same thing? If not, why not?

YOU DO REMEMBER HOW WE ARE GOING TO PAY FOR ALL YOUR STUFF, DON'T YOU?

Everything was really coming together with the strategic planning process. We were making progress on all fronts. The multi-year strategies were complete, and we had assigned an Executive Committee member to be the captain for each strategy. We were making progress on developing a financial process to vet each initiative from a cost and benefits standpoint. And finally, we were creating a more enhanced process for assigning and tracking IT resources.

I really could not believe how things were aligning so quickly. I was excited to give an update to CEO Michael Rouleau. As always, I sent him a copy of the things I would like to discuss a couple of days before our meeting. And also, as always, he would have a topic or two that trumped my list.

He was standing at his whiteboard with a marker in his hand and told me to sit down on a chair in front of him. He did not look mad, but he also did not look happy. I was getting surprisingly good at reading his body language, but as he stared off into space for a moment, I just could not get an idea of what was wrong. Then with one question from him, I knew exactly what was bothering him.

He said, "You do remember how we are going to pay for all of your stuff, don't you?" I knew him well enough to know that he did not want an answer. He wanted to preach a little, so I just kept quiet and listened. "I really like the progress you have made on getting everything moving like lightning with the strategic planning process. You have done a fine job, maybe too fine. We cannot forget how we not only pay the day-to-day bills but also how we are going to pay for all these initiatives.

"We cannot be so distracted that we forget we can get better at everything we do without one nickel of investment. You and I need to come up with a way to define and track all the day-to-day priorities. Then you need to make one of your fancy consulting slides (that was a shot, but I moved out of the way, and it just grazed me a little) to show the team."

"I could not agree more," I said, "What do you have in mind?"

We brainstormed for a while, and then he said, "What the day-to-day priorities are doing is enabling us to invest in our future." A new name was birthed.

We called these priorities "enablers." They focused on three areas: Sales & Gross Margin, Store Expenses, and DC Inventory/Expenses." We listed about 30 enablers and a captain for each on his whiteboard. They included store workload scheduling, fixing broken stores, improving ad performance, corporate employee retention and training, and improving store in-stocks.

We graded each one and set a goal to achieve by the end of 2001. The challenge to each captain was to make improvements with no new investments or no new headcount. You needed to improve each enabler by focus, discipline, communications, and process improvement. The analogy I made is we were a football team that was not going to get a new player; we just had to get better at the basics of blocking and tackling. The focus on the enablers was a tremendous success. Every one of the enabler's grades improved every year without one nickel of investment other than the time of the captain and their teams.

What the enablers also clarified is what was important to the boss. In the fall of 2000, it was crystal clear what his day-to-day tactical priorities and strategic priorities were. The enablers were discussed in every Monday sales and operations meeting, and the strategies were discussed in every monthly Executive Committee meeting. Michael was famous for saying, "What gets measured get done." He kept showing the company how simple but powerful that statement was.

What does your company's management think is important? To succeed, make sure everyone in the company is crystal clear on the day-to-day and strategic priorities.

WE WERE ROWING IN CIRCLES

We seemed to be making progress on all fronts. We had identified about a dozen strategic initiatives and developed a list of thirty day-to-day tactical enablers. The enablers focused on continually improving the day-to-day operations. The strategic initiatives were investments to enhance our longer-term operational capabilities dramatically. We had put together a strategic and financial planning process and an associated meeting structure that aligned the entire organization, but I still felt something was missing.

I could not put my finger on it. Then I had an update meeting with my boss. He asked me a couple of questions about how my objectives aligned with those of the other Executive Committee members. As I was trying to explain why there might be a gap, the lights went off in my head with the brightness of 1,000 suns. "I have no idea of progress on the other executive's objectives because the process is done completely in a vacuum. Every process in this company is cross-functional except this one."

He sat back and thought about it for a moment, then handed me a couple of the other executives' objectives. As I read them, it became even more clear this could be a major missing link. One who was supposed to be working with me to help improve our Vendor Community relations did not have one sentence written concerning this strategic initiative. Another executive's entire organization was key to the successful implementation of perpetual inventory processes, and he only had one or two lines about our most important strategic initiative, and there were a few statements in direct contrast to each other!

It was like each executive was working for their goals, not the company goals. "Michael," I said, "This is like we are all in a rowboat and rowing in a circle. We have to get everybody rowing in the same direction."

Without hesitation, he said, "I guess you have a new process to develop," and he gave me copies of all the current year's executive's objectives and told me to put something together for our next meeting. "Let's make sure we have the new process in place for next year's objectives."

I built a spreadsheet highlighting each executive's objectives and the percentage they put on the importance of each. I inserted what I believed was missing from everyone's objectives—and it was significant. Putting on my strategic planning hat, I built a spreadsheet of what I thought the next fiscal year's objectives should be for each executive. It took me a couple of hours, and when I was done, I walked it back to Michael's office.

He loved it! That spreadsheet and a few tweaks to our company calendar became the foundation of how the executive objective process ran until I left the company. Michael and I would determine the high-level objectives for everyone; then, they would fill in the details. We spent hours making sure we were all aligned down to the period on a sentence. Then these objectives cascaded down through everyone's organization. It was a thing of beauty.

Is your organization rowing in a circle or entirely in sync with each motion speeding you across the lake? There is no better way to get everyone in the boat rowing in the same direction than to make sure it will impact their potential performance review and future wage increases and bonuses. It is a twist on what gets measured gets done. **When designed properly, incentive programs can increase performance and drive organizational success. They can shape people's behavior by highlighting what's important to an organization and providing positive reinforcement to those who actually make the organization successful—the people on the front lines.**

FOLLOW THE YELLOW BRICK ROAD

Michaels was set to rock and roll in early 2001, after being on the edge of bankruptcy three and a half years earlier. The company had solidified its financial position, and sales were rising, as was the store count. During that time, Michael had hired me to lead the effort with my consulting firm to build a solid foundation of efficiency through process improvement. Michaels was now ready to take the next step—begin making $250 million of investment over the next five years.

Michael had preached for years that his company was 25 years behind modern retail in managing inventory at a world-class level. He kept saying that we would have to make up five years every year for us to catch up. Most of the people in the organization thought he was nuts. Many were long-time Michaels' employees, so they had never been exposed to what great was or how to get there.

Just like Dorothy in the *Wizard of Oz* followed the yellow brick road to happiness and her dreams, Michael was going to follow the yellow brick road paved by the best companies in the business—Wal-Mart, Target, Home Depot, Lowe's, OfficeMax, etc. All had spent the last quarter-century building their capabilities in managing inventory, store standards, supply chain, and supplier relations. They had spent hundreds of millions of dollars and countless hours and years of blood, sweat, and tears to become great at everything we were about to invest in. It was Sam Walton's version of copying, but we were going to copy them.

Michaels had some advantages with this "Yellow Brick Road" strategy. One, CEO Michael Rouleau had worked for Target and Lowe's, and he ran an office supply company he eventually sold to OfficeMax. He had been through all of this before. Another advantage was that Rouleau had a person with experience in his one weak spot—vendor relations. I spent seven years at the Haggar Apparel company dealing with all the supplier requirements that companies like Target and Wal- Mart had for the Vendor Community. Together we had experience with what it would take to implement all of our multi-year strategies.

One final advantage we had going for us was the Y2K effect. In the late 1990s, every major company was racing to beat the Y2K deadline to get your systems up to new standards caused by the coming year 2000. All systems applications and hardware companies were upgrading all of their systems not only to remove the Y2K issue but also spending hundreds of millions on enhancements. They had worked out all the bugs, so we could now get the best systems available, plus avoid all the implementation pitfalls the other retailers had struggled with.

Michaels had it all. Experience at where we were going, a road paved by the best retailers in the world, and newly upgraded applications to choose from. The stars aligned for us, and there was not one doubt in Michael Rouleau's mind that this was the path we were going to take. By 2005 we became the most dominant player by far in the Arts & Crafts Industry and were as good or better as related to the management of inventory, our stores, and our supply chain than the best retailers of the day.

Some CEOs would come to a fork in the road and might be too prideful to say that the path paved by others is the path to choose. They want to show they are smarter or believe that they have a special new way to make a retailer or company successful. Many times, the next CEO is explaining why the previous path did not work. Athletes learn by watching the Hall of Fame players. Actors learn from Oscar-winning performances. Doctors learn from watching the best physicians in the field. Why shouldn't you do the same and learn how others are successful?

ATHLETES LEARN BY WATCHING THE HALL OF FAME PLAYERS. ACTORS LEARN FROM OSCAR-WINNING PERFORMANCES. DOCTORS LEARN FROM WATCHING THE BEST PHYSICIANS IN THE FIELD. WHY SHOULDN'T YOU DO THE SAME?

HOLD IT; I HAVE TO CHECK
THE WEATHERVANE

During my three years at EDS and three years at CSC, I always got the impression that whoever was responsible for the company's strategic plan had a weathervane right outside their office. Every year it seemed we had a new direction, a new incentive program, and different organizational structures. It was like the wind in Texas, just wait a minute, and it will change direction and strength.

For example, EDS decided to form a consulting group with about 1,500 management consultants, only to spend $600 million a year and a half later to buy an entire consulting firm called AT Kearney. CSC was the same way. It seemed every year we would have a new direction on how geographic regions interacted with competency-specific consulting groups (ex. Strategy, Supply Chain, etc.).

I was five layers from the senior leadership group and was in a constant state of whiplash. The best you could do was focus on being valuable and hope your strengths aligned with what the leadership wanted and where they were going. I promised myself that if I ever were responsible for setting a company's strategic direction, we would do our homework and pick a lane. The other promise I made to myself was to find a CEO who held the same conviction.

I found both at Michaels. Michael Rouleau had trained his entire career for the opportunity to run a retail chain. After being passed over for the top jobs at Target and Lowe's, he finally got his shot at Michaels. He knew exactly what he wanted to do and how he wanted to get there. The only reason he ever cared if the wind was changing was if it impacted a flight he was about to take.

Michael had the experience and the conviction for the way he wanted the company to move. No matter how much he was pushed or pulled by the board, vendors, employees, shareholders, or the press, he was not going to be moved by a phone call or a hallway conversation. Facts on the ground and his experience would be the key ingredients for a shift or course correction.

He knew from his experience that he needed to hire someone who was 100% responsible (a Pitbull, so to speak) for helping to set the direction and implement all the strategic initiatives necessary to reach the company's goals. He did not delegate this to another Senior Executive who would have to balance all their other responsibilities and strategic initiatives. This was too important for a part-time commitment. He was the boss, and I was his Pitbull.

It was so much easier for me and the organization to get the multi-year initiatives successfully implemented when you knew that the direction was not going to change with the wind. Are you a committed leader, or do you change with the wind? As an employee, do you suffer whiplash as your company seemingly changes direction all the time? **For sustainable success, organizations need to stop looking at the weathervane and instead choose a course based on facts and experience they can rally behind and follow over multiple years. Not just the fad of the moment.**

HOW DO YOU PROPERLY SPEND $250M?

We had a focused set of day-to-day tactical enablers that we needed to improve on every single day to pay the bills and cover the costs of all the strategic initiatives. We had our strategic plan. We had a process to update our strategic direction continually. We had our multi-year strategies. We had a high-level five-year financial plan. We had a roadmap to follow from the best companies in the world. We had a CEO that had set the direction with conviction. What we did not have was a proper process to scope, run cost/benefits analysis, staff, and fund strategic initiatives.

We were about to spend $250M over the next five years, and we were missing a key process. The company had never done anything like this before, so we needed to make sure it was built with the appropriate amount of discipline and with enough incentives for everybody to buy in to the process. The CFO, Bryan DeCordova, had been thinking about this for weeks and came up with a one-page slide that became the foundation for our funding tower process until we were sold to a private equity group in 2006.

On one side of the slide, it had a high-level net income calculation. Bryan had a tower-like image separated into three areas: base budget, growth initiatives, and strategic initiatives. On the far right, he had another tower-like image with different initiatives stacked on top of each other with an arrow showing the prioritization that went from bottom to top. The concept was very straightforward.

- **Base Budget**—Every year, each Senior Executive would have to fight for their money during the budget process. We challenged every headcount, every penny to make sure we were lean and mean. If we knew that an area had become more efficient because of a process update or we were just getting better at execution, we wanted that headcount back or denied a headcount addition. The philosophy was it was company money, not your division's money. It was not zero-base budgeting, but it was close.

- **Growth Related**—If funds were left over from the base budget process, our priority was to fund new store growth. Our ROI on stores was tremendous, and the new stores quickly added additional funds for other investments. Plus, it helped us continue to build our market share.

- **Strategic Initiatives**—If money was left over, then we would fund the prioritized initiatives. The initiatives were sequenced, but we also analyzed the cost (capital and expense during a project, ongoing expenses once implemented, benefits and timing). There were cases where an initiative was not a top priority, but it had such a tremendous and fast payback, we might fund that project to get more cash for future initiatives. When the money or resources were gone, initiatives would have to roll forward to another year.

We challenged the organization to drive higher sales and profits on the lowest cost structure possible. We were a lean, mean fighting machine. If there was any fat, we found it and either invested back into the company, our people, or gave it back to shareholders. As initiatives were implemented, they provided significant increases in sales and margin along with expense savings which were then captured in the base budget. After the first few years of investments began to realize their benefits, the expenses began to leverage (or go down) compared to the increase in sales. We were printing money like the Federal Reserve!

The funding tower process plus a CEO fanatical with expense management gave us the foundation for building a great and profitable company. The incentive for the organization was wage increases, stock options that went to the manager level, and the knowledge you were working for a great company. **A financial funding tower process that forces you to prioritize goals and objectives and allocates money wisely is a system that will work for any individual, business, or organization.**

———————•●•———————

CELL PHONE COSTS

The numbers were in, and they were horrible. It was not surprising, but it was disappointing, to say the least. After months of planning and direct instructions from the CEO, the management team had turned in an absolute mess—the initial roll-up of our base budget for the following fiscal year was tens of millions of dollars over the targeted number.

It was our first run-through of the new base budget process. The process was quite simple. The CEO and CFO gave each Executive Committee member the goals for the next year, including sales, gross margin, operating income, net income, headcount parameters, percentage targets for selling, general and administrative expenses, and targets for capital expenditures. The management team was told to take those parameters and challenge every line item 1,000 times before submitting their initial budget.

As I was looking over the numbers that the CFO gave me, I received a phone call asking me to come to CEO's office. When I arrived, he was on fire, "Why hasn't the team responded to the new process and my specific directions?"

"It looks like they are playing the usual budget process game—asking for more money up front so when it gets cut, they get what they are really asking for even though that number will still be too high," I answered.

"Bull%$#@!" he exclaimed, his fist came down on his desk for emphasis, "You are probably right, but we don't have time for this. I told them what I expected, and that should be enough. If they will not listen to direction and specific instructions, I might need to find someone who will. I will deal with this in the next meeting."

I knew Michael better than that. He was not going to wait. He was, however, going to do some homework before the meeting.

It was Monday morning. As the entire Executive Committee entered the room, everyone was aware of the mess we had created and wondered how Michael would react. It did not take long to find out. Michael skipped a few items on the agenda and began by taking everyone in the room to task. He was sunspot hot, and he let everyone know just how unacceptable the rollout numbers were. For about ten minutes, he was relentless, asking rhetorical question after rhetorical question. No one attempted to answer.

He handed out a one-page document to everyone in the room, saying, "I know all of you are going to give me excuses for why you did what you did. I don't care. I am going to show you that there is waste all over the budget if you are willing to go after it." He held up the paper, "This page represents a little homework I did with our cell phone costs. Last year we spent about $120,000. I got on the phone, called our provider, and negotiated a better rate based on the idea that we would be adding more cell phones in the future. I saved $15,000. The budget number for next year is now $105,000 with more phones in the plan. That is a 12.5% decrease."

He looked around the room with intensity and challenged us, "If I can find a 12.5% decrease in one line item of a budget with hundreds of line items, why can't you? We can do this one of two ways. You can get the budget numbers back in line, or I will."

It was another Michael lesson. He always had a way to show how futile the effort was to try and slip something past him. He just had too much experience and always seemed to find simple examples to understand and remember. His philosophy, **"Don't tell them, show them."**

We react faster to visual stimuli. Management teams always, and I mean always, challenge the boss when it comes to the budget. There are so many lines of data in a major corporation's budget that it can be easy to hide a few dollars here and a few more there. They all add up. As the CEO, you have to challenge every line—I mean *every* line.

Scrutinizing the budget is a boring, non-glitzy task for the boss, but it is not something to delegate. If you don't take it seriously, you will live to regret it.

———————•●•———————

NINE WOMEN CAN'T MAKE A BABY IN ONE MONTH

I had to update my boss, but I did not know how to broach this topic. Four short years ago, Michael Rouleau was begging vendors to keep shipping to his stores, pleading with lenders not to cut him off, and asking Wall Street investors not to jump ship before he even had a chance to identify all the issues facing his new company. When he came on board the listing ship, his company had lost millions of dollars in the previous couple of years and was bleeding cash.

After an incremental leadership effort and a dedicated team of individuals, we now had Michaels positioned to make significant investments in people, technology, and infrastructure. We could now build our future. It was a great story. I decided to do what I have always done—just give him the facts.

When we got to that agenda item, I did not blink, I did not stutter, and I did not break eye contact. I took a deep breath and said, "Michael, we cannot do everything in the pipeline right now. You have this company positioned so well; we actually have more money to invest than the ability of the organization to implement everything successfully." In my head, I was thinking; *I just told this very impatient man that had worked his @$$ off to be in this incredible financial situation to be patient with how much we could successfully take on as a company.*

He did something unusual. He did not react. He just asked me if I could explain my comments in more detail. I asked if I could go to his whiteboard. I drew a circle and wrote the word Retek in the middle. Retek was our system of record for items, inventory, sales, etc. Almost everything we did from a systems implementation standpoint either had to get information from Retek or give information to Retek.

I said, "Our first ten projects have to do with inventory, and there are only so many people that can be working on the inventory code at one time. It is like an old gold mine shaft; even if you had thousand people available, you could only get a few people in one area. We have worked on an aggressive sequence and timing plan that considers these types of scenarios, and we can still implement our projects significantly faster than other companies, but we won't do it by just indiscriminately throwing bodies at it."

Michael did not like the answer, but he knew from experience that throwing money at a situation can cause unexpected problems. He told me to continue to work with the team to get these things implemented as fast and successfully as possible. He then reminded me that was the number one reason he hired me. "It is engraved on my forehead," I told him, "and I see the message every time I look in the mirror."

In 1975, Fred Brooks wrote a book called *The Mythical Man-Month: Essays on Software Engineering.* Its central theme is "adding manpower to a late software project makes it later." His first reason was the indivisibility of tasks. Hence the headline of this story. Some tasks cannot be broken up. His second reason was ramp-up time. Getting new people up to speed is not only difficult, but it can distract from the current project team. The final reason was communication overhead. With every additional headcount, there is an exponential growth in the communication necessary to keep everybody on the same page.

WHEN YOU ARE TEMPTED TO THINK THE ANSWER TO GETTING PROJECTS DONE FASTER IS ALWAYS TO JUST THROW MORE BODIES AT IT, REMEMBER THIS—NINE WOMEN CANNOT HAVE A BABY IN ONE MONTH.

After 25 years of doing systems projects, it is always a challenge when people believe you can just throw more bodies at the problem. In many cases adding more bodies actually had diminishing returns. Spend more time upfront discussing and managing the resources necessary, along with the sequence and timing of every project. When you are tempted to think the answer to getting projects done faster is always to just throw more bodies at it, remember this—nine women cannot have a baby in one month.

IT IS ALL ABOUT SEQUENCE AND TIMING

I updated the Executive Committee on the strategic initiative/project selection process. When your company is twenty-five years behind modern retailers, there isn't a lack of initiatives that have to be implemented. There was not an area of the company that did not need some type of technology enhancement. Even after we had improved every process, we knew that technology would allow us to gain the efficiencies necessary to bring us into the 21st century.

We had to develop a filtering system that prioritized the literally hundreds of potential projects and initiatives. We came up with three categories:

- **Legal, Fiduciary, Compliance & Maintenance**—An example of this would be a new accounting rule or cyber security. Things required to stay compliant with federal, state, or local laws or general maintenance issues to ensure the computers came on every day.

- **High Short-Term ROI** – An example of this would be that Michaels had a manufacturing division that you could give $150K for a new updated machine, and they could give the company back $500K in savings within the current budget year.

- **Longer-Term ROI** – These were initiatives that aligned with our five multi-year strategies. Some of these could take years to fully implement and therefore take a while to see the benefits from the investment.

After a couple of months of discussion with all the appropriate players in the company, we developed an initial list of initiatives and projects totaling about 35. It was way too many. We did not have the resources to invest in all of them in the upcoming fiscal year. As I presented this fact to the Executive Committee, CEO Michael Rouleau spoke up.

"Anyone can come up with a list of things to do. Every company I have worked at all have lists. The companies that are the most successful are the ones who can properly sequence and time their initiatives. I have seen companies make major mistakes implementing something out of sequence. It always causes delays and reworks. I have experienced four-month projects that become 12-month projects. It is all about sequence and timing." Point made!

I used my huge whiteboard in my office as a five-year view of all of our plans. We spent the next several weeks working on how all these initiatives fit together. What begot what? Every time I thought I had it, someone would come into my office and tell me something was out of order. When there were no more objections, I presented the plan to the IT Steering Committee and the Executive Committee. We had it!

Of all the parts of the strategic planning process, I would argue that our fanatical focus on sequence and timing was the most important. If you think about building a house, you don't paint the walls first; you lay the foundation. You don't hang ceiling fans next; you put up the frame of the house. It is the same thing when selecting the sequence and timing for initiatives for your company.

Like Michael, the companies I worked with or consulted for all had implementation issues because they did not spend enough time on the sequence and timing discussion. To me, it came back to leadership. Do companies fund the cool stuff first, fund things based on squeaky wheel gets the grease, or fund projects based on how they fit together? **To successfully implement initiatives and complete projects on time, start and finish with a properly focused, discipline discussion on the sequence and timing process. It is amazing how much you will be able to successfully implement when you know what comes first and, more importantly, what needs to wait.**

EVERYBODY WAS ON THE SAME ... FIVE PAGES

It was red, orange, yellow, green, blue, indigo, and violet, and it was a thing of beauty. It was carried by every Michaels' associate that had anything to do with our growth and strategic plans. With this in your hands, there was no doubt in anyone's mind what we were doing and when. It was the main document I used to manage every strategic initiative and project. What was it? It was a five-page multi-year timeline for every investment the company was making over the next five years.

We had spent months working through the new strategic funding tower process, which helped determine what projects were to receive funding. Then we spent several weeks working through the sequence and timing of the list of priorities. The output of those two processes led to the development of this critical document.

It was broken down into seven categories: new store openings, the five multi-year strategies, and IT maintenance and enhancements. I added a section for our subsidiaries in future years because most of their projects tapped into the Michaels IT Team. The different colors represented different types of activities. Anything that was purple was an IT activity. Light blue represented a process or training activity and highlighted when we would need to hire associates to help support the initiatives and so forth.

Every project had a detailed project plan that could have thousands of steps. For example, when we opened up a new distribution center in the Chicago area, that timeline needed a three-inch thick binder to hold all the documentation. I would then take the major milestones to populate on my rainbow timeline.

If anyone, and I mean anyone, would ask me a question about the sequence and timing of our initiatives, I had the answer. When is the new distribution center going to be operational? When is the first test for perpetual inventory? When is the first go-live date for EDI with a vendor? How many new stores will we be opening in three years from now? What are the main projects scheduled for four years from now? If you had this document, you could answer all of those questions.

There was one other reason for the success of this document. I was the only person who could officially adjust or update the timelines. We did not want to go ditch to ditch with the project teams, the organization, the management team, the board, or Wall Street. We had a process in place where any movement of dates would have to be discussed in the IT Steering Committee and, in some cases, the Executive Committee. Then and only then would I update the document.

Literally, everybody was on the same page (or I should say five pages)! One of my proudest moments came when I was interviewing a potential new director in the IT department. During the interview, I grabbed the timeline to explain how we sequence and time projects. He politely interrupted me and said, "Everyone in the IT department I have interviewed with already told me about this document. In my 15 years of working in IT, I have never seen a document that showed a roadmap of what we would be working on. I wish all of my companies had such a crystal-clear roadmap—we might have completed more projects!"

It was a heck of a compliment, but I knew it was true. You may see IT project timelines or R&D project timelines, but have you ever seen a comprehensive document that had all major investments captured? **A company leader cannot possibly keep track of what you are investing in, working on, or when things are planned to be completed without a multi-year timeline. It's like a head coach who doesn't have all of his plays documented.**

WHY DOES IT HAVE TO BE SATURDAY MORNING?

I was getting more and more concerned that we were losing momentum. It had been a little over a year since I joined Michaels. We had made a tremendous amount of progress since my start date, but I was growing more and more concerned that the management team was not dedicating enough time to the strategic initiative process.

It is so easy to get sucked into the day-to-day running of the business. This fact was emphasized even more because Michael Rouleau, arguably one of the best retail operators in the business, was constantly pushing the organization to hit its sales numbers, drive down expenses, find efficiencies, and reduce headcount wherever possible. The results were showing his focus and relentlessness were paying off.

There was one big challenge. We were only about $40M into what would be $250M in investment spending, and we were only discussing the strategic plan and the initiatives for about 30 minutes or so once a month in the Executive Committee meeting. It was not enough time. So, in my next update meeting with Michael, I planned to propose a change. I knew this would be an uphill battle with Michael, so I knew my best bet was to use his own words against him.

"Michael," I began, "do you still believe you need to spend more time thinking about buying a car than thinking about buying a hot dog?" A couple of years earlier, he told a story about how his wife spends the same amount of time on both buying decisions, but you can't do that; you have to put more time into things you are going to spend a lot of money on. I wanted to see if he still believed in his statement.

"I sure do!" Michael responded, "My wife hates it when I tell that story!"

I had him.

"Then, why are we only spending 30 minutes a month discussing $250M of spending?" I could see his mind wanting to call me a few names or tell me to leave his office, but he refrained.

With a challenging tone, he said, "What do you want now?"

"I would like to have a once-a-month strategy meeting on a Saturday morning." Before he could respond, I continued, "I want to get everyone away from their phones and day-to-day duties so they can concentrate 100% on our strategic initiatives." I was recommending four hours a month out of the hundreds we spent running the business. We went back and forth for an exhilarating 15 minutes before Michael finally agreed with my recommendation. I know everybody did not like me very much that I had taken one Saturday a month away from them, but it proved an invaluable practice.

How much time do you spend on your strategic plan? Does it get pushed to the side to run the day-to-day business? Is your future really a priority? If so, then give it the appropriate time throughout the year.

I like this quote: "Living your best life means spending your time in a way that accurately reflects your priorities." This is true in life and in business. This is a head-down reality. An organization notices when a leader spends too little time on the company's future, and no one is surprised when the organization runs right off the proverbial cliff.

"LIVING YOUR BEST LIFE MEANS SPENDING YOUR TIME IN A WAY THAT ACCURATELY REFLECTS YOUR PRIORITIES." THIS IS A HEAD-DOWN REALITY. AN ORGANIZATION NOTICES WHEN A LEADER SPENDS TOO LITTLE TIME ON THE COMPANY'S FUTURE, AND NO ONE IS SURPRISED WHEN THAT ORGANIZATION RUNS RIGHT OFF THE PROVERBIAL CLIFF.

IT WILL SHOWCASE
EVERYONE'S TALENTS

When the new monthly Saturday strategy meeting was announced, you could hear the groans from across the entire office building. I was not the most popular guy that day, but the CEO backed the idea 100%. He told the Executive Committee, "We needed to spend this time focusing on our future. We are spending hundreds of millions of dollars. Everyone in this room will eventually have a project or initiative, so you need to understand the importance of designing and helping to manage our strategic plans and priorities."

He continued, "These Saturday meetings send a message that strategic planning is important to the entire company." It sent a powerful message that the boss thought this was important. In most organizations I have worked with or consulted for, if the boss did not publicly announce his support for a particular topic, it could be the final nail in the coffin for that idea. "As for Saturday," he told the team, "get over it! Our stores are working today, so we can too."

I was responsible for the agenda, presentation slides, and facilitation of the four-hour Saturday sessions. As we got the strategy meetings up and running, Michael wanted to make sure he and I were on the same page to make sure the meetings were productive, and the Executive Team realized their importance. A couple of weeks before the meeting, Michael and I met to discuss the agenda.

I handed Michael the draft agenda, and it did not take him three seconds to have a problem with my thoughts. I had been working with him for almost five years now, so I anticipated that he would have this problem, and I was prepared with my response. His challenge was with the additional attendees I wanted to invite to the meeting. They included directors and vice presidents, who were the people leading the projects on a day-to-day basis. Michael wanted to know why I needed them in this meeting. He thought it was for the Executive Team only and wondered why I could not do all the updates myself.

I responded, "I could give the updates, but I thought this was a great way for other associates to get exposure to the Executive Team. They are project leaders, and the success of each of the projects falls on their shoulders. I believe this will give them extra incentive to push for a successful project knowing that they will be sharing the updates with the Executive Team each month."

I could see he was about to push back, so before he could respond, I kept talking. "We had such success with the consulting projects I ran before joining Michaels because we showcased the project leaders and their teams. It just makes sense to continue to let the Executive Committee be exposed to the talent that works in this organization. In my experience, running a successful project could be a road for a promotion. It is an excellent way to assist that path by letting the Executive Committee see the people in action."

Michael listened intently and then said, "I agree. But," he emphasized, "you need to make damn sure these people are prepared for this meeting!"

They were. It was one of the best things I ever did in my career. I could have hogged all the spotlight, but I wanted everybody to get their due for the success of the projects. It worked to perfection. The project teams' members continued updating the Executive team in these Saturday meetings for the next four years. They loved the idea of getting exposure for their hard work, and it did help get some people promoted. I believe it was a key reason we were so successful at implementing our strategic initiatives and projects.

Companies should expose people to the Executive Team, especially on important strategic investments. These could be the future leaders of the organization, and what better way to help with their career than to give them access to the people who will eventually decide their fate within the organization.

THE ENVELOPE THEORY

Michael always liked me to interview new executives. He valued my opinion and wanted me to make sure potential employees knew the expectations to work for him and his company. So, I was interviewing a potential new SVP Supply Chain candidate.

The interview was going very well when he asked me about our strategic priorities, specifically, about a new Transportation Management

System. I said, "It is envelope 150." He looked at me strangely and did not understand what I was saying, so I explained my statement.

In the early days of the turnaround, we struggled to set the company's strategic and operational priorities. We had so many opportunities that it was challenging to say which ones should go first, second, third, or 100th because most of them had exceptionally good value propositions associated with them once they were implemented. The reality was we needed a lot of things in those early days, but we could not pay for all of them, and we surely could not work on all of them in one year.

Sometimes this reality is hard for companies, boards, and the investment community to understand. Approving and then successfully implementing strategic initiative investments takes time and, of course, resources—dollars and people. At the same time, you still need to run day-to-day operations. It is a challenging balancing act.

An equally challenging part of an initiative process was communicating this to the board, the investment community, vendor community, and the associates. We were struggling with this message because everybody had their own ideas of what was important. The answer happened on a roadshow with Wall Street analysts where our CEO was being peppered with questions about other priorities than the ones we had selected. His response was legendary.

"I have a box of envelopes sitting on my desk," he said. "In each envelope, there is an initiative, and on the outside is written a number for that initiative based on where it is in our sequence and timing order of importance." He looked at one of the analysts and said, "I have explained our top 10 initiatives that we will be working on; your initiative is in envelope 392." The analyst got the point. His initiative suggestion was not a priority and would not be for quite a while.

It was such a simple way to get people to understand what was important to us from a strategic investment standpoint. You would always hear executives, associates, board members, and Wall Street analysts reference "The Envelope Theory" when discussing our initiative process. There was never a doubt when using this simple talking point about what our priorities were. It aligned everyone as to what was important and, more importantly, what was not.

This process enabled us to successfully run the day-to-day operations and at the same time successfully implement over $250M in capital investment over seven years. How do you communicate with crystal clear clarity what is important and what is not? Focusing an organization like this is critical for success. **A simple initiative envelope system of ordered priorities completely eliminates opinions and ambiguity on what is important. It governs what projects are the highest priority and those that need to wait. What is in your envelope number #1? More importantly, what is in envelope number #192?**

————— • • • —————

NOT JUST WHAT BUT WHY

I was preparing a PowerPoint for my boss when a friend who worked in merchandise planning came into my office. He asked me how the strategic initiative selection process was going. I told him, "Strategic priorities are set. After a six-month effort, we are now ready to fund and begin working on the prioritized initiatives and projects. We began with more than 100 initiatives, and using the new financial funding tower and the strategic roadmap I was responsible for creating, we made the final selections."

I ticked off the list of nine initiatives we chose for the fiscal year 2001. "Let's see, there's perpetual inventory, expansion of our Lancaster, CA distribution center, a new distribution center in the Northeast, major enhancements to our Retek system (Enterprise Resource Planning—ERP), new merchandise allocation system, Web EDI (Electronic Data Interchange) for our Vendor Community, a new Decision Support reporting tool, bringing our vendor website in house, and an enhancement to the vendor website for gathering vendor contact information."

He said, "That is a heck of a lot to work on."

I nodded in agreement and said, "Most companies would only tackle about half of these projects, but I believe that our history proves that we can successfully tackle all of these and still run the day-to-day operations."

He agreed, then asked me the $64,000 question, "Why did you select these over the other projects?"

"These projects all align with our six multi-year strategies. They are sequenced to help us tackle the priorities of managing inventory better, lowering our distribution costs, improving our Vendor Community capabilities to grow with us, making the stores more efficient, and enhancing key merchandise processes." Then I shared the three filters we used to help categorize our priorities:

- **_Yes_**—The initiative is funded, the resources are committed, and it is on the implementation timeline.
- **_No, not now_**—The initiative would not be worked on now but at a later date.
- **_No, not ever in our lifetime_**—All work, discussions, or meetings associated with this initiative must stop.

When I was finished, I asked, "Does that make sense?"

"It is perfectly clear to me," he replied.

"Do you think the rest of the organization will understand my explanation?"

"Absolutely!"

"Great, because that is what I am putting in this presentation for the boss!"

We had selected nine initiatives, so that meant at least 90 projects were not getting funding. The filters helped explain what we were working on now, what was in the queue for later, and what would never happen. The filters helped communicate why these initiatives were selected and why others were not. When the list was announced, the people who got their projects funded were ecstatic. The people who missed the cut were upset, but each told me they understood why the other projects were selected at this time. Telling what and why aligned the entire organization and was key for the buy-in for this process.

When communicating to the organization, it is not enough to just tell them what the priorities are; you have to tell them why. You will gain instant buy-in and gain credibility from the organization about your selection process.

.

THE FAINTEST INK IS BETTER THAN THE BEST MEMORY

A few minutes into a meeting discussing the implementation of Electronic Data Interchange (EDI) capabilities with our Vendor Community to automate the process and eliminate faxing and emailing purchase orders and invoices, things started to go off the rails.

Though EDI had been around since the early 1960s, it did not take hold in retail until the mid to late 1980s. As with many of our initiatives, we were not on the cutting edge of the technology evolution. We just had to be smart enough to copy what others had been doing and not try to reinvent the wheel.

Things were spiraling out of control as people circled around phrases like, "I remember we discussed that we should do it this way," or "I don't remember us agreeing to that," and "I remember it another way."

As the leader of the meeting, I had to put it to a stop. I asked if anyone had taken notes in the last meeting. Of the twenty people in the room, only two had taken notes, the project manager and myself. I let that fact go for now and asked the project manager to read his notes. When he was done, I read mine. Our notes were the same on the subject. After reading the notes, we were able to get to a final agreement on the main point and then move on to other topics.

IT project leader, Mike Wind, whispered a phrase under his breath that I heard, but the entire room did not. I asked him to repeat it. He said, **"The faintest ink is better than the best memory."** I let the comment sink in for a few arduous seconds.

This project was one of the first I ran without my old CSC teammates. As consultants, you always take notes and publish them after every meeting, presentation, or discussion. It is a little bit for "CYA" purposes, but its main function is to have everybody understand not only what happened on a project last week but six months ago.

At the end of the meeting, it was clear we had to go back to the discipline of everybody taking notes. I did not care if they were handwritten, typed into a computer, or etched in stone. Afterward, we would designate one person to publish the notes within hours of the meeting, make any corrections based on the team's input, and store them on a company-owned shared drive.

People are so busy that it is hard to remember what you had for lunch, let alone some meeting that took place a week ago or six months ago. I learned this lesson incredibly early in my career. I had a boss who would say that you did not attend his meetings if you did not take notes. I am old school. I still like handwriting my notes. I will go through three or four composition books a year. Besides meeting notes, I would write down something I read that day, a question I wanted to ask after a meeting, or a note I should send out to someone. It was just to help me remember.

I am surprised how many individuals don't take notes. **You never know when you will have to recall a conversation, meeting, or encounter. Take great notes, and you won't have to worry about how good of a memory you have.**

<hr>

FAILURE IS NOT AN OPTION

In the middle of 2001, I was talking with my former boss from CSC, Steve Biciocchi. He was checking to see how my transition was going with Michaels and if we needed any help. I told him that my transition had gone much better than I anticipated, and that was due completely to the support I was getting from my boss, Michael Rouleau. He had given me the necessary cover to continue to push the company just like I did when I was a consultant, and he was my client. Michael stated continually what I was hired to do, and his actions showed he was true to his word. Steve said, "As long as you have a CEO like Michael in your corner, you will be able to accomplish a lot for him and the company."

Steve then put his mentoring hat on, reminding me that a high percentage of company projects that include technology fail. He said, "You have an awful lot of exceedingly difficult and complex projects going on at one time. If you don't remember all of those reasons you learned the past three years at CSC, you could be on the list of project leaders who failed. "

I asked Steve if he had seen the movie *Apollo 13*. He said he did, so I reminded him about a scene when the NASA team discussed how to get the astronauts back to earth after an onboard explosion to their spacecraft. The actor who played Fight Director Gene Kranz said, "Failure is not an option" for bringing the astronauts home. I said, "Failure is not an option here either."

During my first six months, I had checked off every major issue that causes projects to fail. These included CEO support and buy-in, integrated timelines, detailed communication plans, one person in charge of all the initiatives with the power of the office of the CEO, detailed resource management for all projects, and weekly updates with teams and management.

The final piece fell into place as we were working on our executive cross-functional objective. I needed to have each Executive Committee member be the captain for any project in their area of responsibility. We needed their active participation. If they were the ones who wanted the project funded, they would own the responsibility of making sure it was successfully implemented. We also assigned an IT Director to every executive to be their partner in this effort.

We wanted to make sure that from the management team on down, these were company projects, not IT projects—both equally responsible for making sure we got a return on our investment. **"Too often, technology projects are deemed 'IT' projects and relegated to the IT department, regardless of what the project actually is. But for any project to work, it needs strong leadership from the top down. If a project doesn't have buy-in and support from C-level executives as well as specific department leaders, it's hard to get employees on board and hard to know who is in charge when leadership questions arise" (Forbes 2016).** I could not have written it better.

———————•●•———————

YOU GOT YOUR CHANCE

In one of the last conversations I had with Michael before I officially joined the company, we discussed the new Vendor Relations Team, and I told him almost everything was in place to kick start this new division.

I reminded him that he had accepted the recommendation to form the new Vendor Relations Team, agreed to the new headcount requirements, and agreed that the initial focus was for this team to help inform and train the Vendor Community on their new requirements, not fine them for non-compliance. There was one thing missing. Who would lead this new group report?

I told him that this group reported to the buyers in some organizations, and in others, they reported to the Supply Chain Organization. Still, in others, the group reported to the Finance Team because the foundation of those teams were chargebacks and fines. The recommendation of my consulting team and me was still that this new organization should report to someone independent of any of these organizations.

Our reasoning was fairly straightforward. Michaels was about to start a massive investment program that would cause significant changes in every division. The leadership in functional areas like the buyers, supply chain, and finance were about to be up to their eyeballs in alligators for the next three to four years of technology implementations. They would not have the time to dedicate to starting and running a brand-new organization.

Also, these organizations had just spent the last few months lobbying for a chargeback program. We believed that could slant anything they did with this new team toward the eventual fining of vendors. Michael was completely on board with all of our recommendations. In fact, the conversation was going too easily for my liking. Normally with conversations like this, it could be a struggle to get us to see eye to eye. We would go back and forth like we were playing a game of tennis. After the next few rapid-fire questions, I realized that Michael was ten steps ahead of me.

He asked me if I thought it would be good to have a former vendor running this new division? I said, "Absolutely." He then asked if we had any former vendors in the company right now. I said, "Except for myself, I don't believe so."

"Who was it that pushed this recommendation more than anything else for the last year or so?"

I said, "I guess that would be me."

"Do you still believe we can change the Vendor Community doing it differently by not using a terribly divisive chargeback program?"

"There is not one doubt in my mind," I said with conviction.

"Congratulations," he said, "You now get your chance to do it differently. I want you to head up this new division. It checks all of your boxes."

With those words, I realized I had just added starting a new division to my new job responsibilities. After years of frustration being a vendor having to deal with the likes of May Company, Wal-Mart, and Target, I was now going to have a chance to see if I could get vendor compliance without the fear of fines. It wasn't easy, but I was proven right. In fact, because of how differently we treated our Vendor Community, we became a case study at the Kellogg School of Business.

Most business relationships today are more adversaries than true partnerships. The word partnership has come to mean, "What more can I get from you, or I will find another vendor?" Whoever has the most power in the relationship usually pushes the supposed partner to get every ounce of blood from a turnip. We proved you could do it differently. **You can use honey instead of vinegar with your vendors and third-party business organizations and build partnerships based on mutual respect and benefit, not the fear of a financial fine. I wish more companies would realize this and do the same.**

SOMETIMES YOU HAVE TO SHOCK THE SYSTEM

When Michael hired me to join the team, he did it with one simple premise—that I would move the company farther and faster with the successful implementation of all of the strategic initiatives, or he would fire me. He wanted me to break down roadblocks, eliminate issues, push through personality conflicts, and leave no stone unturned to help Michaels make up for the technology, process, and infrastructure deficit he had inherited.

Then he added a new twist. He asked me to build a new Vendor Relations Division. I expressed concern that it could complicate my other role because that team would be asking for several strategic initiatives. In a strategy meeting, I might be asking for money and also running the process to tell others why they couldn't have money. Michael told me he trusted me to make the right decision for Michaels. Well, I put that comment to test a few days later.

One of the recommendations was for the Vendor Relations Team to put up a new vendor website. We wanted to take baby steps at first by populating the site with links to our new vendor manual, forms, and a newsletter. The vision was to build this to mirror the Wal-Mart Retail Link site that provided everything a vendor could possibly need to do business with them, including sales information. But the CIO was putting up roadblock after roadblock about why his team could not put up this site.

They were the typical reasons, but this was exactly what Michael had hired me to overcome. That is exactly what I was going to do. In my next update meeting, I showed Michael a plan to have the website up and running in one week with a small internet company for about $2,500. The ROI was off the charts because sending a 250-page vendor manual binder to about 1,000 vendors would cost an arm and a leg compared to having each vendor print the copies themselves from a link on the site.

I said, "Michael, I have heard you say at times that you need to shock the system. I know I have been on the job for just two days, but I have an idea about how we can do just that."

He listened, and after thinking about it for a few seconds, he said, "I love it. You have my full support." Fast forward two weeks, and I was making my first presentation to the Vendor Community at the annual Vendor Conference. Michael kicked off the presentation to make sure everyone knew the new team had his full support. Michael also purposely invited the CIO to the breakout session.

We began with basic information about how we would work together to make each of us more successful. Then came slide 17. I said. "To help with our communication between companies, we are announcing today the new michaelsvendors.com website" The moment the slide came up, I looked down and saw the CIO was about ready to blow his top. I continued, "We put this website up in one week, and this is the type of fast-paced implementation you are going to be seeing from Michaels on all our strategic initiatives. This is our expectation for our team, and we hope it will be for your team as well."

When the presentation was over, the CIO wanted a piece of Michael and me. Michael let him blow off some steam for a few moments and then said, "You better get used to this. No more excuses, no more telling me why you can't do something. This is an example of why I hired Jeff. If you guys work together, we can get a lot of stuff done. You need to know that I approved the website *and* announcing it in this session."

Sometimes you need to shock the system a little to get an organization to realize business as usual is not going to be tolerated. At certain times they need to know it is business UNUSUAL. This meeting set the tone for the next five years of successful IT implementations and cooperation between me and the CIO. Do you need to shock the system? It might be just what the doctor ordered!

————————— • ● • —————————

THE BEST AUDIBLE EVER

We had planned for this Vendor Conference for six months. It rallied the entire organization and Vendor Community around a theme for the coming year, provided updates since we last met, and set the strategic and operational direction for the coming year. When we left this meeting, everyone involved with Michaels was on the same page.

As always, we had contingency plans for everything from backup video equipment to three people who had backups for all of the presentations, a rehearsal with every speaker the afternoon before the big show to a dry run-through with the pro shop for the golf outing, plus we had done a walk through with the resort one week earlier. The only thing that could mess things up is if Mother Nature did not cooperate, and of course, she gave us the biggest rainstorm Dallas had seen in quite some time.

We had planned for a shotgun start for the golf tournament at 8:00 am the day before the Executive Presentations. Even though rain was in the forecast, the head of security for the resort gave us the approval to take to the course. With his guidance, we sent 132 golfers out onto the golf course to begin the tournament.

I was on the first tee when it happened. Standing on wet ground with a long metal object in my hand, the biggest bolt of lightning that I had ever seen lit up the sky. Within a split second, the loudest boom you will ever hear ripped across the golf course. I looked at the shock in my playing partners' eyes and said, "That was way too close!" The horn sounded to tell all the golfers to get off the course, but it really was not necessary. As the golfers drove back to the clubhouse, the skies opened up, and the lightning continued.

Luckily, everybody was safe. However, it not only wrecked the golf tournament but also all of our plans for the opening night dinner. We normally gave out the golf awards and had some fun telling stories of what happened on the course. That was out the window now.

I was talking about the storm with two members of the Vendor Relations Team, Jeremy Hazelwood and Phillip Anderson. They asked me what I was going to do at the opening ceremonies. I told them I was open to any ideas. Then one of them made a joke using a line from the movie *Caddyshack*. We all looked at each other and said, "That's it!" This was pre-YouTube, so if you wanted a video clip, you had to go to Blockbuster and get the VHS tape.

I was the Master of Ceremonies for the evening's festivities. No one knew what I was about to do, not even the CEO. I started out by saying that we were planning on doing something a little different this year for the golf tournament. We had hired a crew to film everyone on the course. Even though we were rained out, I wanted to show you some highlights from the event. I sold this like you cannot imagine. I even looked at the boss, and he had this look of anticipation on his face.

We then showed the famous scene in the movie where the bishop was playing the best golf game of his life in a rainstorm. As the storm intensifies, he continues to play. The two-minute scene was a perfect description of the day's events. As the video played, you could hear the laughter in the audience. When it ended, there was a hearty round of applause, including from the boss. It was one of the best audibles I had ever called, thanks to Jeremy and Phillip.

Sometimes the best-laid plans have to be adjusted. You have to have the flexibility to adapt based on new circumstances and new information, and some of the best ideas come from people who work with you or for you. You have to be willing to listen to all ideas. They just might turn into an applause-worthy result.

BETTER THAN A POUND OF CURE

In 2000, Michaels Stores had 15% to 20% of their newly received orders from vendors sitting in a problem area at their distribution centers. It could take upwards of 75 days to investigate and then find a resolution. It impacted upwards of 5M cases out of the approximately 25M the four distribution centers (DCs) received each year.

In addition, about 35% of the orders shipped directly to their stores. The same issues they had receiving product at the four DCs were also happening in hundreds of stores. It was unacceptable, and if it was not fixed, Michaels could never reach their sales or efficiency goals. It is hard to make your sales numbers when you have millions of dollars of freight sitting in a problem area.

There was one additional problem. If we could not receive it, we would not pay for it. Vendors were screaming at anyone who would listen inside Michaels that they needed to get paid for these shipments. Hours upon hours of phone calls were taking place trying to resolve the issues to get the product to the stores and pay the vendors.

It was an absolute nightmare scenario. We focused on getting the problems resolved, but they would show up again when the next shipment arrived. We were firefighters, and we had to become problem preventors. The mission of the Vendor Relations Team was to work with the Vendor Community to learn the requirements that would prevent these problems from happening in the first place. Simultaneously we had to clean up the problem areas in the store and DCs. We had to get that freight onto the selling floor.

Four main categories made up 95% of our issues—carton configuration errors, overages, UPC errors, and items not on a purchase order or having a substitution. Dramatic improvement was possible because we did not just concentrate on resolving the issue and getting the freight out of the problem area. We went to the root cause of the issue and trained vendors on how to prevent the problem in the first place. It worked.

The results were outstanding. By the end of 2001, we had reduced the error rate from 20% to 4%. By the end of 2002, the error rate dropped to .5%. By the end of 2003, we had a 99.8% accuracy rate. By 2004, the accuracy rate was 99.96%. We also dropped the time it took to get an order out of the problem area from 75 days to 7, and we were paying the vendors on time.

In 1736 Benjamin Franklin wanted the citizens of Philadelphia to remain vigilant about fire prevention. He said, *"An ounce of prevention is worth a pound of cure."* He meant it is clearly better to prevent fires than having to fight them. It is still relevant almost 285 years later. How many occasions has it taken two times, five times, ten times more effort to put out a fire than it would have taken to have spent the time to prevent it?

> **USE YOUR RESOURCES TO PREVENT PROBLEMS, NOT BECOME FIREFIGHTERS THAT CONTINUALLY PUT OUT THE SAME FIRES OVER AND OVER AGAIN.**

Pay me now or pay me double later. Take the time to investigate the root cause and determine what it takes to prevent problems in the first place. Use your resources to prevent problems, not become firefighters that continually put out the same fires over and over again.

IF WE CAN'T TAKE THEM TO THE PROBLEM AREA...

When they first saw it, they could not believe their eyes. A couple of vendors commented that this area was bigger than their entire distribution building. There were cartons as far as the eye could see. You could not have made a more powerful case that something had to change and change quickly. These were some of the first Michaels' vendors to tour our Dallas Distribution Center (DC), standing in front of our purchase order problem area.

We had to overcome this terrible logjam where freight sat in this problem area far too long, causing inventory issues for stores and timely payment issues for our vendors. To address this situation, we began a vendor training class to show them "How to do business with Michaels." I knew that over the course of a few years, the training would yield dramatic improvement in reducing inbound freight problems. The challenge was neither Michael Rouleau nor I were patient people, so I had to make significant progress and fast.

While preparing for the upcoming Vendor Conference, I asked my team if they had any ideas on how we could replicate the impact of the training class tour of the DC since a three-hour field trip was not going to work. Then someone said, "If we can't take them to the problem area, can we bring the problem area to them?" That is exactly what we did.

Outside the main ballroom at the Four Seasons Resort, we put up examples of the hundreds of issues we had to deal with every day. We categorized each issue and also put the name of the vendor responsible next to each example. But we did not stop there; we asked the CEO to stand right by the displays during the opening night meet and greet before dinner.

He was spectacular! Being the CEO, everyone wanted to get a piece of him, even for a brief moment. That night it was not niceties and cordial conversations; Michael was a man on a mission. Any vendor who came up to say hi or talk to him, Michael would turn to the displays and ask the vendor if they had product there. If they did, he asked them why they could not clean up their act. It was like he had the training class memorized.

These were the CEOs, Presidents, EVP's, and Owners of our top 500 vendors. It was a tad bit embarrassing for them to have their products displayed in the problem vendor area and have the retailer's CEO you are selling to point it out to you. An unexpected benefit came from Michael's response to vendors who did not have a product in the problem area; he made it a point that whoever was waiting to talk with him heard him praise that vendor for a job well done.

During the next year, our accuracy rate rose from 90% to 99.5%. Bringing the problem area to the Vendor Conference was a big reason why. After seeing all the issues staring them in the face, the executives of our biggest vendors realized they had a problem they could no longer ignore.

Sometimes the only way to change behavior and get someone to admit they have a problem is to put the problem right in front of the person responsible for fixing the issue, even if that means a moment or two of embarrassment.

PRESS HARD, WRITE CLEARLY, AND FILL OUT THE WHOLE FORM

I was sitting in the lunch area at the Michaels' Vendor Conference when Michael Rouleau came to my table and sat down. I was hoping he would congratulate my team and me for a great job with the conference, but I knew him too well. The look on his face meant he wanted me to do something.

He did give my us a nice compliment but quickly changed topics, asking if I had talked with any vendors about the mess the marketing dollar contract process (we called it the entitlement process) was. I said, "Yes, I have heard about it for the last few months from vendors that came to the training class."

He cocked his head, "Have you ever taken a deeper look at it?"

I knew what was coming next, so I just said, "When do you want me to start?"

He laughed because we knew each other so well. I was his "fix-it" guy. If there was a problem in the company somewhere, he came to me to find the solution. He had talked with our CIO and said, "There is a $1M technology solution that could fix many of the issues, but you know we have other priorities." Then he asked, "Do you think it can be fixed with a process improvement effort?"

I nodded, "That is always the first place to start."

A couple of weeks later, I had a cross-functional team of about 20 Michaels' associates laying out the current process and discussing how to make improvements. It took us about two months to develop a new process, but when it was done, we had addressed all the major issues. As with all processes, there were tasks out of sequence, roles and responsibilities that were not clearly defined, miscommunications, and inadequate understanding of how the entire process fit together. Knowing one's role isn't enough; you must also see how the team works in tandem.

Another major issue was our use of a six-part carbon copy form (hey, it was 2002)! For those of you who might not know what that is, it's a form with six back-to-back pages, and as you write on the first page, it transfers the writing to all subsequent pages. We wanted a technology solution for this, but we had other more pressing priorities. We needed to find a low-tech, no-dollar fix for the problem now.

During a later update with Michael, I told him that the team and I had resolved all the major issues and would soon announce the findings. Our solution was a perfect example of why we could delay spending $1M today.

At our next Vendor Conference, I told the audience we had improved the process, and there were three keys to solving all of our problems. Everybody in the audience was waiting in anticipation for this huge climax to how we were going to solve the issues. I said, *"You need to press hard, write clearly, and fill out the whole form."* Yes, that was it. No million-dollar IT project. Just do those three simple things, and 95% of the issues go away.

Without a clearly written form with all the necessary information filled in, it caused all the phone calls, emails, and high levels of anxiety for all involved. This effort bought us time, and we were much better prepared when the technology solution was funded years later.

Great management never misses the opportunity to improve everything everywhere. Solutions to many of a company's problems don't have to be high-tech/high-dollar solutions—especially when money is tight. Maybe management just needs to designate a fixer who can find low-tech solutions instead.

I FORGOT TO FEED MY PITBULL THIS MORNING

It had become personal. I had spent a lot of my political capital telling everyone who would listen that Michaels could get their vendors to follow their requirements manual without a chargeback program. We had made great progress on our issues with receiving, but we now expected more from our vendors. At the time of the 2003 Vendor Conference, about 75% of our vendors had not completed our basic requirements. I was p@%%ed!

As the Executive Team considered what we were going to say at the upcoming Vendor Conference, I reluctantly offered that we might need a Vendor Chargeback Program as part of my presentation. There was more than one "I told you so" from the group. We prepped and rehearsed to time the speeches and make any last-minute tweaks. I read through my speech notes, but everything about my delivery changed the day of the event.

Below is a piece from my actual notes that day, and you'll get the clear message being sent. However, on that day, I made these words come alive—I lit up that room to show how disappointed I was to have to say these words to the audience.

"I was asked two years ago if Michaels would institute a chargeback program, and I stated that as long as we did our job educating you on our requirements and you followed those requirements, we would never have to go there.

One year ago, I described to you a different and better way for retailers and vendors to inform, educate and interact with each other. I stated we would not go to the dark side if we worked together.

In January, Michael gave a speech to many of you at HIA where he said, 'Many retailers use chargeback programs; we will not have to go there unless you back us into a corner.'

After two years of effort to get you to comply with the basics, it pains me to say that you collectively have backed us into a corner. As of today, only 156 of you have complied with our request to complete the Big 6, let alone put in the quality assurance checks that we have asked you to implement.

We will not be your quality assurance department; with that said, Michaels will implement a Vendor Compliance Program."

You could hear a pin drop. I glanced over to see Michael's reaction. He was not pleased I had changed my tone so dramatically from how I had rehearsed it—if looks could kill. Shortly after my speech, we took a break, and Michael waved me over to talk. Before I could get to him, at least ten vendors got to him first. Each one said they agreed with all I shared, and it was about time we had said it.

They said, "We were all in compliance two years ago, but your buyers keep buying from vendors who don't follow your rules." They really took it to him, which is good because those ten vendors probably saved my job! When they left, Michael reminded me of his dislike for surprises. "I know, and I'm sorry, I just believed a message had to be sent, and we needed to shock the system."

After the break before the next scheduled speaker, Michael went to the podium and said, "As all of you know, Jeff is my Pitbull. Every company needs one. The problem is that this morning I forgot to feed him!" Pure poetry that brought a round of laughter that cut through the tension in the room. Four months later, the remaining 477 vendors completed their Big 6, and Michaels never implemented a chargeback program on my watch.

Every company needs a Pitbull—someone not afraid to get tough when the situation requires an unrelenting stance. Management must be willing to give this person the latitude to tell the organization, the senior leadership team, or even the CEO, the truth without repercussions.

WE CHANGED AN INDUSTRY

When we first started the Vendor Relations Team, our original intent was to concentrate on those who were selling or would be selling their products to Michaels. We had an error rate of almost 20% when product was received from our vendors, and we had no time to think about fixing anything else.

That changed in late 2001. At a Hobby Industry Association (HIA) meeting Michael attended, he learned about a concern. If the entire industry did not begin to follow the supply chain standards we were implementing at Michaels, it could harm its growth potential.

At the time, the industry was over $32B, and the expected growth rate was about 10%. A lot of that was driven by the growth in Michaels. We were the dominant player in the industry, bringing more and more people to the world of arts and crafts. As we got better so did our competition. Hobby Lobby, AC Moore, and JoAnn's, to name a few. Also, as our sales and profits went up, Wal-Mart and Target started adding more and more space to our categories. All boats were rising from a sales standpoint.

Our industry's greatest strength was also our greatest weakness. The strength of the vendor base was this unimaginable creative ability. The people in this industry were, without a doubt, the most creative people I had ever met. They had to be because our customers thrived on getting new and exciting creative ideas to feed their crafting passion.

The weakness was a myopic focus on creativity alone. The retail world was changing not only for the major retailers but also for the small mom and pop stores that still made up most crafts sales. Everyone wanted to make more money from their product offerings. The way to do that was to spend an equal amount of time on supply chain standards to ensure their products could get to the stores for the customers to buy more cost-effectively.

Michael was so pleased with my team's progress with our vendor base; he told me that day he had volunteered me to help lead the Industry Standards Committee. For the next few years, we basically followed the Michaels' Vendor Relations Playbook. We established the industry standards for issues like EDI, UPC bar codes, and carton labels. We put up a website for the entire industry to get all the necessary information to implement the standards. We developed a marketing campaign called "I'm On Board" and followed that up with an industry-wide email campaign.

One of the proudest moments of my career came a year later when I was walking the floor of the annual HIA show. I was walking from booth to booth to see what was new in the industry and finding friends that I knew who sold to Michaels. A woman came up to me and asked if I was Jeff Wellen. I answered, "Yes."

She said, "You don't know me because we don't sell to Michaels now, but because your committee pushed us to get on board with those industry standards, we just got our first order from Wal-Mart." It was the same message I heard from many of our Michaels' vendors. The work my team and I did helping the Vendor Community balance their creativity with new supply chain standards changed the industry forever.

At this moment, I realized that my passion to be a leader of a company was crossing paths with my passion for coaching and mentoring others. It gave me a bigger rush than implementing a new initiative, discovering an improvement to a process, or helping figure out a way to save millions of dollars. I was impacting people and their lives.

Few things are as rewarding as the ability to impact someone's life, career, or business in a positive way. Paying it forward creates more of a lasting legacy than chasing corporate titles, money, or trophies on a wall.

———————•—•—•———————

IS THIS THE REAL JEFF?

In late 2002 I had just gotten back to my office when my administrative assistant Diana Gosser came in. She had just talked to a professor who wanted to speak with me about the Vendor Relations Team. I had no idea what this could be about, so I dialed the number on the message note and called Professor Anne Coughlan.

She thanked me for getting back to her so soon. "No problem," I said, "your message has piqued my interest."

"I am the Professor of Marketing at the Kellogg School of Business at Northwestern University in Chicago," she began, "and one of my lesson plans teaches about 'Channel Conflict.' The premise of the teachings is that whoever controls the power in the channel controls the relationship. That channel could be Boeing Company to its suppliers. John Deere tractor to its suppliers. Or Wal-Mart to their suppliers.

"One evening during the Executive MBA class, one of my students, Wayne Marsh, raised his hand and said, 'Not everyone deals with their suppliers the same way you are teaching.' Now mind you, I have taught this class for more than 15 years, and I use numerous case studies to validate this concept. But this student told me about your company, Michaels Stores in Dallas, Texas, and said you are not using your power over your vendor base in a coercive manner. He told me you were *training* them instead of *fining* them. Is that true?"

Wayne had first-hand knowledge of what we were doing because he was the Vice President of Marketing for one of our top vendors. Anne continued, "It is such an unusual occurrence that I want to come and talk to you and possibly write a case study to use in my class. Would that be a possibility?"

It took me a moment to catch my breath. Here was a professor at one of the finest Business Schools in the country wanting to do a case study on our Vendor Relations Team. "It would be an honor," I fumbled, "I would be delighted for you to come and check out the team and our direction."

It did not take her long to realize that we were, in fact, doing something completely different than she had ever seen before. We were the big gorilla in the industry, yet we were expending money on a team and training class not only to help our vendors but the entire industry. Within three months, she had a draft case study done. After a few minor edits, the Michaels Stores case study was added to the full-time MBA and Executive MBA program.

But that isn't even the best part. Professor Coughlin asked Wayne and me if we would be guest speakers once a semester so the students could hear from a vendor and the retailer. We both agreed. The first time Anne taught the case study, we were both ecstatic to be in attendance. She introduced Wayne first and told his background story about being a student and telling her about Michaels.

Then she introduced me as the person who started the Vendor Relations Team with a new vision based on my experience as a vendor. Before we started our presentations, one of the students raised their hand. The student looked at Anne and said, "Is this the real Jeff from the case study?"

"Yes, this is the real Jeff," she chuckled.

"That is awesome," the student replied. It was one of the coolest moments of my life.

For the next several years, I was a guest speaker to her class. I originally went to college to be a teacher before changing my degree to marketing, but I never stopped wanting to impact people's lives— especially young people. For those brief 90-minute sessions, I was in heaven. The Kellogg case study showed that you could do things differently with a vendor base. I had been chasing the dream to be part of running a company and mentoring people in their careers for as long as I could remember. The intersection of those two dreams was incredibly special.

Life can take many crazy twists and turns. Even when the road gets rough and you cannot see around the next corner, don't stop chasing your dreams. With determination and persistent pursuit, they can come true.

REMOVE EXCUSES

In late 2001, Michael wanted me to turn over the reins of the Supply Chain Information Technology (SCIT) Steering Committee meeting to the IT leadership, and I was not a happy camper. The SCIT committee meeting was one of the last reminders of the CSC consulting projects I ran for Michaels a year and a half earlier.

At that time, I was responsible for any project that had anything to do with improving inventory management and the effectiveness and cost-efficiency of the supply chain. It made sense to have it report underneath my role, seeing that the consulting engagement projects were the predominant focus of the IT Team at the time. In my opinion, that was still the case because 95% of the strategic investments I was responsible for were focused on inventory management, store operations, vendor relations, and the supply chain.

My biggest concern was this might give the IT leadership just enough wiggle room for excuses for why they could not get something done or why there would be a delay in a project. I told Michael, "Even though our IT Team is outstanding, I swear sometimes there must be a college class that all Computer Science majors take on how to make excuses for why a project is delayed."

He said, "My experience has been the same. That is why I hired you. You know how all these projects and timelines fit together. Plus, you have all that experience at big Tech firms like EDS and CSC. Put everything in place, so you take away all of their excuses." That is exactly what we did. We put a structure in place that held both IT and the company accountable. Here are the key principles we followed:

- CEO sponsorship was critical, and the CEO had to be an active participant in this process.

- SVP or EVP sponsorship was required for all projects and participation on the IT Steering Committee.

- The Office of the CEO was a role created to facilitate that strategy execution got accomplished in an integrated way.

- Finance, Strategy, and Human Resources all had to be aligned on the funding of projects and human resource requirements for project implementation and when projects became operational.

For example, before we even funded a project to replenish our stores automatically, we determined how many Replenishment Analysts and Managers we would need over the next three years. Those numbers were added to the budget for those years.

We needed active Business Owners who knew IT and IT Directors and Managers that knew the business.

In many companies, the IT group knows so much more about the business than the business knows about IT. So many business leaders' only concern about IT is if something works, not how it works. We brought in business owners (many times before a project kickoff) that had been on successful implementation before to team up with the IT group.

- All scope, budget, resources, and timelines were signed off by both IT and the business.

- Any adjustments to the above were discussed and approved by the IT Steering Committee, and if needed, we immediately raised it to the CEO level.

- Excessive communication was the order of the day.

- We were fanatical about making sure everyone was on the same page.

These principles ensured that we did not have IT projects; we had company projects. We gave the IT leadership the sponsorship, financing, structure, and business ownership to help them be successful. Many companies like to put the world on top of IT and then blame them when they fail. We worked hand and hand, so the company was successful. **When implementing any project or initiative within an organization, both the business and IT Teams love making excuses and pointing fingers at why things aren't successfully completed. Remove everyone's excuses and just get stuff done.**

————— • ● • —————

GET UP, GET OUT, AND LOOK UP

Every time the CEO of Michaels thought people were getting a little too comfortable with our progress, he would find some reason to stir the pot. He had so much experience; it was like he had a file cabinet full of lessons ready at a moment's notice to teach the team. We were in the Monday Sales and Operations Committee meeting, and the results were okay, but not what he thought our potential truly was. Our six-store Zone Vice Presidents (ZVPs) started the session by discussing the many issues they were still dealing with across the country. As they were talking, I could see Michael was getting more and more agitated. One of the ZVPs was in mid-sentence when he had had enough.

He looked around the room at every non-store person and asked a simple question. "When is the last time you were in a store and looked at it through the eyes of the store manager or customer?" Crickets! He then took aim at every Executive Committee member in attendance. He looked at the EVP of merchandising and said, "How often do all your buyers get in the stores?" It was a stumbling and bumbling answer. He looked at the SVP of Logistics and asked, "Do your DC people ever actually go to a store and unload a truck they have packed and see what it takes at the store level?" Another stumbling and bumbling answer.

He finally got to me and asked, "How many of your Vendor Relations Team visit the stores to see what they need from the Vendor Community."

"Not enough," I replied. Point made.

"All of you are too comfortable working the cushy 9 to 5 corporate life while our store associates are on the front lines working 80 hours a week." Then he screamed, "You can't learn a **damn** thing just staring at the computer screen! It is like trying to fight a war without going to the front lines. You all have to get out to stores and see the repercussions of your actions. You have to see the experience of the store associates. That is where retail happens!"

He paused for effect, then finished with the quote of the century for all corporate office retail associates. He said, *"A bad store manager can affect one store. A bad district manager can affect 15 stores, but a bad decision at the corporate office affects 800 stores!* I want you all to work with the Store Operation Team to get out of the corporate office and learn how your team can make the store associate's life better and the customer's experience better. Stop looking at it through your eyes, and look at things through their eyes!"

From that moment on, each Executive Committee member worked with Store Operations to get out to stores with a dramatically different perspective of what we all should be looking for. Michael took the lead by arranging an annual trip to the Northeast every Christmas season. He took about 50 people from the corporate office, including every area of the company he took to task in that meeting. The lessons learned were invaluable. Those trips dramatically accelerated the progress in making our store an environment better for our associates and a better shopping experience for our customers.

Now more than ever, we spend too much time looking at a screen. We believe that is the real world. It is not. Whether you work in a retail brick and mortar environment, a manufacturing environment, a hospital, are a politician, or are a hedge fund investor, the computer screen in the four walls of your cube or home office can tell you only so much. You have to get out and experience the real world to see the real impact of your decisions.

As for life itself, get out and see the world. Take road trips to see America and experience the world. Meet new people. Investigate different cultures. Sample new cuisine. Investigate our collective history by seeing and touching it. **Get up, get out, and look up. You will be amazed at what you can experience and learn when you look up from your computer or cell phone screen and get out into the real world, how it will change your perspective, add to your knowledge base, and how you will thirst for more.**

––––––––––– • • • –––––––––––

WHAT'S AROUND THE CORNER?

We seemed to have found a nice rhythm of running the business. Every Monday, we had a Sales and Operations Meeting that included the leadership of every operational discipline in the company. We discussed last week's results and determined what needed to be adjusted, fixed, or implemented to make sure we hit or exceeded our numbers for the upcoming week.

On the other hand, we also had a Strategic Planning and Initiative process that looked out into the future. It included the current budget year and extended out an additional four years. We had a strategy meeting, an Executive Committee meeting, and a weekly IT Steering Committee meeting to select, monitor, and make any necessary adjustments to ensure the successful implementation of our strategic initiatives and projects.

Our sales were up, as were profits, processes were all working well, projects were all on schedule, and the team was working together very well. We had a tactical view at the ground level of running the business day-to-day and a strategic view ranging from 5,000 feet to 30,000 feet above the ground to look into the future. But there was a gap somewhere in our processes, and I could not put my finger on it. Being the process guy, I was supposed to be the person to help identify gaps and how to fix them. I was stumped.

Certain topics were becoming more of an every-week discussion, not just a once-in-a-while issue. In the Monday meeting, someone brought up an issue related to product that was in the Sunday sale—the same issue that we had come up two weeks ago and four weeks before that. It hit me; we were resolving issues and not preventing problems.

The CEO asked, "How many times over the last two months has this issue arisen?" The answer was about 3 or 4. "We just preached to our vendors to prevent problems, but then on issues like this, it seems we just fix it for the next week and move on. What is the root cause of this issue?"

After a brief discussion, we realized there was a miscommunication between the Marketing and Inventory Management areas. We found the root cause, but Michael wanted the team to start thinking in broader terms about everything related to running the day-to-day business. He said, *"We need to move beyond a week-to-week focus and start looking 30, 60, 90 days out with a glance around the corner."* He added, "If there is a tweak to a process, let's fix it. If you just need to communicate something to this team, we will put it on the agenda. We can't keep coming in here every week discussing the same issues over and over again."

That is what we were missing. We had become too myopic in our view of the day-to-day or week-to-week business. We were not looking out into the short-term future to anticipate an issue and then prevent it. The 30, 60, 90 day around the corner phrase was so easy to understand. We needed to take a step back from the trees just a few steps to avoid being blinded by the narrow view of only the next week's results. We needed to keep our heads on a swivel to identify and anticipate anything that could impact us in the next quarter or two.

When you run a business, it is easy to get dragged down into the mud every minute of every day fighting a trench warfare battle. You are so exhausted that you don't have a chance to look beyond the next day, let alone 90 days or five years into the future. Great companies can do it all, and we wanted to be great. **Whether in business or in life, take a step back from the day-to-day grind to look all around you and make sure you are heading in the right direction and avoiding the numerous potholes that could derail your future.**

———•●•———

DIAMOND IN THE ROUGH

It is an almost impossible situation. How do you hire people to come to a company that has had two straight years of losing money in an industry that people don't know much about? That was the challenge for Michael Rouleau in late 1996 when he took the reigns at Michaels. In 1995 the company lost $20.4M and had an earnings per share of $(.95). In 1996 the company lost $31.2M and had an earnings per share loss of $(1.34).

At that time, the Arts & Crafts Industry was not seen by Wall Street analysts or most people in the retail industry as a sexy or cool place to be. Wal-Mart, Target, Home Depot, Bed, Bath and Beyond, Toys "R" Us, May Company, Macy's, Kohl's, The Gap, Limited, Victoria's Secret, Best Buy, Circuit City, and Barnes & Noble are just a few of the places people wanted to work for and invest in.

When I told my friends in the retail industry I was going to do some consulting work for Michaels in 1997, they either said "Who?" or "If you do help them, it won't look good on your bio." When I joined Michaels as an executive, my friends and colleagues thought I was nuts. One said, "Except for my wife, who else knows anything about the Arts & Crafts Industry? Consulting for them is one thing, but working for them is a totally different scenario!"

In 1997 two CSC colleagues and I did an in-depth strategic analysis of the Arts & Crafts Industry, Michaels' financials, Michaels versus their competition, and Michaels versus the best specialty retailers in the country. I will admit that I was not very confident about the entire situation when we were done. It just seemed like it was too much of an uphill battle that included land mines seemingly with every step. I struggled to see where the upside for this company could possibly come from.

That was before I met the CEO, Michael Rouleau. I remember telling my two colleagues, "I don't know why but I think that guy is actually going to make Michaels into something special. His drive, passion, and intensity are second to no one I have ever met. He also has a crystal-clear vision of what the company can be and of how to get it done. When he speaks, he has five answers for every challenge with no hesitation or doubt in his voice."

Rouleau was the secret sauce, and those characteristics of his were what many people that joined Michaels in 1997-99 told me sold them on Michaels. They all knew what I knew about the company and the industry. They all knew that this whole thing could crash and burn and be a dark mark on all of our resumes. Almost to a person, they said the difference was that after spending time with Michael; you just believed that this man was not going to fail.

Years later, I asked Michael what he saw in Michaels Stores that others missed. He answered, "When I first walked a Michaels store in 1996, I saw a diamond in the rough. They lacked standards, processes, and systems that all had been implemented by other retailers 15 to 25 years ago, so that was not my concern. The key was even with all the warts, the customer loved crafting, and they loved Michaels. It just needed the right leadership, team, and vision to produce the real beauty of the stone. Some people just saw the rock; I saw the potential for a beautiful diamond."

You can find hundreds of definitions for visionary people or leaders. I like this one, "Visionary leaders are driven and inspired by what a company can become." In 1996 that was Michael. **Not everyone has the leadership capabilities or talents to see things in a visionary way, and not everyone wants to take a chance on helping to turn a rock into a diamond. However, if you want the thrill of being a diamond cutter, attach yourself to someone who can see what a company can become and then enjoy the ride with them.**

GREY HAIRS OR NO HAIRS

I was talking to my boss, and something was bothering him. We were discussing progress the company had made since he showed up in late 1996. At the end of 1999, we had 12 straight quarters of sales and earnings increases. Our stock price had risen from $3.25 in 1996 to $26.75 per share at the end of fiscal 2000. It was a far cry from the just three years earlier when Michaels Stores recorded two straight years of net losses.

Finally, we talked about how the once-maligned Arts & Crafts Industry had a gale-force wind in its sails. We both agreed we were no longer the company and industry that family, friends, and investors were dismissing a few years earlier. We were on a roll, and everyone had taken notice. Everything all seemed great, but I asked what was keeping him up at night now.

He said, "Two things. First, most people in the organization have never seen great. Most associates have only worked at Michaels, and that is all they know. They have never worked for a great company like Target or Wal-Mart. Second, most people in this organization have never been through the transition we are about to undertake. They have zero experience with all the new systems and infrastructure projects we are about to invest $250M in over the next five years."

He kept going, "Jeff, we need more people who have been there and done that. We don't have time to wait for the entire organization to learn. I need people who know where the landmines are, know what mistakes to avoid, and what it takes to be great. When we blend the best of the current team and experienced individuals, we will have the best of both worlds."

The is what we did. At the Executive Committee level, we brought in people who had 25 to 30 years of experience working at some of the great retailers of the day. At the VP, Director, and Manager level, we hired people who had already lived through the systems and infrastructure implementation we had on our strategic timelines or had years of experience operating those same systems.

The biggest change was going to be in our store organization. In four short years, 90% of what they currently were doing surrounding ordering merchandise directly from vendors would become centralized in the corporate headquarters. Their fundamental role would transition to operating the store and taking care of the customers. Due to the coming transition, we started hiring managers and assistants who had worked with centrally driven retailers like Target, Bed, Bath and Beyond, and Home Depot.

We could never have had the success between 2000 – 2006 if we did not hire all those people with years of experience. It would have been cheaper in many instances to hire less-experienced people, but the overall costs to the company would have been incalculable. Most companies today take the more affordable and less experienced route. They look at a person with 20 to 35 years of experience as too expensive or set in their ways. So, they hire incredibly talented younger but less experienced individuals for less money and discard all the expertise and knowledge to the side of the road like an old Coke can. Then they watch the organization make the same mistakes over and over again and wonder why it is happening.

It is such a tragic mistake. **Every generation thinks they are the first to ever experience something. I believe that is the reason history repeats itself.** I would not be where I am today if it weren't for the grey-hair or no-hair individuals who shared their wisdom, discussed the pitfalls of going down a certain path, or saved me from making a big mistake. **Don't discard experience; learn from it. Don't just kick all the individuals with years of wisdom to the side of the road to save a buck or two. Find a few grey-hair or no-hair people and get them on your team. It will be well worth the investment.**

THE MICHAELS' WAVE OF REALITY

In a weekly update meeting with my boss, Michael told me there was a candidate for an open SVP position coming in for interviews next week, and as usual, he wanted me to be part of the interview team for key hires.

He expected my honest opinion of the person. He counted on me to explain our strategic plan initiatives process and our current project list to the candidate. Finally, he wanted me to test the candidate's ability to handle Michaels' culture and the pace with which things were changing and evolving. The words he would use are, "Scare them straight."

Michael really wanted me to scare this person straight. You might think that is a crazy thing to do with a potential candidate, but there was a method to his madness. Michael wanted to hire more experienced individuals at all levels of the organization, and he did not have the patience to wait for someone to learn on the job. He wanted people who had been there and done that.

As with most things, there is always an issue or two with any strategy. The company was rolling, but we were also undergoing a massive amount of change. The pace was off the charts, and you had to be able to stay up with it. Many interviewed had plenty of knowledge and experience, but the pace of change would have buried them.

We also had an environment still missing many things, particularly in the area of technology. That is why we were investing hundreds of millions of dollars to rectify. It would take us five years to get it all completed, so the candidates would have to do without many of the technology solutions that their current companies already had for decades. We needed to know if they could still be productive without the safety net of technology until we had all our systems projects implemented.

That was the backdrop of my interview with (I will call him Joe). "Joe" worked for a great company and had a great deal of the experience we were looking for. After the standard set of interview questions, I shifted to the topics Michael wanted me to cover. I asked Joe to think that back to the year 1985 and where his current company was without all the technology investments they had made since.

He asked, "Why would I want to do that?"

I said, "Because that is where Michaels is today." His eyes grew wider, and he showed a brief glimpse of fear. I continued, "We have made improvements, so we are no longer 25 years behind modern companies; we are only about 15 to 20 years behind. We are still missing so many things, especially in your area of responsibility, and you won't have any of those things for years. Can you handle going back to 1985?"

At that moment, the Michaels' wave of reality hit him. The sales and profit headlines were outstanding, but the reality of what we were missing was a shock. This person did a good job answering the questions, but the eyes never lie. He did get hired and lasted a few years, but he struggled mightily with the pace of our environment and with the technology gap.

When you investigate a company you would like to go to work for, you have to go beyond the headlines and the numbers. You need to explore the culture, a day in the life of your job, the pace of work, what is there but also what is missing. Perform this due diligence, or you could get swallowed up with a wave of reality you might not be able to recover from.

• ● •

ANYTHING BUT HUMANE

It was the week the Green Bay Packers had to cut their roster from 90 players to 53. Their General Manager (GM) was interviewing with the press, and he was describing his philosophy about how he was going to make the final roster cuts. He talked about how he had to look at the potential of each player to weigh keeping one player at one position versus another player at a different position.

He continued saying they talk to the coaches to get their input on the pros and cons of each player. They weigh past performance, growth potential, the character of the player, and whether the person has a positive or negative locker room locker presence. The bottom line is 47 players were going to be told they were not good enough to make the team.

Seven days later, the final roster was approved. Each of the 53 players who made the NFL roster was relieved—that is *unless* the GM could find a better player. Forty-eight hours after you believed your dream had come true, the GM could let you know that you were cut, and a new player could be announced to take your place on the roster. It did not end there. For the next sixteen weeks of the season, the GM held tryouts with 5 to 6 players or more a week. If you were a player on the team, you had one eye trying to get ready for the game and one eye on the tryout process to see if you would be replaced the next day or maybe that afternoon. It is a ruthless business.

As a fan, you want your team to get better in hopes of winning a Super Bowl. You cheer when a marginal player gets cut, and a supposed better player is signed. You act like these players are a disposable commodity. All you care about is winning. If you don't already know, this is what corporate America does every day.

Until I became an Executive at Michaels, I did not realize the entirety of the excruciatingly painful Human Resource process. Before I joined Michaels, I just executed the plan that the Executive Team and HR gave me. Now I was part of the entire process from strategy to budget, where we can cut and who we can get rid of. It was a ruthless black and white approach to finding a way to win.

Like the NFL, corporate America is constantly looking to turn the so-called bottom 10% to 20% of their roster. As a fan, you love it, but just like the players, you always look over your shoulder to see if you are the next one to get cut. There is a reason it is called Human Resources and not Humane Resources. The definition of humane is "having or showing compassion or benevolence." The process to build and maintain a talented organization and stay within the budget parameters is anything but humane. The sooner you realize that, the better off you will be.

First, if you love what you're doing and the company you work for, make sure you are doing something that makes you too valuable to cut. Don't give the company a reason to let you go. Volunteer to be on a project team, check and triple-check your work, or maybe give the boss an analysis that they did not expect. *Second, look for ways to further your education.* Maybe getting certifications or taking a finance class, for example, gives you more knowledge than the person next to you.

Third, have a good locker room presence. Don't get labeled a person no one gets along with. *Finally, always keep looking for something else every day of the year.* Never get complacent. If Hall of Famer Peyton Manning can get cut, so can you. DO NOT depend on the corporate world to take care of you. In a 2018 *Fortune* article titled "HR is Not Your Friend," they had a couple of pertinent quotes. "It's important to remember that HR exists primarily to serve top management—not you!"

DO NOT DEPEND ON THE CORPORATE WORLD TO TAKE CARE OF YOU. HUMAN RESOURCES PRIMARILY SERVES TOP MANAGEMENT— NOT YOU!

DON'T TELL ME WHAT YOU THINK, TELL ME WHAT YOU KNOW

They were brutal. I had heard about these meetings, but it was worse than I had been told. The Sales and Business Development Team were on one side of the table, and a team of representatives from different functional areas within EDS sat on the other side of the table. At one point in the meeting, I thought the salesperson was going to break down in tears. What was this meeting about, and why was it so painful?

It was a meeting to discuss a potential contract between EDS and a new client for a $100M deal to outsource the technology department for the client. At the time, outsourcing was a major percentage of the annual EDS sales figure. These contracts were complex, incredibly detailed, and could be very risky for both EDS and the client. This meeting was to make sure the Sales and Business Development Teams had dotted all the i's and crossed all the t's. It was standard for all contracts, but especially important for new clients.

The meeting was painful because the Sales and Business Development Team could not get past two words they kept using—"I think." Every question asked was answered with, "I think ..." Then the team representing the different functional area would bounce on the Sales Team and say, "Don't tell me what you think, tell us what you know! We cannot sign a contract if we don't know the answers to these basic questions." After the meeting, the salesperson told me he thought he was prepared, but obviously not. The next time his team made a presentation, those two words were never spoken.

It was harsh to watch but a great lesson in setting expectations for any future conversation I would have. *No one cares what I think! They want to know what I know—facts, statistics, and quotes that prove I know what I am talking about.* Five years later, I was sitting in the boardroom of Michaels. We had just put in a new process for the buyers to explain their plans in detail for their departments. It was new to Michaels, but standard practice for all major retailers.

We wanted the buyers to develop their own strategic and tactical plans for their departments. It included a vision, historical and future financials numbers, consumer trends, competitive analysis, etc. On one side of the boardroom table sat the buyer, their boss, merchandise planner, other inventory management personnel, and a vendor relations person who supported this area. On the other side were executives from inventory management, finance, strategy, store, and logistics.

It was their first time to go through the process, so we told everyone that we knew this was as much gathering information to make decisions in support of the buyer as it was to see how the process worked. Unfortunately, Michael Rouleau did not remember getting that memo. The reason for his anxiety, two words— "I think!" When questions arose, the buyer continually said, "I *think* the customer wants this ..." or "I *think* my sales will go up if ..." or "I *think* if you give me two more end caps, I can produce $10M in sales."

Rouleau said the same thing the EDS internal team said, "How can I give you millions of dollars to spend on product when you don't *know* all of the answers to basic questions?" Just like at EDS, you could hear crickets from the Buying Team. Even though it was just a first trial run, his question hit the nail right on the head. We finished the meeting, and word traveled at light speed around the building. Never use the words "I think," and you better *know* the answers to the questions.

How many times in your life have you started a sentence with "I think"? Even if you are the smartest person on the planet, most people would still challenge the rest of the statement. **Don't get caught being unprepared, and never begin your answer with the words "I think." Know your subject matter. Be prepared to answer questions with facts, quotes, or references to support why you are saying something.**

———————•●•———————

NO GOING BACKWARD

Debi worked frantically to finish so we could start the meeting on time. She knew anytime Michael went out of town, he was handing her this impossible Monday morning project, but knowing it was coming made no difference in getting the job done.

It did not matter whether his trip was business or personal; Michael Rouleau always found time to visit two or three Michaels locations and as many nearby competitors as he could pack in. When he returned, he would hand the camera filled with pictures of his trip to his Executive Assistant Debi, and she would spend Monday morning putting what could be hundreds of photos into a slide presentation.

Retail was in his blood, and Michael knew the only place to see if we were really making progress was how it impacted our stores and our customers. So, any Monday Sales and Operations meeting following any trip he made began with a slide show to present his findings before we started checking off any other agenda items.

When he first started doing this a few years earlier, it was a painful but necessary process. It showed not only the issues but also the potential of what we could become. No one was immune from his slide show. The pictures spoke louder than any notes from a store, call from a vendor, or letter from a customer. The photos validated our to-do list or exposed new issues to add to the list.

After a few years, we had made tremendous progress. When Michael showed pictures now, he could say we use to have this problem, but now it is fixed. For an instant, you felt a sense of pride that he admitted we had done something good. But just when you thought he might leave it at that, he would show hundreds of slides of new issues and problems he discovered. He would then show slides of the competition and ask, "Why aren't we doing this?" or "How come they can do this, and we can't?"

The final straw came when he bought a video camera. He would go into our stores and interview sales associates. We knew some of the scenes were set up, but they still told a powerful story. He would say to the associate, "Tell the people at corporate why this end cap is horrible," or "Tell the logistics people why they need to fix the way they load a truck." You had to laugh but at the same time pull the knife out of your back.

Michael never wanted you to be comfortable. *He wanted you comfortable being uncomfortable.* He would always say that everyone and everything can get better. He believed any progress you made set the new standard for the organization, and now you needed to build upon that. No going backward was his motto! Like a great football coach, he was always raising the bar for the team. He did not want to see all the progress to date fall apart. He wanted to build on top of the new foundation, not let cracks form that could destroy our future goals.

The visuals were a tool in his toolbox that easily showed progress and opportunities, but the message was always to push yourself to set a new standard of excellence. **Once you reach a new level of achievement, set a backstop so you don't go backward. Then do everything possible to build to a new level, so that becomes the new standard.**

Great coaches and great players are never satisfied. They are always looking to raise their game to the next level. Tiger Woods, in his prime, would practice 10 to 12 hours a day. Michael Jordan would spend an entire summer lifting weights to make him strong enough to take on the toughest of defensives. **Never stop trying to improve yourself. No matter your age, find ways to improve your health, your business acumen, your personal life, your knowledge, or an activity you are passionate about. Continue to raise your personal bar—and no going backward!**

———————•●•———————

A COUPLE OF OLD GUYS AND A TEN DOLLAR BILL

CEO Michael Rouleau, SVP of Store Operations Ed Sadler, and I were standing by the customer service desk at a store called the Christmas Tree Shop. We looked a little out of place—two sixty-something guys and one forty-something standing in a store shopped by 99% women. We were on our annual fall trek to the Northeast to check out our stores and our competition. Besides the normal investigative work we did on these trips, Michael would set a new objective to focus on each year.

The mission of this trip was to find individual items that could sell hundreds of thousands of units in the 8 to 12-week holiday period. They are hard to come by, but when you hit on one, it is a wonderful joy ride. Our Buying Team had spent the last few years improving our merchandise selection of basic arts and crafts suppliers. This meant we had a better assortment of craft paint, artist paint supplies, and kids' crafts made up of hundreds or thousands of items, not one single item.

Now they had to learn how to find that one item that could sell on its own. Little did the Buying Team know that they were about to get a master's degree in finding a key item that could sell millions of units.

Michael was a former buyer and Senior Merchant at Target almost 30 years ago, but he had not lost his touch or dulled his instincts one bit. He had done some homework before he went on this trip, and he told Ed and me to be on the lookout for a little $1.00 2" x 4" ceramic cake pan. He had heard Christmas Tree Shop had sold a ton of these items, and he knew with the traffic in Michaels Stores, the sky was the limit on how much we could sell.

We had been to two other Tree Shop stores, but they had already sold out. We had the same bad luck in this store until I noticed a woman standing in the return line. In her hand was one of her cake pans and a return receipt. I nudged Michael and Ed, and instinctively Michael said, "Let's buy it from her."

"Buy it from her?" I asked, a little confused.

"Yes, buy it from her!" he repeated.

"How much should we offer her?" I asked.

Michael said, "At least $5 or $10, so we make it worth her while." Not a bad return for a $1 item.

We all went into our pockets, and of course, I was the only one that had anything less than a $20 or a $50 bill in their pocket. Michael took my $10 bill and went up to the lady, explained who he was and that he had been looking for that item all day. He asked if he could buy it from her for $10. I think if Michael had not had a dress shirt and tie on, she might have called the police, but he convinced her to sell it to him—and he had his item!

That night in the hotel, all the buyers showed what ideas they had found. There were one or two possibilities, but the real show was just about to happen. Then to the amazement and amusement of everyone in the room, Michael told them our buying story. No one believed it at first until Ed and I confirmed that was exactly how it happened. That little ceramic dish went on to sell millions of units the next Christmas season. It was a lesson in how great merchants will dig and dig until they find that one home run. It just happened to be from the CEO, who had not been a buyer for decades!

Leading by example is a phrase many executives use, but few really follow. **Leaders need to be great teachers and mentors. They have all these years of experience and lessons learned, but if they don't share it with the organization, what good is it?**

Michael led by example. He was never afraid to roll up his sleeves and get his hands dirty. Is your leadership the ivory tower leadership, or do they lead by example? It might be the difference between your company being successful or not.

THE WORLD IS SIX FEET UNDERWATER ON AVERAGE

We were in a merchandise planning meeting with one of our Buyer Teams to hear how the area was doing and plan for the following year. These discussions would feed our upcoming annual budget process and determine what areas would get new planogram sets in our stores, so we had to make sure the numbers made sense.

The challenge in this meeting was that I could not reconcile the numbers. As the buyer talked, I scoured through the entire presentation deck, and the answer was not there. I pulled up a few reports I had run to prepare for the meeting and compared them to the presentation deck. As I frantically went back and forth between my numbers and the buyer's, I finally found the answer. The buyer was talking in averages which did not paint the entire picture.

The buyer's presentation said:

- Average store sales were up 10%, but she did not say that 40% of the stores were flat or down in her area.

- Average classification increased by 10% as well, but the increase came predominantly from only 25% of the classifications.

- Average margin expansion was 2%, but it again came from only 25% of the classifications and a single item that sold very well during the holiday season.

I was sitting next to our new CFO, Jeff Boyer. Jeff had joined us recently and was taking part in his first merchandise planning meetings. I leaned over to him and pointed out the disparity in the numbers. He smiled and said, "The world is six feet underwater on average." I wanted to burst out laughing, but I held back from making an outburst. His comment was perfect.

I have never been able to confirm the statement geologically, but I don't care. It is a perfect metaphor for how incredibly careful you have to be when using averages. Businesses use averages all the time to discuss financial results, vendor base, store metrics, and more.

- Average store sales were up 5%, but we could have 25% of the chain flat or down.

- The average in-stock position was 98%, but we could be out of stock in key items in half our chain.

- The average size of our vendor base was $30M, but we had 30% of our vendors who had volume less than $10M.

The old saying that the devil's in the details hits the nail on the head when using averages to paint the entire picture. You see this in our everywhere daily lives. The average American in a poll, the average NFL football player, the average rainfall, the average college student, or the average person eats so much chocolate, etc. The average means nothing to the individual circumstance.

Be incredibly careful accepting averages or any number that is defined as the absolute fact about a situation. **Numbers can lie. Challenge to find the details behind those numbers to see if the reality is something different than the black and white number. If you blindly accept an average number, you might find yourself like the world, six feet underwater on average.**

POUND THE TABLE

Something had changed, and frankly, I was getting tired of it. Invariably someone would come into my office to discuss an issue they had with something in the company. I had built a reputation over the last five years as a fix-it man at Michaels. People would seek me out to share something they thought should be a priority of the company or me to fix.

In the beginning, I took it as a great compliment that individuals would trust me to share their ideas and knew that often, we found a way to address their problem. Most were very polite and would bring me detailed facts to back up their comments. Their information gave me a sense of how big an issue something was and whether it was worth my time or the company's time to look into.

For some reason, something had changed about six months ago, and now it seemed like every time someone came into my office or at every meeting I took part in, there was some sort of outburst or emotional diatribe. Rather than constructive discussions, things had deteriorated into just another rant.

On one occasion, after a few sentences, I stopped the conversation and said, "Where are your facts? Show me a document, show me an email, show me pictures from the stores, show me a survey of the entire chain ... but show me *something* to support what you are saying. It is not that I don't believe you; I just can't determine if this is a 2 out of 10 problem, or a 10 out of 10 problem. Get me the facts, and then we can talk."

When I went home that night, I told my wife about the incident. "I would like to put a sign behind my head that says, 'Bring me the facts or get the heck out of my office!'" We laughed, then she said, "Why not put something on your desk that says something about facts?" That was a perfect suggestion.

We went to a store in the mall specializing in engraved items and found a glass desktop nameplate. Instead of my name, we engraved the words *"Manage by Facts"* on it. I put it on my desk where anyone who entered my office could see it. If anyone started down the ranting and raving path, I pointed to the sign. It worked. Soon people brought documents, pictures, notes, etc., when they wanted to talk with me about a problem. The conversations were 100% more productive and helped find many important issues we needed to address.

Carl Sandburg is quoted as saying, *"If the facts are against you, argue the law. If the law is against you, argue the facts. If the law and the facts are against you, pound the table and yell like hell!"* It doesn't just happen in law; it happens at home, business, sports, and of course, politics. When you don't have the facts, you get emotional and hope that carries the day. It doesn't. Pounding the table is only a distraction.

Do your homework and get your facts straight when having a discussion. No emotion. No outburst. No ranting. No pounding the table. Just the facts!

I FELT LIKE TONY STARK

After struggling the year before, the Packers' number one draft choice had another outstanding game. In fact, he had now put together an impressive string of five games. It was his second year, and he looked like a totally different player from his rookie season. After the game, the press surrounded his locker and asked him to explain the dramatic difference in his play from last season to this season. He said, "The game has slowed down for me. I am no longer thinking so much. I see things faster; I can process things faster, and I am now playing faster than I could last year."

This simple phrase has been utter thousands of times by athletes who make a leap from an unproven player to a worthwhile pro and maybe even a superstar Hall of Famer. There is no time machine that a player can enter and actually slow down time, but because they have more experience and repetitions to draw from, they can then translate these images in their minds to their actions faster than when they were less experienced.

That is exactly what had happened to me in my second year at Michaels; the game slowed down for me. During my first year, everything seemed so fast and that my hair was on fire every minute of every day. I had been given a tremendous amount of responsibility from my boss, but 75% of my job I had never done before.

I had never started a division from scratch. I had never been responsible for $250M of capital investment. I had never been hired to move an entire company farther or faster, and if I did not, I would be fired. I had never been asked to help change an entire industry. In the beginning, I just worked harder and longer hours to make sure I did not let one mistake happen on my watch.

Just like the rookie draft pick, in my second year, everything changed. I understood my role in the company better. I understood the playbook for the company better. My teammates trusted me more, and I could now visualize things before they even happened. It was like I had this hologram in front of me that showed all the processes I helped build, our systems and infrastructure projects, the investment capital, the timelines, and how it all fit together.

If you are a Marvel fan, it was like when Tony Stark would be working in his lab, and he would produce a holographic display in front of him. He could move things around with his hands and do what-if scenarios or see if his calculations worked out. I felt the same way. I had a crystal-clear image of how all the dots within Michaels fit together. I felt I could see things others could not, identity things faster that could potentially be a problem, predict how one project today could impact another project two years into the future, and stop us from potentially going off a cliff.

When you are young and inexperienced, you can struggle with your new role or company. Don't let it get to you. Everyone has been there at some point in their career. The challenge for you is to learn and gather as much knowledge as you can every day. If you do your homework and continue to gain valuable experience, someday, the game will slow down for you. When it does, you will be much more productive, and the job will be much more fun.

————— • ● • —————

AND I'LL DO WHATEVER IT TAKES

My wife entered our home office and asked when I was coming to bed. I said, "I am not sure because we are still editing the presentation."

She put her hands on my shoulders and said, "When did you start working on this with him?"

I rubbed the back of my neck and answered, "I got a call about 8:30 pm, and I have been doing it on and off since then."

Lisa said, "Does he not realize it is 11:30 pm the day after Christmas? Does he not realize that this is supposed to be your day off?"

I did not have to answer the question because she already knew the answer.

Of course, he knew. The "he" we were talking about was my boss, Michael Rouleau. Both my wife and I knew what I signed up for when I joined the company. Michael had extremely high expectations for me because he knew I would always deliver for him. For over seven years now, we had worked together, and he knew I would do whatever it took to help him make his dream for Michaels come true, and in return, he was helping me make one of my career dreams come true.

This evening would last another three hours. Back and forth we went. He was old school, so he would make changes on a paper copy of the document and then fax it to me. I would then update the changes in PowerPoint and fax the edits back to him. Twenty minutes or so later, the fax machine would start humming again, and we would continue the process.

It was about 2:00 am my time and midnight in Seattle, where he was spending the holiday weekend, when the fax machine started churning out pages again, but this time the last page was not from the presentation. It was a handwritten note from Michael. It read, "My wife said I should let you go to bed. Thanks for all your help and good night." He signed it with his signature smiley face and his initials M.R. Of course; I did not go to bed until I had made the last set of changes and sent them back to Michael.

This was not a one-time incident. There was the time he called me on vacation because he wanted to get my opinion on a potential change that he wanted to make to the Senior Management Team. He was on vacation in Hawaii, and I was in Telluride, Colorado. He was talking on the balcony of his hotel while his wife was in the shower. I was standing on the balcony of my hotel room with my boots and ski jacket on because it was 15 degrees outside, and my wife was also in the shower. We both got busted by our spouses, but he got my opinion. I have hundreds of examples of stories like this.

When I was about 24, I set a goal to be a Senior Executive helping run a company or be the company's CEO and become become financially secure in the process by the age of 40. At 39, I joined Michaels with the title of Office of the CEO, and Michael gave me a backstage pass to almost everything he did daily for the next six years. I had more influence and accomplished more in those years working with Michael than at any other time in my career. I was off by a couple of years on the financial piece, but in 2003 at the age of 42, I exercised my first stock options. I had accomplished my dream.

You, too, can accomplish your goals if you are willing to stretch yourself, take risks, be willing to fail, be open to mentorship—especially from more experienced individuals—and doing whatever it takes. It is not an easy journey and definitely not a straight line up, but once you arrive at the summit and realize what you have accomplished, it is an amazing feeling. In 1996, Gloria Estefan recorded a song for the Atlanta Olympics called *Reach*. Her lyrics are a perfect way to end this story.

> *Some dreams live on in time forever,*
>
> *those dreams you want with all your heart*
>
> *And I'll do whatever it takes,*
>
> *follow through with the promise I made*
>
> *Put it all on the line;*
>
> *What I hoped for at last would be mine.*

I'LL JUST HAVE TO GET NEW DOGS

It was becoming a pretty animated Executive Committee meeting. We were discussing our corporate turnover numbers—a contentious topic because even though we were on a roll, we had a reputation of being a tough place to work. This made it harder for the Executives and their teams to recruit quality individuals and have the right team in place to meet Michael's high expectations for each of us in the room.

After a few back-and-forth discussion points, Mike Greenwood, President of our Artistree Custom Framing Division, spoke up. Mike had been with Michaels since 1992, so he had been through a lot of changes over the last decade. He was concerned that we were pushing our organization too hard and that it would burn people out.

Mike said, "Michael, I am going to make an analogy to my bird dogs. If you beat the dogs too much, they won't hunt."

Before we could laugh, agree, or even breathe, without hesitation, Michael said, "I guess I'll just have to get new dogs!"

Whatever chance we had to make a point that we might want to create a different aura about Michaels in the marketplace was gone. It also hit home for every Executive Team member because Michael had been through numerous Senior Executives during his tenure.

In Michael's nearly ten years at the helm, we had gone through two HR execs, two CFOs, five Marketing Leaders, three Chief Merchants, four CIOs, five Heads of Supply Chain, four Leaders of Inventory Management, two COOs, and three Heads of Store Operations. It was like President Lincoln changing Generals during the civil war. Michael was always searching for someone who would understand their role and execute his plan. If there was a hint that you could not do the job, he would move on.

Besides Mike Greenwood, only two executives lasted throughout Michael's entire tenure, the EVP of Real Estate, and me. Mike and the head of real estate were both on sort of an island unto themselves. They were incredibly good at what they did, and their areas of responsibility were not a broken mess or needed huge strategic investments when he joined the company. So, they did their jobs, and Michael left them alone.

As for me, he knew I had been extraordinarily successful building the rock-solid process foundation he wanted for the company. He believed that the processes were strong enough to withstand the turnover, even though it created chaos within many of the divisions to have a new leader every other year. He also knew I would run through a brick wall for him, and if needed, I could pinch-hit for him when there was an executive opening. It worked. Even with all the executive turnover, we never missed a beat hitting all of our financial targets every year until we were put up for sale in 2006.

I would not suggest you turn your Senior Executive Team as often as we did at Michaels. It creates havoc for the company and for those who uprooted their lives to join the organization only to be moved out in a short time. Some turnover is good and some of the decisions were correct. However, you began to wonder if we had crossed a line of being ridiculous.

I am more of a Golden Rule kind of guy, "Do unto others as you would have them do unto you." People are not replaceable

TO SURVIVE, FACE THE FACT THAT IT IS A DOG-EAT-DOG WORLD. KEEP YOUR RESUME UP TO DATE, YOUR SKILLSET GROWING, AND YOUR RESILIENCY HIGH.

parts or disposable parts. They have feelings and families, and they should be treated with a level of respect that you would want for yourself. However, I know the reality of the corporate world is a very cutthroat place, so in most, the Golden Rule does not exist. If you are to survive in the corporate world, you have to face the fact it is a dog-eat-dog world. Keep your resume up to date, your skillset growing, and your resiliency high.

IT WAS A COMPLIMENT AND A CURSE

A few years in, I broached a subject with my boss. I wanted to be put in charge of a new area to expand my experience and run a larger part of the organization. I reminded him that I had started the Vendor Relations Team from scratch, and the results were outstanding. We had flipped a product received error rate as high as 20% down to just 0.2". We now had a 99.8% accuracy rate! The average time to resolve an issue went from 75 days to 7. And the Kellogg School of Business wrote up a case study on my team!

I sat on an Industry Standards Committee and helped lead the effort that changed an entire industry to balance product development and sales with compliance to supply chain requirements. I also was responsible for building and improving every process in the company, and we ran like a finely tuned machine.

I was responsible for developing the strategic initiative funding and implementation process from scratch as well as for the successful implementation of $50M of capital every year. We were on track and not missing one deliverable. Michael now trusted me so much that whenever there was a Senior Executive opening (and we had a lot of openings), he would ask me to pinch-hit until the position was filled and then help onboard the new executive. I had built a track record of success.

For six months after our meeting, Michael avoided the subject as best he could. Then one day, he said, "Jeff, you have done outstanding work for me going all the way back to 1997 when you first showed up as a consultant. I would be hard-pressed to find anyone who has helped the company more than you over the last six years. Every time I needed something done or fixed—you're my guy!"

It was a great compliment. However, I knew there was a but coming. " ... but," he continued, "I need you to do things for the company and me that no one else can do. I know you want to run something, but I can get anyone to do that. I have turned the Executive Team over three times, and we have not missed a beat. The processes you built with the team are so strong that they almost seem to run themselves."

I took in a deep breath, knowing where he was headed. "Do you know how many resumes I looked at for the open CFO position last year? Hundreds. There are hundreds of people who can do that job, just like hundreds of people can run stores or run the supply chain. But in the 40 years I've been in business, I have met only one or two other people who can do what you do." He paused, and I sat still. In all my years working for Michael, praising people was not a core competency. Part of me knew it was a sell job, but he normally just told people what he wanted.

"Jeff, I need you to take over running the next biggest initiative, and that will be a full-time job." This time Michael wanted me to know how valuable I was to him and the company. It was a great compliment but also a curse. I knew continuing in this role might pigeonhole me with any future company, but I loved what I was doing, and I still had a lot of stock options in my portfolio yet to vest. I had helped build this place, and I wanted to enjoy some of the fruits of my labor, so I accepted his new challenge.

Life is made up of thousands of choices. The bigger the decision, the more difficult the choice is to make. Like all big decisions, I did my homework, talked with my wife and a few other people I respected, prayed, and once I made my choice, I never looked back.

Once you make a decision in your life or career, if it works out, pat yourself on the back. If it turns out not to be what you wanted, don't waste any energy regretting your choice. Use that energy to regroup and move forward.

I NEVER KNEW THE CARPET CHANGED

When Michael asked me to take our next big initiative, he made a couple of adjustments that impacted my responsibilities—and my seating assignment. First, he took the Vendor Relations Team away from me, which really stung at first. This was my baby that I had grown from an idea to a force in the company and the entire industry.

The other change was Michael wanted me to move into the office next to his. We were going to be spending a lot of time on this new initiative, and he did not want me at the other end of the building. I did not like being that close to him, but I did like the idea of the bigger office I was getting. You have to take the good with the not-so-good, right?

It took a few days to get me totally set up with office furniture, my trusty whiteboard, and all the technology configurations. I liked how the office was laid out, and most importantly, I had more space to conduct meetings. In my other office, things were a little more cramped.

After a few days, I realized something that happened all the time in my old office had not happened once since my move. No one came by to talk, shoot the breeze, tell me about an issue happening in the company or update me on a project. In my old office, this happened at least 25 times a day. My administrative assistant would try to play traffic cop, but people still got by her. I didn't dwell on the missing exchanges but kept my head down, getting a handle on my new responsibility.

I heard a knock on my door. I looked up and saw Jeff Mitchell. I had known Jeff since I first showed up six years earlier. He had worked on many of those project teams, and we had become good friends. He was valuable, not only while doing his day job, but he also helped me with various new project teams.

We talked for a few moments about my new office and my new role, and I told him that he was the first person to come by and see me since I moved. He replied, "Of course, they are not going to come see you now because of the carpet change."

"Carpet change?" I exclaimed, "What the heck are you talking about?"

"Follow me," he said. I walked outside my office, and sure enough, ten feet away, the carpet did change. I was told it was from a renovation of the executive area years before, and they could not match the carpeting. I looked at Jeff and asked, "Who cares if the carpet changes?"

"Everyone," he answered. We all know if we come down here, Michael might see us and start asking questions."

Not two seconds later, Michael walked into my office, looked at Jeff, and said, "You are far away from your home, aren't you?" Jeff smiled at me and left my office.

I never noticed that the carpet changed. I never knew that people knew it or that they used that saying about avoiding executive row. Because I worked with Michael daily for years, I had become immune to that reality. I had forgotten what it was like to be an employee five or six layers down from the boss. Where the carpet changed became a great reminder for me of what my dad always preached. Never forget where you came from, and always remember what it felt like as you work your way up the corporate ladder.

No matter how high you climb, stay aware of yourself and others, and make sure you remain accessible to people on every rung of the ladder. Never get too big for your britches.

———————•●•———————

PURSUING PERFECTION

One of our original six multi-year strategies was called the "Idea Store" concept. It focused on having outstanding merchandise assortments, an inviting store environment, informed and helpful sales associates, and classroom programs to assist our crafting community. It was a very customer-centric strategy.

However, before we could focus on this strategy, we had to make sure our stores could keep products in stock, build a more efficient and cost-effective supply chain, get our Vendor Community to comply with our supply chain standards, and take numerous tasks away from the Store Operations Team so they could spend more time with the customer. After three and a half years of effort, we were closing in on all the key initiatives that supported those strategies.

In another eighteen months, we knew 80% of the heavy lifting would be complete, so we could turn our attention to shifting our strategic plan to consider this reality. After a disastrous first attempt, Michael asked me to take over the leadership role and develop a more encompassing strategy than just redoing the physical store. I presented Michael a three-pronged approach:

- **Merchandise & Merchandise Layout**—Based on the customer insight, sales analysis, vendors, merchant team, and store operations, we wanted to standardize our store layouts to create an easier and more satisfying shopping experience.

- **Expand the Shopping Experience**—We wanted to compliment the merchandise with more classroom programs, demonstrations, how-to project guides, and significantly expand our Michaels.com website.

- **Creating Demand**—We were now ready to move beyond Sunday newspaper circular advertising and dramatically increase brand awareness using radio, TV, magazines, Internet, and public relations efforts.

For 2004 it was a pretty forward-thinking strategy. We wanted to create the best Internet and physical store environment possible to learn and to shop. No matter where a customer interacted with us, they would have the same incredible experience. Then we could shout from the rooftops to tell more people to come and have fun with us and create something special. This was our plan to realize Michael Rouleau's dream of getting the company to $5B in sales.

The Idea Store headline was no longer going to cut it. We needed something fresh and catchier to stretch the imagination. About two weeks after our initial meeting, I got a call from Michael, and with the voice of an excited child, he said, "it's 'The Pursuit of the Perfect Store!'" We had our new name for this initiative, and it did exactly what we wanted. It set an expectation for the entire organization that we were now ready and capable of chasing a new direction!

You always need to continue to reevaluate the entire landscape of your business and make the necessary operational and strategic changes to stay competitive and relevant in the marketplace. You also need to have a great understanding of the organization's abilities to shift its focus without making a huge strategic error. It is a delicate balance and one that needs strong and steady leadership dedicated to driving that change. We had both, and we were now going to pursue perfection.

Vince Lombardi, former Packers' coach, once said, *"We will chase perfection, and we will chase it relentlessly, knowing all the while we can never attain it. But along the way, we shall catch excellence."*

To catch excellence, continually chase perfection.

———— • ● • ————

DON'T THROW THE BABY OUT WITH THE BATHWATER

I was putting the finishing touches on my August 2005 Vendor Conference speech. It had been a little over 18 months since Michael asked me to lead this effort after a disastrous first attempt that was too narrowly focused on only enhancing our store's merchandise assortments. It had been run by the Chief Merchant with little input from outside the Buying Team. We had broken every rule and process we had used to become a world-class operations-driven company. It was time to do it the right way.

First, we created a vision statement: *"Michaels will be THE source where people looking to express themselves find ideas, inspiration, information, education, and the merchandise they want."* Next, we defined the three pillars for success: Merchandise & Merchandise Layout, Expand the Shopping Experience, and Creating Demand.

Next, we developed an Executive Steering Committee that included the CFO, CEO, and heads of Stores, Merchandising, Store Planning, and Marketing. We put together cross-functional project teams from every functional area of the company. We developed detailed project plans, timelines, deliverables and held a kickoff meeting where Michael set the expectations for the team where he told everyone he owned this project, and I was in charge of ensuring we were successful.

Since I was put in charge eighteen months before, we developed a test store lab environment—five different standardized layouts for the five different size stores we had across the chain. Those were developed in coordination with store operations, store planning, the buyers, vendors, and marketing. The layout had specific financial and customer metrics to determine if the changes met the ROI standard.

We had identified five markets and five stores within those markets to test the new "Perfect Store." We also determined five markets that would be our control group to measure our results against.

Before we began, we spoke to over 1,000 customers in the five test markets to get a baseline of their desires for the perfect store. Then we went back to those markets and talked to customers after the changes. These surveys included Senior Leadership, Store Operations, Merchandising, Marketing, and Store Planning. We also began testing some new marketing vehicles to see how we could create more demand for this exciting new environment. Finally, we evaluated the ROI on the cost to not only roll this out to new stores but to retrofit the entire chain.

It was eighteen months since we regrouped, and we were ready to announce to vendors and the world that we would be rolling out the Perfect Store concept. All new stores (45 per year) would get the new layout; we would remodel 450 stores, and then we would retrofit the rest of the chain. In my speech, I said, *"By 2008, the plan is to have our entire chain standardized with the perfect store assortment and layout."*

I can't say we picked up the entire lost year, but we sure came close. By using the process and discipline that we had used for all major strategies, initiatives, and projects since 1997, we able to work effectively at lightning speed.

Many times, senior leadership gets antsy and believes they need to make a change "just because." They end up throwing the baby out with the bathwater and doing more damage than good. Sometimes there is no school like the old school.

———————•●•———————

SINK OR SWIM

The annual Christmas dinner was supposed to be a nice celebration of last year's accomplishments and a thank you to the Michaels Senior Leadership Team and their spouses. It started out so beautifully. CEO Michael Rouleau and his beautiful wife Susan had opened up their home for the party. The house was immaculate, and it seemed like every room was decked with holiday decorations.

At a function like this, there is always some concern that conversations will invariably turn to business. My wife would always make me promise not to make her stand and listen to war stories she had no interest in at a Christmas party. I believe Susan Rouleau must have told her husband the same thing because Michael was 24/7 business—including holidays and celebrations. At this event, however, he was on his best behavior.

There were round tables situated in an open area of the home that each sat six people. When the dinner bell rang, Lisa and I were seated next to Michael and Susan. The dinner was great, and the conversations at each table were lively and fun, then it took a sudden turn. At the table to our left sat our newest SVP of Marketing. She was having a conversation with the wife of one of the executives, and as the conversation slipped into business, I saw both Michael and Susan's ears perk up.

The conversation was about a marketing event our new SVP had recently done. I watched as Susan slowly took her hand off the table and gently moved it to Michael's leg. I knew what she knew, that this was the first Michael was hearing about this. To make matters even worse, the spouse innocently told Michael how cool this was and asked why he was not doing more of this. Susan's grip tightened.

Sometimes leaders have to put on a performance. Well, Michael performed well that night. He laughed it off and said he would have to look into it. On the way home, Lisa and I talked about what happened. "She could be gone within a few months," I said. "She broke both of Michael's top two rules: no surprises and no going solo. This might not be the only reason she's in trouble, but you can't give Michael ammunition like that—especially when you run the marketing area."

Within a few months, we were looking for our fifth SVP of Marketing in eight years. She did break two major rules of working with Michael, but I don't know if anyone ever sat her down and gave her the guardrails of how to deal with Michael, navigate our company's culture, the executives, or her team. She came in with an SVP title and knew she needed to make things happen. She probably never even knew she was out of bounds.

A 2017 Harvard Business Review article survey results showed that only about 2% of global companies have an onboarding program that stresses fully assimilating an executive into the culture to help them make a successful transition. *In the same survey, 68% of executive respondents said they had a poor grasp of how their organization worked after their initial onboarding process.* It is hard to run a division if you don't know the rhythm of the company. It is a sink or swim attitude.

It is not just executives who get this treatment. In my experience, employees at all levels mirror these survey results. **When interviewing for a position, it is critical that one of your questions is about how they onboard and assimilate new people. If you get the sense it is sink or swim, exercise caution. You might need to pass unless you believe you can succeed in that environment. Get that answer before you make a final decision, or you might be sunk.**

* ● *

MOVING LIKE A TREMENDOUS MACHINE

I was talking with a few Michaels' associates who had been with the company since the mid-1990s. We were nearing the end of fiscal 2005, and we were discussing the progress made since Michael Rouleau showed up in late 1996. When we started to list the accomplishments, it was the difference between night and day.

In 1996, they were losing money and bleeding cash like crazy. From a systems, process, and infrastructure standpoint, they operated like a company did in the late 70s or early 80s. In the first three years after Michael took over, he righted the ship, built a solid foundation of processes, installed a couple of key systems, and began bringing on more experienced talent. At the close of 1999, Michaels had 12 straight quarters of sales and profit increases and was ready to take their game to the next level.

In 2000, the company shifted into high gear by developing a Five Year Strategic and Financial Plan—the first in the company's history. With the help of my old consulting firm, we solidified an investment roadmap that would spend over $250M over five years. I joined the company as the Head of Strategic Planning and Initiatives, Office of the CEO. My main objective was to move the company farther and faster, or Michael would fire me, so I chose farther and faster.

In five years, we documented and continually improved every process in the company, we opened three new distribution centers and expanded another one, we put in major systems MMS allocation, EDI, Perpetual Inventory & Automatic Replenishment, Transportation Management, Human Resource Information System, upgraded systems in all of our Subsidiary Divisions, Store Payroll, Peoplesoft Financials, Michaelsvendors.com, and Michaels.com.

We started new organizations from scratch, like the Vendor Relations Team and the Automatic Replenishment Team, and added significant talent across the entire organization. Lastly, we had finalized plans for our future to execute our "Pursuit of the Perfect Store." Here's a snapshot of where we started and to where we had come:

	1996	2005
Gross Sales	$1.4B	$3.7B
# of Michaels Stores	453	1066
EBITDA Margin	Low Single Digits	13.60%
Earnings	($31.2)	~$255M
Stock Price	$3.25	$144 *Split Adjusted
Cash	Bleeding	$500M
Returned on Invested Capital	12.2% *(Year 2000)	28.60%

In 1973, Secretariat was running in the Belmont Stakes and was attempting to win the Triple Crown of Thoroughbred Racing. Through the first half-mile of the mile and a half race, Secretariat was neck and neck with his rival, Sham. As they approached the halfway point, Secretariat took off. Chic Anderson was the broadcaster for the event and uttered one of the most famous lines in sports history. *"Secretariat is widening now! He is moving like a tremendous machine!"* Secretariat won the race by a record 31 lengths.

Michael Rouleau and his organization had built a tremendous machine by the end of 2005. There is no better feeling than being part of a winning organization. I had set a goal at a young age to someday help run a company. In 2005, I realized I played a significant role in helping to build a retail powerhouse, and it was an incredible feeling.

Never stop believing that you can do great things. The journey is not easy. All the blood, sweat, and tears. All the missteps and mistakes. All the long hours and sleepless nights—it is all worth it!

———————•●•———————

I ALWAYS FAVOR THE MAVERICKS

Michael and I were having a challenging discussion. Over the length of our business relationship, we had hundreds of these types of conversations. I knew I was getting remarkably close to crossing that invisible line between a nice gentle pushback and getting fired. I always wondered when that day would come when he had enough and said, "You just aren't worth it anymore." Thankfully, today was not that day.

We were discussing his continued desire to copy from one of our competitors, AC Moore. They had been his nemesis since he joined Michaels almost eight years ago. They had set the standard in the industry for dominant arts and crafts assortments and averaging upwards of $6M a store. We had spent most of the last eight years trying to copy their assortments. It was an old trick Michael learned from Sam Walton, founder of Wal-Mart, who famously wrote in his book, "Most everything I've done I've copied from someone else."

My problem was AC Moore was no longer the Gold Standard. We were. I had the numbers to prove it, but Michael kept repeating, "They do 20% more per average store."

I shared with him some of the reasons. "They carry 25% to 30% more inventory per store, they have 25% more payroll expense, and they are nowhere near as profitable as we are." Then I hit him with my ace in the hole, "Vendors I trust are telling me that AC Moore is copying **us** now."

AC Moore was no longer the "A" student. We were copying from the wrong person. Michael and I continued to go for another few rounds, and then I threw in the towel. As I was leaving his office, he said, *"You know you are still the biggest pain in the a#@, but I respect you for always being honest with me and being willing to tell me things you know I don't want to hear."*

I smiled and said, "I will continue to do it until you tell me to pack my bags."

Sam Walton once said, **"I always favored the mavericks who challenged the rules. I may have fought them all the way, but I respected them, and in the end, I listened to them a lot more closely than I did the pack who always agreed with everything I said."**

That, in a nutshell, is my relationship with Michael Rouleau. I consistently challenged him and the status quo. I was relentless in trying to find ways to make us better and move the company to reach our goals faster. **There are yes men and women, there are the "hangers-on," those who pick and choose their battles, and then there are the mavericks. You cannot have a company of mavericks, but you better have a least one or two to keep you honest.**

As a leader, you have to have the courage to allow someone to tell you, "The emperor has no clothes." As the maverick, you have to have the courage to tell the emperor that fact, time and time again. Likewise, you need someone in your life who you trust to tell you the God's honest truth, and there will be a time where you have to have the courage to tell someone the same thing.

Being a maverick can be a tad bit risky at times, but I can tell you it is a lot more fun!

———— • ● • ————

HOW BIG OF SHIP DO YOU WANT TO SAIL?

We longed for the good ole days when we were nimble and had a great deal of maneuverability. We could make quick decisions or do an immediate course correction without having to worry too much about the repercussions. The challenge was we were no longer a fast, highly maneuverable Navy destroyer. We were a huge 1,000-foot aircraft carrier that could no longer turn on a dime.

In 2005, Michaels had close to 1,100 stores and $3.7B in sales. We invested heavily in building infrastructure, systems, and processes, enabling us to keep 35,000 items in stock in all our stores and provide our customers with an outstanding shopping experience. As we grew from 450 stores to 1,100, we also added thousands of new employees, 15 to 20 new systems to maintain and upgrade, and three additional distribution centers to run.

The bigger we got, it was natural to become more bureaucratic. It is not necessarily because of rules and regulations; it is because it is just harder to maneuver a large organization. Like an aircraft carrier, when you want to make a course correction or attempt a quick turn, you have to be incredibly careful of what you leave in your wake. You have to become more cautious in your actions because the repercussions might take out a region, many of your vendors, or cause great stress on the organization.

Also, because you are much bigger, you have a much better chance to hit something in the open ocean. Think Titanic. If they were a smaller ship, they would have had much better maneuverability to miss that iceberg. You have to be on the lookout at all times for something that could cause you to rip your company apart. It could be a faster, nimbler competitor or a new disruptor enters the marketplace; maybe people get sick of crafting and turn to playing video games, or a global pandemic hits the world. You are just a bigger target.

Once you made a decision, understood all the potential ramifications, notified anyone who would be affected, you still had to make a successful turn. Five years ago, we might have been able to make the turn in a day or a week tops. Now it might take a month or longer.

Bigger companies will be more bureaucratic, slower to change, more set in their ways but also more stable and predictable with more infrastructure and support. Smaller companies are less bureaucratic, can and do change things quickly. They have less structure, but they can be less stable, and you might have to be both the chief cook and bottle washer.

What size company can you be comfortable in and, more importantly, thrive in? It might take working in both large and small environments to decide, or you might find your niche right away. Find that perfect size ship you want to sail on and head out to the open seas.

ROME WAS NO LONGER BURNING

We had put out all the fires and repaired every building that had been damaged. We had added significant new capabilities and infrastructure to our once broken city. Gone were the days of living with your hair on fire. Gone were the days when you put out one fire, and ten more would start. Gone were the days you feared that the entire city would be destroyed no matter how much you tried to save it.

After almost nine years of intense work, Rome was no longer burning. It was now a shining city on a hill. By 2005, the turnaround of Michaels Stores was complete and a perfect example of how to rebuild a broken company. Michael Rouleau had helped lead what many thought was an impossible effort. If you had the top ten reasons for why Rome was no longer burning, the top five would be Michael.

He loved the chaos. He loved dealing with the unknown. He loved the thrill of the roller coaster ride of emotions that happens when you inherit a city on fire, and 25 new fires start each day. He not only loved it, but he also thrived on it. It was as if the more chaos we had, the better he was. He was the perfect person for the job in 1996. Now the situation had changed, and so had the needs of our leadership.

At the end of 2005, we were now a normal retailer, dealing with normal retail issues. I used to use the analogy that in 1997 when I first showed up at Michaels, the environment was like a ball bouncing back and forth at the speed of light (670,616,629 mph). In normal retail, the ball only bounces back and forth at the speed of sound (761.2 mph). 762 mph is still incredibly fast, but it was not light speed.

Instead of a list of 500 items to fix, we had 50 to-do's to keep the city operating at full efficiency. We weren't totally building a new skyscraper or rebuilding a burned-out area of the city; we were just ensuring we maintained the beautiful structures we had built. I felt at times that Michael was now bored and sometimes tried to create chaos, just so he could fix it.

I say this not to disparage him, but because he and I are so much alike, and I was getting a little bored myself. All the processes, systems, and infrastructure I was responsible for leading the effort to implement successfully were done. It was now up to each division head to get the maximum performance out of our investments and their teams. Here is an example of the difference for me.

For the previous five years, I managed projects to open multiple distribution centers, implementing three or four systems a year when most companies would implement only one and starting a new division from scratch. It was a thrill ride every day. In late 2005, Michael asked me to help fix the phone system to be more automated when customers called our 1-800 number. I could do that with both hands tied behind my back, with a blindfold, and hopping on one leg. When we talked, I felt Michael felt the same way about what he was doing.

It takes a drastically different skill set to turn around a company successfully, just like it takes a different skill set to be an entrepreneur and start a successful company from scratch or run a mature business. I did not know what the future held, but my radar was turned up to full power, and I was trying to see what could possibly be coming around the corner. I felt a change was coming, so I was beginning to prepare myself. I was not going to be blindsided.

If you sense something is in the wind, crank the radar up to full bore. **You always have to keep your radar on and keep analyzing what might be coming at you that could impact your job. Do not be caught off guard because you did not want to face reality or thought the situation might just disappear. Be proactive so you won't be a victim.**

THE STORIES WERE GETTING OLD

You could see it in their body language. For as long as I can remember, I always sat in the same spot in the Michaels' boardroom. Michael Rouleau was always at the head of the huge horseshoe table. I would always sit at the end of the horseshoe on his right side. I would bring my chair over a couple of feet close to the center of the room because I could then see everybody in the room.

I did it that way for two reasons. One, I was able to look everyone in the eye if I was speaking to anyone at the table. I also did it because I wanted to watch everyone's reaction to the comments and conversations going on at the time. To me, the eyes and the body language always gave away the true feelings of the participants.

Michael was speaking to the leadership team about expenses. It was the budget time of year, and he wanted to set the ground rules for this year's process. The story he told was about how he could reduce cell phone costs across the organization, and if he could find savings for the one-line item in the budget, everyone in the room could find savings in their budgets.

The first time I heard it was such a great message. Everybody in the room got the point and was given the challenge to find the money. If the boss could do it, so could you. But now, I had heard this story seven or eight times before. I knew it was coming, and it did not get anywhere near the response as it did when I heard it the first time.

The body language of everyone else in the room was saying the same thing. They were tuning out the boss because his stories were getting old. His challenge was the same as a professional football coach that can last 8 to 10 years. Players and people who work throughout the organization begin to tune out the coach. Even if they are off the charts successful, it is only natural for people not to want to hear the same story for the fifth or tenth time.

As a coach, mentor, or parent, you have to understand that this can and will happen the longer you are talking to the same group of people. For example, college coaches can stay at their institutions for 30 years because every four years, 25 % of the team leaves due to graduation. Most businesses do not turn over their entire organizations that fast— nor should they.

A generational divide was also happening. Michael was still telling stores from when he worked at Target in 1966, nearly forty years before. He was in the business world longer than 75% of the organization had been alive. It does not mean you can't relate; you have to change with the times.

Mike Krzyzewksi (Coach K) is the 74-year coach of the Duke Blue Devils. He has coached the team since 1980, won 5 NCAA championships, gone to 12 final fours, and has a record of 1084-291. After 47 years in coaching, Coach K decided that 2022 would be his last year in coaching. He was a model for being able to continue to be successful on the court by adapting and changing with the different needs of the players throughout his career.   He was also flexible enough to have coached three Olympics teams made up of the best NBA players to Gold medal victories.

As you gain experience and become one of the older people in the group, you have to adjust with the times. It does not mean you change the core of who you are; it means you have to adapt. You have to give different examples and stories your audience has not heard before. You have to make the points relevant so as a leader, you can still inspire any generation. Then you can last as long as Coach K.

———————•◦•———————

DO THEY EVEN KNOW WHAT IT TOOK TO GET HERE?

I was tweaking a presentation that I would be giving to the February 2006 Monthly Strategy Meeting. There was a knock at my door. I looked up, and it was my boss asking if I had any plans for lunch. "I am headed to the cafeteria and getting a sandwich to bring back to my office," I stated.

"Forget that plan, and let's eat in the cafeteria."

"Sounds great," I answered. This was not the first time Michael asked me to have lunch with him. We had done it hundreds of times the past nine years. But it was always a working lunch, never pleasure. He would bring a document, notes, or presentation he wanted us to work through while we ate. We would get the same sandwiches, go to one of the farthest tables from the food line, sit down, and go to work.

Today was different. He did not have anything in his hands. I asked him if I needed anything for our discussion, and he said, "No, not today." I got this strange feeling something was up.

As we walked to the cafeteria, Michael started reminiscing about his almost ten-year run at Michaels. He reminded me of the early days and what it took just to keep the company afloat. He talked about all the things that were terribly broken or did not exist in 1996. As we approached the cafeteria, he said, "I remember you telling me when you came here as a consultant that you did not think we were going to make it. Didn't you tell me that you told your boss you did not want to work here?"

I had to admit that at the very beginning, that was true, and we both laughed. We got into the food line, ordered our usual sandwiches again, and then proceeded to our back table. As we continued to talk about everything that had happened over our time together at Michaels, a couple of new employees came walking past our table. I had met them both a few days earlier. They said hello and proceeded to another table.

Michael looked at me and asked who they were. I told him, and he replied, "You know I used to know everybody. Now we have so many new people I can't keep track."

"You're right, but remember they are all here because of your leadership. They have jobs because of you," I told him.

I don't think he heard me because he was gazing across the entire cafeteria. He said, *"Do these people even know what it took to get here?"*

"They don't have a clue," I answered. I gave him a couple of examples of what people were complaining about now and how trivial it was compared to what he had to deal with in the early days. He agreed. We finished our lunch and then walked back to our offices, where Michael said, "You are a good man." I thanked him for the comment and also for letting me be part of this fantastic ride.

One month later, Michael announced his retirement, and the board announced they were "Exploring Strategic Alternatives." That is Wall Street code words for they were putting Michaels up for sale. Our conversation all made sense now. He must have been negotiating his departure while the board was making plans to sell. He had built a great company that market capitalization had improved from $1.5B to a private equity sale price of $6.2B.

Employees rarely have a clue about the people who really built the company except for the history section on their website or a picture on a wall. But great companies don't just happen. Take a moment to find out what those who paved the way did and how they did it. They are why you have a job.

GREAT COMPANIES DON'T JUST HAPPEN. TAKE A MOMENT TO FIND OUT WHO PAVED THE WAY— WHO REALLY BUILT THE COMPANY— AND HOW THEY DID IT. THESE PEOPLE ARE THE REASON YOU HAVE A JOB.

ALL GOOD THINGS MUST COME TO AN END

One of the board members was standing outside my office. I had known him since 1997, and we had a cordial relationship. He saw me coming and knew what I was going to ask him. It was the number one question everyone working for or associated with the company wanted to know—why was the board recommending selling Michaels?

I shook his hand, and he said, "Timing."

"Why is the timing right?" I pressed.

"Private equity players have tons of money they can get their hands on, and they are looking for companies like Michaels to invest in. It is almost like they have monopoly money, and when the environment is like this, you have to look at the best thing for the shareholders and the company. We just need the process to play out and see if someone is willing to buy us and at what price."

On March 20, 2006, the announcement read, "Michaels Stores Announces Decision to Explore Strategic Alternatives for Enhancing Shareholder Value." And with that, the Executive Team without the now-retired Michael Rouleau would spend the next several months selling the company to prospective private equity companies or consortiums. This was my first time going through something like this, so I just tightened my shoelaces a little tighter because I knew it was going to be a heck of a roller coaster ride.

When the announcement was made, our CEO retired. Instead of naming a new CEO, the board named two individuals as Co-President. In the blink of an eye, we went from one person who had successfully run the company with an iron fist for ten years to a two-headed organization. Talk about shocking the system.

It was a very unusual move to have Co-Presidents. In sports they say, "If you believe you have two starting quarterbacks, then you have none." That is exactly how it felt. Whether you liked Michael's leadership style or not, there was never a doubt who was in control of the company. No one knew—including the two Co-Presidents—how this was going to work.

These two had to keep the day-to-day business going and also lead the effort to sell the company. We could not miss a beat with our financial situation, or it would affect the sale price. The board estimated the process would take about six months. I knew that Michaels was such a smooth-running machine that it could almost run itself for a year.

For me, it was the worst-case scenario. I knew this day would eventually come. In 2006, Michael was 67 years old. He had mentioned to me he hoped to be able to run Michaels for another five years. I always told him to give me at least a six-month heads up when he was going to retire, so I could start looking for a new job. Because of my relationship with him and the Pitbull role he had me play, I knew that new leadership might not want to keep me around. I used to joke with him that I was an acquired taste.

On October 31, 2006, the headlines read, "Michaels Stores Announces Completion of Merger Agreement with Bain Capital and Blackstone Affiliates." On June 4, 2007, another headline read, "Brian C. Cornell Named CEO of Michaels Stores." In my world, the headlines should have read, "All Good Things Must Come To An End!" It was a hell of a ride, and I enjoyed every single minute of it. Six months later, I left Michaels.

Nothing lasts forever. Do not take anything for granted because it can come to an end in a blink of an eye. If you have a great situation going, savor every single moment. EVERY SINGLE MOMENT!

———————— • ● • ————————

ALL GLORY IS FLEETING

Everyone was asked to take their seats. The room lights dimmed as the presentations were about to begin. It had only been a couple of months since the announcement that Michaels was exploring strategic alternatives (being put up for sale). Post the retirement of Michael Rouleau, the new leadership structure was doing its best to keep the company running and leading the effort to put together a sales presentation for prospective buyers.

Today was the day to show off the greatness of Michaels, so one of the many private equity firms would buy us for an estimated $5B to $6B. I had been part of the development and rehearsal process and knew what was going to be presented. I knew it had to be done this way, but it still sucked. When Michael retired, the board's conscious decision was to focus on the new management structure and not mention Rouleau's name. The post-Michael era had begun the moment he retired, and there was no time to reminisce about the past.

Unless, of course, 100% of the reason the company was in the position to sell themselves was because of one man—Michael Rouleau. He had rebuilt the company starting in 1996. All except one presenter did not even know Michaels existed in 1996. The reason I know that is I interviewed all but one of them. Here are the start dates for their positions for the nine presenters: 1 – 1990, 2 – 2000, 2 – 2003, 2 – 2004, 1 – 2005, and 1 – 2006. Most of them did not have a clue what it took to get to this day.

The presentation was surreal. There was only one reference to Michael Rouleau in the entire thing, and that was a backhanded bull$#!@ comment, which said something to the effect that the former CEO, Michael Rouleau, was hired in 1996 and focused nearly exclusively on the company's operational issues. No kidding! That was something the old Board, Wall Street, the vendors, and everybody associated with Michaels already knew. One throwaway line is all the guy who built the place could get!

My nausea was about to worsen when it came to discussing all the investments we made in key strategic areas of the company. It showed the top initiatives we had successfully implemented over the last five years (all public knowledge). They included Supply Chain, Vendors, Processes, Systems, and Organizational Change. These were all the areas my consulting team had identified as needing to be addressed, and Michael hired me to fix them. They mentioned that they were all implemented without business disruption.

It should have been the proudest moment of my career, but I was not even mentioned. As Head of Strategic Planning & Initiatives, I was the person directly responsible for all of the initiatives written on that page. I did not run stores, marketing, or supply chain; I ran the initiative process. Heck, the former CFO and I built it—but there was not **one** mention.

In the entire presentation, the guy who built the place got only one casual comment, and the guy he hired to implement $250M worth of initiatives successfully got no mention at all. General George S. Patton tells a story about the conquering Romans returning from war to parades and accolades. He said, "A slave stood behind the conqueror holding a golden crown and whispering in his ear a warning: that all glory is fleeting."

You see it all the time. A great sports legend is quickly forgotten when the new star is born. An Oscar-winning actress can't find a role because she is considered a has-been. A former rock legend plays on the oldies station. A business leader has been pushed aside for the next generation. It happens to the best of them. **Enjoy every moment you have in the spotlight. Relish your moments of success. No matter how good or valuable you are—or think you are—there is always someone who can replace you. It is one of those unfortunate facts of life.**

———————•●•———————

GREED IS NOT GOOD

When I first heard a rumor that Michaels might be sold, I thought about how the sale would impact employees and shareholders who owned Michaels' stock. Then I sat back and thought about my knowledge of these types of deals, and I got genuinely concerned. The shareholders might be happy, but what about all the employees, vendors, and customers who depend on Michaels. My apprehension grew even higher.

My impression of private equity or leveraged buyouts dated back to the late 1980s. The headlines back then usually had the term "Corporate Raiders" in the title. A corporate raider would raise large amounts of money and buy a large stake in a corporation. Then they would undertake certain measures meant to increase shareholder value. Many times, these new measures were polar opposites to what management wanted to do. These would include downsizing operations, liquidating the company, or selling specific pieces and parts of the business.

The focus was not really on making the company better. It was focused on making money at whatever cost, period. In the 1987 movie *Wall Street*, the main character Gordon Gekko gives a famous speech to the shareholders of a company he wants to take over. He said, "The point is, ladies and gentlemen, that greed—for lack of a better word—is good. Greed is right. Greed works. Greed clarifies." Gekko was based on several real investors of the 80s, and that reputation is something the Private Equity firms wanted to change.

By the mid-2000s, Private Equity (P/E) firms had changed from stripping companies to make a profit to investing in companies they thought they could improve and then sell in 3 to 5 years. At least that was the goal. For the shareholders, it was usually a fantastic deal. For example, the winning bid of $44 per share for Michaels represented a 30% premium since the date the company had put itself up for sale.

Here is the challenge. When the sale was complete, Michaels went from debt-free and hundreds of millions of dollars in cash to having over $4B in debt. As of 2018, they still showed $2.7B. It is a huge anchor for any company with that much debt to make any major investments. You spend most of your money paying the interest and then struggling to pay off the principal. The debt is because it limits the amount of cash the P/E firm has to put up itself. It places all this burden on the company. Then the real fun begins.

The P/E firm then starts taking things like management fees or dividend payments to make a return on its investment. Then they bring in a slew of consultants to try and find ways to cut expenses, sell assets, replace management, etc., to make the company's financials look better when they try and sell it a few years later. But is the company really better, or are just the financials better?

A 2018 *Retail Dive* article said, "That since 2002, $116.5B had been spent on 95 retail acquisitions." Here is the money quote, "More than two-thirds of retail bankruptcies in 2016 and 2017 were P/E owned or controlled companies." If you look at the fine print of many of those deals, the P/E firm still made money or got their money back. Good deal. Make money and destroy a company.

In my book, greed is not good. There are too many examples where corporate or Wall Street greed wrecked companies, destroyed towns due to environmental concerns, or even brought the world's economy to its knees. The balance sheet needs to have wealth creation on one side and the impact on everyday people's lives on the other.

PAWNS IN SOMEONE ELSE'S GAME

"That is the dumbest thing I have ever heard." My investment advisor said this when we discussed the announcement that Michaels Stores would explore strategic alternatives. His statement was not about the decision to put Michaels up for sale. He knew that the Private Equity (P/E) market was hot, and Michaels' financials were a great candidate to sell in this climate.

It was not about the fact that Michael Rouleau, who had rebuilt Michaels into a retail and financial powerhouse, had retired. He knew that many CEOs, especially ones with 45 years of experience, were not going to want to work inside the structure world of P/E. It is hard for CEOs who ran their own show for years to now have to run everything by a 30-year-old MBA.

So, if it wasn't the announcement to sell and it wasn't Michael's retirement, what did he think was so dumb? The board did not select a CEO to succeed Michael; they announced that the company would be run by Co-Presidents. While we were talking, he tried to think of an example of this in all his years of investing. Neither of us could come up with an example. He asked, "Why would the board do that?"

It could be one of two reasons. One was that the board really believed both of these men could be CEO and wanted to give them a chance to prove it to the new owners. The other possibility was that they knew Michael would not help with the sale of the company, so they just put these guys in as placeholders through the sale, knowing the new owners would bring in their own CEO. I believed the latter because I knew they were being set up for failure with this decision.

Put yourself in the board's shoes. You knew Michael built the company and ran it with an iron fist. They never had a true succession plan. There was no one waiting in the wings to take over the job; no one had been groomed or prepared. Both Co-Presidents were extremely smart, talented, and had all the capabilities to run a company. I just thought they were being used.

The board had also been majority shareholders for over 20 years, and they wanted to cash out. Who could blame them? Their leadership took Michaels from seven stores in 1983 to over 1,000 in 2006. They were the ones who grew the company into a national footprint by buying small crafts chains across the country, and they also brought in Rouleau to build it into a retail success story. I figured once the ink was dry, they would be satisfied with what they had done and then count their money.

Internally the decision caused all kinds of strife. People who believed this was a true horserace began to pick sides. They figured they needed to be in one camp or another. Within 24 hours after Michael left the building, we went from what is best for the company attitude to everyone being selfish trying to pick the winner. Also, for ten years, only one man had made all the critical decisions. Now we were going to make decisions using the rock, paper, and scissors method. All things considered, the Co-Presidents did a great job, but in my opinion, they were purposely put into a no-win situation.

Unfortunately, I was right. Less than eight months after the sale was official, the new owners named an external person to become CEO. Shortly after, one of the Co-Presidents resigned. The other one left about nine months later. After spending time with the new owners, I never got the sense that these two men ever had a real chance to be CEO. They did what the board wanted—got a high sale price, and ran the company until the paperwork was signed.

The reality is that in the corporate world (public or private), we are often just pawns in a game of chess. As the boards and management play the game, you need to be playing the game as well. **Just like a great chess player, you need to think 5 to 10 moves ahead. If you feel your situation is deteriorating, make your move before the other player says checkmate.**

I LEFT EVERYTHING ON THE FIELD

Though it was official on October 31, 2006, we had actually been working on a transition plan for almost a month. Bain Capital and Blackstone Affiliates were now the owners of Michaels Stores. They were not going to waste any time putting an action plan in place. I struggled because it seemed like their intent was not to make Michaels better for the long haul.

In my opinion, it was to make enough changes and improve a few key metrics so, in 3 to 5 years, they could sell the company at a profit. This is typical of many Private Equity (P/E) deals. Add in the yearly management fees and other P/E goodies, and you have yourself a nice financial return on investment. You take your money and run and let the new owners worry about the company's long-term future.

It was a different philosophy than the one we had lived under for the last ten years. Our former strategic plans and investments had the same 3 to 5-year horizon, but they never had a definitive end date. It was a rolling plan that was adjusted every year. We cared that all boats were rising, including employees, vendors, shareholders, and customers. The management was building a company to last, not to sell. Obviously, our former board had a different idea.

The first thing we did was put together a 100-day transition plan for the new ownership group. Due to my knowledge of our strategic plans and timelines and my project management background, I was asked to lead the 100 Day plan effort. I worked with three individuals (two from Bain and one from Blackstone) called sponsors to develop and manage the plan. Two were Harvard MBAs, one was a Columbia MBA, and all three worked for McKinsey Consulting. Superb pedigree and really great gentlemen.

Their role was to help gain a quick understanding of Michaels, help validate or adjust our priorities and assess the Michaels' management team. It was a typical assessment that I had done for years as a consultant. It gave the new owners their first chance to take a look under the hood, and depending on what they found, it would determine our path forward.

They brought in Bain Consulting and Kurt Solomon & Associates to look at a few areas they prioritized. Being a former consultant, I knew who they were reporting to, and it was not our two Co-Presidents. They were reporting to two new owners; senior management was a spectator in this new game.

At first, I figured I would give it my best shot to see if the new owners wanted me to stick around or not, but it became apparent early on that I was a short-timer. Once the new owners solidified their plans, they brought in a new CEO from the outside to take the company forward in their new direction. They had spent $1.8B of their money and another

$4.2B or so in debt to buy Michaels; they could do anything they wanted. After spending a couple of months uploading things to the new CEO, it was time for me to leave.

A 10-year relationship with the company where I had been able to check off my top two goals for my business career had come to an end. I could not have been more satisfied with what I gave to Michaels and what it gave back to me. I left everything on the field on every play. When I left the company, I knew I had played an important role in making Michaels a rock-solid company. What more could you ask for?

My dad gave me great advice when I was younger that fits this situation perfectly. **Give the company everything you have, no matter what. If you can't, you are cheating them and cheating the skills the Good Lord gave you, and if you no longer can, then it is time to find a new place where you can.**

———————•●•———————

DON'T EVER PAY FOR THE SAME JOB TWICE

When the announcement was made, I knew I was in trouble. We all figured it was going to happen sooner rather than later. Two Private Equity firms had purchased Michaels Stores for $6B eight months earlier. You spend that kind of money; you want your own handpicked person to run the company. Brian Cornell was named the new CEO of Michaels on June 4, 2007. He had a heck of a background, most recently being the EVP and Chief Marketing Officer of Safeway, Inc. He not only ran merchandising, marketing, manufacturing, and supply chain, he also had been a key architect for Safeway's new store format.

So why did I think I was in trouble? Brian not only had a tremendous track record running operations, but he had an eye for strategic planning, obviously was a great marketeer, and he had played the key role in developing a new store format for Safeway. I was the current strategy and initiative guy who had a marketing background to go along with my process improvement experience. I was leading the effort to remodel our stores called "The Pursuit of the Perfect Store."

Though Michael Rouleau had retired, his "Rouleauism's" continued to influence my career. One was, "Don't ever pay for the same job twice." Michaels did not need two people doing strategy or working on a new store concept, especially when one of the people was the new boss.

This lesson was something Michael preached relentlessly. He was fanatical about managing expenses—the guy who negotiated his haircut to save $50 a year. If you thought he was tough when managing capital investments and expenses, he was 1,000 times more difficult when you wanted to add headcount. It was almost like you had to give up your firstborn to get an additional person in your division. If you ran a division, you experienced Michael challenging you to the nth degree to add additional headcount to the organization.

He called adding headcount the easy way out for a manager. He was not against adding people, but he wanted each manager to make sure they had done everything in their power to finds ways to make their area more efficient before adding personnel. He would always get into the minute details to make sure a manager had thought through their entire organizational plan. He would compare your headcount requests with other managers' requests to see if he could hire one person to satisfy both roles.

An example of this was when both store operations and logistics wanted to hire an Industrial Engineer. He approved one to work for both organizations. It was yet another lesson in the MBA School of Michael Rouleau. Labor is usually at the top or near the top of most companies' expenses. It is such a balancing act for an executive to want to do the right thing and employ as many people as you can to represent the "Human" side of Human Resources, with the reality that if you still have to make your budget numbers work.

Throughout Michael's ten-year run, he hired thousands of new employees in our store organization, distribution organization, and corporate office. He added entire new divisions like the Vendor Relations Team, a new replenishment organization, and a merchandise planning team. He did not want to make a duplicate hire in one area that caused him not to have the available funds to hire in the right areas. **As an executive, challenge every hire. Never pay for the same job twice and always do what is right in the long-term interest of the entire organization and your people.**

BUILT TO LAST

It was on my Honey-Do list from my lovely wife, Lisa. On the list was a visit to a Michaels Store to pick up a few items for a project she was working on. It had been about five years since I left Michaels. I am not a crafter, so the only time I would visit a store was with my wife or to run an errand for her.

When I walked in, I could see they had shifted the layout slightly since I ran the "Pursuit of the Perfect Store." They were not major changes, but I could understand why they made these adjustments. Before I looked for the items Lisa wanted me to pick up, I walked the entire store. It is an old habit I got from walking stores when I worked for the company. I used to have a checklist of things that included in-stock position, signage, top-shelf inventory, aisle and end cap displays, etc., that I would focus on to see how the store manager was performing.

I obviously could not officially grade this store manager, but retail is in my blood, and it reminded me of the good 'ole days at Michaels. As I was walking down the back aisle, I ran into the store manager. He saw me coming and asked if I needed some help. I thought for a split second to say no, but something made me say, "I used to work for Michaels several years ago, and I still know my way around the store." It was the perfect opening for me to as a few questions.

He asked what I did, and I told him I worked at the corporate office. I did not tell him what I did since that was not the point of my questions. "How long have you been with the company?"

"About a year now."

"How do you like it?"

"It's great. Everything is so organized compared to the company I came from," he said, then went on to list about ten things he loved about Michaels.

After each example, I got a big grin on my face. He asked, "Why are you smiling?"

"Man, it is just nice to hear that the corporate office is still trying to make the store manager's life just a little less hard," I confessed. It is so hard to manage a retail store. After my brief stint managing a store section at Gimbels, I will always have a tremendous amount of respect for managers. But that is not why I was smiling.

I was smiling because every one of the examples he mentioned was something I had helped put in place during my tenure at the company. It was such a rush of pride to know that a small part of my legacy of work was still being used five years after I left. I was also smiling because one of our goals was to build the company to last. We did not want to be a typical turnaround where a new management team comes in and uses smoke and mirrors to make you believe they have fixed things.

They would run new marketing campaigns, introduce new product lines, or change the logo. The problem was nothing got to the root cause of why they were in a turnaround in the first place. As of the writing of this story, Michaels is still a dominant player in the Arts & Crafts Industry.

If you only make superficial changes and never get to the root cause of a problem, your situation can never truly get better. It will continue to rear its ugly head up again and again. When rebuilding a company or even your life, identify the root cause of issues, focus like a laser on fixing them, and build a rock-solid foundation around them. Consistently nurture it, so the problem never comes back again. Then you have built something to last.

WHEN REBUILDING A COMPANY (OR YOUR LIFE), IDENTIFY THE ROOT CAUSE OF ISSUES, THEN FOCUS LIKE A LASER ON FIXING THEM. BUILD A ROCK-SOLID FOUNDATION AROUND THEM. CONSISTENTLY NURTURE IT, SO THE PROBLEM NEVER COMES BACK AGAIN. THEN YOU WILL HAVE BUILT SOMETHING TO LAST.

NAVIGATING A NEW JOB THAT SEEMED TOO GOOD TO BE TRUE

After an extraordinarily successful run at Michaels, I never thought for a moment that I could catch lightning in a bottle again. Then I received a phone call that Fossil was in the market for someone to do almost exactly what I had done at Michaels.

These stories discuss how to handle the growing pains of an ever-expanding company, creating a strategic direction for a company that never had one, and what to do when a position seems too good to be true. In addition, I will share how I handled a dramatically different leadership structure than I was used to and how I coped when things just didn't work out as planned.

THE DAY I MET OWEN WILSON

In the spring of 2008, a few months after leaving Michaels, I was on the golf course when I received a call from my friend Jeff Boyer. Jeff and I worked together at Michaels for years and had become great friends. He was now a Board member at Fossil, Inc., the watch and accessory company. He told me he might have an opportunity for me.

We exchanged a few pleasantries, then he began, "Fossil is a $1.5B multi-brand, multi-channel global company, and they are looking to double in size over the next five years. Interested?"

"Absolutely," I responded.

"Well, Fossil has undertaken a strategic planning and initiative process, but they are struggling with how to proceed. They need help prioritizing and implementing initiatives. I was talking with management and realized they need someone like you—someone to do what you did for Michaels."

I took a deep breath, remembering what a ride that had been, but my curiosity was piqued.

"The Chairman and the President/COO are already totally on board, and the CEO is coming around to the same conclusion. So, listen, Jeff, I have already mentioned your name to them, and if you want to kick the tires, I will help set up an interview to meet the main players."

I replied, "Let's do it!"

About a month later, I was sitting in the lobby of Fossil, Inc., ready for my interviews. I interviewed with CEO and the President/COO. Both conversations went great, and they both assured me that they supported this new role.

My last interview would be with the Founder and Chairman, Tom Kartsotis. Jeff had told me that Tom was a free spirit and might show up in a t-shirt, jeans, and flip-flops. He warned me that my interview with him might be a little unorthodox and to be ready. He was not kidding! I soon noticed a tall man with shaggy hair wearing jeans and flip-flops approaching the door.

Tom walked into the office and said, "You must be Jeff." We shook hands, and he sat down. "I have heard outstanding things about you from Jeff Boyer, so I only have a few questions."

I nodded and settled in to answer whatever he wanted to ask. "Oh!" he interrupted himself, "before I forget and before we get started, in about 5 minutes, a good friend of mine is coming to meet me, and I would like to introduce you to him. Is that okay?"

I had no idea where this was going, so I said, "Of course, that sounds fine."

He asked me one question about Michaels, and then his phone rang. He held up his finger and said, "Hey, this is my friend; I'll be right back." Then he got up and left. I waited a couple of minutes then saw Tom and his friend approaching. I did a double-take because I could not believe who it was. Tom waved at me to come out of the office and said, "Jeff, meet Owen Wilson."

"Owen, Jeff is going to be the next employee at Fossil."

Owen looked at both of us with a strange look and asked, "Are you interviewing right now?"

I'm sure my eyebrows lifted all the way to my hairline, and I said, "In fact, I am."

"I bet you didn't plan for *this* part of the interview!" he joked, and we all laughed.

A few minutes later, I told Owen it was nice to meet him, and as Tom and Owen walked away, I went back into the office, trying to figure out exactly what had just happened.

When Tom returned, he said, "I really don't need to know anything more about you. I trust Mr. Boyer, and I like the way you reacted to our interview. I think you will fit in nicely here at Fossil."

One month later, I received an offer to join Fossil as their SVP Strategic Planning.

You never know how interviews are going to go. This one was by far the most unorthodox in my entire career, but it was not the only time something unplanned happened. I have been asked to name my favorite color, if I like roller coasters, and whether I am a cat or a dog person, and early in my career, they watched how I ate! **You never know what might happen during an interview. Many interviewers are just as concerned with how you react to the situation rather than how you answer their questions. You have to be flexible, never flinch, and answer as honestly and confidently as you can.**

GROWING PAINS

In my brief interview with Tom Kartsotis, Founder and Chairman of Fossil, Inc., he said one thing that really resonated with me. He referenced a conversation with one of their newest Board members, Jeff Boyer, my friend. Jeff knew how I had helped transition Michael's by driving the strategic initiative process and had recommended me because he believed that Fossil's management and Board were ready to implement similar disciplines.

"Fossil needs to be a more balanced company now," Tom began. "At our core, there has been and always will be an entrepreneurial spirit. That's how I started the company and how we have grown over the last almost 25 years. I like what Jeff told me about what happened at Michaels. We also need to add more financial, strategic, and operational discipline to our company. In no way do I want to hinder or put a roadblock in front of the foundational spirit, but I do want to enable the organization to be more efficient and gain higher profits."

Fossil started in 1984 and was the classic entrepreneurial American success story. Tom Kartsotis was a college dropout operating a ticket scalping business in Dallas. His brother and current CEO was a merchandising executive at a Dallas Department store at the same time. His brother told him about the potential to make large profits importing fashion watches. So Tom took all his savings and his half of the ticket business company and went to Hong Kong. He brought back 1,500 watches to sell in the States, and the rest is history.

The brief conversation with Tom was similar to the one I had eleven years earlier with Michael Rouleau, CEO of Michaels. Like Fossil, Michaels had also grown up with great entrepreneurial drive. When I joined their ranks, Michaels needed to make more strategic, process, and infrastructure investments to take the company to the next level.

Before I accepted the job, I called Michaels' new CEO, Brian Cornell (Current Target CEO). Even though I left Michaels after Brian came on board, he said if I ever needed any help to give him a call. I knew that Brian had international experience and wanted his opinion on the opportunity at Fossil. Brian gave me some great tips on working in the international arena and recommended a great book to help me.

The book was called *Growing Pains: Transitioning from an Entrepreneurship to a Professionally Managed Firm*. It was written by

Eric G. Flamholtz, a professor at UCLA, and Yvonne Randle, a VP at a consulting group in Los Angeles. It seemed to be written just for me and the perfect roadmap for what I was about to undertake at Fossil. Brian did tell me one thing to watch out for, however. "Jeff," he said, "this only works if everybody is on board. If there is any dissent among the leadership, it will be exceedingly difficult or impossible to make the transition." He did not know how prophetic that statement would prove to be, but I was all in on joining Fossil for the moment.

Everybody experiences growing pains. The transition from high school to college or directly into the business world. From college to the real world. From being single to getting married. From being married to having kids and many other life stages. Just like making a change within a company, it can be difficult, and many times people want to give up because the challenges seem too great.

The best thing to do is leverage people (friends, family members, mentors, teachers, etc.) who have been down this path before. **Let me emphasize as strongly as I can—*you are not the first to go through most challenges in life you will face.* Be willing to listen and be open to advice from others who have been down the same path. Learn from other's mistakes so you can successfully navigate the potholes and roadblocks that you will encounter. When you succeed, and you will, you can help the next person with their growing pains.**

---

846 PRIORITIES

It was one of, if not the main reason, the Board of Fossil wanted someone like me to join the company. They had nudged management to put together a strategic view of the future. In the previous 25 years, they had never done anything like this before. Fossil found three talented people within the organization and gave them the entrepreneurial challenge of putting together a five-year strategic and financial plan.

Fossil had numerous examples of this throughout the organization and its history. They would take someone who worked their way up from maybe working in the warehouse to running a brand or a company division. It was one of the best things about Fossil. At the core of their culture was enabling anyone to succeed and move up the company's ranks, no matter where they started from in the business. It had worked for them for years, but as I discovered with this strategic process, this philosophy also had its pitfalls.

When the initial presentation was made to the Board, they were concerned with one number. It was a number that told them that maybe Fossil needed someone who had done this before. The number was 846. That was the number of initiatives that came from the initial five-year planning process. It was the first document I was handed on my first day with the company. The CEO and COO asked me to help prioritize this list. After conducting interviews with 35 members of management from 21 different countries, I understood how the company got to this place. The results of the discussions were threefold.

First, they loved the idea that Fossil was taking a more strategic view. Second, there was no top-down guidance to determine what a strategic initiative was, what was day-to-day business, or what could be done through their yearly operational budget. The 846 initiatives were more of a wish list from around the globe. It included everything from mini blinds, office furniture, and new laptops to a new office building and a new distribution center. In addition, everything seemed to have an equal level of importance. And finally, like most companies, the process was 85% financial and only about 15% how can you make the numbers happen.

I presented my findings to Senior Management along with about eight recommendations. Every recommendation was right from the playbook I used at Michaels. So, with the blessing from the leadership team, I went to work. I immediately separated the 846 initiatives into four buckets: Information Technology (IT) maintenance, facilities, marketing, and strategic initiatives. Within a month, we had established business and financial rules within the annual budget process to handle the first three buckets. Then I recommended using the Michaels' funding tower process to prioritize, fund, and track the strategic initiatives.

It worked like a charm. When the process was completed, we had 22 strategic initiatives, and about 800 or so of the initial "wish list" items were funded through the annual budget process. The remaining initiatives were moved out to future years. We also added more structure to the capital spending process. In addition, we added a return on investment calculation to make sure we were spending the company money wisely. Finally, management agreed to have a strategic planning workshop with Senior Executives from around the world.

Priorities can be determined by wish lists, hallway conversations, pet projects, or the squeaky-wheel-gets-the-grease mentality instead of what will actually move the company forward operationally and strategically. **There are many reasons strategic plans and initiatives fail. One main reason is the lack of courage of the leadership to properly prioritize their initiatives. The sooner companies realize this, the more time they will spend on the "must-haves" compared to the "nice-to-haves," and they are more likely to succeed.**

--------·●·--------

THEY DON'T TEACH YOU THIS IN BUSINESS SCHOOL

The timing could not have been worse. It rocked the entire world, and no one was spared from its wrath. It began with headlines as early as the spring of 2007, and things just kept building from there. It seemed like every day over the next year and a half; there was another headline about the building crisis. Then, in the summer of 2008, it seemed like every headline had the words "subprime mortgages and mortgage-related securities."

As I was interviewing for the SVP Strategic Planning position at Fossil, Inc., I had one eye on everything I could read about Fossil and another eye on the Wall Street Journal. I was concerned that the entire world's economic situation would continue to deteriorate. I was also selfishly worried it could impact Fossil's willingness to hire a new executive. But Fossil did extend an offer, and I accepted without hesitation on September 15.

A couple of weeks after joining, one of the largest brokerage firms, Lehman Brothers, declared bankruptcy involving over $600B in debts. In October, the Dow Jones suffered its largest one-week loss to date. Throughout the remainder of 2008 and into 2009, the headlines did not get any better. The world was crashing around Fossil like every other company, but I was hired to help build a 3-year strategic plan. Talk about bad timing!

No one knew what was going to happen from day to day, let alone how to plan for the next few years. It reminded me of a situation we had at Michaels when on September 11, 2001, the terrorist planes crashed into the World Trade Center and the Pentagon. No one knew what was happening or what to do on the infamous day. Then after the initial reaction, management led the effort to get the company through those difficult days. We used to say, "They don't teach how to handle this type of situation in business school." I felt the same way now.

Fossil's management team did an outstanding job navigating through uncharted waters. They had to make some exceedingly difficult decisions to cut expenses, including layoffs. It was a blow to their tremendous culture, but everyone knew it had to be done. The management, especially the CEO, did an outstanding job making sure everyone knew this was the best for the company even though it ripped his heart out to do it.

I was only with the company for a few months, but it seemed that the way the leadership handled this situation caused the organization to rally around the boss. At the same time this was going on, both the CEO and COO told me to continue working on what I was hired to do. They believed this would pass, and they wanted to be ready to take advantage of the post-recession world. So that is exactly what I did.

Whether it was the 9-11 attacks, numerous financial crises, or the Covid-19 global pandemic, each caused headaches for even the most seasoned leaders. I have lived through all of these, and there are a few common themes to be a successful leader in a crisis. **First, you need to show you are in control with a steady hand at the wheel. Second, you need to be adaptable to the constantly changing conditions. Third, you have to be creative. This is business unusual, not business as usual. Finally, you have to communicate often and honestly with the organization.**

These are the same qualities you have to use when managing a crisis in your life. Maybe it is a death in the family, a loss of a job, or a serious illness affecting a family member. **There is no class you can take that truly prepares you to deal with all the emotions and daily struggles when a disaster happens. Lean on your faith, family, and friends to help you get through the difficult times. Keep pushing forward every day, and you will find the light at the end of the tunnel.**

IF IT SEEMS TOO GOOD TO BE TRUE ...

I was taking a break from the Managing Director's meeting. It was a chance for all the countries worldwide to come to Dallas and hear from the company leaders and see the new product offerings. It was similar to the national sales meetings I took part in when I was a sales representative for Haggar. Like at Haggar, this meeting was meant to get the sales teams fired up about the upcoming season's sales possibilities. Also, like at Haggar, it worked.

I was only on the job for a couple of months or so, and it was my first time to see the entire display of product offerings that Fossil brought to the marketplace. It was breathtaking to see a multi-brand and multi-product line company have such a breadth and depth of product offerings. In addition, it was an opportunity to meet people I would be dealing with from around the globe. My start date and the timing of this meeting could not have been more perfect.

During the break, I returned a call from my former administrative assistant, Laurie, at Michaels. She had heard I started working at Fossil and was checking in to see how I was doing. I went to my car to make the call to ensure no one could overhear my conversation. After a few minutes of catching up and reminiscing about how much fun we had working together, she asked me how it was going at my new job. I hesitated for a second, and she knew something wasn't right.

She knew me too well. She also knew that I had a fairly good batting average of knowing when a situation wasn't exactly what it seemed. I told her the truth. "It is too good to be true. Most people never find the perfect job in their entire career, and I had it for almost ten years working at Michaels. Is it possible I have found another one?"

"What concerns you about Fossil?" she prompted.

"Honestly, even though the Chairman, COO, and CEO have told me continually that they support this role, everyone else in the company is telling me a different story. For example, one gentleman who works in our Far East region told me that I am the fifth or sixth person from the outside that had similar objectives when they were hired. Not one of them lasted more than a couple of years. So, that is a little concerning," I said.

"He told me there was a lot of initial momentum, but management always reverts to their comfort zone. 'Tree huggers,' I call them. The new hire and management get frustrated, and they part ways. He did say that most love the idea of what I could do for them but that I should know what I am up against."

Laurie said, "That is a little different than the 100% support you received from Michael Rouleau, for sure. So what are you going to do?"

"Well," I told her, "I love the challenge of doing something other people have failed at, and I like the chance to prove people wrong. I have taken my fair share of risks in my career, and the worst thing that can happen is I give Fossil everything I have, and we still decide to part ways. I'm just going to give it my best shot."

Here I was a couple of months on the job, and the natural progression of going from unknown optimism to known pessimism had just hit me. I had seen this countless times in the past, but this was the first time I was the one going through this particular scenario. *Was this situation too good to be true?* I wondered. *Was I being set up to fail?*

When that reality hits you, do not ignore it. Be a realist about your situation and deal with it head-on. Also, don't let it weigh your performance down like an anchor. Deal with it and do your job to the best of your ability! If you get the sense that you have passed this initial phase, fantastic. However, **if you feel that things just aren't right with your job or company and might never be, it might be time to update your resume. Do not be naïve to believe management and HR won't make a move. The faster you realize that sometimes things just might not work out, the more successful you will be managing your life and career.**

—————•●•—————

POLAR OPPOSITES

I talked with a friend I had worked with at Michaels about my new position at Fossil. He wanted to know how I was doing, and I told him Fossil was remarkably similar to my days at Haggar when product and sales were number one and operations were second. It was fun being part of such a creative environment, but it was taking me some time to make the adjustment.

He said, "... unlike your days at Michaels?" I laughed but had to agree. Even though we sold arts and crafts to highly creative customers, we were an operations, process, and systems-driven organization. We never were quite able to tap into the creative side of our brains. It was efficiency first, second, and third. My friend knew I was 100% correct. He then asked the million-dollar question, "How different is your new CEO compared to Michael Rouleau?"

My answer—"Polar Opposites."

"You are kidding!" he laughed.

"I'm not," I promised, "the companies are the exact image of their leaders for good and not so good."

"What do you mean?" he asked.

I started with the person he knew. "Michael was first and foremost a fantastic retail operator. His expertise was store operations, supply chain, processes, systems, and financial discipline. You could make the argument that he was one of the best ever. His history at Target, Shopko, Lowe's, and Michaels all leveraged his greatest strengths. He definitely had merchandise and marketing experience, but those were not his sweet spot. He knew it and could have been equally as great at it, but he made his living making companies operationally efficient and much more profitable because of it."

"All true," my friend agreed, "but what about Fossil's CEO?"

"Fossil's CEO is like the mad creative genius. He was a merchant executive earlier in his career and brought the merchandise first mentality to Fossil. Sometimes I believe that he has a hologram that only he can see about where he sees the product direction for the company. That is one of the reasons I know I could never be a great merchant. I do not have the gene," I answered.

I worked with so many buyers and merchandise executives at Gimbels and product development people at Haggar that always amazed me— the way they could seemingly see the future of fashion 18 months in advance of it hitting the sales floor. That was Fossil's CEO. It was his greatest strength.

Just like Michael's weakness was the Fossil's CEO's strength, his weaknesses were Michael's strength. Fossil's CEO obviously knew operations, finance, systems, and supply chain, but he was more comfortable with the goods. These individuals were perfect examples of the difference between being left-brained (analytical and methodical) or right-brained (creative, artistic, and intuitive).

> **DO AN HONEST ASSESSMENT AND BE ABLE TO RECOGNIZE AND ADMIT YOUR STRENGTHS AND WEAKNESSES. PUSH YOUR SKILLS LIKE HECK TO BECOME GREAT AT THEM, AND MITIGATE YOUR WEAKNESSES AS BEST YOU CAN. WHEN YOU BECOME THE BEST YOU CAN BE, IT HELPS YOU RISE TO THE TOP OF YOUR PROFESSION.**

As you can see, these polar opposite individuals were equally successful. They just did it in different ways by leveraging their greatest strengths to take them to the top of the corporate world. It took me a number of years to really find out what my strengths were, and once I found them, I did everything I could to leverage them in my life and career.

Everybody has strengths and weaknesses. The key is to do an honest assessment and be able to recognize and admit yours. Push your skills like heck to become great at them, and mitigate your weaknesses as best you can. When you become the best you can be, it helps you rise to the top of your profession.

———•●•———

WHAT TIME IS IT?

Bringing Fossil's senior leadership team together for a strategic planning meeting was nine months in the making. It took every ounce of skill I had to persuade them that this was vitally important to the future of the company. They had never done it before, but they needed to do it on a more consistent basis. This was especially true in 2009, when the world was still trying to work its way through the Great Recession. The financial crash was a significant emotional event that shook the whole world. Now Fossil, Inc. had to take a look at an entirely new economic landscape.

Organizations around the world were doing the same thing in reaction to the world crisis. Now Fossil was bringing their entire senior leadership team (including the leaders of our international regions) to Dallas for a two-day strategic planning meeting. I hoped this session would be as productive as a session I ran ten years earlier with the Michaels' leadership team. That meeting had led to a clearly defined strategic roadmap that enabled Michaels to increase sales from $1.8B to $3.7B over six years.

Fossil's pre-Great Recession goal was to double their sales from $1.5B to $3B in five years. The number one question for the participants was, is this still a realistic goal? If it was, then we had to determine the tactical and strategic priorities to get there. There were so many unknowns, but for me, the answer was crystal clear. I just did not know if the team would agree.

Every participant had homework assignments, and they all did an outstanding job preparing for the meeting. I introduced the session; then, each executive had about an hour to discuss their section of the business.

It started a little slow, which was natural for the first time, but the conversation got a little livelier and more engaged as time wore on. As the meeting drew to a close, I recapped the notes I had taken throughout. To my surprise, the team had agreed with my going-in assumption. The top two priorities were to maximize the global wholesale sales distribution network by emphasizing the still underdeveloped big three: watch, leather, and jewelry businesses.

It seemed obvious, but the company had spent a lot of money, time, and focus on other initiatives that had not yet produced the level of sales and profits as did the big three. An example was the apparel business. They had tried for about ten years to make that work, but in my mind, it had not yet produced enough to be one of the top priorities. It was not a politically correct thing to say because it was a goal of the CEO to make this work. The purpose of the meeting was not to stop additional business opportunities like apparel, retail, the internet, or new watch technology but to determine how to triple the business over the next five years.

In fact, a quote from my notes of that meeting says, "As it relates to watches, the phrase cash cow was used." With this renewed focus and a post-Great Recession boom in the fashion watch business, Fossil's sales increased from $1.5B in 2009 to $3.2B in 2013. Their net income rose from $139K to $378K during the same period. Now that is a cash cow!

It is so easy for companies to get distracted by the new shiny object. There are so many examples where those shiny objects distract management from their core money-making businesses. Great companies can balance first maximizing every ounce of sales and profits from their core competency while looking around the corner for the next opportunity.

THE AIR COVER DISAPPEARED

I was standing at the copy machine one afternoon when Fossil's Chairman walked by and said hello. Ever since the first day I met Tom, I really like talking with him. He had been a supporter of my role from the beginning, and I knew I needed his support now more than ever. After my initial honeymoon period and the craziness of the early months of the Great Recession, the company was drifting back to the pre-Jeff days.

Before I arrived, most decisions were made in a decentralized manner. A hallway conversation, an impromptu meeting in the parking lot, or a few extra minutes at the end of a scheduled meeting could all be places where decisions on strategic priorities were taking place. It was the entrepreneurial spirit at its best and worst.

During my initial onboarding, one of our SVPs told me other executives had been hired to tackle similar issues. Initially, there was a lot of momentum, but then the company reverts to their decision process comfort zone, and the person gets frustrated and leaves. I was not surprised when this scenario began playing out for me.

I could never really get anywhere near as close to Fossil's CEO as I did with the CEO at Michaels. But it was not because I did not try every trick in the book. My only hope was that the Chairman and President would remain in my corner. While talking with the Chairman, I did not directly come out and tell him my thoughts. I did, however, try to give him a sense of what was happening. His comment solidified the nail in my coffin, "Going forward, Jeff, you need to get the CEO completely on board with your process."

He said nothing else, but he did not have to. I had heard rumors that he was thinking of leaving the company. Who could blame him? After 25 years with Fossil, why wouldn't he want to try and find something new to sink his teeth into. My intuition said something else was going on. His comments to me that day were so different from the positive statements made during my interview and since I joined the company.

A few months later, on January 5, 2010, the headlines in *The Dallas Morning News* read, "Fossil Founder Leaving Company's Board." In the third paragraph was the key sentence. "Kartsotis, Chairman since 1991, told the board he wouldn't stand for re-election and was not the result of any disagreement with the company or its management." Why was this statement in the press release? Why not just say it has been a blast, and now I am off to do something else? I thought there must have been some tension at the top.

I immediately went to see President/COO Mike Barnes. Mike was my boss and one of the original Fossil employees. In my ten-minute conversation, I got the sense that Mike had one foot out the door as well. I knew that I had just lost any air cover I had with the company. On September 30, 2010, the headline read, "Fossil President/COO Michaels W. Barnes Resigns." This news seemed to validate that there was something else going on at the top of the organization.

In-between these two announcements, I left Fossil. I had a blast and learned a great deal during my short tenure and knew I had given them everything I had. I am disappointed I could not help them more, but there are no hard feelings on my part. Sometimes you have to realize that not all situations will work out. In this case, the two principals who supported my role the most and provided me cover left the company. With no air cover is it hard to fight the ground war.

If you get caught up in a situation outside of your control, here are a few tips: First, understand that you can only control the controllables. Focus on doing the best you can in the difficult situation. Second and just as important, if you realize that no matter what you do, the problem won't change, begin to identify options to move you to a different environment or situation. Do not just hope that it will change. Be proactive before the situation deteriorates even more. Finally, do not blame yourself. S%@t happens. Learn from it, but don't let it define you.

WIPEOUT

When I was a young boy, I would watch surfers on TV and marvel at their athleticism and fearlessness. I could not believe how they could stay upright when the water was crashing all around them. Surfers call the biggest waves a "bomb," and they ride it for all its worth when they get one. The ride would end in three ways. One, the surfer would give up. Two, the surfer could ride the wave successfully until it lost its energy, or three, they could wipe out. Unfortunately for Fossil, after the fashion watch wave ended, they had a massive wipeout and still have not recovered.

As the economy slowly recovered after the Great Recession, the fashion watch business was a massive "bomb" wave. People started looking at a watch as a fashion accessory compared to just something that could tell the time. Consumers bought a white watch for one occasion and outfit, a black watch for another, and a rose gold watch for another. It became like changing a tie for men or a pair of earrings for women. It took off like a rocket.

At that time, Fossil was perfectly positioned to take advantage of this trendy wave. They had a variety of brands, were excellent at product development, an outstanding sales distribution network, and their prices were perfect for a post-recession period. In addition, after the 2009 strategy session, management wanted to stress their three core categories—watches, jewelry, and leathers. Their decision could not have been better timed. These trends don't happen often, so when you get one just like a surfer, you ride it for whatever it is worth.

There is one big problem with a trend. Just like in nature, a real wave will run out of energy, so will a trend. You just don't know when, but you better have a plan for when it does. Fossil did not. Once the wave slowed, they were not prepared for the post-trend era. From the peak of $3.5B in 2014, their sales declined to $1.6B in 2020. Starting in 2017, they had net losses of $748K, $3.5K, and $52.3K, respectively. The stock price peaked in 2012 at $139.20 and crashed to below $4 in 2020.

The trend crashing was one thing, but two other forces also began working against the company's leadership. The first was the dramatic rise of E-Commerce and the impact on brick and mortar retail, especially department stores. The department store business accounted for more the two-thirds of Fossil's business. So when this part of retail suffered, so did Fossil.

The second major force working against Fossil was the rise of the Smartwatch. Apple Watch was introduced in 2015 and has dramatically changed the watch landscape. In a bit of irony, Fossil should have been prepared for the Smartwatch revolution. In 2009 they had a division dedicated to researching Bluetooth technology. However, they sold it in 2011.

Their business was leaking before the Covid pandemic, and that has only helped accelerated the decline. A headline dated August 13, 2020, in *The Dallas Morning News* read, "No Talk of Bankruptcy Here." That is a massive wipeout when you go from the talk of the industry to a headline with the word bankruptcy in it.

It happens to the best of them. My favorite team, the Green Bay Packers, won five championships in nine years in the 1960s and then struggled for close to 30 years until they won a Super Bowl 1997. Sometimes you focus so much on winning now, you forget to plan how to keep the success going. Never stop analyzing where you are going and what could be around the next corner that could challenge your company or industry. Keep investigating what is happening in your environment that could cause a major wipeout. Remember—the perfect time to plan ahead is during the best of times.

NEVER STOP ANALYZING WHERE YOU ARE GOING AND WHAT COULD BE AROUND THE NEXT CORNER THAT COULD CHALLENGE YOUR COMPANY OR INDUSTRY. KEEP INVESTIGATING WHAT IS HAPPENING IN YOUR ENVIRONMENT THAT COULD CAUSE A MAJOR WIPEOUT. REMEMBER—THE PERFECT TIME TO PLAN AHEAD IS DURING THE BEST OF TIMES.

CHAPTER 9

RUNNING A SIGNIFICANT PART OF A COMPANY

I achieved my goal of being a senior leader of not just one but two different major companies. After I left Fossil, Inc., I set my focus next on running a company—or at least a large slice of one. That moment arrived when Michael Rouleau, my former boss and the previous CEO of Michaels, offered me the chance to help turn around yet another failing company. This opportunity allowed me to have more direct operational responsibility than I ever had before in my career.

These stories discuss how I handled the additional responsibility, the steps used to turn this broken company around, changed yet another corporate culture, and navigated the complexities of a strong and engaged Board of Directors. I soon realized, however, that running day-to-day operations was not all it is cracked up to be. I learned I was born for chaos. It turns out that I love the action of righting a sinking ship or fixing broken area(s) of a company. When that thrill ride disappeared, I actually got bored.

WHO YOU GONNA CALL?

It was so unexpected. We had stayed in contact for the last six years since my former boss had retired from Michaels. Our calls were cordial—basically checking in on each other. But all that changed in the fall of 2012, when my wife and I were driving home after a fun day at the Texas State Fair. My phone rang, and this call had a familiar feel, but I knew Michael Rouleau so well I could tell there was something different about his tone. We exchanged pleasantries, then the real reason he called came out.

"Are you ready to get back to work?" he asked.

Since I left Fossil about a year and a half ago, Michael kept bugging me about getting back in the ballgame. He knew I had turned down several positions that would have required me to move my family. I was willing to commute, but I did not want to transfer my son now that he had entered high school. I had seen too many examples in my career where people uprooted their families only to survive a couple of years with the new company.

I knew how hard this was on their kids, especially those of high school age. High school is hard enough without having to change schools a couple of times. Michaels had been particularly good to me financially, so I passed on those offers and just kept looking for something local or where I could commute. That something happened with this call.

"Jeff," Michael said, "there is a very good possibility that I will be named to the Board of Tuesday Morning. In my initial investigations of the company, I think they need your skills. They are in pretty bad shape right now, and they need help turning this once great company around. I told the Chairman of the Board and management that very few individuals can do what you can do, Jeff. You are a perfect fit. What do you say?"

"I don't know," I answered. "I will need to do some homework, but after Fossil, I am hesitant to join another management team where my skills are thrust upon them. That experience did not end well because my main support came from the Board and not the CEO."

"Don't make a quick decision right now," he encouraged. "Go do some homework on the company. I'll get back to you in a few weeks."

When we hung up, my wife said, "He needs you again! You know Michael well enough to know that if he does get on the Board, he will not be a passive participant. It is not in Michael's nature not to take control of any situation he is in. If I'm right, Michael knows how good you are and what you can do to help him. So, the next time he calls, ask him why he called you and if he called anyone else."

As always, I listened to the wisdom of my wife, and a month later, Michael called me back. In my hands was the press release stating he had been appointed to the Tuesday Morning Board of Directors, *"We are pleased that he has joined the Board at this time and look forward to his active and involved Board role."* My wife's instincts were right on. I did ask Michael why he originally called me, and he reiterated that my unique skills to help companies in chaotic situations were perfect for Tuesday Morning's situation. When I asked him if he called anyone else first, he said, "No, why would I?"

Ghostbusters hit the big screen in 1984. It was a wacky comedy about four individuals fighting ghosts in New York. The lyrics in the theme song said, *"If there's something weird and it don't look good, who you gonna call?"* When a company is in trouble, and it didn't look too good, he called me. Out of the thousands of people he had worked with and the hundreds of executives that had worked for him, he called me.

Over the ten years I worked with him at Michaels, I had made myself valuable because of my particular skill set. **Consistently go above and beyond your job description to make yourself a valuable asset to the company. Make yourself stand out from the crowd by doing the little extra things that the bosses aren't expecting but will greatly appreciate that you were able to accomplish. Strive to do this in your career, so when management needs something done, they will call you!**

———————— • ● • ————————

EYES WIDE OPEN

It was surreal. I was living out the exact same situation, except it was with a new company. A friend of mine joined the Board and then called me to say this new company was an ideal situation for my skills. I talked with the Chairman of the Board, and he liked what my friend told him about my skills. I interviewed with the CEO, and he had reservations but was willing to take my friend's word. He offered me a job with a newly created position.

Instead of Fossil in 2008, it was Tuesday Morning in 2012. It was déjà vu all over again—except for one particularly important difference. This time I did not go into the opportunity believing this could be a long-term position. I looked at it more like a consulting project that could end at any time. I set my expectations differently, so I would not be surprised if and when the situation on the ground changed.

The circumstances over the last six months had been very chaotic at the Board and Senior Management level. On June 5, 2012, Becker Drapkin Management filed a Securities and Exchange Commission form 13D which served as an opening volley of a potential fight between the company and activist investors. Tuesday Morning did not put up a fight, and Steve Becker put himself and another person on the Board.

Within a month or so, they fired long-time CEO and three Board Members and the Chairman left. Becker became the Chairman and added my former boss Michael Rouleau and another retail industry veteran to the Board. He also added a new CEO, who brought in a few of his friends in senior-level positions. It was a dizzying number of moves, but something you often see with activist hedge fund investors.

I had experienced a small dose of this kind of chaos when two private equity firms bought out Michaels. Within a year of that sale, many Senior Management individuals left. We had a completely new Board and a new CEO. As an employee, your head spins, not knowing when the next shoe will drop.

With all of this said, I was still interested in giving it a shot. My initial research showed many similarities between what was broken at Tuesday Morning and what had been a mess at Michaels. I thought the worst-case scenario was that I attempt to help management, and some time into the future, they could decide my services were no longer needed. The best-case scenario was to help fix what is broken and give the company a fighting chance to survive.

To sweeten the deal, corporate headquarters was only seven miles from my house. As a result, I did not have to worry about moving my family, which was very important to me. I understood what was happening at the management and Board level and knew what challenges this posed for me when I accepted the job offer. I was going into the situation with full awareness.

Never go into a situation blindly. Do not assume that things will get better. Investigate the issues. I don't care if it is getting married, picking a college, or joining a new company; you need to have as good an understanding of the actual situation as possible before you say yes. Perform your due diligence to understand exactly what you are getting into before you commit. Go in with your eyes wide open, and you will never be blindsided by a situation.

PERFORM YOUR DUE DILIGENCE TO UNDERSTAND EXACTLY WHAT YOU ARE GETTING INTO BEFORE YOU COMMIT. GO IN WITH YOUR EYES WIDE OPEN, AND YOU WILL NEVER BE BLINDSIDED BY A SITUATION.

I CAN FIX IT

It was the first time she had ever done store visits with me as a retail operator. We had shopped in stores together before, but this was different. I wasn't browsing to buy something; I was there to see what problems needed to be addressed. Then I would determine if it was possible to fix them and how long it might take. Finally, I needed to know what, if anything, was positive about the company I could glean from visiting stores.

My wife, Lisa, was helping me perform due diligence before accepting or rejecting the offer to join Tuesday Morning stores. She had been a loyal customer for over 30 years, and I wanted her to give me that consumer view of what she liked and disliked about Tuesday Morning now.

We visited about five Dallas locations, and I walked every aisle of every store. I talked my way into the backrooms of every store and also found out that some of the stores had storage containers that held additional merchandise. I spoke with every associate and customer who would answer my questions. What we found was an unmitigated disaster with a few rays of hope.

The stores looked horrible and were unshoppable because they had way too much inventory. My wife commented that she was worried that the merchandise would fall on her head in many of the aisles. Every stock room was filled with new products that they had no space to put on the floor, and there were three-year-old holiday items still sitting on the floor while the new seasonal product sat in boxes in the stock room.

When I talked with the associates, they could not stop telling me about all of the problems. The trucks never show up on time, the merchandise was ticketed wrong, the quality of the inventory continues to drop, the buyers continue to ship in more of the stuff that doesn't sell, and the corporate office never visits the stores, so they don't know what is happening. These are only a few of the hundreds of issues that kept coming up at each store.

With all the doom and gloom, I found two rays of sunshine. First, even with all of this mess, every customer I talked with loved Tuesday Morning. I asked each, "If we fixed some of these issues, would you shop here more?" 100% of them said, "Yes!" Second, the associates had all worked for Tuesday Morning for 10 to 25 years. They were passionate about the company, and they wanted someone to help fix these issues.

After the last store visit, I asked my wife's opinion of Tuesday Morning now that we had looked at the store from a different perspective. "The issues seem insurmountable, but what do you think?" she asked.

"I can fix it," I smiled.

She smiled back and said, "I thought you were going to say that!"

In the 1982 cult classic movie *Fast Times at Ridgemont High*, Sean Penn played a character named Jeff Spicoli, who got into a car wreck. The vehicle was a mess. Cinder blocks sprayed all over the hood, the engine was steaming, and the front end was all caved in. After inspecting the damage, Spicoli confidently announces, "I can fix it."

I was confident that the issues were not, in fact, insurmountable. Challenging, yes, but I had seen similar problems at Michaels that we were able to resolve. Also, because of the passion and love for Tuesday Morning displayed by the associates and customers, I was pretty sure they might just stick with us through the challenging turnaround phase. I put the odds of success at 50/50, but that was good enough for me.

You have to be wired a little differently to work in seemingly helpless situations. Emergency rooms, working in underdeveloped countries, or working on finding a cure to a disease are examples of these. Some people look at a situation and call it helpless, while others see the same situation as an opportunity to help. Not everybody can work in these environments. The ones that do should be praised and honored for their desire to bring people hope. That is what I wanted for the associates of Tuesday Morning.

---•●•---

NOT FOR LONG

They gave me two months to conduct an initial assessment of the current situation and help the new CEO deliver an update to the Tuesday Morning Board in early February. They wanted me to dive into every nook and cranny of the company, lay out the issues, and provide a roadmap to address each and every one. It was a tall order but doable. I just had to put on my consulting hat and get to work.

I was conducting the assessment with the new CEO, and I wanted to make a great first impression on him and the Board. From my first day on the job, I hit the ground running. I interviewed close to 100 associates, including people from every corporate department, our stores' organization, and the distribution center. I received hundreds of documents and reports that I had to wade through.

Finally, I compared notes with the CEO, and then we proceeded to put the Board presentation together. What we found was not surprising for a company that had been underperforming for years. In the final presentation, we had five pages of issues. Headlines included being a completely dysfunctional organization and culture, upwards of $100M overstocked, 25% of the stores located in extremely poor locations, no real IT infrastructure investment over the last five years, and a general denial that the organization was in trouble.

We also included five pages on what we were going to do about these issues, including a list of tactical priorities with timelines for how long it would take us to complete each task. On the actual summary page, it had three key takeaways: (1) This was a monumental undertaking,

(2) We needed to peel back and establish a solid foundation, and (3) We needed to take five steps backward so we could then move forward faster.

We wanted to let the Board know the reality of the situation and that it could be fixed in time. *"In time" were the key words.* The Board Chairman was a Hedge Fund investor who had already shown signs he lacked patience with his newest investment. Within the first few months of his ownership, he had fired the CEO and COO and took over the role of Chairman. I felt good about what we had told the Board, but I had the feeling that something was brewing beneath the surface during the entire meeting. I could not put my finger on it, but there just seemed to be a lot of tension in the room.

Exactly one month later, a headline in *The Dallas Morning News* validated my intuition. It read, "Tuesday Morning CEO Brady Churches resigned." That was the headline, but the second sentence was the real news—Michael Rouleau was coming out of retirement at 74 years old to be the interim CEO. My first thought was, *Wow, that was fast!* Sports fans joke that the first letters of the NFL stand for "Not For Long" because players and coaches are hired and fired so quickly. Obviously, this Chairman had similar tendencies to owners in the NFL. Michael Rouleau would be the **third** CEO in just six months.

You hear it all the time when a coach gets fired, "It is a cruel business," and "This is a 'what have you done for me lately' league." Well, the business world is exactly the same. It is especially true of Senior Executives and corporate turnarounds. Many people think it is so cool to be a boss with all the perks and privileges, but you always live with "Not For Long" running through your mind. You wonder if you miss a quarterly earnings report or you make a mistake, then today might be the day they will ask you to leave.

Don't let this scare you from wanting to be a Senior Executive. **When seeking a Senior Executive position, you have to understand the challenging realities of that role. If you do, you can have a highly successful career in senior management. If not, the pressure of the job can drive you crazy. Some love it, and others can't take the pressure or the volatility. If you want a job at the top, understand the nature of the beast and go after it with all you've got!**

IT WAS IN HIS BLOOD

could not believe he did it. He had retired in 2006 at the top of his game. Michael Rouleau had just led Michaels Stores on a ten-year run of consistent sales and earnings increases, culminating in a private equity sale of over $6B. When he arrived at the company in 1996, the stock was in the low $3 range. At the time of the sale, it was $176. Why, at the age of 74, would you not only come out of retirement but do it for an incredibly troubled company?

It was the first question I asked him after reading the announcement that morning. I walked into his office without even knocking and found him talking with his new executive assistant about the things he needed for his office. He looked up and saw me standing in the doorway, waved me in, and asked his assistant to leave.

After telling him he was crazy, I asked him why he was doing this. He said, "I have played all the golf I can play and seen the world over the last six years. *I just wanted to get back into the action again.* I still have more to give to the world of retail, and I think this is a great opportunity to see if I can fix another company."

I asked him, "Is your wife on board with this decision?" I knew her very well, and I could not believe she wanted him to do this. When he retired, she told me that it was now their time to spend life together after dedicating his life to his job for so many years.

"I'm still working on my wife," he admitted, "it may take a while, but she knows I love doing this, and I was getting bored at home."

"Are you moving back to Dallas?"

"I'm not." He answered. "Because this is an interim position, I will commute."

"From Seattle or Phoenix?"

"Seattle in the summer and Phoenix in the winter."

"You are crazy!" I told him. "Seattle is approximately a 4-hour flight, and Phoenix is a little over 2 hours." Those kinds of flights were hard when I was a consultant traveling every week at 35 years old, let alone 74. "You're nuts!" I joked.

"Everyone keeps telling me that," he laughed, "but I just had to get back in the game one more time."

As he talked, I remembered my first job as an Executive Trainee at Gimbels Midwest Department Stores when the CEO, Tom Grimes, gave his opening remarks to the class. He said, "Retail is a very tough but equally rewarding business. The determining factor of whether you survive is one simple thing. *If it is in your blood, you will have a successful career.*"

There could be no doubt that retail was in Rouleau's blood. From being one of the first Target employees in the early 1960s to his outstanding run as the leader of Michaels, retail had been his life. He loved every minute of it and wanted to taste the craziness one more time.

This situation reminded me of a great athlete who comes out of retirement for one last hurrah. They miss the crowd. They miss the lights. They miss the attention, and they miss the competition. Nothing in retirement can provide that adrenaline rush. It is the same for great leaders in the business world. You want a piece of the action one more time.

People work hard so they can eventually retire. Then after three months of playing golf, cleaning the garage, and finishing all the chores around the house, they are bored out of their skull. Their minds are still sharp, and they have the energy of a 25-year-old. They want back in the action, but will anyone want them?

Don't be in such a hurry to hang up your uniform. Retirement is not all it is cracked up to be. If you do retire, make sure you have a plan to keep your mind sharp and yourself busy. If it is in your blood and you find an opportunity to get back in the game one last time, enjoy every moment. Then you can retire for good.

ONLY IF I CAN RUN SOMETHING

I had gone into the situation at Tuesday Morning with the mentality that this could be nothing more than a short-term consulting engagement. My eyes were wide open to the reality of working for a company that was an absolute mess and aware that the Chairman was an impatient Hedge Fund activist investor.

My former boss at Michaels was on the Board, but I did not know how much influence he would really have over the CEO. I figured I could help them as best I could, and if someday the Board had enough of me, I could go on my way. No harm, no foul, as they say in pickup basketball games.

Now my former boss, Michael Rouleau, was just announced as the interim CEO. The announcement changed everything. The short six-month tenure of the previous CEO was over. My mind was going 100 mph as I was trying to wrap my arms around what had just happened, and Michael and I spent the next three hours together mapping out the next 12 to 24 months for the company. It was almost like what we had done at Michaels Stores for nearly ten years. The key word was *almost*.

As we sat at a big table in his new office, Michael wanted to dive right into the meeting. "Before we tackle the challenges here at Tuesday Morning," I told him, "I need to get a few things straight. At Michaels, I was your pit bull. I accepted that role under one simple statement: to move the company farther and faster, or you would fire me."

I had no problem with the role. I was really good at it, and I loved to see all the progress we were making due to my abilities and Michael's support for me in that role. The one challenge was that he would never let me transition to a different role. I wanted to hire someone new for my position and asked Michael continually to let me run a part of the business. He would always say the same thing, "You are too valuable to me in your current role." I did not like his answer, but I accepted it because I loved what I was doing, and I had a huge financial incentive to stay with the company.

Now it was different. Michael had called me to get me involved at Tuesday Morning. He needed my help more than I needed the headaches we were about to incur. I was in a much better negotiating position than I was in the past, and I leveraged it. *"I do not want to be only the pit bull/fix everything guy for you. I want to prove that I can handle the responsibilities of a division or two."*

I also wanted to prove I could be his replacement. He was interim, and I knew I could run a company. I wanted Michael to give me a chance. "If I fail, I fail," I said, "but I will only stay on to help you if I can run something." To my pleasant surprise, he agreed.

"Jeff," he said, "you will have to pull double and sometimes triple duty, but I know you need this opportunity to show your stuff."

I became the new SVP, Supply Chain, Inventory Management and Process Improvement. I was now responsible for the distribution center, domestic and international transportation, merchandise planning and allocation, order entry, and every process in the company. No one had more responsibility except Michael. There was one caveat to this decision. He was very blunt in telling me that the Chairman was on his side now, but neither of us should get too comfortable that his support would last. He would end up being prophetic.

During any negotiation, it is important to understand who has the real power. You see it all the time in contract negotiations with professional athletes. If they are the number one player at their position, they have the power. If they can be easily replaced, they have little to no power. If you are in a position of power with your current company or a new company, use it for whatever it is worth. Do not take less when you hold all the cards.

---·●·---

BEEN THERE DONE THAT

As the meeting wore on, Michael Rouleau and I realized how much easier this conversation was compared to those we had in the early days of the Michaels Stores' turnaround. Even though he had over 35 years of retail experience, there were times at Michaels that he faced an issue for the first time. As for me, I had never been part of a turnaround before, so everything was new to me.

Now, as the new interim CEO and the new SVP for Tuesday Morning, we felt like it was getting back on a bike you had not ridden in a while. There was no panic. There were no questions about what we should do first, second, or third. We had been there and done that, so we had the turnaround plan complete in a matter of a few hours, and we were ready to get to work.

It helped that I had been on the ground for the past four months or so, looking at every part of the organization from top to bottom. For many of the items on the to-do list that we presented to the Board a month ago, I had already begun to improve under the previous CEO. The plan now included many of the things I thought were important, but the previous CEO had said no to. As in the past, Michael and I were in 100% agreement, or we worked through the issue until we gained a consensus.

The first thing you have to do in a turnaround is manage cash levels. If you run out of cash and cannot pay the bills, your tenure as a senior leader will be noticeably short. You need to stop the bleeding and stabilize the patient. The most important thing to do is find ways to cut expenses. Before we had arrived on the scene, Tuesday Morning had identified $2M - $3M in expense savings. These included areas like waste management services, company supplies, and UPS charges. In three months, I reported to the Board we were going to realize close to $3M in savings.

Within the first year, my process teams had redone the budget, seasonal, advertising, fall peak season, markdown, physical inventory, new and relocation store, and merchandise planning process. What took me years to do at Michaels took me months because all I did was copy what we did there. In a matter of one year, Tuesday Morning had received almost $5M in consulting work done for free. It made us instantly more efficient and helped us run the organization with a minimum amount of people, which was critical during those early days of the turnaround.

We also took the one-time new CEO markdown charge to clean up about 90% of our overstock and aged inventory problem. Our stores were now shoppable again instead of cluttered from ceiling to floor with boxes of stuff. At the same time, I put on my old strategy hat and worked with Michael on developing our new marketing, supply chain and inventory management, real estate, and information technology strategies. We knew if we could survive a year, we wanted all the longer-term plans to be ready to go on a moment's notice.

In the first twelve months, we had reset the foundation of Tuesday Morning. This had taken three years to do at Michaels. Everyone was taking notice—the employees, the Board, and even Wall Street. One of the best emails I ever received was from one of our merchandise VPs. His note said, *"No one in the organization ever believed that you could accomplish so much in such a short time ... you saved the company."* It was a great compliment for Michael and for me.

When you have a plumbing problem, you don't hire an electrician. If you have a broken leg, you don't go to a heart surgeon. When you need new tires for your car, you don't go to see a dentist. It is the same in business. If you have a company in trouble, you don't hire a person with zero experience turning a company around. Hire someone with the expertise to accomplish what needs to get done—someone who has been there and done that. You might think you can't afford to do it. I will tell you that you can't afford not to do it.

—————•●•—————

TEXAS TWO-STEP

We had to find money, and we had to find it fast. The company was bleeding cash, and if we did not stop the hemorrhage, our tenure as the new leadership team would be very short. Consultants call this finding quick hits. Something that you can identify and get an almost immediate return. The challenge for us was the situation was so dire that an almost immediate return might not be fast enough.

We did not have time for system projects or a new consulting project. We only had time to identify a possible area for money and get it now. One of those areas was our annual spending on FedEx shipments, $1.6M. Our goal was a 20% actual savings for this expense category. We were going to approach it from two different angles. First, we were going to renegotiate the contract.

Everybody and their brother does this when they are looking for expense savings. You put the contract up for bid between UPS and FedEx, and you will always get a price reduction from one of them. I have been on projects in the past where you renegotiate the contract and announce to the world that you will save $1M. Then, you actually spend $1M more on Fed Ex charges by the end of the year.

Then the Senior Executive over this budget item will say, "I told you my savings number was only based on last year's spend. I always said if we have more packages, my negotiations will be more cost-avoidance than actual savings you can take to the bank." The executive does the Texas two-step, and the company has a $1M expense surprise at the end of the year.

My Texas two-step is different. Along with contract negotiations, I put new rules in place to dramatically reduce the amount of FedEx shipments that happened in the first place. We were a company close to bankruptcy, yet everyone was sending packages overnight express even when 75% of the boxes did not have to arrive for two days. We were allowing our vendors to use our FedEx number to send us samples of their products. We even allowed employees to send FedEx packages using the company expense account!

In less than four weeks, we had developed new guidelines for every area of the company and stopped all of these practices and about 25 more. Some people did not believe I was serious about these changes. After implementation, I instructed the mailroom not to make any FedEx shipments unless they had a signed authorization with my signature on it for the first month.

By the end of the year, we had actual savings of $368K. A savings of approximately 23%. That is how you find money to let you fight the other turnaround battles for another day. It was tough love, but it would have been much tougher to tell everybody we had to close our doors because we ran out of money.

This same scenario plays out every day with individuals who are in a financially challenged situation. They work like crazy to consolidate their debt, shift to a lower interest credit card or take out a loan from the bank, but they never change their spending habits.

DO THE FINANCIAL TEXAS TWO-STEP: PAY DOWN EXISTING DEBT AND LIMIT SPENDING. IF NEEDED, GET SOMEONE TO SIGN OFF ON ALL YOUR EXPENDITURES TO KEEP YOU ON TRACK. THIS CAN PROFOUNDLY CHANGE YOUR FINANCIAL SITUATION.

When you struggle with your personal finances, you need to do a Texas two-step. Step one: pay down your current debt payments, and step two: put tough love rules in place to limit your spending. To enforce the new rules, you may need to get someone to sign off on all your expenditures to keep you on track. This will profoundly change your financial situation. The biggest benefit of this process is that it shows you that you can, in fact, live without many things you thought were must-haves but were really just nice-to-haves.

WHO'S ON FIRST?

I knew I was in trouble when each of them brought in more binders and reports to a meeting than I had ever seen before. I had seen them in action before in different meetings or one-on-one conversations, but today was a different scenario. Today was the first time for my new direct reports to give me an update.

My responsibilities were wide and deep when Michael agreed to allow me to run a significant part of the business. My team's responsibilities included merchandise planning, purchase order writing, store allocations, vendor relations, international and domestic transportation, distribution centers, and all processes from the backroom of the stores to the POS register.

With this promotion, the only thing that I did not have direct responsibility over from an operational standpoint was buying the product (Buyers did this) and the running of the store's sales floor operations. It was a lot, and I knew I had inherited a hornet's nest of problems. The first topic on my agenda was to get a correct answer to some very basic questions to see if my team was on the same page.

After a few opening comments, I got right down to business. I wanted an update on how we did the week before and how we were looking for the upcoming few weeks. The first question I asked was, "How many units did we ship last week?"

Four individuals scrambled to find this report within their stack of documents. The head of the distribution center (DC) answered first. He said, "2,317,987." Within a split second, the head of merchandise planning said, "No, it was 2,295,346." Another split second later, the head of DC reporting said, "It was 2,365,987," and the head of transportation said, "2,341,666."

I did not react at first to the discrepancies. I just asked another question. "How many units did we allocate last week?" The exact same process ensued—scrambling for a report and four different answers. I then took one more shot. "Okay, how many units are we planning to ship next week?" The same thing happened again. It reminded me of the classic 1945 sketch by comedians Abbot and Costello called "Who's on First?"

The skit still stands the test of time because it illustrates a universal truth we all understand and have experienced: the slightest misunderstanding in simple common terminology can lead to a complete breakdown of communication. For me, it was not "Who's on First?" but *"What number is correct?" The answer was all of them. That was what was maddening.*

Each was correct because of where the person pulled the data from, when they pulled the data, or what days they included in the analysis. After the third question, I said, "We will not have this happen again. We can't run a company with dueling reports. This group will work together to get one version of the truth, period." That is exactly what happened.

Within five weeks, we had worked through all the issues and now had, for the first time ever, all relevant information on one page. We weren't done. We came up with three first-time-ever reports to track seasonal selling by store and by item, track all advertising purchase orders, and our inventory plans versus actuals by week. Within three months, we went from five versions of the truth to one. We could now begin to manage the business and report to the rest of the company on our performance.

I knew from my initial assessment that the organization was terribly dysfunctional, and I had to change that quickly if we were going to have a chance to save the company. **One of the first things a new leader has to do is get everybody on the same page. There cannot be dueling reports, individual priorities, or arguments over whose facts are correct. You have to set the tone early and make sure everybody knows they are working for the same team.**

NO SURPRISES

It was Friday at about 3:00 pm. I was still the new guy and was still dealing with the dictatorial nature of the last person to hold my job, so I did not want to explode. People were still hesitant to be completely open with me because the previous person would have really taken them to task. They were like a puppy who had a bad owner before you and now hides when they think they will have bad things done to them.

I did my best to remain calm, but I could not understand how we could not have known that we would miss shipping to about 50 stores their allocation of merchandise for the advertisement that was running this Sunday. For the first five minutes of the conversation, they told me ten different reasons for the mishap. All of them understandable considering the level of dysfunction the entire organization was dealing with for the last few years.

I did not care that we were not yet perfect. I had told them the "Progress not Perfection" motto, and we had made tremendous progress as a team. We continued to go round and around in circles for a while when I asked the million-dollar question. "*When* did you know?" No one spoke. I looked into all of their eyes and knew the answer already, so I asked another question. "Did you know when we all talked on Tuesday?" Again, no response.

Then one person spoke up and admitted they all knew earlier in the week that we had a problem but were unsure if I would want to spend the extra dollars to expedite the merchandise to these stores. Instead, they tried to process the orders through our dysfunctional distribution centers, and the product got missorted for the 50 stores in question. He said, "We are now here telling you because we can still get the merchandise delivered, but it will cost even more to FedEx the shipments."

When he was finished talking, I took a breath and reminded them that Michael and I said that we wanted no surprises like this. We knew things would happen, but when bad news surfaces, we need to react instantly. Then we can all pitch in to help.

They all admitted that they heard us say this more than once, but they were still hesitant because of their experiences the last few years. I completely understood. I knew about most of the horror stories of the past management team. I also knew that Michael's title was "Interim CEO," and they did not know whether he and I would be here two more days or five years.

I told them I knew Michael and I still needed to earn their trust and that we would do everything we could to show we were different. It started with this issue. I went to Michael's office and interrupted a meeting. I told him the situation, and he was upset as well, but asked what we could do about it. I informed him that my team had already made the arrangements to expedite the product and told him what it would cost.

Under the umbrella of no surprises, I told Michael that the current cost was triple what it would have been if we had known earlier in the week, and we would try and find dollars in the budget to make up for this mistake. He agreed and told me to remind them, "No surprises." When I went back to my office, I told the team to ship the units. It was a painful and costly lesson, but one that helped us grow as a team.

Nobody likes bad news. **The mark of a great leader is how you react to the bad news. Do you berate your team? Do you beat them up one side and down the other? Or do you create an environment where bad news can be discussed promptly and addressed as a team? Organizations that learn to work together to resolve any issue, and more importantly, work to prevent it from happening again in the future are usually at the top of the best places to work list.**

———————•●•———————

I MADE HIM INTO A CARTON OF MERCHANDISE

In the Spring of 2013, about two weeks after he became the interim CEO of Tuesday Morning, I said to Michael, "So, you don't believe me?" In the 15 years we had known each other, he had never accused me of lying or stretching the truth to make a point. Now he was accusing me of doing what many other executives had done to him in the past—make up an excuse for not becoming more efficient in their area of responsibility.

As always, I pushed back. I told him, "If you don't believe me, let's get in the car and drive over there right now." I pulled my keys out of my pocket and said, "I will drive, and I will bet you lunch that I am not lying or even stretching the truth a 1/16 of an inch." He knew me well enough to know that if I pushed back like this, he might need to take a look.

He said, "Let's do it tomorrow, and I will take your bet."

At 11:30 am sharp the next day, I stood in his office, ready to show him the truth. I was about to reveal the most inept and dysfunctional distribution center (DC) process he would ever experience in over 50 years in retail.

On the drive, he asked me again to explain how things worked. "You really have to experience it," I told him. "I am going to make you into a carton of merchandise and show you how many times we need to touch you before we ship you to our stores."

"I'm game, " he said, "but I want to know the number."

"Well, for our fastest process, we can touch the product 15 times. If we have a certain issue, we can handle a box 22 times."

He shook his head in disbelief and reiterated, "That is impossible."

Over the next two hours, I walked Michael through our process with him as the carton of merchandise. In a normal DC process, it is pretty simple and straightforward. You receive the product, put it away in a rack, pick it, pack it, and ship it. Five touches, maybe six, and it is on its way to the stores. Not here. We had three different DCs within a mile radius of each other that all performed those same five touches.

One of our buildings received the merchandise. Then when we were ready to process the goods, we had to pack them up in that building and send it to another building. They received it and also processed the merchandise. Then they would put it in a truck and drive it across the street to our shipping building. The product was unpacked again, sorted by store, and then finally shipped to the destination store. Many times, the process took too long, and we would miss the outbound truck. When that happened, we put the cartons in a storage area and shipped them out the following week.

When we were at the end of the tour, Michael was speechless. That was a first. He could not believe what he had just experienced. He said, "Who the heck would design something like this?" Only he did not say the word heck.

I told him, "Not only did they design it this way, but the Warehouse Management System is also coded to make this as efficient as it could possibly be!"

While we were discussing the tour during the lunch he paid for, he said, "We have to show this to the Board."

"The only way they will believe it will be to do what we did today. We need to make them a carton of merchandise," I said, and Michael agreed. It took us a few months to coordinate the tour with the Board, but we did show them an animated PowerPoint presentation at the very next meeting. They were speechless. A few months later, we took them on the DC tour. They told me they did not want to believe my earlier presentation, but it was even worse seeing it live.

Pictures, videos, eyewitness testimony, or slick presentations can only do so much. **There are times that the only way to convince somebody of something is to have them experience it first-hand. When they can get all of their five senses into the actual environment, it is hard for them to argue that you are stretching the truth about the situation. Although it can be fun watching them squirm, it is more rewarding to gain their trust and get them on board with your solutions.**

---·●·---

IT IS OUR HOUSE TO CLEAN NOW

We were on our way back from our tour of the distribution center (DC). Michael was still trying to get over how dysfunctional a process the former management team had allowed to be put in place. He had never seen a setup where you have three distribution centers within a one-mile radius, all doing separate processes. Normally you have one building where everything is done under one roof. Due to the configuration of each building, we actually had six roofs. It was a mess.

Michael asked me how the DC management team was doing. I told him, "If you thought my direct reports had built silos and were challenged to work together, the DC team is 1,000 times worse. Each building is run like it is a separate DC in a different city. They do not talk much; they have their own reports, and when things go wrong, out come the knives!"

"What are you going to do about it?" he challenged.

I told him about a couple of ideas, but he did not like any of them. Instead, he said, "Why don't we do something that gets them to work together and show a sense of pride in the DC team. Within the next few days, we had agreed on our plan of action.

It was a two-pronged plan. The first was to clean the distribution centers of $4M of old and distressed inventory. The second part was to clean out the old junk located in all three buildings. This included old conveyor equipment and parts, LP and HR records dating back 15 years, old buses that hadn't run in years, and office furniture from the 1960s. The goals were to build pride in accomplishing something by working together and free up 15% of DC space currently cluttered with junk.

In three months, these once siloed teams had worked together to clean up every inch of those buildings. Not only did we get rid of the old inventory and all the other junk, but we also established new standard operating procedures to keep the centers safe and clean. During the cleanup process, I would go over to the DC every day and pitch in. I would pick up a broom to sweep or walk the DC floor and pick up garbage off the floor.

I wanted them to know I was with them. I was not sitting in an ivory tower barking orders to the troops and then not join them on the front lines. I wanted them to see it was not beneath me to roll up my sleeves. The entire process met and exceeded our goals. The before and after pictures of the DC space were dramatic. Every excess piece of distressed inventory and junk was gone.

We had also instilled a great sense of pride. They saw what they could accomplish as a team and not as workers from individual buildings. It was a beautiful thing to watch, but that was not the best thing that happened. I was touring the DC with Michael when the project was complete when I saw a couple of pieces of plastic lying on the ground. I went down to pick them up when one of the employees started yelling, "No, no, no!"

He came over and took the plastic out of my hands and said, "You don't need to do this anymore. You showed us the way; it is our house to keep clean now." Mission accomplished. After being beaten down for so many years, these wonderful employees just wanted someone to respect them and show they were one of them. With the newly instilled pride, we saw a nice productivity increase.

Treat people who report to you with respect. You don't need to beat them to get them to do their jobs. Lead by example. Show them you are willing to roll up your sleeves and pitch in to help. Never forget you were once an employee reporting to a senior leader. Build pride in the team and thank them for a job well done. You will be amazed at how positively the team will respond.

GOLDILOCKS

In March 2013, we had the first store District Manager meeting since Michael had been named interim CEO and had promoted me to SVP, Supply Chain & Inventory Management. To a person, everyone in attendance thought I was nuts, and many came up to me after my presentation and told me directly to my face. They said things like, "You are going to kill the company," or "I thought you guys knew what you were doing," and one or two said something like, "In my 25 years in retail, no one would make the statement you just made."

Again and again, I responded, "I accept your challenge. In less than six months, you will be thanking me for what we are about to do." I had just told them we were going to reduce our current inventory position by at least 25% and that we would not lose one dollar of sales. In fact, I told them, our sales would increase.

My positive attitude was not based on conceit or arrogance. It was based on the fact that we had done the same thing at Michaels Stores 15 years earlier. All the associates there thought the decision to cut overall inventory was crazy until we showed them that the key is not just to buy a lot of stuff and hope it sells. The key is how to manage inventory to make the most money.

Buying inventory (merchandise) is the largest annual investment a retailer makes. It is an obvious and amazingly simple equation but extremely hard to execute. You need to buy the right amount of merchandise in the products consumers will buy so you can make enough profit to pay all of your bills and have a little left over to continue to invest in the company. Too little, and you can hurt sales. Too much, and you can hurt profits. You need to get just the right amount.

It is just like the classic story of *Goldilocks and the Three Bears*. One bowl of porridge was too hot. One was too cold. The last bowl was "just right." Managing inventory is part art, part science, part experience, and part gut feel. We were about to show an entire organization that we did know what we were doing.

Six months later, I made a presentation to the Board about what would be announced shortly to the organization and the public. Page 4 of my presentation had two bullets with letters in 60 pt. font size. One read, "$94 Million Less Inventory," and the second read, "10% Comp

Sales Increase YTD." It was only a 22% reduction in inventory, but we weren't done.

Fast forward another eight months, which was fourteen months after I told the organization about our inventory reduction goals, and I again reported our progress. Page 18 said, "25% Less Inventory Than Last Year" and "Sales up 5.7% YTD." The bottom line was we knew that the excess inventory was, in some cases, three years old and taking up valuable space in our stores and tying up millions of dollars we needed to run the business. Once we got rid of that inventory, the new fresh merchandise was able to be displayed properly on the shelves, and the customers responded. At the next District Manager meeting, the tone of conversations I had with the attendees changed completely.

FIND THE BALANCE IN YOUR LIFE THAT MAKES YOU HAPPY, GIVES YOU ENERGY, AND PROMOTES A HEALTHY LIFESTYLE. NOT TOO MUCH, NOT TOO LITTLE, BUT JUST RIGHT.

In the world of retail, you are always challenged to find the right level of inventory. In the real world, you have the same challenges. How much is just the right amount of drinking, partying, surfing the Internet, eating, exercising, watching TV, or playing video games? If you go overboard, you could end up being a dysfunctional mess like Tuesday Morning. You need to find the balance in your life that makes you happy, gives you energy, and promotes a healthy lifestyle. Not too much, not too little, but just right.

THEY WERE HEROIN ADDICTS

When my boss asked my opinion, I told him it was not sustainable. I said if we did not address it immediately, we had no chance to save Tuesday Morning. We had to stop it, and we had to stop it now. "When I show you my analysis, you will agree with me 100%." When I showed him just one example, he immediately called a meeting with the head of Marketing to discuss how we should change this situation.

I had just shown him an analysis of the only true advertising vehicle that Tuesday Morning used to draw traffic into their stores. It went back to the company's early days when the founder, Lloyd Ross, would buy left-over inventory from brands and retailers and invited the public to shop in a warehouse-type setting at extremely discounted prices. He used a simple postcard that was lime green to tell the customers to come and check out his deals.

He chose the color to differentiate from all the other mail items. The legend of the Green Card advertisement was born. Over the years, the advertising grew in size and scale from one small postcard to a 12-page ad circular with upwards of 100 items. The reason for the growth is a natural phenomenon in retail. I call it being a "Heroin Addict."

A retailer wants to generate more sales, so it advertises one special item to attract more customers. It works, and they increase sales by 10%. Fast forward to the next year, and now they have to beat last year's sales. They now run two special items plus a special 10% discount on an entire category of merchandise. Now the drug addict needs more sales, so they keep adding more and more to their advertisements.

Then they go from advertising once a month to twice a month, then every week. The more they need to boost sales, the more advertising drug they need to take, even though it was really killing them. That is what was happening at Tuesday Morning. The analysis I gave Michael showed sixteen weeks after the last sixteen Green Card advertisements; we still had an average of 42% of the merchandise remaining in our stores.

Over three-quarters of our excess inventory was old Green Card merchandise that did not sell. To make matters worse, there were numerous cases where the buyer would purchase the same item for the next year even though the markdown area was full of the exact same item. As you can see, the illicit drug of trying to beat last year's sales at all costs can cause people to make very poor choices.

We immediately changed the process for item selection, the number of items we put in the ads, and the quantities we purchased. The buyers hated us, but we had to go pretty close to cold turkey to save the patient. It worked. Our sales still rose, and our left-over inventory was dramatically reduced. In some cases, we actually sold out of the advertised items. Selling out meant we were going back to the early days when the customers flocked to our stores to get the best deals before someone else did.

When you get addicted to anything, it is really difficult to stop. Ignoring problems only makes them worse. You have to address them head-on. You might be able to stop it on your own, but if you can't, seek out whatever help is necessary to break the bad habit. Do it as if your life or your business might depend on it because it just might.

———————•●•———————

90/10

It hit me like a ton of bricks. I could not believe I had missed something so obvious that anyone could recognize the problem. Little did I know it would become a catchphrase that changed the entire merchandising strategy of the company. It would refocus most of our energy to drive sales every day, not just during the ten times a year we ran promotions.

I was analyzing the amount of floor space we give each category in a typical store, just as I had done when I worked for Michaels Stores. It is a common practice for retailers because they want to get the best merchandise assortments that also produce the most sales and profits.

To make it more impactful, I would get a typical blueprint layout of the store, including the fixtures and the names of the categories by each fixture. I would put the layout in a PowerPoint presentation and then color code the fixtures to represent the different categories. For example, green represented where we put our promotional fixtures, blue designated seasonal areas, and so forth.

I would always make it into what you call a build slide. Each time I hit the button on the remote, a different color would appear on the screen. It worked fabulously. As I was practicing my speech, I was stumbling on the first build slide that showed the space we allocate to our monthly promotional merchandise. As I was struggling to find the correct words, there was a knock at my door. It was one of our buyers. She asked if I had a second to discuss something.

I said, "Of course," and she sat down. She asked me what I was working on, and I told her. She studied the slide for a few seconds then asked, "Is the green color space where we place the advertised merchandise?"

I said, "Yes."

"That looks like it is only about 20% of the store is green, but it seems like we spend 80% of our time on 20% of our sales."

"Honestly," I told her, "it is probably more like 90/10." She did not disagree.

"So, the slide shows that 90% of our sales floor is white space?" she asked. In that moment, the words "White Space" became the driving force behind our merchandise strategy for the next several years. *The white space represented the fixtures I had not filled in yet with their category color.* It was such a telling visual that it almost explained itself when I presented it.

The visual showed that we were spending an inordinate amount of time on ten promotional events of the year instead of how to drive sales through exciting and ever-changing products every day of the year with 90% of our floor space. We spent 90% of our time and energy on about 10% of our business. That had to change.

From that moment forward, the company refocused the organization's effort to drive sales and increase customer satisfaction by focusing the appropriate amount of energy and time on our everyday business in the store. For decades, the company could not see that they were in a slow death spiral and just needed an outsider's perspective to shock the system. This was the main reason we were able to reduce our reliance on the big promotions and drive business 365 days a year, not just several weeks a year.

Business, as in life, is about focusing on the things that matter the most. The challenge is to make sure you can determine what is truly important. Sometimes an outside perspective can help your company (or yourself) with this task. Their viewpoint can help you face the reality that your time and energy are focused on the wrong things. Once adjusted, watch things significantly change for the positive.

ONE TIME PASS

Everything changed when the SVP of Distribution quit. Even though I did not like that I was losing one of the only people in the company that knew how the current processes worked, it gave me a chance to bring in someone from the outside to take a real good look under the hood. That person was Les Gardner. Les and I had known each other since 1997, working together at Michaels.

I placed an emergency SOS call to see if I could convince him to come out of retirement to help me until I could fill the opening. I needed someone I could trust to tell me the truth about the operations and also be able to tell me what needed to be done quickly. I gave him ten days to do an initial assessment.

He asked me to meet him at his office and said, "There is something you need to take a look at ASAP." I thought he was going to tell me that our conveyor system needed to be replaced or half the team was quitting. What he had found was even more concerning. It looked like members of the distribution center team were making money on the side by leveraging their relationship with Tuesday Morning.

He had some evidence, but we needed to find more. We agreed that we should play the new guy card and tell everyone we were just trying to get our arms around what was going on operationally and from an expense standpoint. Les focused on improving day-to-day operations, and I took the expense track and said that for the next several months, I was the only one authorized to sign invoices.

I did not know what I was getting myself into, but it ended up bearing a tremendous amount of fruit. Every day for about six weeks, I would show up at 6:00 am at the DC to review and sign hundreds of invoices. These included everything from office supplies to Gatorade for the workers, maintenance items for our forklifts, and transportation carriers. What I found was disturbing.

We were paying invoices to one member of the management team selling products to us through a multi-level marketing company. I discovered we were paying too much for almost all of our supplies. In some cases, triple what we should have been paying. Finally, we were paying for maintenance supplies like nuts and bolts, yet we had tons of the same items already in the DC.

Now the question was what we should do? By themselves, each offense was a 4 out of 10, but in totality, they were an 8 out of 10. It could take us months of investigative and HR work to determine if it rose to a severable offense. We decided to call a manager meeting and see if we could scare them straight.

In the meeting, I told everyone what we had found. I told them that it was disturbing on the surface, but I knew that it could get really ugly if I went deeper. You could hear a pin drop. I then said, "I can do one of two things. I can start a detailed investigation and see what I find, or I can give all of you a one-time pass." I left that statement sit out there for a few seconds and watched everyone squirm. I then said, "I am going to give you a one-time pass but just remember Les and I are still looking." It worked, and the shenanigans stopped.

It is so tempting to cross that line and tell yourself it is not a big deal to get a little extra on the side for yourself. **Most companies have a Code of Ethics guideline, but you should have your own moral compass for conducting business honestly and with integrity. Live by a higher standard, so you don't have to constantly keep looking over your shoulder to see if someone has found out what you are doing. The bottom line is if it even comes *close* to the line of wrongdoing, just don't. It's not worth it.**

<hr />

20,000 LEAGUES UNDER THE SEA

Unbeknownst to me, they had worked on it for weeks. When they handed me a copy of their report, you could just see the pride in their faces of what they had accomplished. A few weeks before, I mentioned that we needed to do something to improve the number of units we were sending to each store. In retail terms, this is called allocating inventory. If you do this right, you can become a superstar for the company, but you will need to update your resume immediately if you do it wrong.

We had decided to reduce our overall inventory levels throughout the company, but we still wanted to increase our sales. The only way you can do that is to make sure you have just the right amount of product in every store for every item. The people who determine that are some of the most valuable people in retail.

These three had done a deep-dive analysis by item, by category, by region, and by store. It was a tremendous amount of data they had gone through to complete their report. I was extremely excited because they did this on their own, and it was something I knew we needed to have done. My anticipation level to hear the results was rising by the second.

I wanted the answer in the first two sentences of the conversation. I bit my tongue because I knew they wanted me to see the detail of the analysis they had done. The more they talked, the more I realized that these individuals had not just done a deep dive; they had traveled *20,000 Leagues Under the Sea* like Captain Nemo did in the famous Jules Verne novel. They had gone down and stayed down for quite a while, trying to find the answer to this allocation puzzle.

The more they talked, the more I was growing concerned with their analysis. I tried my best not to show my emotions or give them one hint of my feelings. They never knew. However, their boss, who was one of my direct reports was in the room, knew something was up with me. Beth was remarkably similar to my wife. Tough, opinionated, smart, talented ... and she could also read me very well.

When they had completed their presentation, I told them it was outstanding, and I could not thank them enough for all the work they had done. "This is so much information, I need to take it all in, and then we need to figure out how to use it to improve our allocation process." When they left the room, you could see a little hop in their step.

Then Beth got up and closed the door and said, "Okay, what don't you like about what they did?" Before I could speak, she added, "And don't tell me 'nothing' to make me feel good."

She knew me. I asked her one simple question in response, "What decision can I make with that analysis?"

She started to answer, but we both realized that she was talking in circles. After our discussion, Beth and the team tweaked a few things, and based on that; we decided to adjust our allocation formulas which helped increase sales in our top-performing stores.

This scenario is one of the biggest challenges we have today. There is so much data available, and the increase in processing horsepower is exponentially better than at any time in human history. It is so much easier to take a deep and long dive into the abyss. When you surface, do you have an interesting factoid to share at the water cooler or on a Zoom call, or did you find something valuable that could help move the company forward?

You have to be incredibly careful not to get lost in all the data. Don't dive down without a purpose. Don't get caught in analysis paralysis, only to realize you learned nothing really important. Be targeted and focused on solving a business issue or finding that key gold nugget of information to help the company make progress. Then you know your data analysis has been worth it.

MERRY GO ROUND VS. A ROLLER COASTER

As the interview wore on, I realized the person had no real idea of the history of the last 24 months at Tuesday Morning. She did not know that we had a complete turnover of the Board of Directors. Nor did she know that we had three different CEO's in a matter of six months. She did not even know what the closeout business entailed. All she knew is what the headlines said. One headline from October of 2014 in *Chain Store Age Magazine* said, "Tuesday Morning Turning Things Around."

I knew from working at Michaels during the early days of their turnaround that the headlines were much different than the reality of working for the company. Every time I would interview someone for a position, I could tell they believed those headlines. They saw that the company was improving, and that is all the mattered. They completely ignored the fact that they were entering a fast-paced, crazy, frustrating, exhilarating, and exhausting environment.

You would try and be honest with them, but you also wanted good people to join the company to help complete the turnaround. It was a heck of a balancing act. It was the exact situation we were now in at Tuesday Morning in 2014. Since Michael Rouleau and I showed up a couple of years earlier, we had made tremendous progress with the mess we inherited, but we still had a difficult road ahead of us.

Many of our candidates were currently working at the other retailers in the Dallas/Fort Worth metroplex. These included Pier One, Radio Shack, JCPenney, Neiman Marcus, and Michaels. Even though they all had some issues of their own, they all were more established names in the marketplace with processes and a culture that went back decades. At Tuesday Morning, we were ripping everything down to the foundation so we could build it back up on much more solid ground.

I needed to explain the difference in their current environment to what they could expect when they joined Tuesday Morning at this time. During a conversation with one of my direct reports, I hit on an interesting little riff, which became my go-to explanation. "The difference between your company and Tuesday Morning is the same as the difference between riding a merry-go-round or a roller coaster. Your company has been doing pretty much the same processes forever. There was a little tweak here or there, you might have a few ups and downs, but it is a safer ride. Tuesday Morning, on the other hand, is a wild and crazy ride. It is the most frightening, exhausting, and exhilarating experience. You will go up and down. You will go fast, slow, and then faster than ever. You will be going in a straight line, and then just when you think you can breathe, you will take a terrifying dive or are thrust into a loop-de-loop set of turns. Then the train finally comes to a stop, and the safety harness rises above your head."

I would look them in the eyes and say, "If your first thought is, 'I am never doing that again,' then Tuesday Morning is not for you. However, if you say, 'That was an absolute blast,' and you want to get in line and do it again, Tuesday Morning is exactly the place for you because this is what happens in a typical eight-hour day here." This particular person accepted the job offer and told me after their first week that I was not lying!

Many individuals are completely satisfied with a life like a merry-go-round. That is fantastic! For others, that life would bore them to death. They are the thrill-seekers and the X-games participants who need that adrenaline rush every day. It does not matter which group you fall into. What matters the most is you are honest about which ride is the right one for you and then putting yourself in an environment that mirrors those desires. Then and only then will you truly be happy.

JUST ONE THING

I talked about it from the first day I arrived on the job at Tuesday Morning. I said it to anyone who would listen. It should have been the number one priority from the very beginning. It did not matter if we saved the company from the brink of bankruptcy and gave it a rock-solid process, systems, and infrastructure foundation—this was not Michaels Stores. This was a totally different type of retail, and if we could not get significantly better at this one thing, none of our efforts would mean anything.

That one thing was recapturing what had made the Tuesday Morning a success in the first place. The one thing was the essence of the treasure hunt retail shopping experience. Tuesday Morning was founded on the ability to find ever-changing great merchandise deals so enticing that customers would flock to their stores to see what the company was offering that day. You had to shop often because you knew they bought limited supplies, and you did not want to miss out on something wonderful.

The customer felt like a treasure hunter, roaming up and down every aisle searching for something different, special, or unique. It was the thrill of the hunt as much as it was actually finding something. They had this magic through the mid-2000s, but to this day, they have not been able to recapture that exciting merchandise deal environment.

It is a dramatically different retail environment than shopping at Michaels or Wal-Mart. Upwards of 80% of their merchandise is basic everyday items that don't really change that much. Selecting those goods is important, but once they are on the shelf, the systems are in place to keep them in stock every day.

Compare that with off-price stores like TJ Maxx and Home Goods, which have done an outstanding job for decades because they knew if they could not continue to create that treasure hunt environment, they were done. The key is to have an ever-changing assortment that they buy in limited quantities to force consumers to shop them early and often. The customer never knows what they are going to find. That is what makes them special.

In the 1991 movie *City Slickers,* three friends from New York go through a mid-life crisis, so they decide to vacation to New Mexico for a two-week cattle drive. In one scene, Mitch talks to a crusty old cowboy named Curly. The following conversation takes place.

Curly: "Do you know what the secret of life is?"

Mitch: "No, what?"

Curly holds up his hand with his forefinger raised: "This ... one thing, just one thing. You stick to that, and everything else don't mean s#@t!"

Mitch: "That's great, but what's the one thing?"

Curly: "That is what you gotta figure out."

As I write this book, Tuesday Morning has not yet figured that out. During my three-year run with the company, 90% of the conversations with the Board were about supply chain costs, expense savings, store labor, real estate, or corporate headcount. In the big scheme of things, they did not mean s#@t because the one thing that really mattered, they ignored. Current headlines reveal they have just come out of bankruptcy and are taking on a new CEO. Perhaps that will get them refocused.

FINDING YOUR "ONE THING" DOES NOT MEAN YOU MYOPICALLY FOCUS ON ONLY THAT ONE THING. IT MEANS THIS: IDENTIFY THAT ONE FUNDAMENTAL THING UPON WHICH YOU BUILD EVERYTHING ELSE. IT IS THE FOUNDATION OF WHO YOU ARE. FIND THAT ONE THING AND BUILD IT AS A DEEP AND SOLID ROOT SYSTEM THAT WILL HELP YOU GROW.

Finding your "one thing" does not mean you myopically focus on only that one thing. It means this: Identify that one fundamental thing upon which you build everything else. It is the foundation of who you are. Find that one thing and build it as a deep and solid root system that will help you grow. If you were a tree, the tree trunk is the "one thing" that allows all the other branches to grow. Like Curly says, "That is the secret of life; you just gotta figure it out."

GETTING THE BAND BACK TOGETHER

I remembered it differently. Michael Rouleau was reminiscing about our glory days without remembering it was only glorious for a few of us. He wanted to forget that he was a challenging and difficult boss to work for at times. He didn't want to admit that many executives did not enjoy their experience working for him. I reminded him he fired close to 20 executives during his tenure at Michaels. I was concerned that if anyone from the old management team joined us at Tuesday Morning, they might come out of a need for a job, not loyalty for him.

The challenge was that we did not have time to recruit new employees and train them quickly enough to understand the rhythm of his leadership style. We only had about an 18 to 24-month window to right the sinking ship and show the Board we could take the company to the next level.

Basically, it came down to the devil you know is better than the devil you don't. So, we went through the list of potential people that could join us, identifying those willing to come to work for Michael (more than who wanted to come work for Tuesday Morning). The appearance was people reached out to us to join the company, and we were going to put the band back together. The truth was that we had to do some recruiting.

As former Michaels team members came on board, they were hit with two realities. The first was how messed up the company was and how much work had to be done to fix it. The second was Michael Rouleau had not changed at all in his six years of retirement. That was great for 90% of his style, but the other 10% mixed in drove many people crazy. There is a reason why some of the greatest bands in history fail at "getting the band back together" after a breakup.

A 2013 *Forbes* article talked about this scenario. *"Bands break up for many reasons. Usually, like other kinds of teams, they reach the end of their life cycle. They find that the sum is no longer greater than the parts, and they move on. If enough years go by and they decide to reunite, they may discover, to their dismay, that the same problems that led to the breakup are still there. They are not the band they were at their peak. They are a greyer version of their own dead end."*

I wish I would have read that when it was printed because no matter how hard we tried to make it work, things were just not the same. We could not recapture that spark between us and with the culture of this new company. Even with these struggles, we were still able to reposition Tuesday Morning to have a fighting chance to survive before many of us decided to leave the band once again.

Most of us have some version of "glory days" where we fondly remember being at our peak. We long for those days and wish we could find a way to recapture, if only for a second, that feeling of success. It is a natural desire to want to recreate that special moment when we did our best work.

When you are on a roll and enjoying great success personally or professionally, enjoy each and every second. Don't take anything for granted. Soak each ounce of pleasure from the experience, and if you are never able to recapture it again, who cares! You have a great memory that will last with you forever.

———— • ● • ————

CLASH OF THE INDUSTRY TITANS

From the very first Board meeting, I knew this would be a 180-degree difference from what we had experienced at Michaels. All you need to know is that the Chairman of the company was an activist investor who had taken over the Board and had already fired two CEOs in six months. One was the long-time CEO and one he had hired to replace her.

I wondered if Michael would be able to adjust to the activist Board mentality. During his ten-year run at Michaels Stores, from my perspective, the Board always had their strong opinions, but I never got the sense that they wanted to be on the management team. As long as we performed to their high standards, it was never their desire to get into the weeds of running the company day-to-day.

I was having a conversation one day with Charles Wyly, the Chairman of the Board for Michaels. Somehow the conversation shifted to the role of a Board. He said, "You will have a problem with a company if the Board thinks they are management. The Board is there to guide and challenge, but if we don't like what they are doing, we get new management. We will not become management."

Tuesday Morning was totally different. The Tuesday Morning Board took their lead from the new activist Chairman. He did not know much about the retail business, so he brought an incredible array of retail talent to the Board. Former CEOs, COOs, Presidents, and EVPs. They all had been remarkably successful in their careers, resulting in them getting to the top of the corporate ladder. A couple had almost as much experience in retail as Michael himself, and just like Michael, a few had just retired.

It was truly the Clash of the Industry Titans. It seemed like they forgot they were Board members and thought they were still the CEO or COO of the company. Our discussions felt more like an update meeting with your boss, who needs to know things in minute detail. It was hard to argue or disagree with their points because they were so successful and talented, but it made it exceedingly difficult when they seemed to cross the line into acting like they *were* the management team.

If you looked at the makeup of the Board, it looked like a Senior Executive Team—a former CEO, COO, CFO, Supply Chain expert, and a Chief Marketing Officer. It was brilliant for the Chairman to surround himself with experts in an industry he had little knowledge of. It was, however, a pain in the butt for the real management team.

Michael never spoke directly about this to me, but I knew him too well not to understand how frustrated he was. Because he commuted every week, he was a bachelor at nights, so I would go out to dinner with him once or twice a week. My sense was initially; he had been given more leeway to run the business as he saw fit. This was remarkably similar to what he had experienced at Michaels. Then something changed after about a year and a half into his tenure.

From my observation, the incessant questions and inquiries were beginning to wear him down. I could see it in his body language. I just felt that he could not run the company on his terms and wondered when he would say he had enough. That day came in September 2015 when Michael retired once again. The Board had won the Clash of the Titans.

Even when you rise to the highest position in the corporate world—CEO, you still have a boss. You have to deal with the emotions, opinions, priorities of the Chairman, other Board members, and Wall Street, just as all your employees have to do reporting to you. It is an interesting irony for the most powerful position in the company.

In my opinion, you need as much or more political ability as you do the knowledge, skills, and experience to successfully run a company. That is why many times, the people who get to the top are the ones who can win the political Clash of the Titans.

GROUNDHOG DAY

At the start of each week, I could tell almost to the minute what was going to happen the following seven days. You could set your clock by it. It started Sunday night when I would receive the sales reports for the weekend along with reports on shipments, DC labor costs, inventory levels, and sales through reports for any seasonal activity.

On Monday, I would get to the office early to get the updated versions of all of the reports I received the night before, plus about twenty-five others on various subjects. I would analyze them for any issues and make phone calls to address my concerns. I would walk the hallways and talk to the head of stores, marketing, and merchandising to get updates on their reaction. Then the rest of the day would be spent in meetings.

First, I met with my team and then with the Sales and Operation committee, where we would discuss all the reports and issues that had surfaced the week before. We would then create an action plan to resolve existing issues and prevent problems in the future. I spent Tuesdays at the Distribution Center and following up with my team about issues address in Monday's meetings.

Wednesdays and Thursdays were made up of buyer meetings, updates with my direct reports, following up on our strategic initiatives, and conducting specific project team meetings. Friday mornings, we called our Store Operations Team to prepare for the weekend sales. Friday afternoons, I would check with my team that we had, in fact, completed all of our tasks for the week and began initial inquiries about the next 60 to 90 days. Saturdays, I would visit stores and then start the routine all over again.

I was living the movie *Groundhog Day* where a TV weatherman, played by Bill Murray, finds himself living the same day over and over again. The film takes place in Punxsutawney, Pennsylvania, where he reports on the annual Groundhog Day event. No matter what he did, each day started and ended the same way. That was how I felt in 2015 at Tuesday Morning.

For most of the past 18 years, my career was like riding a completely different roller coaster every day, and I loved it. My role for much of that time was to help companies deal with crazy and chaotic situations. First at Michaels, then at Fossil, Inc., and now at Tuesday Morning. I thrived on chaos. It gave me energy to know that each day could and would present so many new challenges that your head would spin. I loved looking back a month, a year, or a couple of years later and see that we not only survived that chaos, but we were also thriving.

When I joined Tuesday Morning, I made a deal with the interim CEO that I wanted not only to be the fix-it guy, but I wanted to run a part of the organization to see if I could show that I could be his successor. At first, I loved it. I had more responsibility than anyone other than the CEO. After about a year and a half, we had made so much progress fixing the mess I inherited that we were dealing with normal retail day-to-day issues. I was bored out of my skull.

Even though I believe I did a very good job running the day-to-day business, I knew I was experiencing the exact scenario I would tell people about during their interviews with me about joining Tuesday Morning. I would tell them some people are completely satisfied having a career like a merry-go-round—a few ups and downs, but otherwise pretty safe ride. Others like myself needed the thrill of a roller coaster. In fact, I sometimes needed it to be a different roller coaster every day.

Everybody has to find what environment makes them happy. Some people like a *Groundhog Day* situation. Predictable. Steady. Maintaining what is working. That is great! Others thrive on chaos and need something different every day. That is also awesome! Know what makes you happy. Find a career that feeds your taste for risk and reward, mayhem and maintenance, and you will enjoy the ride.

THE OLD MAN AND DEATH

It just never stopped. No matter what we did, the Chairman could not stop undercutting the Senior Leadership Team. We had saved the company from going into bankruptcy and entirely rebuilt the foundation in a little over two years. It had taken us twice as long to do this at another company 15 years earlier. Our sales were up $50M, and the stock price had risen from a little under $4 per share to more than $21.

The Chairman's Hedge Fund had pocketed a reported $13M profit in the same period. It was not enough to stop the constant nitpicking coming from the Board. It was a miracle what CEO Michael Rouleau, CFO Jeff Boyer, and I had accomplished with this company in such a short time. We were all hired to replicate the success we had at Michaels. We were on pace to do just that, but the Board could not leave well enough alone.

None of us needed this. At 74 years old, Michael had come out of retirement. Jeff Boyer is one of the best CFOs/COOs you will ever find. As for myself, I was financially sound and could pick and choose where I spent my time and energy. We wanted to help 10,000 people who depended on Tuesday Morning surviving. If we had failed, they all would have lost their jobs. We did not fail our employees. We gave the company a fighting chance, but it was inevitable that the Board wanted to take the company in another direction.

The first domino to fall came on April 30, 2015. The headlines read that Tuesday Morning had appointed a new President and COO, and it was not Jeff or me. This was a Board hire and a finger in the eye to all three of us. Then on June 30, 2015, the second domino dropped. Jeff Boyer resigned from Tuesday Morning and took a similar position with another local retailer. About six weeks later, I left the company, and finally, on September 30, 2015, Michael resigned.

In Aesop's fable, *The Old Man and Death*, a very old man had a heavy load of firewood on his back. As he walked home, he became tired, and in desperation, he called out loud to Death, "I cannot bear my burden any longer. Please come and take me?" Much to the man's surprise, Death appeared before him, carrying a scythe. The old man was terrified when he saw Death standing right in front of him. Now that he could see Death with his own eyes, he realized he did not want to die! **The moral of the story be careful what you ask for; it just might come true.**

When someone asked me what happened at Tuesday Morning, I would say, "The Board wanted to go right, so we all left, and it got exactly what it wanted. Total control." In mid-July, the Fiscal 2015 numbers were announced. Sales were up almost $100M to $906M, which was just shy of their 2007 record. The company also reported a net income of $10K. That was where we left the company.

On December 31, 2015, the activist Chairman finally got his wish. He was appointed CEO of Tuesday Morning. He and the Board got what they wanted—full control of every decision in the company without anyone interfering in their desired direction. The fact is that the company has been in a slow death spiral ever since. Even though sales had slowly risen between fiscal years 2016 to 2020, the real story is net income. In 2016 net income fell to $3.7M, then from 2017 to 2020 they reported net losses of ($32M), ($22M), ($12M) and ($166M).

The reason for the big loss in 2020 was that the company went into bankruptcy. The stock had tanked to the low $0.20 per share range, and Death was at their door staring them right in the eyes. On January 19, 2021, a headline from *The Dallas Morning News* read, "Retailer Tuesday Morning Seeking New CEO after Bankruptcy." By May 2021, Tuesday Morning had named a new CEO.

BE VERY, VERY CAREFUL WHAT YOU WISH FOR IN LIFE; YOU JUST MIGHT GET IT, AND YOU MIGHT NOT LIKE WHAT YOU GET.

Be very, very careful what you wish for in life; you just might get it, and you might not like what you get.

DREAMING OF TOMORROW

"WE MAKE A LIVING BY WHAT WE GET, BUT
WE MAKE A LIFE BY WHAT WE GIVE."

—WINSTON CHURCHILL

MISSION ACCOMPLISHED

The continued onslaught of online retailing alternatives and now the devastation caused by COVID-19 has left the industry I worked in most of my career in tatters. The headlines are littered with bankruptcies, store closures, and thousands of personnel being laid off. Amazon keeps swallowing up market share, getting bigger and more powerful every day. I know that I can still assist companies across the retail and wholesale spectrum, and I am still an asset to help them respond to and navigate the current retail environment. But what do you do when you are 60 years old and so many players in your industry are on life support?

Some settle for the current fate. Others complain about the situation or become armchair quarterbacks. Still others resign themselves to deciding their best days are behind them and retire. Not me. I determined to do what I have done for my entire career—look for options and take a few risks.

I decided to put all my efforts into making yet another shift in my career path by becoming an author and then looking for branches off that new tree to propel me into the next phase of my journey. When I first decided to write a book of stories, there were four main inspirations:

- First and foremost, I wanted to give my son a helping hand as he embarked on his life after college. I wanted to provide a guidebook for him to know some of the things he would encounter during this new, exciting, and mysterious adventure.

- Next, I originally went to college to be a teacher, and even though I chose a different career path, I never lost the yearning to help and mentor individuals. I hoped these stories would help inform and inspire others to learn from my successes and failures. I wanted to provide them a roadmap to guide them on their journeys.

- Third, I wanted to see if, at the age of 60, I could again do something I have never done before—become a published author. I was a B- writing student at best, and I even changed my major because I was so challenged as a writer. I wanted to prove to myself and others that you can accomplish great things even if the barriers seem insurmountable.

- Finally, I wanted to use this book as an opening to begin a more focused effort of inspiring, mentoring, and teaching people and companies how to improve.

After more than fifteen months, I can say "Mission Accomplished" to all four. Where this next phase of my adventure takes me, I don't know, but I am as fired up as ever to take the new long and winding road.

Stories from leaders and mentors stayed with me through the years. Their experiences resonated with me, and when they shared real-life situations and how they handled them, I learned lessons far more valuable than anything ever taught to me in any college course I ever took. Because of the positive impact stories had on my growth and development, I felt compelled to share my stories as transparently as I could, in the hopes that they would impact you with valuable lessons, humor, and guidance.

Hopefully, you are more informed about what lies ahead after reading my stories. As you continue your journey, remember that there is much knowledge and experience surrounding you every day. **When you are younger, know that you don't have to learn the hard way by fighting life's challenges alone. Bury your pride and seek out assistance from a parent, grandparent, older sibling, a manager, a teacher, or refer back to this book. Help them help you!**

For those who are older and a little more experienced, I hope you nodded your head again and again as my stories highlighted events that happened in your life or career, and you knew exactly what I was talking about! I believe there are still nuggets of wisdom for you to find in this book that will not only help you as your adventure continues but also perhaps help you find language to mentor someone else.

You have so much wisdom and experience to share—be willing to help and mentor someone. **You don't have to write a book to help someone close to you. Just be there for them. Listen to them, and be open to helping them through their issues. Don't take all the knowledge you have and let it go to waste—share it! If you can help just one person with a story that changes their lives, you too can say, "Mission Accomplished."**

MY LAST STORY

J ust like yours, it is yet to be written ...

MINDSET AND PRIORITIES

PERSONAL DEVELOPMENT AND FAMILY

MONEY AND FINANCES

———— • • • ————

INSPIRATION AND MOTIVATION

LEADERSHIP

LEADERSHIP CONTINUED

MENTORING AND COACHING

EXPERIENCES, FUN, AND BUCKET LIST

FAITH AND PROVIDENCE

PERSONAL AND CAREER DEVELOPMENT

PERSONAL AND CAREER DEVELOPMENT
CONTINUED

PERSONAL AND CAREER DEVELOPMENT
CONTINUED

A C K N O W L E D G M E N T S

REMEMBERING THOSE WHO HELPED YOU ALONG THE WAY

When I began this new journey to write a book, I knew I had been incredibly fortunate to have so many people assist me throughout my life and career. With each passing word I wrote, I quickly realized that the number of individuals and their influence on me was so much greater than I could have ever imagined.

I want to acknowledge those special individuals, who without their help, love, compassion, guidance, and support, I could have never accomplished what I have achieved.

- **Dave Levey** was my first buyer when I received my promotion to Assistant Buyer at Gimbels. He taught me so much about retailing and how to transition from college student to a young professional.

- **David Lazovik** was my SVP, General Merchandise Manager at Gimbels. Through his support, David gave me the confidence that enabled me to believe I could become whatever I wanted to be if I was willing to put in the work and effort.

- **Don Franklin** was the head of personnel at Gimbels. If it weren't for his timely meeting with me to discuss how my priorities needed to shift away from my college days' activities and into my career, I don't know if I would have even survived my first job.

- **Mr. J.M. Haggar** was the founder of Haggar Apparel Company. As a trainee with the company, I was asked to drive this wonderful 93-year-old man around Dallas. His kind words of encouragement and wisdom gave me more knowledge than any MBA could have given a 24-year-old young man.

- **Mr. Ed Haggar** was the founder's son and became a mentor to me during my time at Haggar. Just like his father, his willingness to assist a young aspiring trainee provided me a solid foundation of knowledge upon which I built my entire career.

- **Mr. Joe Haggar III** was President of Haggar Menswear and the founder's grandson. He showed me how a leader could assist you not only professionally but personally. His acts of kindness to invite me to play golf with him when I originally moved to Dallas got me through some very lonely weekends.

- **Jimmy Palasota** was one of the many great salespeople and people of Haggar. During my days as a trainee, my time in my first territory, my shift to a new division, and my eventual decision to leave Haggar, Jimmy was always in my corner. He opened up his home to me and made a young man 1,000 miles from his family feel like I had become part of his family.

- **Jim Herman** was another one of the many great people of Haggar. When I moved to Phoenix for my first sales territory, Jim opened up his home to me because he knew I was a scared newbie. His children were like my younger sisters and brother, an invaluable support network and one of the main reasons for my success in my new position.

- **Corbett Howard** was the final member of my Haggar trifecta. I cannot even begin to explain the lessons I learned from Corbett about selling, relationships, working with Wal-Mart, friendship, family, faith, and the willingness to share all that he knew with me.

- **Chip (Charles) Humphrey** is my best friend. We met as Haggar trainees in 1985 and became instant friends. Neither years nor miles have diminished our friendship. It's the kind that lasts a lifetime.

- **The wonderful men of Haggar who influenced my life and career.** In addition to the men listed above, I want to mention the following individuals who provided me more than a young man deserved. Mr. Joe Haggar, Jr., Frank Bracken, James Thompson, Rich Norwood, Greg Baloyan, Jeff Morrow, Randy Bartlett, Steve Carter, Greg Whyte, Tim Lyons, Doug Moore, Jerry Cornelison, Randy Lockard, Milton Hickman, David Barber, Jerry DeJulius, Bob Firkens, Jimmy Haggar, Larry Tolini, Tom Kilroy, Sylvan Landau, Clay Huston, Ted Demerle, Tom Sample and Mark Bannon.

- **The wonderful women of Haggar who influenced my life and career.** What does a 24-year-old young man miss the most when he moves away from home for the first time, his mom? Just as the Lord blessed me with the Haggar men who provided me guidance, he also blessed me with the perfect blend of motherly influence, business knowledge, and friendship from the wonderful woman of Haggar. Bobby Bodmer, Bobbie Schmidt, Donna Harrington, Gracie Thomas, Opal Roberts, Dale Kimmel, Edna Morris, Dana Tullos, and Phyllis Neie.

- **Marvalee Nakata** was my buyer at Goldwaters in Arizona when I became a first-time sales representative for Haggar. She helped put me on the map and enabled me to realize that I belonged in the new world of selling.

- **Charles Jones** was my first Managing Partner in the consulting world. He took a chance on a young, ambitious non-MBA consultant and gave me the break I needed to help fulfill my career dream.

- **Amir Hoda** was my partner for most of my time as a consultant at Computer Sciences Corporation (CSC) and our work together at Michaels. He is one of the smartest people I have ever met. He was a confidant and a supporter when times were sometimes exceedingly difficult. If there is a picture in a book that says surround yourself with talented and wonderful people, Amir's picture would be in that book.

- **Steve Biciocchi** was my partner at CSC and always supportive of my career. If Steve had not talked me into still coming to CSC after the head of the division quit one week before I was supposed to start, my story would be dramatically different.

- **Joe McKinney** was a partner at CSC. He helped pave the way for me to succeed as a consultant with the Michaels' account. He was always in my corner and willing to help at a moment's notice.

- **The talented and outstanding people at CSC.** I have never in my career been associated with such a talented group of individuals in one place at the same time as I did during my time at CSC. Many of them were Senior Consultants like me, but went on to have careers as VP's, SVP's, Presidents, COOs, and Partners of companies. I thank you for sharing your knowledge, skills, and friendship with me. Rob Howell, Will O'Brien, Lee Whitaker, David Toth, Maria Cramer, Dennis Heppner, Jeff Langenfeld, Lou Baylog, Vishal Jain, Steve Bogart, Peter Ilgenfriz, Derrick Walker, Cheryl Doggett, Steve Caulkins, and Sharla Miller.

- **Michael Rouleau, CEO Michaels.** I don't have enough space to recognize what Michael did for my life and career. For some to-this-day-unknown-reason, he allowed me to work at his side for almost ten years at Michaels and another three at Tuesday Morning. He let me in on all the inner workings of being a CEO during the challenging days of a turnaround and then building a company to last. It was like I received ten Ph.D.s working with him, and I will be forever grateful.

- **Bryan DeCordova** was the CFO at Michaels during my time as a consultant. He was integral in supporting my three years of consulting work and was one of the main people who helped me leave consulting and join Michaels when I wanted to stop being a road warrior.

- **Jeff Boyer** became the CFO when Bryan left the company, and we became fast friends. That friendship has lasted to this very day. Jeff has always been in my corner with much-needed and timely advice and counsel.

- **Mary Kuniski** was my partner as we developed the Vendor Relations Team from scratch. She always gave it everything she had and helped us change an entire industry related to supply chain efficiency and effectiveness. Without this division, Michaels would never have been able to reach the heights it did.

- **Les Gardner** is a great friend and was the key player at Michaels who enable us to build a truly world-class supply chain from almost nothing. Though we went through about six SVPs during my time at Michaels, his consistency throughout all the change was key to our success. His support was critical in enabling us to make more progress in a shorter time than anyone thought possible.

- **Harvey Kanter** and I worked together at Michaels and have remained friends. Harvey was very inspirational in helping me take one more shot at writing after his book, *Choosing to Lead*, was published. He was also so kind as to introduce me to his editor, who I would be lost without.

- **The great people of Michaels I worked with from 1997 to 2008.** We could not have turned around Michaels and made it into a great retail success story were it not for all the outstanding people in every division and part of the company. This also includes the wonderful Vendor Community. I want to thank you all. I want to specifically recognize Gale Binder, Vicki Hilzendager, Jeff Mitchell, Sam Laboi, Eric Dickenson, Tom Roush, Matt Fisher, Larry Fine, Iris Allen, Tom Bazzone, Greg Sandfort, Robin Moore, Tom Peterson, Chris Howard, John Martin, Brian Jansen, my entire Vendor Relations Team, and the entire IT team.

- **Mike Barnes** was the President and COO at Fossil and was integral in bringing me on board as the SVP of Strategy. Mike was always in my corner as we tried to navigate not only the transition of Fossil to be more of a strategic company but also the craziness of the 2008 and 2009 financial crisis.

- **Ron Spencer** was my partner and main supporter during my time at Fossil. His continued guidance assisted me in assimilating into the Fossil culture and was the main reason I had the success that I did during my tenure with the company.

- **The wonderful people who worked at Tuesday Morning.** I joined Tuesday Morning during a challenging time to try and help these great people succeed in keeping this company from going out of business. Thank you to everyone I worked with during my time with the company, specifically Beth

Alonzo, Brian Turner, Don Williams, Tom Sangalli, Jenna Hawkins, Shirley Garrison, Claudia White, Amy Folmar, Mike Rollando, Shellie Sheehan, and Sandie Pembroke.

- **Tim Grantham** and I began our relationship as financial advisor and client. Today he is not only my advisor but a close friend. His support in the early stages of writing this book was integral to give me the confidence to continue to type. His thoughts and words of wisdom helped me make the appropriate shifts in the critical days of writing my first draft. It gave me a much-needed wind in my sails.

- **Alan Marek** has been a colleague and friend for almost 20 years. His positive comments and words of encouragement throughout the entire book process enabled me to keep pushing through when times were challenging.

- **Professor Anne Coughlin and Wayne Marsh**. I was introduced to Anne by Wayne (a Michaels' Vendor and one of her students). She wanted to write a case study about my Vendor Relations Team for her MBA class at the Kellogg School of Business. The case study was a wonderful compliment for our work, but that was not the best thing Anne did for me. She allowed me to come and speak to her students every semester for about three or four years. Those sessions were some of the best days of my career. She planted a seed in me that I could inspire people with my words.

- **Wendy K. Walters** is my editor and my friend. When we first met, I knew God had put yet another wonderful person in my life at just the right moment. Through all the challenging times you have when editing and then publishing a book, she has never wavered in her support and guidance for my desire to shift my career at the age of 60.

MEET JEFF WELLEN

STRATEGIST, SENIOR EXECUTIVE, MANAGEMENT
CONSULTANT, ENTREPRENEUR, SPEAKER, AND AUTHOR

Jeff is the son of a truck driver and a first-generation college graduate who rose from a retail trainee to Senior Executive leadership, including serving as the right-hand man of a CEO for a $4B company. He is a straight talker who has worked for some of the best brands in America—Michaels, Fossil, and Haggar.

From jumping out of an airplane at 13,500 feet and bungy jumping off a 143-foot river bridge to leaving a great job with a great company to see if he could become a successful entrepreneur, Jeff is not afraid to take a risk. Wellen is a gifted storyteller and captivates his audience with humor and authenticity, seasoned by a lifetime of experience and the incredible privilege of working closely with great mentors who helped him along the way. His stories are timeless, relatable, and so entertaining that you almost forget you are learning valuable principles for business and life. Spend a little time walking down his path, and you will find confidence and clarity to guide you as you walk your own.

You can book Jeff to speak at your conference, college, or university. Or, to connect with him for executive and management consulting or career coaching opportunities, please visit:

JEFFWELLEN.COM

Bungy jumping from the
Kawarau Bridge in New Zealand

Taking a leap from 13,500 feet!

*"Success and failure are judged only
by those who are willing to try."*

Providing a steady, experienced, firm hand at the wheel

Made in the USA
Coppell, TX
18 February 2022